TOMORROW A NEW WORLD:

The New Deal Community Program

Published under the direction of the American Historical Association from the income of the Albert J. Beveridge Memorial Fund.

For their zeal and beneficence in creating this fund the Association is indebted to many citizens of Indiana who desired to honor in this way the memory of a statesman and historian.

Tomorrow a New World:

THE NEW DEAL COMMUNITY PROGRAM

By Paul K. Conkin

PUBLISHED FOR THE

American Historical Association

CORNELL UNIVERSITY PRESS

ITHACA, NEW YORK

© 1959 by the American Historical Association

All rights reserved, including the right to reproduce this book, or portions thereof, in any form.

CORNELL UNIVERSITY PRESS

First published 1959

PRINTED IN THE UNITED STATES OF AMERICA BY THE
VAIL-BALLOU PRESS, INC., BINGHAMTON, NEW YORK

Acknowledgments

AMONG the many people who assisted me in the preparation of this book, I especially want to thank Dr. Henry Lee Swint of Vanderbilt University for his guidance, criticism, and inspiration. I also received generous assistance from almost all members of the Vanderbilt University History Department, from the staffs of the Joint Universities Library in Nashville, Tennessee, and the Southwestern Louisiana Institute Library in Lafayette, Louisiana, and from Stanley Brown of the National Archives. The illustrations were possible because of the aid and permission of the following journals: *Landscape Architecture, Architectural Record,* and *Architectural Forum.*

P. K. C.

Contents

Introduction 1

PART ONE: *Of Men and Their Ideas*

I The Land—Our Refuge and Our Strength 11
II Bringing the Town to the Country 37
III Bringing the Country to the Town 59
IV From Acorn to Oak 73

PART TWO: *Of Bureaus and Bureaucrats*

V The Subsistence Homesteads Program 93
VI The Federal Emergency Relief Administration Communities 131
VII America Resettled 146
VIII The Community as a Locale for a New Society . . 186
IX The Old Society Reasserts Its Claims 214

PART THREE: *Of Individual Communities*

X Arthurdale—An Experimental Community . . . 237
XI Jersey Homesteads—A Triple Co-operative . . . 256
XII Penderlea Homesteads—Something Less than a Rural Paradise 277
XIII Granger Homesteads—An Escape from Modernity . 294
XIV The Greenbelt Towns 305

In Retrospect 326
Appendix 332
Bibliographical Note 338
Index 341

Illustrations

1 Penderlea Homesteads, North Carolina 283
2 Greenbelt, Maryland . . . . . . *facing* 312
3 Greenhills, Ohio . . . . . . *facing* 314
4 Greendale, Wisconsin . . . . . . *facing* 316

TOMORROW A NEW WORLD:

The New Deal Community Program

Introduction

THE depression that began in 1929 was a powerful catalyst in the modern American reaction against the idea of individualism and against the well-established institutions which gave that idea reality. This reaction was well under way by the end of the nineteenth century, but did not attain the proportions that it reached during the period of the New Deal. Never before had it so permeated the federal government or led to so many attempts at institutional reforms. The reaction was rooted in the vastly altered physical environment, which is generally attributed to a technological, a scientific, or an industrial revolution, and in a greatly altered intellectual environment, which was closely related to scientific advances and which quite completely destroyed the intellectual foundations of nineteenth-century rationalism, liberalism, and individualism, even as it gave a philosophic basis for the modern social sciences. This reaction against individualism, or this movement toward a new collectivism, is not at all synonymous with the New Deal, which reflected other, more traditional currents of thought; it was, however, a major element in the New Deal, shaping a large part of its program.

The most important American political tradition was rooted in an earlier reaction—a reaction against political systems or social systems that suppressed and inhibited the individual, against oppressive governments, powerful monarchies, and the restrictive mercantilistic economic system. This earlier reaction was most defiantly stated in the Declaration of Independence. It drew its metaphysical support from the current rationalism, which, while not repudiating authority itself, used a rationalized and all too perfect picture of the natural world as a new authority to defend the individual against either Church or monarch, the two most firmly entrenched threats to individualism. Although in many ways a retreat from the near anarchy of the Declaration of Independence, the Constitution and its first ten amendments implemented much of this individualistic reaction by its rigid separaton and division of powers and its guarantees of individual rights, despite the then powerful influence of those disciples of Hamilton who still retained a reverence for the stability and efficiency of European governments. This stress on individualism, on equal opportunities for all, on special privileges for none, on small, limited, and localized (and therefore nonoppressive) governments was complemented, or perhaps almost necessitated, by an open, inviting, and largely rural environment. Strangely enough, the idea of individualism found further support in puritanical American Protestantism, which, though based on metaphysical suppositions that directly opposed the deism of the rationalists, tended to give the same support to individual aspirations. Out of the American Revolution and the revivalism of the early nineteenth century came a political system based on consistent natural law and a religion based on a highly supernatural God, yet both joined hands to become, in the minds of most Americans, coequal progenitors of a set of values which, perhaps inevitably, lost their revolutionary characteristics and, even as the environment changed, became traditional dogmas themselves.

The individualistic tradition—nineteenth-century liberalism—found its most exact expression in the Democratic parties of Jefferson and Jackson, although heresy entered even Jefferson's administration. This liberalism was countered, though never in all its aspects, by the parties in the Hamiltonian traditions, which were nationalistic at the price of state rights, which, whether explicitly or no, embraced the idea of a qualitative distinction between men, and which were not averse to a strong central government representing the privileged interests of the country. The slavery controversy saw the individualistic tradition most heartily defended in the South, but nevertheless weakened by the paradoxical acceptance of slavery. The Civil War

Introduction

ended with the ascendancy by force of the Hamiltonian tradition and the reign of privilege, which was already securely garbed in the verbal clothes of liberalism and individualism. It was opposed by the true Jeffersonians, by the "purists," who wanted a return to equal opportunities for all and a limited government. The purists, most rigidly adhering to the liberal tradition, dominated the Democratic party during most of the years before Wilson's administration, but were reduced to a rather hapless minority by the time of the New Deal. With Theodore Roosevelt and his New Nationalism, the beginnings of a new tradition found its first important, though never clear-cut, political expression. It was the modern, collective reaction against individualism and was to grow rapidly.

Industrialization, centralization, and urbanization created a new society that was alien to the liberal and individualistic tradition. Concentrations of people, wealth, and power made necessary new limitations on individual freedom. A new class, the unpropertied proletariat, became large enough to be politically important. The very existence of the new society had partially depended upon governmental privileges—on corporate rights, franchises, land grants, and tariffs. Ideas such as free enterprise, private property, equality of opportunity, and competition became almost meaningless to many men, even though completely accepted. At the same time those ideas became crutches for the use of a privileged few. The purists saw this and fought back. They wanted to return to decentralization in government and in the economy, to equal opportunities and really free enterprise, to pure competition, and to an age long past. They continued to believe, and do yet today, that the liberal tradition remains valid. In a polluted, indistinct form the liberal tradition remains the dominant political ideology in America today.

Meanwhile the problems of the new environment were being approached from a new angle, first in Europe and then in America, where the individualistic tradition was most firmly entrenched. The new environment was embraced, not repudiated. Industrialism, urbanization, concentration, and centralization were not of necessity evils. But for the new environment new institutions were advocated in order to render the new society more democratic. It had to be controlled by the masses, democratized, collectivized. Governments of privilege had to be replaced, not by less government, but by governments of all the people—functioning, efficient governments, capable of regulating and controlling the economy in such a way as to insure a rewarded honesty for all men. This was a new and disruptive political creed, ranging from Marxian Socialism to its mildest form, interventionism, which predominated in the United States.

The new political creed sprang, most obviously, from the problems created by the new environment, but it was either partly rooted in, or else created for itself, conducive philosophies. Since the rationalistic and liberalistic tradition was so often warped and molded to fit the needs of the new privileged groups, especially the capitalists, it had to be refuted and replaced, even though the purists were sometimes acknowledged as friends because of a common enemy. The Newtonian world view, essential to the naturalistic rationalism, swayed before evolution and practically succumbed before relativity. Marx, with his historical interpretation and complete materialism, provided a dogmatized philosophy that was seized upon by many collectivists. But, in the United States, the growth of pragmatism and, in particular, the ideas of John Dewey were the most important intellectual supports for interventionism and a degree of collectivism. The new philosophy broke completely with all past authorities, placed man in a neutral universe, and gave him a method or a tool, radical empiricism, for coping with his environment. It was idealistic in its view of man, had a high moral content, was extremely practical, and made a religion of democracy. It thus had much that could be related to traditional liberalism, even as it destroyed the foundations of that liberal tradition. When vulgarized and widely disseminated, few noticed how thoroughly it destroyed or undermined some of the most cherished ideas in American life, even including the theological content of Christianity. Very important also, it was relatively new and untried in the social realm, lacked the conviction of a less intellectualized and more dogmatized faith, and had unexplored implications to mankind and to the whole structure of Western European civilization, which had always been based on certain traditions and on some degree of authority. This radical empiricism, separated from metaphysical certainties and from past authority, provided the framework for most of the modern social sciences, including all of, or significant groups within, the disciplines of economics, sociology, psychology, political science, and anthropology. It greatly influenced educational theory,

Introduction

historiography, and jurisprudence. It thrived most purely in the colleges and universities, but affected the lives of almost everyone. It is extremely significant that such a large number of professors, who were familiar with or openly espoused this pragmatism, were active in the New Deal.

At the time of the election of 1932 three important political philosophies were vying for recognition, although most individuals represented mixtures of two or three. One philosophy was that of the purists, who still believed in Jeffersonian liberalism but saw through the superficial espousal of this liberalism by business groups. The purists were anticapitalistic, antimonopolistic, antibureaucratic, and were for state rights, governmental economy, decentralization, and restored competition. Another philosophy was that of the modern Hamiltonians, who welcomed a centralized, functioning government, but who, out of sincere conviction or from self-interest, wanted the government to represent the "best" class of people, who distrusted the "vulgar" masses, and who wanted the government to perform certain services for the dominant, business class, believing that such favoritism would eventually benefit every group. They were more and more using the iconography of Jeffersonianism to win wide support to their viewpoint. The other philosophy was advocated by those who desired a democratization of privilege or who, in other terms, wanted to use Hamiltonian methods to serve Jeffersonian purposes. They wanted more and more socialization and more intervention on the part of the national government, which meant less and less individual freedom but more economic security. Their ideas had received verbal support from Theodore Roosevelt, had been advocated by minority parties, were partially implemented by a professing Jeffersonian, Woodrow Wilson, but had never been dominant in national politics. They were anticapitalistic, but not anti-industrial. Their views were more representative of labor and of urban thought than of rural philosophies.

The New Deal was a grand mixture of political faiths that managed to come together for a considerable, if inconsistent, program. In his earliest campaign speeches Franklin D. Roosevelt acclaimed Jeffersonian ideas, even as he advocated a precedent-breaking program of national planning and even as he showed that he was distinctly sympathetic to business. Not so charmingly eclectic were many of his advisers and followers, ranging from Hugh Johnson, who represented a business point of view, to Rexford G. Tugwell, an urban liberal, pragmatist, collectivist, and somewhat of a revolutionary. Yet the early program of the New Deal was seemingly an almost complete vindication of the anti-individualistic, anti-Jeffersonian, collectivist approach. The emphasis on economic planning, the accretion of federal governmental powers, the declining importance of local and state governments, the privileges granted labor and farmers, the broad controls over banking, finance, and business, all indicated a trend away from Jeffersonianism. Collectivist ideas were made more explicit than ever before. Still there was no complete victory for the new ideas. Many of the programs were enacted entirely because of the desperation of the depression and were later repudiated. Many were supported by the old liberals as second best. Countertendencies were evident. Early planning measures were largely accepted by big business or by big farmers because of hopes for control or a desire for economic gains. Most important, the ideological foundations of the new policies were never completely understood and, except for darkest depression days, never broadly embraced. Jeffersonian ideas, used sincerely or prostituted to self-interest, still claimed the greatest loyalty. The older ideas were more and more asserted by Congress after 1937, with both the purists and the Hamiltonians joining in an alliance against collectivism. Individualism, while apparently slowly losing its hold in the minds of men, even as the physical world denied it any such free expression as it had in the past, was still king on a well-shaken but still-standing throne.

One of the smaller programs of the New Deal was the construction of approximately 100 communities. Yet, from a standpoint of conflicting ideas, these communities represented one of the more significant programs. They were a focal point of ideological clashes. Although their initiation was much influenced by a reactionary, quasi-Jeffersonian agrarianism, their development reflected one of the most open breaks with the individualistic tradition in American history. The very word "community" became a synonym for a form of collectivism and an antonym of individualism. These communities were to be examples of a new, organic society, with new values and institutions. Their story is a fascinating adventure in idealism and disillusionment.

Any account of the New Deal communities is confusing because of

Introduction

the many governmental agencies that were involved in their development or management. In one sense the story of these communities is a part of many stories, for in many cases they were closely related to other activities carried on within the same agency that fathered or managed them. The term "community" is the one unifying concept, but it is a term with considerable content. The first communities were planned and initiated by the Division of Subsistence Homesteads in the Department of the Interior. This was the only New Deal agency devoted exclusively to community building. Almost simultaneously the Federal Emergency Relief Administration initiated a group of communities as one small aspect of its relief program. In 1935 all but three of the communities initiated by these two agencies were turned over to a newly created, independent agency, the Resettlement Administration, which itself initiated several additional communities. Yet the communities represented only about a third of the total program of the Resettlement Administration. Three of the Federal Emergency Relief Administration communities were retained by the Works Progress Administration until 1939. In January, 1937, the Resettlement Administration became a part of the Department of Agriculture. In September, 1937, it was replaced by the Farm Security Administration. Neither change materially affected the communities. The final disposition of some of the communities was carried out by the Farmers' Home Administration, the Federal Public Housing Authority, and the Public Housing Administration, but by the time they came under these agencies the whole community program had been repudiated.

These 100 communities, aside from reflecting a conscious break with individualism, remain monuments to the reforming zeal of their creators. In an age of depression, when many believed that economic progress had reached its limits, the reformers yet reflected a spirit of optimism and high idealism. In an age of cynicism many of the reformers would be considered naïve. Even so, an oddly spaced group of small white homes dotting a West Virginia hillside or an imaginatively planned little city sitting in the midst of a very green belt of Maryland forests, despite all the misdirected or wasted effort that went into their creation, will remain vivid reminders of a time, not so long past, when Americans still could dream of a better, more perfect world and could so believe in that dream that they dared set forth to realize it, unashamed of their zeal.

Part One

OF MEN AND THEIR IDEAS

I

The Land—Our Refuge and Our Strength

FOR many people in the United States of 1932 and early 1933 hope for an early economic recovery, overstimulated by too many optimistic predictions, turned to deep despair. As men desperately searched for security, the tinsel trappings of the machine age seemed to tarnish. The glittering lights of the great city now only too often bared men's aimless, hopeless wanderings in search of employment. The powerful urban magnet, which had drawn millions of farmers into its enticing fold during the twenties, had lost much of its attraction. As progress slowed, many men turned their eyes back to the land, to the old homestead, to security, to a memory. The deserted farms, the mountain shacks, the tenant cottages became repeopled. Most often the country-bound pilgrim found his dream of a pastoral haven to be of the illusionary nature of most dreams. The grim shadow of depression also darkened the rural scene, but in the cities men still spoke longingly of the land. In the tremendous back-to-the-land sentiment of the depression the idea of subsistence farming, or of subsistence homesteads, which was as ancient as farming itself, became a unifying concept that bound together a multitude of individuals with widely divergent philosophies. Industrialists, agriculturalists, land economists, agrarians, physical culturists, politicians, economists, social workers, and city planners all had schemes for moving the unemployed and discontented back to the soil. Many thought in terms of temporary relief; some envisioned a return to a simple past; a few dreamed of a new order for society. Out of this confusion of ideas, if not of tongues, came the first New Deal communities. A few men took a term, "subsistence homesteads," and converted it into a physical reality and in so doing led the national government into the role of community building. The reality could please only a few of those who had acclaimed a term, or an abstract concept, but nevertheless it was their advocacy of a term that made the reality possible.

The back-to-the-land movement was not entirely a child of the depression. With less urgency it had existed long before the depression and had other justification than temporary relief. The United States began its history as an agrarian nation and, in its folkways, had largely remained one. From Jefferson and his fellow democrats, especially John Taylor of Caroline, the United States inherited a philosophy of agrarianism.[1] The virtues of agricultural pursuits, the greater political responsibility of a landowning citizenry, and the dangers of urbanism and of a propertyless proletariat remained axioms for many twentieth-century Americans. Agrarian ideas and ideals continued to color Americans political utterances, though hardly in the consistent form voiced by John Taylor. At times this agrarianism found partial expression in the nostalgic, romanticized memories of the many country boys who came to town to live or in the city boys who read and sang of rural delights. For discontented idealists, who could see only the ills and ugliness of a complex industrial society, the country often became an avenue of escape, an avenue to nature and to simplicity. These expressions of what was most often only a nebulous idea can more easily be studied in the context of specific back-to-the-land movements, whether originating as relief measures in times of depression or in a convinced agrarian philosophy.

It is almost anomalous to talk of a back-to-the-land movement before the Civil War, for an overwhelming majority of Americans lived on the land. The line between town and country was often far from sharp. Regardless of how effective the frontier was as a safety valve,

---

[1] Thomas Jefferson, *The Writings of Thomas Jefferson,* ed. Andrew A. Lipscomb (Library ed., 20 vols.; Washington, 1904), II, 229–230; John Taylor, *An Inquiry into the Principles and Policy of the Government of the United States* (Fredericksburg, Va., 1814).

The Land

it was an ever-present reality in the minds of the people, who strove mightily for a more liberal land policy. Soldiers, after each war, had received land as a reward for their service. The Union veterans were to profit from the Homestead Act of 1862.[2] Yet, in the period from 1820 to 1850, scores of communitarian colonies were founded in America. Most of these represented a desire for a peaceful separation from an increasingly complex and, to some, sinful world.[3] All were concrete attempts to make real the perennial longing for a Promised Land, "into which, like Moses, man will never be permitted to enter, but which gives rise to this heroic and never-ending adventure that is none the less pathetic."[4] The largest number of communities originated in the socialist philosophies of Robert Owen and Charles Fourier, both of whom reacted against the evils of industrialism and of the economic order. Both envisioned a new communal order to be realized in an agricultural setting or in a return to the land.[5]

The other important motivation for communistic experiments was religious. The Shaker colonies, the Rappite communities, the Amana villages, and the Oneida colony represented attempts to preserve certain religious ideas in self-contained communities. Of all the religious communities, those founded by the Mormons were by far the most numerous and influential. The Mormons were the first irrigators in the United States, laboriously developing by hand many of the techniques later used by the Bureau of Reclamation.[6] Through Milburn L. Wilson, the first Director of the Division of Subsistence Homesteads in the Department of the Interior, the Mormon communities were to influence directly the government-sponsored subsistence homesteads.[7]

---

[2] Russell Lord and Paul H. Johnstone, eds., *A Place on Earth: A Critical Appraisal of Subsistence Homesteads* (Washington, 1942), pp. 4–5.

[3] R. W. Murchie, *Land Settlement as a Relief Measure* (Day and Hour Series no. 5, University of Minnesota; Minneapolis, 1933), p. 6.

[4] Charles Gide, *Communist and Cooperative Colonies*, trans. by Ernest F. Row (London, 1930), p. 18. See also Arthur E. Bestor, *Backwoods Utopias: The Sectarian and Owenite Phases of Communitarian Socialism in America* (Philadelphia, 1950); Alice Felt Tyler, *Freedom's Ferment: Phases of American Social History to 1860* (Minneapolis, 1944).

[5] Gide, *Communist and Cooperative Colonies*, pp. 22–23.

[6] Alfred R. Golzé, *Reclamation in the United States* (New York, 1952), p. 46.

[7] Milburn L. Wilson, *Farm Relief and Allotment Plan* (Day and Hour Series no. 2, University of Minnesota; Minneapolis, 1933), p. 49.

The Mormon farm village, as perfected in Utah, represented a large-scale departure from the isolated farm pattern that had characterized American rural development. Unlike isolated farmers, the Mormon villagers enjoyed a rich social life, could more easily acquire such amenities as electricity, telephones, and running water, paid less for their roads, automatically escaped the small one-room school, easily developed responsible government, and, as most often argued by exponents of subsistence homesteads, could combine small manufacturing and handicrafts with their farm work. Their village form of settlement has been attributed to a harsh environment, to a need for protection against Indians, to a necessity of sharing irrigation works, to loneliness, and to a common religion. Back of these practical factors was the vision of Joseph Smith, who planned a City of Zion while the Mormons were still in Ohio. It was not only to be the home of the Mormons, but was to be the future dwelling place of the soon-returning Savior. Possibly inspired by the biblical New Jerusalem, by Robert Owen's New Harmony, and by the current rectangular land survey, his plan provided for large ten-acre blocks, each containing twenty families. In 1847 Salt Lake City was settled with ten-acre blocks, but with many farm families receiving as much as two whole blocks. Other Mormon farm villages provided one- or two-acre subsistence plots for each settler.[8]

After the Civil War back-to-the-land schemes appeared with increasing frequency. In 1870 Horace Greeley promoted a successful land colony at what became Greeley, Colorado. This colony utilized irrigation and became fairly successful, although it was not back-to-the-land for the destitute, since the colonists had to have money to attain membership.[9] During the depression which began in 1873, Archbishop John Ireland of St. Paul developed five agricultural colonies for the Catholic urban poor on land purchased from the railroads in Nebraska and Minnesota. Partly because of the isolated farm method of settlement in the United States, the Catholic Church, with a scarcity of priests, had long advised Catholic immigrants to remain in the cities where they could be under the watchful care of the

---

[8] Lowry Nelson, *The Mormon Village: A Pattern and Technique of Land Settlement* (Salt Lake City, 1952), pp. 10–13, 15, 25–38, 96–101; Golzé, *Reclamation in the United States*, p. 8.

[9] Golzé, *Reclamation in the United States*, p. 10.

Church. These agricultural colonies founded by Archbishop Ireland marked the beginning of a rural movement in the Catholic Church, partly caused by the fact that city Catholics were believed not to be reproducing themselves.[10]

The much-publicized Greeley colony and the work of Archbishop Ireland helped influence three congressmen to propose government-supported colonies for the relief of the Eastern workingman. In October, 1877, General Nathaniel P. Banks, Representative from Massachusetts, introduced a bill which would have created a private colonizing corporation under government supervision. Under the provisions of this bill, deserving, unemployed laborers were to be transported and settled in groups of twenty-five upon the public lands, receiving $400 in credit. The bill, which was never reported from committee, provided for an appropriation of $10,000,000, one-half in bonds and one-half in greenbacks, the latter inflationary measure being one of the objects of the bill.[11] Also in October, 1877, Hendrick B. Wright, Democrat-Greenbacker Representative from Pennsylvania, introduced an almost similar colonization bill, which was to be administered by the Public Land Office.[12] Wright, as a member of the Committee on the Public Lands, spared no efforts to get his bill enacted. He secured the support of Terence V. Powderly, head of the Knights of Labor, and solicited petitions from over 20,000 laborers. As a result of his efforts he was scorned in newspapers, branded a Pennsylvania communist, and forced to see his bill defeated by a vote of 210 to 23.[13]

By far the most intricate and detailed colonization bill ever introduced in the United States Congress was sponsored in 1878 by General Benjamin F. Butler, Representative from Massachusetts. Under the direction of the army, large groups of settlers were to be located on the western frontier in close proximity to army posts. Quite appropriately for Butler, the bill excluded any settlers from any of the

---

[10] Raymond P. Witte, *Twenty-five Years of Crusading: A History of the National Catholic Rural Life Conference* (Des Moines, 1948), pp. 1–2.

[11] Albert V. House, Jr., "Proposals of Government Aid to Agricultural Settlement during the Depression of 1873–79," *Agricultural History*, XII (1938), 47; United States, *Congressional Record*, 45th Cong., 1st Sess., 1877, p. 169. (Future references to the *Congressional Record* will be cited as *C.R.*)

[12] House, "Proposals of Government Aid," p. 48.

[13] *Ibid.*, pp. 52–60; *C.R.*, 45th Cong., 3d Sess., 1879, p. 771.

Southern states. An appropriation of $420,000,000 in greenbacks was to be used to resettle on 45,000 sections exactly 333,333 people from the unemployed or insufficiently paid laboring class.[14] Butler argued that this unemployed group, then a labor surplus, could become a prosperous class of consumers and producers when placed upon the land. Each settler was to receive free transportation, $1,250 in equipment, and a forty-acre plot of land containing exactly six and two-thirds acres of timber. The bill required a meticulous land survey before locating a colony and prescribed a detailed list of equipment for each settler, including the seed to plant and the amount of lumber to carry along. An army physician was to be detailed to each colony. Butler's bill was never reported from committee despite the great effort that went into its preparation.[15]

The demands for government-directed resettlement of Eastern laboring classes were repeated in 1885, a year of heavy unemployment and of business recession. At a special hearing on the relation of capital and labor conducted by the Senate Committee on Education and Labor, the Reverend Heber Newton, a Christian Socialist, stated: "As a practical aid to the re-establishing of better relations between labor and land, I would suggest the organization by the National Government of colonization. Colonization has always been the natural relief of overcrowded centers. In this way surplus labor has gone back to the soil." [16] He believed that the masses of workers who most needed colonization were also the ones who most needed guidance and supervision in their resettlement. For the government to relieve the East and build up the West by leading the dull ones "back to the land" and making them self-supporting was, to him, "a wise work for the state." [17] At the same hearings, Fred X. Heissinger, a landscape and garden engineer from New York City, urged the states and the national government to co-operate in establishing colonies and "founding new homes and towns in the West and South" for emigrants and laborers. He wanted to form a company or an association to find land, establish

[14] *C.R.*, 45th Cong., 2d Sess., 1878, pp. 4381–4382.
[15] House, "Proposals of Government Aid," p. 50; *C.R.*, 45th Cong., 2d Sess., 1878, pp. 4381–4382.
[16] Senate Committee on Education and Labor, *Investigation of the Relations between Labor and Capital*, 48th Cong., 1885, p. 575.
[17] *Ibid.*

The Land

model farms, finance purchases, secure clear deeds, and provide farm machinery.[18]

Around 1890 a school garden movement was started in several cities, usually for the purpose of promoting the physical, mental, and moral growth of children. After the depression beginning in 1893 this movement was expanded and its leaders began to see in it a method of permanently guiding young people back to the country, thus removing the surplus in the cities. One ever-present assumption of the back-to-the-land movement was that there were too many people in the cities for complete employment. The school garden movement was based on the assumption that many city children would grow attached to agriculture, as well as learn its arts, and would migrate to farms when they became adults, relieving the labor surplus in cities. By 1906 thirty-five cities had school gardens, while many normal schools introduced courses in gardening.[19]

In the depression that began in 1893 the mayor of Detroit originated the idea of vacant-lot cultivation as a relief measure for the idle poor. As a temporary measure it was tried in twelve or more cities with excellent results. In Philadelphia, in 1896, it had a new birth under the leadership of R. F. Powell, who was "an enthusiastic single-taxer." [20] By 1904 over 800 people were cultivating gardens in Philadelphia's vacant lots. Powell saw his movement as a training school, whose graduates would go to the country as farmers. Eventually, Powell believed, the vacant-lot gardens would open people's eyes to what he believed to be the root iniquity of the existing economic system, the unearned increment. Under single-tax inspiration, a similar vacant-lot association was developed in New York, and one was planned for Cincinnati.[21]

In 1898, to combat what it considered the greatest evil of the day, the drift of population into the cities, the Salvation Army began colonizing the destitute of the cities. Utilizing $150,000 raised by bond issues, the Army started farm colonies at Fort Amity, Colorado; Fort Romie, California; and Fort Herrick, Ohio. At Fort Amity the

[18] *Ibid.*, pp. 1340–1352.
[19] Florence F. Kelly, "An Undertow to the Land: Successful Efforts to Make Possible a Flow of the City Population Countryward," *Craftsman*, XI (1906), 308.
[20] R. F. Powell, "Vacant Lot Gardens vs. Vagrancy," *Charities*, XIII (1904), 26.
[21] Kelly, "An Undertow to the Land," pp. 302–307.

fourteen original settlers were sold twenty-acre plots on twelve-year terms and were lent money for seed and livestock on five-year terms. Many settlers were so poor that transportation had to be provided. Despite difficulties with poor soil, Amity was a success, containing thirty-two families by 1906, each with an average worth of about $1,200. The colonists settled compactly and had the advantage of social life and mutual help. Fort Romie was a complete failure at first, but after the installation of irrigation works it became more prosperous than Fort Amity.[22] Fort Herrick was smaller and was used primarily as a home for inebriates. The increased land values in each settlement more than protected the Salvation Army's investment, although about $50,000 in development costs was not charged to the settlers and was considered a loss by the Army. In all cases the Army carefully screened prospective settlers, probably thus insuring the success of their ventures.[23] Commander Frederick St. G. de L. Booth-Tucker of the United States Salvation Army, who had observed colonization methods in other countries, believed scientific colonization would soon take its place beside scientific agriculture.[24]

After 1907 the back-to-the-land movement became a sizable popular crusade. In that year Bolton Hall, inspired in part by the vacant-lot movement, published his very popular *Three Acres and Liberty*.[25] The next year he followed with *A Little Land and a Living*.[26] Both books described intensive farming on small plots, as well as advertised the advantages of rural life. They were also handbooks on subsistence farming, giving needed practical information. These books were followed by many magazine articles giving advice to landward-bound cityfolk. *Country Life* published twenty-four such articles from 1910 to 1912 under the general title "Cutting Loose from the City." Typical of the articles are the following descriptive titles: "How Two Young People—One an Invalid—Found Health and a Competence by Ex-

[22] *Ibid.*, pp. 299–300.

[23] Henry Rider Haggard, *The Poor and the Land, Being a Report on the Salvation Army Colonies in the United States and at Hadleigh, England, with a Scheme of National Land Settlement and an Introduction* (London, 1905), pp. vii, 116–117; Kelly, "An Undertow to the Land," pp. 300–302.

[24] Frederick St. G. de L. Booth-Tucker, "Farm Colonies of the Salvation Army," in U.S. Department of Commerce and Labor, Bureau of Labor, *Bulletin*, XLVIII (1903), 1001–1003.

[25] Bolton Hall, *Three Acres and Liberty* (London, 1907).

[26] Bolton Hall, *A Little Land and a Living* (New York, 1908).

changing City Life for a Little One-acre Home in the Country (near the Maryland line)"; 'How One Woman, Without Family or Means, and Without any Previous Agricultural Experience, Has Laid the Foundation for an Old Age of Peace and Plenty, and at the Same Time Added a Present Zest to Life, by Getting 'Back to the Land' "; "How One Young Couple, Without Capital, Have Really Cut Loose and Are Enjoying Life While They Pay for Their Maine Farm on the Installment Plan, Making Use of Their Former Professions to Help Out Occasionally in Lieu of a Bank Account"; "How a Married Couple, Both in Ill-Health, with Three Children, and in Debt, Have Made Good on a Mississippi Farm. Plenty of Similar Openings in the South."[27]

The most interesting result of the popularization of small, intensive farms was the Little Landers colonies in California. William E. Smythe, a publisher and an expert on irrigation, adopted the motto "A little land and a living" and organized a group of families to settle upon small holdings of one to five acres.[28] His idea was that by concentrating on such farm industries as poultry raising, by growing all needed food, and by a system of co-operation, a group of families could live well on their small acreages and, at the same time, achieve a most excellent social life. The first group, which was organized in 1908, established their colony on 550 acres at San Ysidro, two miles from the Mexican border and near San Diego. The land was controlled by Little Landers, Incorporated. On rather poor soil, the settlers expected a moderate living, security, and freedom. Co-operation was soon realized and a town-meeting type of government was established.[29] The creed of Smythe and the Little Landers was as follows:

THE HOPE OF THE LITTLE LANDERS

That individual independence shall be achieved by millions of men and women, walking in the sunshine without fear of want.

[27] For the complete list of articles see L. O. Bercaw, A. M. Hannay, and E. M. Colvin, *Bibliography on Land Settlement, with Particular Reference to Small Holdings and Subsistence Homesteads* (Bureau of Agricultural Economics, Department of Agriculture, Miscellaneous Publication no. 172; Washington, 1934), pp. 36–37.

[28] "Land Settlement in California," *Transactions of the Commonwealth Club of California*, XI (1916), 425–426.

[29] Henry S. Anderson, "The Little Landers' Land Colonies: A Unique Agricultural Experiment in California," *Agricultural History*, V (1931), 140–142.

That in response to the loving labor of their hands, the earth shall answer their prayer: "Give us this day our daily bread."

That they and their children shall be proprietors rather than tenants, working not for others but for themselves.

That theirs shall be the life of the open—the open sky and the open heart —fragrant with the breath of flowers, more fragrant with the spirit of fellowship which makes the good of one the concern of all, and raises the individual by raising the mass.[30]

San Ysidro failed to vindicate Smythe's faith or to live up to the Little Landers creed. Plagued by dissension, a disastrous flood, and plots too small for economic security, the Little Landers colony was dissolved in 1918, although San Ysidro later became a prosperous town. Two similar Little Landers colonies, Los Terrenitos and Hayward Heath, likewise failed. In February, 1919, Smythe gave up his promotional work with the Little Landers and joined Franklin K. Lane, Secretary of the Interior, to help Lane promote a plan to extend the reclamation movement to the whole United States and to provide farm colonies for returning servicemen.[31]

For the purpose of placing the poor of the cities upon the land, the National Forward to the Land League was founded by Mr. and Mrs. Haviland H. Lund in 1911. The Lunds believed that privately directed colonization on the land was necessary to make the country immune to "the red virus." The National Forward to the Land League was an incorporated, nonprofit agency to secure private financial support to settle, in groups of fifty, the urban poor in agricultural colonies. The League solicited loans from businessmen, distributed government information pamphlets to interested colonizers, sponsored lectures in New York City by members of the College of Agriculture, Cornell University, developed plans for garden cities and part-time farming colonies for industrial workers, asked for and allegedly received support from such influential congressmen as Warren G. Harding, and secured the services of Harvard's political economist, Thomas Nixon Carver, as director of colonization, but never placed a single colonist upon the land.[32]

[30] *Ibid.*, p. 142. [31] *Ibid.*, pp. 142–150.
[32] Haviland H. Lund, "Redistribution of the Labor Now Employed in Producing War Supplies," *American Economic Review*, Supplement to vol. VII (1917), 239–240; House Committee on Labor, *Hearings on H.R. 11055, H.R. 11056, and H.R. 12097, Relief of Distress Due to Unemployment*, 72d Cong., 1st Sess., 1932, pp. 75, 76, 83–84.

The Land

The plans of the National Forward to the Land League were ambitious. Through borrowed money the League was to be able to furnish the inexperienced city colonists with finished houses; free medical insurance; co-operatives for credit, production, and marketing; an expert agricultural adviser; and fully equipped farms. The colonists were to divide their time between their farms and nearby factories, which were to utilize the by-products of the farms. Lund blamed the failure of his League on vested real estate interests and on socialists within the government who preferred bureacratic rather than private colonies.[33] Mrs. Lund later, in a rambling and bitter denunciation, described the League's unsuccessful attempt to get a co-ordinating bureau in the Department of Labor during the Wilson administration. She attributed the lack of success to Frederic Howe, Commissioner of Immigration, and Louis Post, Assistant Secretary of Labor, both of whom wanted government-directed colonization and who, in Mrs. Lund's opinion, were socialists and single-taxers. Mrs. Lund described the Farm Loan Bank, the Farm Board, and the Reclamation Service as communistic. She also bore a particular hatred for certain "scheming" international financiers.[34] Nevertheless, Mrs. Lund claimed credit for two of the proposed soldier settlement bills following World War I and was a lobbyist for subsistence homesteads in 1932.[35]

From 1916 through 1922 there was always at least one colonization or soldier settlement bill before Congress. Since these bills represented much more than a back-to-the-land movement, they will receive detailed attention in a later chapter. The tremendous ovation awarded these proposed colonization schemes, particularly those applying to soldiers, was compounded of many elements—of the idealism of the war to end wars; of the enthusiasm for doing the best for the returning servicemen; of the rampant nationalism inherent in any plan to reclaim thousands of worthless acres, in a sense creating a larger, wealthier nation; of the humanitarianism implicit in the oft-repeated belief that only American agriculture could feed a starving, war-torn Europe; and of the glowing confidence in the future of agriculture, which, just after the war, was reaping the highest reward in history.

---

[33] Lund, "Redistribution," pp. 242, 244; House Committee on Labor, *Hearings on Relief of Distress Due to Unemployment*, pp. 76, 84.

[34] House Committee on Labor, *Hearings on Relief of Distress Due to Unemployment*, pp. 75, 78–79, 81–82.

[35] *Ibid.*, p. 77.

But by no means least, this popular support reflected the strong feeling among perhaps a majority of the population that, for soldiers or for anyone, an independent farm home was the greatest possible blessing, contributing most to the wealth of the individual and to the strength, stability, and safety of the nation. William E. Smythe, of Little Landers fame, jubilantly predicted that "no part of the nation, and scarcely a single state, will fail to feel the new impulse toward the soil." [36]

This impulse toward the soil resulted in one notable private back-to-the-land venture and publicity stunt combined. Inspired by the proposed government colonization schemes, William D. Scott, a Brooklyn sales manager, issued a prospectus in 1921 inviting prospective back-to-the-landers in New York to join him in establishing a farm colony in far-off Idaho. Scott received wide support for his plan, purchased 5,120 acres of land, sight unseen, near Buhl, Idaho, met with delegations of citizens from Idaho, and enlisted colonists for the great migration. To attract attention to the venture, Scott decided that the group should move to Idaho by automobile—no small undertaking in 1921. Only twenty-eight eager colonists were able to pay the $3,000 required for an automobile, equipment, and the first payment on their land. This small caravan of pioneers, modern style, left New York amidst raving newspaper accounts. It was to be a trip of joy, with sports, fishing, theater trips, magical Yellowstone Park, and the acclamation granted only to heroes. Mayors spoke, maidens kissed, farmers stared in wonder, all to be exceeded by the official welcome Idaho heaped upon its newest pioneers. The celebration over, the caravan left Buhl for their new colony, which they had already named Roseworth. They barely were able to cross Salmon Falls River Pass, were now alone in desolate sagebrush, and found only one settler and a few shacks at Roseworth. The soil (really very good) was coated with sand. The disillusionment was complete. All but four of the colonists sold their equipment and returned home.[37]

The Roseworth debacle epitomized the end of an era of popular back-to-the-land sentiment, which had begun as far back as the

[36] William E. Smythe, "New Homestead Policy for America," *Review of Reviews*, LXV (1922), 293.

[37] Albert Shaw, "From New York to Idaho," *Review of Reviews*, LXIV (1921), 179–180; George F. Stratton, "Sundown at Roseworth," *Country Gentleman*, LXXXVIII (Nov. 3, 1923), pp. 7, 32, 34.

The Land

depression of 1893. Then, in times of industrial depression, the movement had been one of relief. Later, with the general recovery, it had become one of sentiment and of small, intensive farming enterprises. With the European war came a new promise of future agricultural prosperity and with this many colonization schemes, public and private. But even as the pioneers left New York for Roseworth in 1921, a changed outlook faced American agriculture. The high postwar prices, which had been so temporary as to seem illusionary, were followed by falling prices and an era of agricultural depression. Meanwhile, industry, if not booming, was prosperous. No such imbalance between agriculture and industry had existed since the two decades which preceded the depression of 1893. Sentimentally, the farm might have retained its halo of desirability; economically, it was the problem child of the nation. A migration to the cities that had been progressing long before 1920, in the face of the dire predictions of the agrarians, became a rushing tide in the twenties. Always there is a great amount of migration both ways, but from 1921 until 1929 the net gain toward the cities varied from approximately 400,000 to 1,137,000 annually.[38] Thus, back-to-the-land lost all but a sentimental value, while the problem of what to do with those on the land became a major concern of the decade. To this problem an industrialist not only proposed an answer but attempted a cure. Moreover, in this decade of agricultural gloom, a number of individuals and groups developed the most complete and formal agrarian philosophy that had appeared in America since Jefferson's day.

It is no exaggeration to say that Henry Ford was one of the most popular men in America in the twenties. When he announced a new scheme for both industry and agriculture, Americans listened. Naturally Ford found the key to a glorious new era within the techniques and policies that he had applied to the Ford Motor Company. To Ford, industry had serious problems, such as poor housing, slums, and temporary unemployment. These evils sprang from industrial concentration and the profit motive. They could be solved, he believed, by the decentralization of industry and by the wage motive, which meant high wages and a greater demand for the manufacturer's product.[39]

---

[38] Pascal K. Whelpton, "The Extent, Character, and Future of the New Landward Movement," *Journal of Farm Economics*, XV (1933), 59.

[39] Henry Ford, in collaboration with Samuel Crowther, *Today and Tomorrow* (Garden City, N.Y., 1926), pp. 135–149.

In decentralizing industry, Ford believed that he could bring salvation to the farmer, who wanted the same money and luxuries as the industrial worker. The family farm was an antiquated island of small business in a world of big business. The farmer was becoming a part-time worker, especially if he were able to afford the new farm machinery. In the future the work of the average farm would take about one month out of the year. The rest of the time the farmer would work in Ford's decentralized factories. This grand synthesis of agriculture and industry was, to Ford, the way of the future. "Industry and agriculture have been considered as separate and distinct branches of activity. Actually they fit into each other very neatly. But first we have to rid ourselves of many traditions." [40]

One of the goddesses of the twenties was prosperity, and the harmonious songs in her praise swelled throughout the land. All men were not prosperous; with all her largess, prosperity had passed by many without heeding their pleading eyes. But still they worshiped her. Farmers, even though they choked on the chorus, sang her praises as never before. The tragedy of their increasing economic ills was heightened by the devoutness of their worship. Perhaps tomorrow even they would find favor in her eyes, and find two cars in their garages. But toward the end of the decade the harmony of this worshipful praise was shattered by the most shocking discord, by heresy no less. In highly literate blasphemy the great goddess prosperity was vilified. From some Catholic agrarians in the Midwest, from a few heretical Southerners in Nashville, even from the midst of the holy city of prosperity, New York, came a clarion call for men to return to their old gods and old ways. Who were these men speaking so? Was Jefferson back on earth, or was it St. Thomas speaking? America continued her song of praise, but many were visibly annoyed, some few disturbed. Many laughed at these quaint eccentrics and called them escapists or incurable romantics, while a few heralded them as prophets. In fervent phrases these fundamental Jeffersonians, these reactionaries, these doctrinaire agrarians, or (as they sometimes called themselves) these distributists continued their plea for men to recognize the insufficiency of their newly discovered idols.

The agrarian movement of the late twenties can be traced back to a small manifesto issued in 1911 by Hilaire Belloc, an English literary

[40] *Ibid.*, p. 218, see also pp. 210–218.

The Land

figure and prominent Catholic. He romantically praised the Catholic, agrarian society of the late Middle Ages, when the majority of men possessed, or had access to, wealth-producing property, and vehemently criticized the modern, Protestant, industrial, capitalist society in which only a few men owned real property. Belloc, as a moralist, advocated a return to a stable culture based on a wide distribution of property, particularly land.[41] Belloc, who used the word "distributist" to describe his economic platform, inspired a back-to-the-land movement in Great Britain and influenced an agrarian, distributist school among American Catholics. The Catholic Rural Life Conference, which was organized in 1923, advocated an agrarianism very similar to that of Belloc's, although they found their ideal agrarian society in Jefferson's America and not in the Middle Ages. The Catholic Rural Life Conference advocated property as a right and a responsibility, denounced farm tenancy, advocated subsistence farming, and, in the depression, attempted to guide the back-to-the-land movement.[42] Father Luigi Ligutti, a leading member of the conference, sponsored and organized one of the first government-financed subsistence homesteads communities, Granger Homesteads in Iowa.

The most heretical protest against contemporary American life came from the South, where twelve academicians at Vanderbilt University took a stand in behalf of their ideal agrarian society, the Old South. A few words can hardly summarize the thoroughness with which they repudiated all the goddesses of modernity—prosperity and her trappings, which, in their hostile view, became cheap and vulgar; industrialism and urbanism, which had engulfed and enslaved the North and now threatened the South with its meaningless technology and coarse materialism; corporate wealth and government bureaucracy, both of which demoralized and enslaved the individual by depriving him of the morally beneficial control of his own economic destiny; and progress, with her offspring of liberalism, progressivism, pragmatism, and relativism that wooed men away from an older, established, quality-conscious, formalized society in which art, agriculture, manners, authority, simplicity, tradition, breeding, leisure,

[41] Hilaire Belloc, *The Servile State* (1st American ed.; New York, 1946), pp. 52–53, 110–123.

[42] Witte, *Twenty-five Years of Crusading*, pp. 60–61; National Catholic Rural Life Conference, *Manifesto on Rural Life* (Milwaukee, 1939), pp. 3, 41, and *Rural Life Objectives*, I (St. Paul, 1935), 21, 34–35.

religion, romanticism, ritual, regionalism, and localized institutions were respected. Their emotionally tinged picture of the Old South, of a delightful, self-assured, relaxed culture, was sharply and, in their skilled literary phrases, brilliantly contrasted with the fast tempo of modern life, with its ceaseless hard work, gross materialism, and vulgar capitalistic rationale. Although mainly an academic protest, the Southern agrarians were aware of Southern problems and advocated a redistribution of property and a return to subsistence farming. Enthroning Jefferson as their political and economic deity, they argued that only men with the actual control of the means of production, preferably farm land, could be independent of other men and, hence, politically free.[43]

One of the most influential agrarians or distributists was Ralph Borsodi, who in 1920 personally started subsistence farming on a small homestead near New York City. By utilizing labor-saving tools and by growing and processing a phenomenal number of foods, Borsodi achieved economic independence and became the supreme exemplar of self-sufficient farming and successful back-to-the-land. Borsodi, who also favored the single tax, aesthetically revolted against the ugliness of the city and found his subsistence homestead an avenue to freedom and independence, but not to leisure. For quality-minded, freedom-seeking individuals, Borsodi proposed subsistence homesteads as an escape, as little islands "of intelligence and beauty amidst the chaotic seas of human stupidity and ugliness."[44] In the depression Borsodi found several to follow him back to the land. When the Division of Subsistence Homesteads was established, Borsodi was already guiding the development of a homestead colony in Dayton, Ohio. The first subsistence homesteads loan went to this project, although Borsodi, who had hailed the subsistence homesteads legislation as the beginning of a new, distributive era, soon became disgusted with government control.[45]

[43] Twelve Southerners, *I'll Take My Stand* (New York, 1930), pp. 12, 51–53, 152, 244; Patrick F. Quinn, "Agrarianism and the Jeffersonian Philosophy," *Review of Politics*, II (1940), 88; Frank L. Owsley, "The Pillars of Agrarianism," *American Review*, IV (1934–1935), 529–574.

[44] Ralph Borsodi, *This Ugly Civilization* (New York, 1929), p. 221.

[45] Ralph Borsodi, *Flight from the City* (New York, 1933), pp. xix–xxii, "Subsistence Homesteads: President Roosevelt's New Land and Population Policy," *Survey Graphic*, XXIII (1934), 11–14, and "Democracy, Plutocracy, Bureaucracy," *Free America*, III (Aug., 1939), 10–12.

The Land

Another influential distributist was Herbert Agar, a historian and newspaper writer who, while in England as a reporter, received his agrarian inspiration directly from Belloc and other English distributists. Back in America, he became an effective advocate of a redistribution of property and a decentralization of industry. Agar looked into history for his ideal but, unlike the other agrarians, did not color his history with a sectional or religious bias. In two excellent historical interpretations, *The People's Choice* and *Pursuit of Happiness*, Agar passionately defended the Jeffersonian philosophy of equal rights for all and special privileges for none, but pointed out how the Jeffersonian ideal had found less and less expression in American life.[46] Agar recognized the kinship between the English distributists, the Catholic Rural Life Conference, the Southern agrarians, and Borsodi. Partly through his efforts, all the agrarian groups participated in a meeting in Nashville in 1936, jointly published a new book, *Who Owns America?* [47] and launched an agrarian, distributist magazine, *Free America,* which consistently advocated decentralization, subsistence homesteads, and co-operatives.[48]

In the twenties Henry Ford expressed the prevailing sentiment when he said that farming, in the old subsistence sense, was an antiquated way of life, since everyone had moved into a money tradition. Yet the agrarians had pleaded the sufficiency and superiority of the traditional farm and had hurled vitriolic insults at the money tradition. After 1929, as the depression deepened and hopes of quick recovery faded, the agrarians apparently were vindicated, for prosperity had certainly been fickle. As industry failed, men, driven by necessity, turned back to the farm, for subsistence and not for money. The exact size of the back-to-the-land movement from 1930 to 1934 can only be estimated, although it was certainly exaggerated by the newspaper accounts which portrayed a veritable flood of population moving to the country.[49] One factor that made the exodus seem so large was the diminishing number of farmers flocking to the city. In one estimate, the Bureau of Agricultural Economics indicated that, in 1930, for the first time, there were more migrations to the country than

---

[46] Herbert Agar, *Pursuit of Happiness* (Cambridge, Mass., 1938), and *The People's Choice* (Boston, 1933).

[47] Herbert Agar and Allen Tate, eds., *Who Owns America?* (Boston, 1936).

[48] Editorial, *Free America,* I (Jan., 1937), 4.

[49] Bercaw, Hannay, and Colvin, *Bibliography on Land Settlement,* pp. 69–104.

to the city. The net gain of the country, according to this estimate, was 17,000 in 1930, 214,000 in 1931, and 533,000 in 1932, after which the trend reverted back to normal, with the city gaining 277,000 in 1933. A later estimate revealed only one year, 1932, in which the countryward migration was the larger, and that by only 266,000.[50]

Regardless of the number involved, never before in the history of the United States had back-to-the-land been so popular, so frequently discussed, and so susceptible to crackpot schemes. Necessarily, there was pathos, humor, and romanticism in the movement. One critical writer described the movement: "The march back home moves to a various inner music, as profound and cleansing as the psalm beginning, 'The Lord is my Shepherd,' and as noisily self-deceptive as a mammy song."[51] The logic of the movement was often very simple: "Here are idle men; there are vacant acres; get them together and Mother Earth and Mother Nature will wipe all tears from their eyes and they shall be happy and satisfied in a primitive acadian simplicity."[52] A realtor's advertisement in the *Wall Street Journal* stated: "Buy an abandoned farm and live on trout and applejack until the upturn."[53] Henry Ford, as his contribution to the public welfare, put out a series of advertisements which proclaimed: "The Land! That is where our roots are."[54] One writer announced that "more log cabins are being built in the United States than at any time since Abraham Lincoln was a rail-splitter."[55] Some of the back-to-the-land movement merely represented farm boys returning to their fathers' farms, or farm laborers who had drifted to town and now drifted back to the farm, or Negroes who had come North and now were returning to the South. Others, and these were more pathetic, were returning to mountain shacks or formerly abandoned submarginal farms barely to subsist on meager diets. Even cityfolk without farming experience were moving to suburban subsistence farms or, tragically deceived, were buying deserted, unproductive farms with their last savings. Many

---

[50] Edmund de S. Brunner and Irving Lorge, *Rural Trends in Depression Years* (New York, 1937), p. 81.

[51] Russell Lord, "Back to the Farm," *Forum*, LXXXIX (1933), 97–98.

[52] Willard T. Davis and Malcolm Cowley, "How Far Back to the Land?" *New Republic*, LXXV (1933), 336.

[53] Lord, "Back to the Farm," p. 98.   [54] *Ibid.*, p. 97.

[55] Arthur Pound, "Land Ho!" *Atlantic Monthly*, CLI (1933), 715.

The Land

voices began to demand reason instead of romanticism and direction and instruction for the prospective back-to-the-lander. Newly created social problems appeared; and the inescapable facts of unemployment remained, with many predicting that because of technological advances employment could never again include all the prospective workers.[56] The "march back home" continued.

One way of relief lay close at hand. The vacant-lot–garden idea was resuscitated. Garden clubs sprang up all over the country, with the Extension Service of the Department of Agriculture reporting that a large share of its work consisted of directing and assisting the new gardeners. In Kansas, a farm state, sixty-three of seventy-eight counties had garden plans by 1933.[57] Many large corporations provided garden space for their employees. Standard Oil, Studebaker, and the American Rolling Mill Company donated land for individual gardens. B. F. Goodrich promoted community gardens, as did United States Steel. Forty per cent of the railroad companies promoted gardens. But it was Henry Ford who went the limit. He sponsored 50,000 gardens in the Detroit area and astonished the nation by announcing that, starting in 1932, no employee of his woodworking plant at Iron Mountain, Michigan, could retain his job unless he grew a garden to supply part of his winter food needs. On his part, Ford promised that the company would provide expert aid and plots for those who needed them.[58] Ford, who had heretofore been unsuccessful in marrying shop and field, decreed that "the man too lazy to work in a garden during his leisure time does not deserve a job." His dictatorial decree was quickly called paternalism and the gardens dubbed "shotgun gardens." [59]

A number of more ambitious back-to-the-land schemes were successfully managed. The Atlanta Chamber of Commerce sent several

[56] *Ibid.*, pp. 716–717, 719.

[57] Department of Agriculture, Agricultural Extension Service, "Subsistence Gardens Flourish," *Extension Service Review*, IV (Nov., 1933), 109.

[58] Warren Bishop, "How Business Fights the Wolf," *Nation's Business*, XX (Nov., 1933), 24–25, 54; U.S. Department of Labor, Bureau of Labor Statistics, "Gardens for Unemployed Workers," *Monthly Labor Review*, XXXV (1932), 495–496; "Ford Promotes His Hobby to Unite Farm and Factory," *Business Week*, Sept. 2, 1931, p. 23.

[59] "Stirred Up by Henry Ford's Shotgun Gardens," *Literary Digest*, CX (Sept. 12, 1931), 10.

selected families back to farms. Los Angeles proposed a "land chest" for its one-foot-in-the-country part-time farmers.[60] In Muscogee County, Georgia, a local relief commission aided city dwellers in returning to tenant farming.[61] In Michigan 300 families from large cities established the Sunrise Co-operative Farm Community on 10,000 acres of land, where they planned to raise all needed food and enough marketable products to procure clothing. They shared everything in common, even making the care of children a community matter.[62] After three years of unsuccessful operation by about seventy-five Jewish families the Sunrise Co-operative Community was sold in 1936 to the Resettlement Administration and became the site of the Saginaw Valley Farms, a rural resettlement community. Across the border, in Canada, both Saskatchewan and Manitoba advanced funds to selected back-to-the-landers.[63] One of the more ambitious schemes in the United States, and one that materially influenced subsistence homesteads legislation, was carried out in Greenville, South Carolina. In 1931 Charles L. Richardson, Commissioner of Conciliation, Department of Labor, was sent to Greenville to assist in relief to the unemployed. With the assistance of Red Cross workers and funds, Richardson placed forty-two destitute families on abandoned farms in the area around the city. Most of the farms were acquired at a small rent from the Farm Loan Bank. Contrary to many predictions the farmers remained on the land.[64]

By 1932 several people were clamoring for some directed program of land settlement. The Salvation Army had complete plans for moving thousands to the country, but insufficient funds.[65] One proposal, based on past plans within the Reclamation Service, suggested that a colony be established in each state, utilizing the engineering ability of the Bureau of Reclamation, the agricultural advice of the Department of Agriculture, and the ready funds of the Federal Land Bank.[66] A more elaborate scheme called for an agricultural army. Enlisted

[60] Back-to-the-Land," *Survey*, LXVIII (1932), 614.
[61] Lord and Johnstone, *A Place on Earth*, pp. 12–13.
[62] "Unemployed Workers Farm 10,000 Acres in Michigan," *American Observer*, III (Oct. 25, 1933), 6.
[63] Murchie, *Land Settlement as a Relief Measure*, pp. 16–18.
[64] House Committee on Labor, *Hearings on Relief of Distress Due to Unemployment*, pp. 35–42; "By Way of the Hoe," *Survey*, LXVII (1932), 538.
[65] *C.R.*, 72d Cong., 1st Sess., 1932, p. 15385.
[66] Alvin Johnson, "Relief from Farm Relief," *Yale Review*, XXII (1932), 64.

The Land

families, officered by skilled agriculturalists, would build log houses, wear homespun, and grow food only for their own consumption. The author of this plan pointed to its small cost and to the fact that the army colonies would become great farm demonstration units and that the agricultural army, permanently organized, would offer a lasting guarantee to everyone of the right to work.[67]

Bernarr Macfadden, physical culturist and publisher of several newspapers and cheap magazines, probably did more than anyone else to promote back-to-the-land legislation in the United States Congress.[68] In 1932 and 1933 he maintained a lobbyist in Washington to develop support for a government subsistence homesteads program. By means of a stream of articles in his publications he defended the idea. To Macfadden the problem was very simple—get the people on the land and they could take care of themselves. In short, he wanted the government to "take people out of the bread line and put them upon land and give them some coarse food and implements that are essential to work the land and enable them to raise their own vegetables." [69] Other considerations about the people's welfare did not matter to Macfadden, who declared that it made no "difference whether the people have much to wear; they will be satisfied with enough to eat." [70] As a result of Macfadden's efforts and in light of relief measures already undertaken in Greenville, South Carolina, and in New York State, Loring M. Black, Jr., Representative from New York, introduced two bills in 1932 providing for government information or assistance to those seeking subsistence living in rural areas.[71] In the Senate, Charles L. McNary of Oregon introduced an almost identical measure in the form of a joint resolution.[72] The Senate resolution called for the Department of Agriculture (the Black bills designated the Department of Labor) to provide information to prospective back-to-the-landers about available lands and sources of finance.[73] One of the Black bills went farther and provided for an appropriation of $10,000,-

[67] Malcolm McDermott, "An Agricultural Army," *South Atlantic Quarterly*, XXXI (1932), 181–183.

[68] Lord and Johnstone, *A Place on Earth*, p. 23.

[69] House Committee on Labor, *Hearings on Relief of Distress Due to Unemployment*, p. 23.

[70] Ibid.   [71] C.R., 72d Cong., 1st Sess., 1932, p. 15384.

[72] Ibid., p. 15381.

[73] Senate Committee on Agriculture and Forestry, *The United Communities*, Report no. 799, 72d Cong., 1st Sess., 1932, pp. 1–2.

000 to be used by the Department of Labor in providing farming opportunities to destitute and unemployed persons with former agricultural experience.[74]

Since these Macfadden bills, as they were referred to in congressional debate, were the most direct antecedents of the later subsistence homesteads legislation and the only bills to receive any attention from the floor of Congress, the committee hearings and floor debate on these measures remain the sole indication of early congressional sentiment toward subsistence homesteads. The Black bill requiring an appropriation of $10,000,000 was not reported from the House Committee on Labor because it had no chance of passage in a penurious Congress.[75] The Senate Joint Resolution, which received a favorable report by the Committee on Agriculture and Forestry, passed in the Senate by voice vote, despite the reluctant acceptance given the bill by Secretary of Agriculture Arthur M. Hyde, who was much concerned about the effect the measure might have upon mounting agricultural surpluses.[76] The Black bills received a hearing before the House Committee on Labor, where the most extensive and objective testimony was given by Dr. John D. Black, Harvard professor and farm economist for the Federal Farm Board. Black cautiously admitted possibilities of temporary relief in idle farms near cities and in city gardens. He also predicted a future need, after the return of prosperity, for the planned development of small, part-time farms near cities, but advised against any extensive colonization plans in a depression, pointing to past failures and prohibitive costs. The other witnesses were largely back-to-the-land advocates who compensated for their vague plans by their sincere fervor. The parade of advocates, many already discussed in former pages, included Macfadden; his lobbyist, Mrs. Edith R. Lumsden; Mrs. Haviland D. Lund, of the former National Forward to the Land League; Edgar Schmiedeler, who represented the views of the Catholic Rural Life Conference; Miss Mae A. Schnurr of the Bureau of Reclamation; Hugh MacRae, a Wilmington, North Carolina, businessman who had established some farming colonies; and others representing Negroes, the Department of

---

[74] House Committee on Labor, *Hearings on Relief of Distress Due to Unemployment*, pp. 1–2.

[75] *C.R.*, 72d Cong., 1st Sess., 1932, p. 15386.

[76] *Ibid.*, p. 13839; Senate Committee on Agriculture and Forestry, *The United Communities*, pp. 1–2.

The Land

Labor, and a back-to-the-land movement within the Episcopal Church.[77]

On the floor of the House of Representatives the Senate-approved joint resolution was subjected to the only extensive floor debate ever accorded subsistence homesteads legislation. Defended on the basis of pressing need by its cosponsor, Loring Black, the resolution was most cogently attacked by Fiorello H. LaGuardia of New York, who described it as worthless without an appropriation. He argued that moving destitute men back to the farm was a "hard, practical, proposition" requiring extensive guidance and financial assistance, for "everything is not what it once was on the farm." LaGuardia castigated Congress for continually seeking inexpensive but ineffective palliatives.[78] Also opposing the bill on very effective grounds were farm-state congressmen who wished to protect the farmer from possible competition by back-to-the-landers.[79]

Most of the arguments contained more eloquence and invective than calm reason. Robert A. Green of Florida declared that it was either back to the farm now or later for millions of unemployed, who were never going to find employment again and who would have to seek relief on the millions of idle acres, where they could "from the breast of mother nature wring an existence." [80] But to Green this was not bad news: "The farms have always produced our great leaders in finance, industry and statesmanship. . . . The vast population must depart from the congested industrial centers and cities and once again become self-sustaining on our vast and fertile farms, pasture, and prairie lands. Herein lies the real hope for the bright destiny of America." [81] Green had a vision of a new America just ten years in the future, when there would be no congested industrial centers and the "choice people of America would live on farms, free, independent and happy, living by the sweat of their honest brows, laboring beneath the blue canopy of heaven." [82] William H. Stafford of Wisconsin declared that on the farm the poor could "have a cow and a pig and the like" and there "make a step toward relieving themselves and those dearest to them by cultivating God's native soil." [83] His colleague from Wisconsin and

---

[77] House Committee on Labor, *Hearings on Relief of Distress Due to Unemployment*, pp. 5–108.
[78] *C.R.*, 72d Cong., 1st Sess., 1932, p. 15385.   [79] *Ibid.*, p. 15387.
[80] *Ibid.*, p. 15386.   [81] *Ibid.*   [82] *Ibid.*   [83] *Ibid.*, p. 15385.

the most bitter critic of the resolution, John C. Schafer, suggested that Macfadden use his wealth to furnish the back-to-the-landers a cow and a pig, as well as a year's subscription to *True Stories* or *True Romances.* Schafer facetiously asked: "Are you going to take these poor unemployed city people with their little children, and put them out on the farms where it is sometimes 22 degrees below zero and where the snow is as high as 10 feet deep, and then say that you are saving them?" [84] Also, "If a neighbor gives them a cow . . . what are they going to feed it? Snow from some of the banks 5 or 6 or 10 feet deep?" [85] By a vote of 75 to 58 the House sent the resolution back to committee. Later it was resurrected only to be tabled.[86]

In New York State a temporary Emergency Relief Administration had actually assisted many people back to the land. This received the approval of New York's governor, Franklin D. Roosevelt. As early as 1913 Roosevelt had suggested that suburban farms should be provided for city dwellers, thereby making city life tolerable and cities places "where people will be pretty proud to hail from." [87] This desire to provide an institutional link between city and country led Roosevelt into an advocacy of both suburban and rural planning, rather than purely sentimental back-to-the-land schemes. But always, with Roosevelt, there was a kinship with the more romantic agrarians. According to Rexford G. Tugwell, Roosevelt "always did, and always would, think people better off in the country and would regard the cities as rather hopeless." [88] In 1911 Roosevelt gave the following statement of his agrarianism: "In fact, I might almost say that the political salvation of the country lies with the country men and boys. Not because they are more honest or more patriotic than their brothers in the cities, but because they have more time to think and study for themselves." [89] Tugwell discovered this rural pattern of thinking in Roosevelt and used it to get close to him. In the "brain trust" days before Roosevelt entered the White House, he described to Tugwell in nostalgic terms his ambition to place the unemployed population on subsistence homesteads. According to Tugwell they "again and again explored the delights of country life, detailed the possibilities of improvement, and

[84] *Ibid.*, p. 15389.   [85] *Ibid.*   [86] *Ibid.*, pp. 15390, 15725.
[87] Rexford G. Tugwell, "The Sources of New Deal Reformism," *Ethics*, LXIV (1954), 276.
[88] *Ibid.*, p. 266.
[89] *Ibid.*, p. 275, as quoted from the New York *Globe*, Feb. 6, 1911.

The Land

speculated about means for introducing rural virtues into cities." [90] Tugwell believed it "sheer luck that I caught the meaning to him of country life" and ascribed his later appointment as Assistant Secretary of Agriculture to his and Roosevelt's mutual exploration of the "emotional paths" of rural life.[91] In 1931 Roosevelt, when commenting on the back-to-the-land movement, asked the following leading question: "Suppose one were to offer these [unemployed] men opportunity to go on the land, to provide a house and a few acres in the country and a little money and tools to put in small food crops?" [92] He believed the idea had implications worth serious consideration.

In 1931, at the request of President Hoover's Committee on Unemployment Relief and of the Federal Children's Bureau, the American Friends Service Committee, under the direction of its executive secretary, Clarence E. Pickett, began extensive child feeding and other relief activities in the bituminous coal fields of West Virginia, Maryland, Kentucky, Tennessee, Illinois, and Pennsylvania.[93] The Friends, in addition to distributing food, decided to try to do some permanent rehabilitation work with the estimated 500,000 unemployed and stranded people. Assisted by the Federal Council of Churches and with some guidance from the United States Bureau of Education and the Pennsylvania State Bureau of Education, the committee began moving miners to subsistence farms elsewhere and, at the same time, started a part-time farming, part-time mining program for the ones remaining in the mine areas. As further assistance, the Friends, working without exact precedents, established handicraft shops and promoted gardening clubs. A Mountaineer Craftsman's Co-operative Association employed fifty men and women in weaving and furniture making in the Morgantown, West Virginia, area.[94]

[90] Rexford G. Tugwell, "The Preparation of a President," *Western Political Quarterly*, I (1948), 132–133.

[91] *Ibid.*, pp. 133–134.

[92] Franklin D. Roosevelt, "Back to the Land," *Review of Reviews*, LXXXIV (Oct., 1931), 64.

[93] American Friends Service Committee, *Annual Report for 1931–32* (Philadelphia, 1932), p. 15.

[94] Clarence E. Pickett, *For More than Bread* (Boston, 1953), pp. 21–22; American Friends Service Committee, *Annual Report for 1933* (Philadelphia, 1933), pp. 16–17; American Friends Service Committee, *Report of the Child Relief Work in the Bituminous Coal Fields, September 1, 1931—August 31, 1932* (n.p., n.d.), pp. 8–10, 15–17.

The experiences of the Friends Service Committee in West Virginia attracted the attention of Eleanor Roosevelt, who visited the West Virginia mining area just after Franklin D. Roosevelt entered the White House. This visit stimulated her interest in the plight of the miners and in subsistence homesteads. Her interest practically assured a government-sponsored subsistence homesteads project for the Morgantown area. It also led to the appointment of Clarence E. Pickett as Assistant Administrator of the Division of Subsistence Homesteads.[95] In addition, the later handicraft program of the Subsistence Homesteads Division was first developed in the pioneer work of the Friends. Many of the Friends' relief workers continued to assist voluntarily after the work was taken over by the government, some living in subsistence homesteads and devoting themselves to community building or to the establishment of co-operative shops.[96] Four of the most controversial subsistence homesteads communities (Arthurdale, Cumberland Homesteads, Westmoreland Homesteads, and Tygart Valley Homesteads) developed from the Friends' activities.

The back-to-the-land movement, springing from the urgency of depression or founded largely in nebulous, romantic, or escapist philosophies, was relatively unimportant in giving direction to the actual administration of the subsistence homesteads and resettlement programs. As a whole, the direction of, as well as part of the motivation for, government communities came from social scientists and from advocates of governmental planning. Although the back-to-the-land movement contributed such men as Macfadden, MacRae, Borsodi, Father Ligutti, and Clarence Pickett to the actual administration or policy making of the Division of Subsistence Homesteads, those men, excepting Pickett, either soon left the movement or exerted a strictly local influence on single projects. But it is almost inconceivable that there would have been any subsistence homesteads legislation without the back-to-the-land movement of the depression period. This fact alone made the back-to-the-land movement an important, even a basic, factor in the entrance of the federal government into the field of community building.

[95] Pickett, *For More than Bread*, pp. 44–45.
[96] American Friends Service Committee, *Annual Report for 1934* (Philadelphia, 1934), p. 15.

❧ II ❦

Bringing the Town to the Country

"BACK-to-the-land" was not the only slogan that influenced the creation of the New Deal communities. After 1929 the concept of "planning" also became a slogan and a proposed escape from insecurity. Just as much as a wholesale return to the land, "planning," if the implications of the term had been fully defined and comprehended, probably implied more a revolution than a mere palliative. But most of the people, businessmen included, who acclaimed planning in 1933 comprehended only their own distress. They no more understood the implications of the term "planning" than many urbanites comprehended the true situation back on the farm. It even seems likely that Franklin D. Roosevelt acclaimed planning without a full understanding of its implications. Yet, as one convinced planner has said, Roosevelt's first historic achievement was that "in his campaign for the presidency, [he] raised economic and social planning to the status of a recognized national policy." [1]

In origin the New Deal communities were very closely associated with this new emphasis on planning. Three related but separate planning movements influenced the entrance of the government into the field of community building and contributed almost all the personnel to the agencies that planned and developed the communities. One very significant movement was concerned with the development of a

---

[1] Louis L. Lorwin, *Time for Planning* (New York, 1945), p. 137.

policy of planned land settlement, directed toward organized rural communities containing many urban advantages. Another was the city planning movement or, more specifically, a certain element in the city planning movement which emphasized the need for developing wholly new towns or communities in a spacious, rural environment. Lastly, and perhaps most important, was the movement, at first largely among economists in the universities, for a broad program of national economic planning which, most important for the New Deal communities, included land-use and agricultural planning. These three movements will be considered in this and the next two chapters.

Before approaching either of the above-mentioned planning movements, a few comments on the term "planning" are worth while. Planning itself denotes purposeful endeavor and is, therefore, an activity possible for all men. To plan is to be human. Individuals are constantly selecting goals and means to achieve them—or, in other words, are planning. But at the time of the New Deal the term "planning" was related not to individuals but to a group of individuals or a whole nation planning collectively. If everyone in a state could agree on ends and means, collective planning would involve no sharp distinction from individual planning, but obviously individuals do not always agree on either ends or means. This fact severely restricts the amount of collective planning possible in a society or necessitates some degree of discipline on the part of individuals. Much of this discipline will be voluntary—in fact, in a democratic society, the degree of voluntary discipline almost determines the extent of collective planning. On the other hand, in any society there is some coercive, involuntary discipline, particularly for small minorities. In all cases some individuals do not share in the planning but are necessarily included in it. The greater the extension of collective planning, the greater is the likelihood that a larger number of individuals will have to be coerced unless some emergency or crisis, such as war or depression, causes more people to be willing voluntarily to acquiesce in common goals and programs. In these instances the planning program, with its restrictions on individual freedom, will last only as long as the crisis unless some method of coercion, such as propaganda or police methods, is instituted.

In 1933 the term "planning" usually implied planning by a government. Collective programs were to be realized through the instrumen-

Bringing Town to Country

tality of government. Actually the very existence of government almost necessitates some type of collective planning. In the United States the government had always implemented certain common goals, either those held by many people or by a few powerful people. Thus, in the New Deal, the real argument was not over state planning but over the extent of state planning, which, in reality, was the old argument over the desirable role and function of a government in a society. Yet the term "government," even in the most representative republics, is usually associated not with the voting public but with the individuals, elected or appointed, who execute public programs. Regardless of the method used in selecting these programs, much of the policy, much of the detailed planning, is left to these public officials. In modern governments the complexities of administration require more and more expert knowledge from the bureaucrats, thus separating them and their work more and more from the voting masses. The bureaucrat becomes not only an agent to implement the goals of the people, but himself plans broad programs which he may or may not have to present to the voters for approval or disapproval. Thus, in the New Deal, the increased emphasis on the term "planning" not only implied an increased role for the State in society but, springing from this, an increased importance for the bureaucratic expert.

Finally, the term "planning" meant, to many people in 1933, a certain "looking forward" activity within a government. This specific activity could be either a part of ordinary action programs or a special branch of government, such as state or city planning boards or commissions. In either case highly skilled professional planners were to be utilized by the government to study future needs and to recommend specific policies or programs. Although their recommendations would be based not only on detailed statistical studies but also on their personal philosophies, this type of planning apparently promised better government, since policies and programs would be selected only on the basis of comprehensive and technically accurate facts. Thus, to some, governmental planning meant better, more efficient government. To others it also meant more government, with new programs being based on the social vision of enlightened planning officials.

When, around 1900, a few individuals began to ask for a government policy of planned and directed land settlement, they were asking for a complete revision of the recent United States policy toward land settlement. In colonial America the public lands in New England were settled under rigid regulations and controls. The townships often were settled under regulations governing the size of family units, the time limits on full settlement, the size of houses, the amount of land to be improved, the provision of church and school facilities, and the ultimate disposition of surrounding land. In 1784 and 1785, partly because of the influence of Thomas Jefferson, much of the New England idea of directed colonization was incorporated into the first land ordinances. Surveys were to precede sales. A section was to be reserved for education. Four sections were retained for the future disposal by Congress, and one-third of the mineral rights were reserved for Congress. Land was to be sold by townships and, to secure compactness, each township was to be completely sold before a new one was opened to sale. Of these early provisions only the requirement of prior survey and the reservation for schools were retained as permanent, though much abused, policies in the nineteenth century.[2]

Apparently the main objective of nineteenth-century public land policies was the most rapid possible disposal of the public lands to private individuals. Even the early use of the lands as a source of revenue was gradually replaced by liberal pre-emption and homestead acts, as well as by huge grants for internal improvements. Except for the idea that ownership should be widely diffused in family-size farms, there were few guiding objectives. Mineral and timber rights were given away or sold at fractions of their value, without awareness of public interest. Even the few regulations as to survey and recording of titles were never enforceable. The people desired free land and little control over how they settled it.[3] The public interest may not have been served, but, in a democracy, who can safeguard the public interest except the public itself?

Even as the better public lands began to disappear, new settlement policies were developed. The short-lived and unsatisfactory Timber Culture Act of 1873, which required all homesteaders on the plains to cultivate a fixed acreage of trees, represented a beautiful dream of dark green trees on the bleak treeless plain.[4] As Secretary of the

[2] Benjamin H. Hibbard, *A History of the Public Land Policies* (New York, 1924), pp. 36–40.
[3] *Ibid.*, pp. 550–551.   [4] *Ibid.*, p. 413.

Interior under Hayes, Carl Schurz recommended the withdrawal of timberlands from homestead entry and requested a law providing for timber culture. In 1879 the United States Geological Survey and the Public Land Commission were established, eventuating in a land conference in the same year. A strong conservation movement developed in the eighties, led by the American Forestry Association, which was founded in 1884. It was ably supported by many young, German-trained economists who united to form the American Economic Association in 1885. They not only had observed German scientific forestry but had learned that the state could safely enter the realm of economic regulation. In 1891 an act to repeal the several timber culture laws led to a virtual revolution in public land policy, for the act permitted the President to set aside public lands as forest reserves. After a century of rapid disposal, a policy of retention was adopted. Under Theodore Roosevelt, a passionate conservationist, the new policy bore abundant fruit, for he set aside 148,346,925 acres; he also extended the policy of retention to oil lands, power and reservoir sites, and mineral lands. This was the beginning of the end for the old public land policies, although it was only on February 5, 1935, that Franklin D. Roosevelt withdrew the last of the public lands from entry.[5]

Conservation marked the negative aspect of the new land policy. The positive side of the new policies involved the development of land resources and the control and direction of settlement. This was, until the New Deal, almost entirely confined to reclamation projects. After several years of agitation for an irrigation program by the national government, the Newlands Reclamation Act was passed in June, 1902. It represented the first time that the government had ever assumed a responsibility for improving the land before sale. The act, which was defended as being similar to river and harbor legislation, became a subject of popular interest, reflecting expansionist and nationalistic sentiments, as well as a neo-Malthusian belief in the continuous expansion of population. It was defended by arguments for conservation, home building, and the relief of congested cities. Like

---

[5] Roy M. Robbins, *Our Landed Heritage* (Princeton, N.J., 1942), pp. 286–290, 422; Leonard A. Salter, Jr., *A Critical Review of Research in Land Economics* (Minneapolis, 1948), pp. 6–7; Hibbard, *A History of the Public Land Policies*, pp. 520–523, 530–531.

all subsequent reclamation or land settlement legislation, it was opposed by the Midwestern farmers who saw, in reclamation projects, government-sponsored and aided competition. They argued that the act was unconstitutional and that the government had the power only to dispose of its public lands, not to develop them.[6]

The Newlands Reclamation Act did not mark a revolutionary departure from the objectives of past land legislation. The government assumed the new task of constructing irrigation works, utilizing funds from the sale of public lands, but the homesteaders on an irrigation project had to repay the government over a period of ten years.[7] Acreage limitations and residence requirements were often abused in practice, but in principle the old idea of complete, fee simple ownership of small farms by individual farmers was honored. In the Newlands Act every possible attempt was made to limit government paternalism to the minimum task of constructing the dams and irrigation works, a task manifestly impossible for an individual settler. As soon as paid for, the works were to be maintained and operated by the settlers, although the actual title remained in the hands of the government. There was no provision for the selection of settlers, for the provision of credit, or for the preparation of the farms to receive water.[8]

Although the Newslands Act was hardly changed until the twenties, a whole new philosophy of land settlement and reclamation, as well as a changed concept of the role or function of government, was developed by individuals closely connected with national or state reclamation agencies. One of these individuals so influenced reclamation and land settlement policies in the United States that he, virtually alone, was responsible for two decades of attempted revision and reform in reclamation. Eventually his ideas, almost in their totality,

[6] John T. Ganoe, "The Origin of a National Reclamation Policy," *Mississippi Valley Historical Review*, XVIII (1931), 48–51; Lewis C. Gray, "The Principles of Land Planning," in *Planned Society*, ed. by Findlay Mackenzie (New York, 1937), p. 167; Dorothy Lampen, *Economic and Social Aspects of Federal Reclamation* (Johns Hopkins University Studies in History and Political Science, Ser. XLVIII, no. 1; Baltimore, 1930), p. 49.

[7] Clarence J. McCormick, "It Can Be Solved," in *Land Tenure*, ed. by Kenneth H. Parsons, Raymond J. Penn, and Philip M. Raup (Madison, Wis., 1956), p. 31.

[8] F. H. Newell and others, "Federal Land Reclamation: A National Problem," *Engineering News-Record*, XCI (1923), 668, 802–807.

were adapted to the rural communities constructed by the New Deal. His name was Elwood Mead.

Elwood Mead, a civil engineer and irrigation authority, served with the United States Engineers and as a college professor before becoming territorial engineer of Wyoming in 1888. From 1897 to 1907 he was professor of institutions and practices of irrigation at the University of California, at the same time serving the United States Department of Agriculture as an irrigation and drainage investigator. In 1904 he received an honorary doctorate in engineering from Purdue University. In 1907 he began the most formative experience in his life as head of the State Rivers and Water Supply Commission of Victoria, Australia.[9] In Victoria, Mead supervised the reclamation and settlement of thirty-two irrigation projects. In Australia the state purchased land, by compulsion if necessary, built the irrigation works, readied and even planted the land, constructed roads and laid out towns, prepared house plans, built fences, and located prospective livestock before the settlers were invited to the project. The settler, after paying one-third of the purchase price of a home, selected his house plan. The government then built his house. The settler received expert advice in purchasing his livestock and in his farming, got his nursery stock from a government nursery, and marketed his products through government-supported co-operatives and with the aid of government dairies, warehouses, and slaughterhouses. He enjoyed the social life of a nearby village or town, which had, very likely, been planned by an English city planner, and received twenty-year loans for up to 60 per cent of his needed improvements. Although the settler purchased his land on long terms, he never received clear title, for he was required to live on and cultivate his own land in order to retain it.[10] Mead enthusiastically endorsed this type of land settlement. It became his ideal. He felt a great compulsion to bring all his newly discovered ideas to the United States and see them applied to what he believed to be a declining American agriculture.[11]

In the words of an admirer, Elwood Mead dreamed "the most

[9] Vernon M. Cady, "A Western Experiment in Land Settlement," *Survey*, XL (1918), 686.

[10] Elwood Mead, "Government Aid and Direction in Land Settlement," *American Economic Review*, Supplement to vol. VIII (1918), 89–91; Frederic C. Howe, "Land Settlement and the Soldier," *Nation*, CVIII (1919), 426.

[11] Howe, "Land Settlement and the Soldier," p. 426.

wonderful dream of social reclamation in America."[12] Mead wished the United States to adopt the Australian idea of an organized rural society. He realized that for the United States to do this would involve an almost revolutionary increase in the role of government. This he welcomed. From his travels he became convinced that the United States was behind the rest of the world in industrial and social legislation. The state should be the great co-ordinating force in industry and commerce; yet it was not so in the United States, where the best leadership and most capable technicians went into business instead of into government. A false feeling that inefficiency and waste were inseparable from self-government had resulted in governmental functions being turned over to private enterprise. He believed that increased governmental functions would enhance rather than limit freedom, for there could be no true freedom as long as want and misery existed in the midst of plenty. He pointed to New Zealand and Australia, where the government operated railroads, telephones, telegraphs, streetcars, and express lines and where it constructed urban and rural housing, as examples of beneficial paternalism. He urged America to give up the idea that the state was purely a political institution with no concern in human endeavor, for the state was, at its best, a business partner.[13] The paternalism "which creates opportunity for industry and thrift, awakens hope, arouses ambition, and strengthens belief in the brotherhood of man, is altogether good in its influence on character and on the prosperity of the state."[14]

Although Mead wanted a new role for government in all realms, he was content to labor for an improved rural life. He was enough of an agrarian to believe that the life of even a modern nation depended upon a prosperous, contented, landowning farm population. Yet, to him, farm life in America was declining as the youth of the country flocked to the cities. Mead believed that the clue to the evil was to be found in the unorganized, unplanned nature of American country life.[15] Past land policies had led to speculation, high land prices, wasted soil, inefficiency, and tenancy and, most important, to

---

[12] U.S. Senate, *Proceedings of the Southern Reclamation Conference,* Document no. 45, 70th Cong., 1st Sess., 1928, p. 31.
[13] Elwood Mead, *Helping Men Own Farms* (New York, 1928), pp. 201–208.
[14] *Ibid.,* p. 207.
[15] Elwood Mead, "Advantages of a Planned Rural Development," *Agricultural Engineering,* III (1922), 42.

Bringing Town to Country

a deplorable lack of the social and community life obtainable in towns and cities. A planned rural development was vitally necessary in order to check political unrest and the migration to cities. As a beginning basis for reform, Mead suggested the implementation of the principle of landownership for those who actually cultivated the soil. Although he advocated tenant purchase laws, changes in tenure, regulated tenancy, and even the single tax to reduce speculation in land, Mead believed that the best starting place for land reform was in the area of reclamation, where fully new communities could be created to demonstrate the best principles of rural planning.[16] The reclamation service had done excellent engineering in the past, but nothing else. Mead wished to combine social reclamation with land reclamation, social engineering with irrigation engineering.

Mead's idea of an organized rural society included many innovations for American agriculture. The first and most basic necessity of rural planning, according to Mead, was group rather than individual settlement. Community settlement meant not only recreational and social advantages, but also co-operative institutions. It required the grouping of the farms around a village or community center, which would contain stores, the church and school, co-operative markets, and a community building. He desired the whole settlement to be planned in advance by agricultural experts, with the land prepared and planted and with house designs available for quick, wholesale construction. Around the village area Mead desired subsistence homesteads of two or three acres for farm laborers, eliminating the problems of migrant labor. After settlement he desired expert direction by agricultural experts. For the village he recognized the possibilities of handicrafts or small industries. He desired some modification of land tenure in order to insure that the settler would remain on his land, although he believed that this would conflict with the American psychology. Finally, he wanted a long purchase contract, with terms up to forty years, as well as credit for improvements and equipment, all this to be secured by a large initial down payment and by a very careful selection of settlers.[17]

[16] Mead, "Government Aid and Direction in Land Settlement," pp. 72–75, 82–85.

[17] Mead, *Helping Men Own Farms*, pp. 187–191; Howe, "Land Settlement and the Soldier," p. 427.

As the Australian land settlements proved successful, at least at first, Mead became more and more desirous of introducing the same methods into the United States. In 1914 he visited the University of California and discussed his ideas with the president of the university, the dean of the College of Agriculture, and the governor and lieutenant governor of California. Hiram W. Johnson, the reform governor of California, along with the others, believed that it would be possible to adapt Mead's type of settlement to the state of California, but not until public opinion was educated to accept what was so radical a change in policy. The educational campaign was launched through the influential Commonwealth Club of California, to which Mead outlined his ideas in May, 1914. In 1915 Elwood Mead returned permanently from Australia to head a state-appointed Commission on Colonization and Rural Credits and to resume his teaching at the University of California. The report of the commission, under Mead's direction, was entirely in favor of California's developing a model farm settlement of approximately 10,000 acres. The proposal, based on extensive studies of existing settlement plans, was sharply debated in the Commonwealth Club. It was defended as a remedy for speculation and for all the human tragedies that had resulted on past irrigation projects because of inadequate preparation, lack of guidance and supervision, absence of credit, lack of settler selection, and inadequate safeguards against tenancy. It was vigorously opposed as an attack on meritorious land agents and private colonization companies, as governmental competition with business, as destructive of democracy, as not recognizing the inefficiency and destructive tendencies always present in government, as subsidized competition against farmers, as the type of paternalism that leads to a shirking of responsibility, as against the American tradition of free and independent farmers, and as subversive of the native spirit of liberty which had led to the universal superiority of the Anglo-Saxon race.[18]

In 1917 the California legislature accepted the recommendation of Mead and his commission and enacted the first land settlement act in United States history. It followed very closely a Victoria, Aus-

[18] "Unemployment," *Transactions of the Commonwealth Club of California*, IX (1914), 682–684; "The Land Settlement Bill," *ibid.*, X (1915), 83; "Land Settlement in California," *ibid.*, XI (1916), 369–373, 397–398, 404–405, 427–428; "The Land Settlement Bill of 1917," *ibid.*, XII (1917), 12–16, 24–29, 33–39.

tralia, law of 1909 and included almost all of Mead's treasured ideas, providing an initial appropriation of $260,000 to begin a 10,000-acre project.[19] Mead became chairman of the Land Settlement Board which was created to implement the act. The board established the first project at Durham, Butte County, on 6,239 acres of carefully selected and surveyed land, which was divided into approximately 110 farm allotments and 30 farm laborers' allotments. The College of Agriculture of the University of California helped in the project, making surveys and classifying soils. America had never before seen what happened at Durham. The happy settler was greeted with fields of growing wheat, by an architect with varying house designs, and by a permanent farm adviser and business manager. The homes, which included electricity and running water, were quickly constructed at wholesale prices.[20] The settlers, carefully selected by Mead's Land Settlement Board, were judged on character and past farming experience. Each settler could purchase his land with only a 5 per cent down payment, with the rest payable in twenty years at 5 per cent interest, along with additional loans for his house and farm equipment. Until paid for, the land could not be sold without the board's approval. The colonist had to remain on his land for eight months out of twelve for the first ten years, a requirement that was not as far-reaching as Mead had desired.[21]

The Durham Colony early appeared to be a great success. By 1919 the state had appropriated an additional $1,000,000 for land settlement and had slightly amended the original act to give preference to returning soldiers. In 1919 the second colony, Delhi, was launched with even greater enthusiasm than had been Durham, perhaps because Delhi was planned for returning soldiers. Commissions and official delegates from more than forty foreign countries and one-half of the states visited the two colonies.[22] In Colorado, North

[19] Mead, *Helping Men Own Farms*, pp. 32, 108.

[20] California Department of Agriculture, Division of Land Settlement, *Final Report, June 30, 1931* (Sacramento, 1931), pp. 3, 27; Elwood Mead, "Buying a Farm in the New Way: The Success of California's New Plan," *Ladies Home Journal*, XXXVI (June, 1919), 37.

[21] Mead, *Helping Men Own Farms*, pp. 215–228, and "Government Aid and Direction," pp. 78–79; Elwood Mead, "The New Forty Niners," *Survey*, XLVII (1921–1922), 653–654.

[22] Mead, "The New Forty Niners," pp. 651, 654; California Department of Agriculture, *Final Report*, p. 27.

Carolina, and South Carolina similar state projects were contemplated but never completed. In Arizona, Washington, Minnesota, and South Dakota projects were actually begun, but all were unsuccessful. In fact, all did not remain well in California. The minimum security for such expensive developments as Durham and Delhi was destroyed by the farm depression beginning in 1921. Durham, well launched and more soundly planned, survived without complete disaster.[23] In 1927 only about one-third of the settlers were seriously delinquent in their payments.[24] Delhi fared much worse. Begun in the inflation of 1919 and managed by overzealous employees of what was referred to as "the academic type," Delhi succumbed to the depression and was an almost complete financial loss to the state. After the expensive improvements, such as a $35,000 pipe factory and a $10,000 community hall, many of the settlers had to pay $400 an acre for their land, much of which was planted in fruit trees which could not bear for several years. By 1928 almost one-half of Delhi's 8,400 acres were unsold.[25] By 1925 the California government, which had become increasingly hostile to farm settlement and which resented the $1,000,000 already apparently lost in the two colonies, was ready to withdraw from the business of land colonization as quickly as possible. Beginning in 1928, a laborious, involved, and embittering process of litigation was undertaken. By July, 1930, the State of California had finally effected a settlement with the colonists at Durham and Delhi. Mead, who had dreamed of four or five colonies each year in California, had to admit certain mistakes at Delhi, mistakes for which he blamed the unpredicted depression, a hostile governor, and irresponsible colonists, but not the ideas that went into the colonies.[26]

The ideas of Elwood Mead quickly spread to Washington, giving

[23] Bertha Henderson, "State Policies in Agricultural Settlement," *Journal of Land and Public Utility Economics*, II (1926), 290–291; William A. Hartman, "State Policies in Regulating Land Settlement Activities," *Journal of Farm Economics*, XIII (1931), 261–262.

[24] California Department of Agriculture, *Final Report*, p. 9.

[25] "The State Colony Settlements," *Transactions of the Commonwealth Club of California*, XVI (1921), 262–263, 267; Hartman, "State Policies in Regulating Land Settlement Activities," p. 261.

[26] "What of the Colony Plan of Land Settlement?" *Agricultural Review*, XVIII (April, 1925), 16–17; California Department of Agriculture, *Final Report*, pp. 11–15.

form to a settlement plan already developed in the Department of Labor. As early as 1915, Secretary of Labor William B. Wilson proposed a new role for the federal government. He believed that the Department of Labor not only should seek jobs for the unemployed, but should create jobs through such utilization of the natural resources as would "tend to make opportunities for workers greater than demands for work and to keep them so."[27] He believed this possible, without a revolution, by properly using the public lands. His program, as then outlined, was general in nature. The public domain should be retained and enlarged by the purchase of unused private lands. Farm lands should be allotted to unemployed laborers, with such tenure arrangements as would prevent inflated land values. Finally, the settlers would be supplied credit, farming education, and marketing services. This program, he believed, would take the place of the antiquated homestead law and the frontier safety valve as a permanent relief for industrial distress.[28] In the reports of the Department of Labor for 1916, 1917, and 1918, Wilson again urgently advocated his plan, especially as a means of caring for the employment needs of the returning soldiers.[29] His most comprehensive recommendation was for a permanent national board to carry out a resources development and colonization program, with duties even more comprehensive than those of Mead's California Land Settlement Board. It was proposed as a permanent source of employment, eliminating the distress of depressions.[30]

Secretary Wilson's colonization scheme was introduced into Congress in 1916 by Representative Robert Crosser of Ohio. The Crosser colonization bill provided for a colonization board, headed by the Secretary of Labor, but including the Secretaries of Agriculture and the Interior. In order to create employment for the urban unemployed,

[27] Department of Labor, *Annual Report, 1915* (Washington, 1916), p. 44.
[28] *Ibid.*, pp. 43–44.
[29] Department of Labor, *Annual Report, 1916* (Washington, 1917), p. 73, *Annual Report, 1917* (Washington, 1918), p. 153, and *Annual Report, 1918* (Washington, 1919), pp. 145–146, 222–224.
[30] Benton Mackaye, "Making New Opportunity for Employment," in U.S. Department of Labor, Bureau of Labor Statistics, *Monthly Labor Review*, VIII (1919), 1067–1068; Benton Mackaye, *Possibilities of Making New Opportunities for Employment through the Settlement and Development of Agricultural and Forest Lands and Other Resources* (U.S. Department of Labor; Washington, 1919), pp. 19–21, 28–33.

the board was to be empowered to examine and acquire land for farm colonies, either by purchase or by reserving public lands. After acquisition a detailed colonization plan was to be submitted to the President. The land in the developed colonies was to be permanently retained by the United States, with settlers acquiring leases only on land which they personally needed for the support of their families. If desired, two or more families could combine their land for cooperative farming. The lease would require a payment of 4 per cent of the development cost each year, for fifty years, and an additional payment in lieu of taxes. The bill provided for a beginning colonization fund of $50,000,000. The colonies were to be of a community type, with public services and government aid to co-operatives.[31] The Crosser bill, which anticipated so much of the New Deal community program, was defended by labor interests in a congressional hearing but was never referred for a vote.[32]

The widespread desire to provide opportunities for the returning soldiers of World War I provided the ideal setting for Elwood Mead to secure a national policy of directed land settlement and rural planning. He found an idealistic and effective ally in Franklin K. Lane, Secretary of the Interior. According to Mead, it was partly because of an invitation from Lane that he returned from Australia to the United States in 1915.[33] In 1918 Mead left his California settlements to join Lane in Washington, where he worked in the reclamation section of the Department of the Interior. Together, Lane and Mead planned and promoted a scheme for soldier settlement that, for a period of over two years, was to secure national acclaim and widespread publicity.

On May 31, 1918, Secretary Lane sent a much-publicized letter to President Wilson in which he proposed a national soldier settlement program. In the past returning soldiers had received bounties in land. Although no frontier existed in 1918, Lane believed that the soldiers of World War I, acclimated to an out-of-doors existence, would still want opportunities to go on farms, not in the old pioneer fashion,

[31] House Committee on Labor, *Hearings on H.R. 11329, National Colonization Bill,* 64th Cong., 1st Sess., 1916, pp. 5–10.
[32] *Ibid.*, pp. 10–11, 23, 31, 41–42, 51–65.
[33] Senate Committee on Irrigation and Reclamation, *Hearings on S. 2015, Creation of Organized Rural Communities to Demonstrate the Benefits of Planned Settlement,* 70th Cong., 1st Sess., 1928, p. 7.

but in the new, Mead-developed methods of colonization, with pre-development, security, and community life. These opportunities could be provided by a large-scale reclamation program, extending beyond arid lands to the swamps and cutover lands of every state in the Union. The soldiers could cease killing enemies and start developing resources, at the same time creating their own future homes. It all should be done, said Lane, upon "a definite planning basis," each project being as carefully planned as "the city of Washington." [34] The plan was endorsed by Woodrow Wilson, who saw in it a part of the enlarged public works program proposed by the Department of Labor. In one of his last statements, Theodore Roosevelt vigorously defended the idea.[35]

Franklin K. Lane combined Jeffersonian agrarianism with a concept of enlarged governmental responsibility. He believed it time that the nation provide not merely soldiers, but every man in the United States, an opportunity for employment.[36] In the Department of the Interior, Lane was most interested in "looking-forward work" or in so planning for the future as to prevent in America "those ills which have fallen upon other lands." [37] This looking forward was, to Lane as to Mead, primarily concentrated upon the agricultural situation. To Lane, the "spirit of democracy does not thrive where men live without the hope of land ownership. There is something peculiarly subtle in the feeling that a bit of the soil is one's own. It makes for a stronger, higher citizenship. It gives birth to loyalties that are essential to national life and to a healthy home life." [38] To be assured a living, as farmers are, is at the very center of "the free life of a democracy." The soldiers, used to a life of doing, of close companionship, of suffering, would return as men, not boys. According to Lane they would want a man's life on returning, or a chance to make their way on a farm. But they would not want the lack of society, the distance between homes, the remote post office and newspaper, and

---

[34] Department of the Interior, *Annual Report for the Fiscal Year Ended June 30, 1918* (Washington, 1919), pp. 24–29.

[35] Senate Committee on the Public Lands, *Work and Homes for Returning Soldiers, Sailors, and Marines*, Report no. 780 to accompany S. 5652, 65th Cong., 3d Sess., 1919, pp. 6–7.

[36] *Ibid.*, p. 30.

[37] Department of the Interior, *Annual Report, June 30, 1918*, p. 3.

[38] *Ibid.*, p. 11.

the poor schools of most rural life. The longing in the heart for contact with the soil had, because of these adverse conditions, often turned to a passion for the city. The only solution to the problem, according to Lane, was to develop a new rural life with all the urban advantages—in fact, to marry the two. He believed that the United States should turn to the farm village, as Europe had, or to settlement around a community center which could contain the advantages of city life. Co-operation could banish isolation; there could be motion pictures and baseball teams, and "there'll be a dance every week in the community house." [39] Lane summed up his dreams in the following picture: "all these farms—which shall not be large, but large enough to support a man, his wife, and three or four children, but not large enough to make a basis of speculation—small farms, intensively cultivated, sufficient for a man and his family; with a central community, and that community having the telephone, and good roads, and the telegraph and the post office, and the good school, and the bank, and the good store all close together, so that the women can talk across the back fence and the man can meet his neighbors." [40]

Lane's soldier settlement idea resulted in a full-scale national debate. As individuals and through the Department of the Interior, Lane and Mead continued to be the spokesmen for the measure, defending it as a means of saving the labor market from collapse, of stopping the alarming movement of people to the cities, of developing American resources, and of setting up throughout the United States examples of the most modern patterns of farm settlement.[41] Frederic Howe wrote a book to raise support for the plan, fervently defending it as a step toward economic democracy in America.[42] The American Legion endorsed the measure, as could be expected.[43] As

---

[39] Henry Irving Dodge, "Back to the Land for Soldiers: An Interview with Franklin K. Lane, Secretary of the Interior," *Country Gentleman*, LXXXIV (Feb. 15, 1919), 46.

[40] Franklin K. Lane, "Bringing Unused Land into Service," *American City*, XX (1919), 318.

[41] Department of the Interior, *Annual Report, June 30, 1918*, p. 6.

[42] Frederic C. Howe, *The Land and the Soldier* (New York, 1919), pp. 5–13.

[43] House Committee on the Public Lands, *National Soldier Settlement Act*, Report no. 216 to accompany H.R. 487, 66th Cong., 1st Sess., 1919, p. 10.

always when reclamation measures were proposed, the farmers and farm organizations were the largest element in opposition. A representative of the National Grange branded the soldier settlement idea as "fundamentally un-American, un-democratic, undesirable, and indefensible." He believed it "paternalistic, socialistic, communistic, bolshevistic, or anything of that kind." He asked why the soldiers had to be set up to compete with farmers; why not in manufacturing or business? Then all the city people would not back it so strongly.[44] Senator James W. Wadsworth of New York cited the then hated Germans as an example of the products of the government paternalism that was implied in the Lane proposal. He declared the whole scheme a fizzle, a publicity stunt to attract the soldiers who wanted something for nothing.[45] Perhaps the most important opinion should have been that of the soldier. By an eye-catching booklet entitled *Hey There! Do You Want a Home on the Farm?* Lane tried to arouse the soldiers' interest, although his method was later severely criticized. From 900,000 of these booklets, which included return postal cards, Lane received 119,000 cards and 65,000 letters, almost all favorable or interested.[46]

At least a dozen soldier settlement measures were introduced into Congress. Only the first of these, a bill that appropriated $200,000 for a preliminary investigation of the public lands available for soldier settlement, ever passed both houses.[47] The most important bill, introduced by Representative Frank W. Mondell of Wyoming, was in part written by Elwood Mead and was very similar to the California Land Settlement Act. It provided for federal-state cooperation and a beginning appropriation of $500,000,000.[48] Soldier settlement bills were extensively debated in committee hearings, were

[44] House Committee on the Public Lands, *Hearings on H.R. 487, Homes for Soldiers*, Part 1, 66th Cong., 1st Sess., 1919, pp. 72–74.

[45] House Committee on Irrigation and Reclamation, *Hearings on H.R. 11171 and H.R. 12083, Aided and Directed Settlement on Proposed Government Irrigation Projects*, 68th Cong., 2d Sess., 1925, p. 47; James W. Wadsworth, "Land Settlement Problems to Be Solved by Self-Help and Not by Government Paternalism," *Sea Power*, Nov., 1919, pp. 237–239.

[46] U.S. House of Representatives, *Farms for Soldiers*, House Document no. 173, 66th Cong., 1st Sess., 1919, pp. 1–2.

[47] C.R., 65th Cong., 2d Sess., 1918, pp. 11590–11592.

[48] House Committee on the Public Lands, *Hearings on H.R. 487*, pp. 3–7, 27.

reported favorably by both Senate and House committees, and one bill was passed in the House in 1920.[49] A surviving version was incorporated into a bonus bill that was eventually vetoed by President Harding.[50] The only substantial reward granted to soldiers was a sixty-day homestead privilege on all public lands open to entry.[51] Thirty-seven states passed some type of soldier settlement legislation, but almost all of these bills were dependent upon federal action. Except for Delhi, the only notable soldier settlement was in conjunction with an agricultural training program for disabled veterans at the University of Minnesota and under the sponsorship of the Veterans' Administration.[52] The twenties were to show that the need for small farm development was not great enough to sustain the early public interest. Even the soldiers preferred cash bonuses to farming opportunities.[53]

Even though soldier settlement failed in Congress, Elwood Mead's prestige did not suffer greatly, for he was still the most prominent irrigation authority in the United States. As such his talents were not tied to politics. Moreover, the first object of his reforming zeal, the Reclamation Service, was still in existence, operating under the virtually unchanged Newlands Act of 1902. But in the twenties the old reclamation program proved inadequate. With the farm recession that began in 1921 and lasted throughout the twenties, many settlers on irrigation projects suffered financial distress, requiring a series of leniency acts to relieve them of monthly payments to the government. These moratoriums prejudiced the whole future of reclamation,

[49] *C.R.*, 65th Cong., 3d Sess., 1919, pp. 4855, 4856; *ibid.*, 66th Cong., 1st Sess., 1919, pp. 4370, 4375; House Committee on the Public Lands, *National Soldier Settlement Act*, Report no. 216, p. 7, and *Hearings on H.R. 487*, pp. 17–18; Golzé, *Reclamation in the United States*, p. 368.

[50] U.S. Senate, *Forestry, Reclamation, and Home-making Conference, 1923*, Document no. 120, 68th Cong., 1st Sess., 1923, p. 14.

[51] House Committee on Irrigation and Reclamation, *Hearings on H.R. 520, Settlement of Returning Veterans on Farms in Reclamation Projects*, 79th Cong., 1st Sess., 1945, pp. 90–91.

[52] Department of the Interior, Bureau of Reclamation, "Nation-wide Approval of Secretary Lane's Soldier-Settlement Plan," *Reclamation Record*, X (1919), pp. 195–196; U.S. Veterans' Bureau, *Annual Report of the Director for the Year Ending June 30, 1922* (Washington, 1922), p. 322; Hartman, "State Policies in Regulating Land Settlement," p. 262.

[53] House Committee on Irrigation and Reclamation, *Hearings on H.R. 520*, pp. 216–217.

which was already under attack because of mounting agricultural surpluses.[54] In 1923 Secretary of the Interior Hubert Work appointed a special fact-finding committee to investigate the whole reclamation program and report their findings. One of the seven members of this committee was Elwood Mead, who had again been in Australia and in Palestine as a reclamation consultant of the British Government.[55]

The report (called the Fact Finders' Report) of the special committee opened a new era for reclamation in the United States. The report was obviously much influenced by Mead's ideas, for it advocated his type of settlement and stressed human factors as well as engineering techniques. In brief, the committee advocated government-developed projects, long-term credit, directed and supervised agriculture, and a careful selection of settlers.[56] In April, 1924, Secretary Work appointed Elwood Mead as Commissioner of the newly created Bureau of Reclamation (the old Reclamation Service), a position that he was to retain until his death in 1936. As Commissioner, Mead tried to implement the Fact Finders' Report and to reorientate the bureau toward a greater consideration of human values.[57] Congress refused to implement all of the committee's recommendations, rejecting bills for aided and directed settlement in 1925 and 1928.[58] It did pass an act in 1926 that permitted a careful selection of settlers by a Board of Examiners.[59] The failure of Congress to approve any further revision in reclamation policy can, in part at least, be attributed to the hostility of agricultural groups and even to the open hostility of the Department of Agriculture. But as Commissioner, Mead had the honor of planning some of the largest reclamation projects in the world, including Hoover Dam on the Colorado

---

[54] Lampen, *Economic and Social Aspects of Federal Reclamation*, p. 61.

[55] U.S. Department of the Interior, Bureau of Reclamation, "Special Advisors Continue Reclamation Analysis," *Reclamation Record*, XV (Jan., 1924), p. 3.

[56] U.S. Department of the Interior, Bureau of Reclamation, "Impending Reclamation Disaster May Be Averted," *Reclamation Record*, XV (May, 1924), pp. 68–69.

[57] Elwood Mead, "What Federal Reclamation Should Include," *Agricultural Engineering*, VII (1926), 237.

[58] House Committee on Irrigation and Reclamation, *Hearings on H.R. 11171 and H.R. 12083*, pp. 1–3, 4–19, 37–87, and *Hearings on H.R. 9956, Aided and Directed Settlement on Government Irrigation Projects*, 70th Cong., 1st Sess., 1928, pp. 1–2, 63–64.

[59] Mead, "What Federal Reclamation Should Include," p. 238.

(the lake was named for him) and Grand Coulee on the Columbia.

Although Mead could not get his settlement ideas incorporated into the regular reclamation program, he found extensive support for planned agricultural settlements in the South. After the failure of soldier settlement, which would have meant projects in the swamplands of the South, many Southerners continued to seek an expansion of reclamation to the South. In December, 1924, Congress authorized an appropriation of $15,000 to be used by Secretary Work and the Bureau of Reclamation in investigating the possibilities of developing arid, semiarid, swamp, and cutover lands. Work used this small sum to investigate opportunities in the South, sending a special advisory committee that was accompanied by Elwood Mead.[60] These advisers called for experimental farm colonies in every Southern state. Except for the lack of irrigation, each was to resemble Durham and Delhi. It was hoped that the colonies, which were to include farmers and farm laborers, would demonstrate the value of a planned, diversified agriculture to an agriculturally backward South. In 1927 a congress of representative Southerners met with Mead in Washington to study the plans, and Southern congressmen introduced appropriate bills in each house of Congress. These bills, which in most details anticipated the rural resettlement communities of the New Deal, were reported favorably, but never came to a vote.[61] President Coolidge opposed them as being against his economic policy.[62] Two of the most loyal advocates of these Southern colonies, Senator John H. Bankhead and Representative William B. Bankhead of Alabama, were later to lead the legislative fight for subsistence homesteads communities.

[60] U.S. Senate, *Proceedings of the Southern Reclamation Conference*, p. iii; U.S. Department of the Interior, Bureau of Reclamation, *Reclamation and Rural Development in the South*, in House Document no. 765, pt. 1, 69th Cong., 2d Sess., 1927, p. 2.

[61] U.S. Department of the Interior, Bureau of Reclamation, *Reclamation and Rural Development in the South*, pp. 1–3, 38; U.S. Senate, *Proceedings of the Southern Reclamation Conference*, pp. iv, 1–5, 8–15; Senate Committee on Irrigation and Reclamation, *Hearings on S. 2015*, pp. 1–3; House Committee on Irrigation and Reclamation, *Creation of Organized Rural Communities*, Report no. 1217 to accompany H.R. 8221, 70th Cong., 1st Sess., 1928, pp. 1–8; C.R., 70th Cong., 1st Sess., 1928, p. 9353.

[62] House Committee on Irrigation and Reclamation, *Creation of Organized Rural Communities*, p. 8.

As reclamation became increasingly unpopular in the twenties, its advocates were forced into a dilemma not of their own choosing. In 1918, with booming agricultural prices and a seemingly inexhaustible foreign market, reclamation and the more intensive farming it required seemed almost a necessity. But during the twenties the prices dropped and the market fell. The advocates of reclamation, mostly from the Western states, and the bitter foes of reclamation, mostly Midwestern or Eastern farmers, were alike influenced by their own selfish interests. Nevertheless the Midwestern farmers were more in line with reality. Whether because of the lingering exuberance of a young, rapidly expanding nation or because of a failure to comprehend the implications of ever-newer advances in technology, many Americans had difficulty in adjusting to the idea of a surplus economy. Yet it already existed in agriculture, which has a much more rigid ceiling of demand than most other industries. Despite Elwood Mead's laudable application of economics to reclamation and despite all his human-centered planning, the inescapable fact remained that, from the viewpoint of the over-all economy, further expensive reclamation projects could not be justified by any need for increased agricultural production.[63] In fact, the reclamation projects were having a demonstrably harmful effect on farm prices. Thus, during the twenties a sizable departmental conflict developed between the Departments of Agriculture and the Interior. The farm economists, from a large, national view of economic trends, constantly deplored any new farm development and questioned the logic of more emphasis upon the small farm. They even referred to the proposed Southern colonies as beginning steps toward economic peonage.[64] It was not that the agriculturalists questioned Mead's emphasis on planning, but rather that they questioned the ability of the Department of the Interior to plan for agriculture. They believed that, from a national viewpoint, a planned reduction of farming acreage and production, not further development, was demanded. Henry C. Wallace, as Secretary of Agriculture in 1924, bitterly stated the farmers' opposition to reclama-

[63] Frank P. Willits, "The Futility of Further Development of Irrigation Projects," *Annals of the American Academy*, CXLII (1929), 186–195.

[64] Millard Peck, "Reclamation Projects and Their Relation to Agricultural Depression," *Annals of the American Academy*, CXLII (1929), 179–180, 184–185; Louis J. Taber, "Reclamation in Dollars and Sense," *Nation's Business*, XVI (Sept., 1928), 69.

tion: "Reclamation policies should grow out of public needs and agricultural possibilities and not out of the dreams of engineers or the ambitions of empire builders who wish to 'develop the country' usually for the benefit of their own pocketbooks and at the expense of the hungry home seeker." [65]

To an optimistic, growing America, Elwood Mead had proclaimed a new type of magic—the magic of governmental planning and organization. This magic, freely applied to the development of rural communities, was to bring salvation to a declining agriculture and, indirectly, to a whole nation. Although the magic did not always work well when tried, as in California, it retained a tremendous appeal for many people. Mead's work in community building, unfortunately for him, was always connected with the reclamation and development of new agricultural resources. But Mead's magic was not necessarily tied to expansion, to optimism, to development, to reclamation. In the New Deal it was to be utilized in subsistence homesteads communities that were born in deepest pessimism over the economic future of America. A little later it was to be applied, in purest form, to rural resettlement communities that, at least theoretically, were to complement a large program of land retirement and population displacement.

[65] Henry C. Wallace, "A National Agricultural Program—A Farm Management Problem," *Journal of Farm Economics*, VI (1924), 6–7.

≽ III ≼

Bringing the Country to the Town

EVEN as Elwood Mead was applying the magic of planning to rural problems, an ever-growing number of people in the cities were attempting to apply the same magic to urban problems. By 1900 a few urbanites were decrying narrow streets and unhealthy slums and were demanding, among other reforms, some public control over future urban growth, as well as the imposition of some plan or pattern on past unregulated development. Thus the group of emerging city planners were confronted with problems never faced by Elwood Mead, for in the case of his reclamation projects the planning agency owned and controlled the land area to be developed. But even in urban expansion the city planning agency usually did not own the land and had to persuade or legally compel private individuals to conform to the public interest as reflected in development plans. Except for limited land purchases by the municipal government, any attempts to remedy past mistakes in city growth immediately confronted entrenched private interests. Faced with these difficult problems, city planners, or city patchers, were usually too concerned with the purely spatial or physical planning of streets and buildings to give much time to the smaller details of social planning, such as cooperation, economic security, and a healthy social intercourse, that typified much of Mead's rural planning. Even as Mead, on the rural scene, had turned from the problems of past misplanning to the freer, more appealing adventure of constructing small models of a new agricultural order, a few city planners turned from the frustrating problems of the older cities to the exhilarating task of building completely new and more perfect towns or suburban communities, each combining the spaciousness and beauty of the country with the social and economic advantages of the city. These latter planners greatly influenced the New Deal communities, particularly the greenbelt towns.

Just as Elwood Mead's crusade for guided and directed settlement was an attempt to resurrect an established policy of colonial New England, so the new emphasis on city planning marked the rebirth of a lost art in America, for in colonial times there had been notable examples of city planning. A zoning law for the Massachusetts Bay Colony was passed under William and Mary. Savannah and Philadelphia were carefully planned by their proprietary founders.[1] This planning emphasis was still potent enough to influence George Washington and Thomas Jefferson to co-operate in the planning of a beautiful national capital which still remains a proud monument to the use of foresight in the laying out of cities. Jefferson carefully studied European cities and dutifully brought back from Europe the plans of eleven cities, mostly French. Unfortunately more Washingtons, more carefully planned cities, were not forthcoming. For some reason nineteenth-century cities grew without objectives or conscious direction. Like Jefferson's ideas on controlled land settlement, city planning also disappeared in the rush to conquer a continent. American cities just grew, and the results were as unfortunate as those of an uncontrolled rural development.

Soon after the Civil War, Frederick Law Olmsted, the pioneer of modern American city planners, began using vision and skill in planning parks and thoroughfares, with Central Park in New York City his best-known monument.[2] In 1869 plans were developed for two completely new towns, Riverside, Illinois, and Garden City, Long Island. Garden City marked the first use of a term which was later to have a very definite and significant meaning in city planning. Alexander T. Stewart, a New York department store owner, acquired 8,000 acres on Long Island where, by the time of his death in 1876,

[1] Thomas Adams, *Outline of Town and City Planning* (New York, 1935), p. 120.
[2] *Ibid.*, p. 167.

he had created a truly spacious village of 102 homes. Garden City later received national fame as the site of a large publishing house.[3] Before 1900 several small towns and villages were carefully planned, including the single-tax colony of Fairhope, Alabama, and the industrial villages of Pullman, Illinois; Sparrowspoint, Maryland; Vandergrift, Pennsylvania; and Hopedale, Massachusetts.[4] In 1893 the beautiful White City exhibit at the Chicago World's Fair led to a revival of interest in city beautification and in the civic possibilities that had been neglected in a period of rapid industrialization. Just before 1900 L'Enfant's original plan of Washington was rediscovered, leading to a revival of the plan by a newly appointed District Park Commission.[5] During the next few years a score of advisory city plans were drawn for cities throughout the country by such emerging planners as John Nolen, Frederick Law Olmsted, Daniel Burnham, and Charles M. Robinson.[6] Just as the century turned, the English garden city added a new perspective to American city planning.

The garden city idea, which was originated by Ebenezer Howard, an evangelical but nonviolent London reformer and court reporter, was quickly adopted and implemented in England by technically qualified city planners. The idea was too visionary for much practical application in replanning older cities, but inspired the design of new towns or additions and eventually provided the pattern for the greenbelt communities of the New Deal. Howard was influenced by the social enthusiasm engendered in England by the Fabians, by Ruskin's economic ideas, by the Christian Social Union and the settlement house movement, and by the ideas of Henry George, Robert Owen, and Edward Bellamy. In a book published in 1898 Howard, utilizing city plans or colonization schemes developed by James Silk Buckingham, Alfred Marshall, Edward G. Wakefield, Sir Titus Salt, George Cadbury, and William H. Lever, proposed an appealing marriage

---

[3] Thomas Adams, "The Planning and Subdivision of Land," in *Neighborhood and Community Planning*, vol. VII of *Regional Survey of New York and Its Environs* (New York, 1929), pp. 257–258.

[4] Adams, *Outline of Town and City Planning*, pp. 168, 177–178.

[5] Frederick Law Olmsted, "The Town Planning Movement in America," *Annals of the American Academy*, LI (1914), 179.

[6] Theodora Kimball Hubbard and Henry Vincent Hubbard, *Our Cities Today and Tomorrow: A Survey of Planning and Zoning Progress in the United States* (Cambridge, Mass., 1929), pp. 5–6.

of town and country by the construction of a city that would be limited in size by, and organically related to, an encircling belt of rural countryside.[7] Howard believed that crowded, slum-infested cities were an evil, but from a visit to a farm in Nebraska, Howard had also discovered the trials of an isolated, unco-operative rural life. Thus he wished to combine the magnetic attractions of both city and country by combining the higher wages, employment opportunities, social advantages, and well-lit streets of the cities with the beauty of nature, fresh air, low rents, bright sunshine, woods, meadows, and forests of the country.[8]

To combine city and country Howard proposed the development of a completely new garden city in a rural setting. In order to realize all of his ideas, Howard proposed that the land for both the city and the surrounding greenbelt be owned by trustees who, as owners, would be able to develop a carefully planned, spacious, well-rounded industrial city of a limited size, set in the midst of prosperous farm land. The city would reap the health benefits and aesthetic rewards of nearby forests and farms, and the equally fortunate farmers would have the ready market and social pleasures of a nearby town. The rapidly rising value of the land, occasioned by a growing city, Howard believed, would result in ground rents sufficient to cover all development costs and, with the original investors receiving only a limited dividend as profit, would also pay for all municipal services. Thus the city dwellers as a whole, and not a few speculators, would receive the benefits of the social increment.[9]

As a model for a garden city Howard proposed a schematic, circular town plan that was probably too unrealistic to be of any value. But the principles underlying the garden city idea became permanent attributes of garden city planning in England and all over the world. The garden city was to be a method of decentralizing both industry and population. It was to be a city of limited size, eternally pro-

[7] Dugald Macfadyen, *Sir Ebenezer Howard and the Town Planning Movement* (Manchester, Eng., 1933), pp. 12, 18, 20–21, 33; James Silk Buckingham, *National Evils and Practical Remedies* (London, 1849), pp. 110–135; James Dahir, *Communities for Better Living* (New York, 1950), p. 110; Frederic J. Osborn, *Green-Belt Cities: The British Contribution* (London, 1946), p. 176; Adams, *Outline of Town and City Planning*, pp. 270–271.

[8] Ebenezer Howard, *Garden Cities of Tomorrow* (3d ed.; London, 1902), pp. 13–17.

[9] *Ibid.*, pp. 20–22, 28–29; Osborn, *Green-Belt Cities*, p. 27.

Bringing Country to Town

hibited from sprawling growth by its greenbelt.[10] The plan of the city would be enforceable through the very effective expedient of a unified or community ownership of all the land. All private homes, all industry, and all businesses were to be constructed on leased land, with certain prescribed building agreements written into the leases. As Howard conceived it, a garden city would be a balanced city of about 30,000 people, including laborers, capitalists, professional people, and businessmen. Except for Howard's desire that the city control retail outlets in the interest of the consumer, the business life of a garden city was to be very similar to that of any other town.[11] Howard envisioned a rapid growth of garden cities. They were to be units in a new civilization, replacing slum-infested cities with beautiful home towns, with parks and gardens, surrounded by green farms. If followed resolutely, this new path to reform would "lead society to a far higher destiny than it has ever yet ventured to hope for," Howard believed.[12] It would be the key "to a portal through which, even when scarce ajar, will be seen to pour a flood of light on the problems of intemperance, of excessive toil, of restless anxiety, of grinding poverty—the true limits of Government interference, ay, and even the relations of man to the Supreme Power."[13] To Howard, garden cities alone could develop better, healthier housing conditions, lead to a higher purchasing power for labor, provide everyone with the amenities of life, and give cultural advantages to agriculture.

Ebenezer Howard never thought of his garden city idea as a speculative utopia. Rather, he saw it as the foundation of a new civilization which could be realized only as his ideas bore practical results. Through his book and public lectures Howard found ready support for garden cities. After one year of personal campaigning Howard formed the Garden City Association in June, 1899. Supported early by single taxers and soon thereafter by businessmen, the association became the nucleus of the city planning movement in England and rapidly raised enough support to construct the first garden city. In April, 1903, a 3,818-acre (later increased to 4,500 acres) plot of land was purchased in Hertfordshire. Here, under the direction of a limited-dividend company, the first garden city, Letchworth, was be-

[10] Osborn, *Green-Belt Cities*, pp. 32–33.
[11] Howard, *Garden Cities*, pp. 72, 76–79.   [12] *Ibid.*, p. 115.
[13] *Ibid.*, p. 13.

gun in October, 1903.¹⁴ Although Howard remained the evangel of garden cities, Letchworth was planned by two technically qualified architects, Raymond Unwin and Barry Parker. Unwin, Parker, and the first secretary of the Garden City Association, Thomas Adams, were to become world famous as city planners. The plan of the city of Letchworth, which was adapted to an undulating terrain, included large open spaces for parks and playgrounds. The industrial areas were placed on the edge of town and separated from residential areas by strips of forest land. The development company retained freehold possession of the land, both in the city and in the 3,000-acre greenbelt, and leased it to individuals or corporations on 99- or 990-year leases.¹⁵ Letchworth grew slowly but steadily into a mixed industrial city of 22,000 people in 1947. Departing only slightly from the ideas of Howard, it became a world-famous model of new city planning techniques. In 1919, under the personal initiative of Howard, a second garden city, Welwyn, was begun. Financed by government loans, Welwyn grew more rapidly than Letchworth and exhibited a greater architectural unity.¹⁶ Though many of the ideas have been widely copied, Letchworth and Welwyn remain until this day the only true garden cities (as Howard defined the term).

The visual demonstration of Ebenezer Howard's ideas at Letchworth led to a world-wide garden city movement. In its idealism appealing to the broadest public, as well as to city planners, the garden city movement led to a virtual renaissance of city planning in England. By 1909 the Garden City Association had become a town planning organization with an emphasis on new towns of the garden city type. From all over the world it received inquiries about Letchworth or about city planning.¹⁷ In 1914 the International Federation

---

[14] Macfadyen, *Sir Ebenezer Howard*, pp. 25, 39; Frederic J. Osborn, "Planning in Great Britain: The Part of Voluntary Societies," *Journal of the American Institute of Planners*, XIV (Summer, 1948), 22–23; Charles B. Purdom, *The Garden City: A Study in the Development of a Modern Town* (London, 1913), p. 31.

[15] Sir Edgar Bonham Carter, "Garden Cities and Satellite Towns and Decentralization," *Journal of the Town Planning Institute*, XVI (Nov., 1929), 14–18; Purdom, *The Garden City*, pp. 291–293.

[16] Frederic J. Osborn, "New Towns in Britain," *Journal of the American Institute of Planners*, XIII (Winter, 1947), 7–8; Macfadyen, *Sir Ebenezer Howard*, pp. 101–102; Dahir, *Communities for Better Living*, p. 117.

[17] Ewart G. Culpin, *Garden City Movement Up-to-Date* (London, 1914), p. 17; Purdom, *The Garden City*, pp. 298–299.

for Town and Country Planning and Garden Cities was formed, with societies in most European countries, in the British Dominions, and in the United States.[18] It was to remain the most important international city planning organization. In England and in other countries the creation of Letchworth led to a flurry of so-called garden cities, garden villages, or garden suburbs. None of these were true garden cities, according to Howard's definition, but each utilized at least one garden city principle. The promiscuous use of the term "garden city" led Howard and others to make unavailing attempts to halt the confusion by more careful definitions. By 1913 there were over fifty developments in England which reflected garden city ideas.[19] The final vindication for Howard came in the influence of garden cities on English national policy, despite Howard's greater faith in private philanthropy. In a succession of laws England moved toward a national city planning and housing program which reflected Howard's emphasis on a unified landownership, decentralized small-town development, and low-priced housing for industrial workers. In England this trend culminated in 1946 and 1947 in the virtual abolition of private land development and in the adoption of the garden city or new towns idea for reconstructing a war-torn England. Long before this Sir Ebenezer Howard (he was knighted in 1927 in recognition of his work for garden cities) had died in his beloved Welwyn.[20]

The garden city idea, which was not to find complete expression in the United States until the appearance of the greenbelt communities of the New Deal, caused a flurry of excitement after it became generally known in the United States, but at first did not seriously affect the developing city planning movement. Garden cities were too visionary for men who were laboring to patch up the mistakes of past misplanning in our older cities. But as a result of the publicity given to Letchworth in popular magazines, many private individuals were impressed with Howard's idealism. In 1906 a Garden City Associa-

[18] Ebenezer Howard, "A Greeting from the President of the International Federation," *City Planning*, I (1925), 31.
[19] Culpin, *Garden City Movement*, pp. 1–2, 19–47.
[20] James W. R. Adams, *Modern Town and Country Planning* (London, 1952), pp. 34, 46–50, 51–52, 56, 66–71, 117; "The British Town and Country Planning Bill, 1947," *Journal of the American Institute of Planners*, XIII (Winter, 1947), 27–28 (reprinted from an article in the *Economist*, Jan. 11, 1947); Macfadyen, *Sir Ebenezer Howard*, p. 158.

tion of America was formed by William D. P. Bliss, an Episcopal minister and Christian Socialist; August Belmont, a New York banker; Bishop Henry C. Potter of the Episcopal Church; Elgin R. L. Gould, president of the City and Suburban Homes Company, an enterprise designed to improve the living environment of New York wage earners; and other interested individuals. It gave highly idealistic support to the garden city idea but limited itself to advising industrialists on how to apply garden city principles to their planned villages. Bliss reported projects in five states, but none even closely resembled Letchworth or Welwyn.[21] For the more realistic professional planners, the main progress was in planning for the older cities. In 1909 the first great advisory plan was adopted by Chicago. On the sponsoring committee for the plan was Frederic A. Delano, whose advocacy of planned cities was later an inspiration to his nephew, Franklin D. Roosevelt, and who was, in the New Deal, to head the National Resources Committee, our first national planning agency.[22] In 1909 the first national conference of city planners convened in Washington. In this and subsequent conferences the city planners heard detailed reports on the English garden cities, but were more interested in the possibilities of zoning legislation.[23] In a milestone in city planning, New York City adopted a comprehensive zoning law in 1916. Zoning was finally upheld by the Supreme Court in 1926.[24]

Before 1920 a few new towns were planned with garden city attributes. In 1910 the Russell Sage Foundation, a long-time supporter of better city planning, financed a model residential suburb in New York City, Forest Hills Gardens, which was advertised as a garden city.[25] In 1912 Torrance, California, was described by its industrialist founder, Jared S. Torrance, as the "greatest and best of the garden cities of the world."[26] In 1914 a small suburb near Boston, Billerica

[21] Royal Meeker, review of *Garden Cities of Tomorrow*, by Ebenezer Howard, *Municipal Affairs*, VI (1902), 287–290; "The Garden City Association of America," *Charities and the Commons*, XVII (1906–1907), 286; "Garden Cities in America," *ibid.*, XVIII (1907–1908), 114.

[22] Adams, *Outline of Town and City Planning*, pp. 202–203.

[23] Senate Committee on the District of Columbia, *Hearings on City Planning*, in Senate Document no. 422, 61st Cong., 2d Sess., 1909, p. 79.

[24] Hubbard and Hubbard, *Our Cities Today and Tomorrow*, p. 7; Stuart A. MacCorkle, *Municipal Administration* (New York, 1942), p. 331.

[25] "Garden City Platted by Russell Sage Foundation," *Survey*, XXV (1910–1911), 309–310.

[26] Dana W. Bartlett, "Torrance," *American City*, IX (1913), 311.

Garden Suburb, was carefully planned, had a limited-dividend corporation, and encouraged resident co-operation.[27] In 1916 John Nolen, one of America's foremost city planners, designed a completely new, diversified industrial town at Kingsport, Tennessee, with rigid zoning laws but no greenbelt.[28] Many other developments used the name garden city, which now had a commercial value, but as yet the United States did not have even a close approximation of Howard's ideal city.

In 1917 the garden city idea received serious congressional attention. Senator Morris Sheppard of Texas secured the acceptance of a resolution praising the garden city movement and requesting a hearing on garden cities by his Committee on Agriculture and Forestry. The hearings led to no legislation, but did provide the Senators with a complete picture of Letchworth as given by an enthusiastic American proponent of garden cities.[29] More important, in World War I the American government, for the first time, entered the field of city planning and public housing. Both the Emergency Fleet Corporation and a short-lived United States Housing Corporation constructed housing for defense workers and used planning experts and garden city methods in some of the approximately sixty projects. The infant program was quashed by a hostile Congress at the war's end, despite objections from planners and housing experts.[30]

In the twenties city planning grew more than in all previous decades. State after state passed enabling laws, many based upon a model law distributed by Herbert Hoover's Department of Commerce. By 1929 over 650 municipalities had planning commissions. Two-thirds of our city population lived under zoning ordinances. Planning was being popularized, planning courses were taught in many public schools, professional organizations were organized, and

[27] Arthur C. Comey, "Plans for an American Garden Suburb," *American City,* XI (1914), 35–37.

[28] John Nolen, *New Towns for Old* (Boston, 1927), pp. 50–65.

[29] Senate Committee on Agriculture and Forestry, *Hearings on Garden City Movement,* 64th Cong., 2d Sess., 1917, pp. 2–14, 18, 33.

[30] Curtice N. Hitchock, "The War Housing Program and Its Future," *Journal of Political Economy,* XXVII (1919), 241–277; Sylvester Baxter, "The Future of Industrial Housing," *Architectural Record,* XLV (1919), 567; Adams, "Housing and Social Reconstruction," pp. 34–35; "The Fate of the War-Housing Projects," *Housing Problems in America: The Proceedings of the Eighth National Conference on Housing* (Bridgeport, Conn., 1920), p. 327; U.S. Housing Corporation, *Report,* I (Washington, 1920), 14, and *Report,* II (Washington, 1919), 23.

professional education was provided at Harvard, at Massachusetts Institute of Technology, and at other engineering schools. The American Municipal League and the American Civic Association backed the crusade for planning, and at least three journals provided planning information to both professional and lay planning boards and commissions.[31]

In 1922 the most ambitious planning effort in the United States before the New Deal was initiated in New York City. A giant advisory regional plan for the whole New York metropolitan area was developed by a private planning committee supported by the Russell Sage Foundation. Frederic A. Delano was chairman of the committee; Thomas Adams, Ebenezer Howard's first secretary in the Garden City Association, was general director of plans and surveys. Most eminent American planners contributed, and French and English planners submitted suggestions. The great project culminated in the publication of a ten-volume survey and plan, which contained literally hundreds of suggestions. Among these was one by Adams proposing several garden cities in the New York metropolitan area.[32] The garden city idea also received new prestige in 1925 when the International Federation for Town and Country Planning and Garden Cities met in New York with Ebenezer Howard and Sir Raymond Unwin in attendance. Howard, who helped organize support for an American garden city, was received along with other planners at the White House by President Coolidge.[33]

The most significant support in the twenties for American garden cities, as well as for planning in a broad regional perspective, came from the Regional Planning Association, an informal association of talented and influential city planners, economists, social philosophers, and conservationists who first began meeting together in 1923. Its membership included Lewis Mumford, a social philosopher and

[31] Adams, *Outline of Town and City Planning*, pp. 247–249; Hubbard and Hubbard, *Our Cities Today and Tomorrow*, pp. 3, 20, 88–97.

[32] Staff of the Regional Plan of New York and Its Environs, *Regional Plan*, vol. I (New York, 1929), pp. 12–13, 126–127; Thomas Adams, *The Buildings of the City* (New York, 1931; published as vol. II of the *Regional Plan* of New York), pp. 568–571; Thomas Adams, *Outline of Town and City Planning*, p. 233, and "The Planning and Subdivision of Land," pp. 254–256; Thomas Adams, "Planning for Civic Betterment in Town and Country," *American City*, XV (1916), 51.

[33] George B. Ford, "The International City and Regional Planning Conference," *City Planning*, I (1925), 124; "Common Welfare," *Survey*, LIV (1925), 337–338.

planner; Stuart Chase, an economist; Charles H. Whitaker, editor of the *Journal of the American Institute of Architects;* Frederick L. Ackerman, a New York architect and city planner; Clarence S. Stein and Henry Wright, a successful team of city planners; Benton Mackaye, a forester, conservationist, and wilderness expert; Robert D. Kohn, who had worked with the housing program of the Emergency Fleet Corporation and who would later direct the Public Works Administration in the New Deal; and Alexander Bing, later president of the City Housing Corporation of New York City.[34] Both Stein and Ackerman had visited England and studied the garden cities firsthand. Under a New York law secured in 1923 by Governor Alfred E. Smith, himself a convinced planner, Stein and Wright completed America's first state-wide advisory regional plan.[35] In 1925 the members of the association, along with Governor Smith and Charles B. Purdom of Letchworth, authored a special regional planning issue of the *Survey,* advocating garden cities and broad regional plans in the nature of the later Tennessee Valley Authority.[36] Lewis Mumford summarized one aspect of the work of the association as follows: "Finally, had it not been for the ideas that the Regional Planning Association . . . had put into circulation during the twenties, the Greenbelt Towns undertaken by the Re-settlement Administration in 1935 would have been inconceivable." [37]

In 1924, with the encouragement of the Regional Planning Association, Bing formed a limited-dividend City Housing Corporation for the express purpose of constructing America's first garden city. The first project, Sunnyside Gardens in New York City, was only a

---

[34] Lewis Mumford, "Introduction" to Clarence S. Stein, *Toward New Towns for America* (Liverpool, Eng., 1951), pp. 3–15.

[35] New York *Times,* April 23, 1925, p. 9.

[36] See the following articles in *Survey,* vol. LIV (1925): Lewis Mumford, "The Fourth Migration," pp. 130–133; Clarence S. Stein, "Dinosaur Cities," pp. 134–138; Frederick L. Ackerman, "Our Stake in Congestion," pp. 141–142; Stuart Chase, "Coals to New Castle," pp. 143–146; Lewis Mumford, "Regions—To Live In," pp. 151–152; Benton Mackaye, "The New Exploration," pp. 153–157; Alfred E. Smith, "Seeing a State Whole," p. 158; Henry Wright, "The Road to Good Houses," pp. 165–168; Charles B. Purdom, "Garden Cities—What They Are and How They Work," pp. 169–172; Alexander M. Bing, "Can We Have Garden Cities in America?" pp. 172–173.

[37] Lewis Mumford, "Introduction" to Stein, *Toward New Towns for America,* p. 15.

trial run, since the city conditions prohibited a garden city.[38] Then, in 1927, Bing's corporation purchased 1,350 acres in Bergen County, New Jersey, for the future city of Radburn, which was to be the closest approximation of an American garden city before the greenbelt towns of the New Deal. Radburn was planned by Stein and Wright in consultation with Unwin, Ackerman, Thomas Adams, and other garden city planners. Only partially completed because of the depression, which forced Bing's corporation into receivership, Radburn was designed as a self-contained industrial community purposefully planned for the automobile age, with pedestrian underpasses, huge forty-acre blocks, and internal parks. By the plan, a person could walk through most of the town by way of the interior park and without crossing a single street. The design was to become world famous; but Radburn was only an approach to a complete garden city. Because of land cost, Bing did not procure a greenbelt, and, in deference to American custom, the lots were sold rather than leased. Since Radburn remained uncompleted, industry never came and the residents, in un-garden-city-like manner, had to commute to work.[39]

The same depression that thwarted the private plans for Radburn created a vast new interest in the possibilities of public planning. The city planning movement had developed the techniques. Now many city planners were prepared to shape the new tomorrow, to design the new phoenix which was sure to rise from the ashes of the old. In Albany, New York, Governor Franklin D. Roosevelt had observed the past work of the planners and had found it good. In 1932 he commented that the work of the Regional Plan Committee of New York City had "opened our eyes to new vistas of the future." [40] Roosevelt wanted to extend public planning to the country and create "wholly new rural communities" with facilities for new indus-

[38] Stein, *Toward New Towns for America*, pp. 21–32.

[39] *Ibid.*, pp. 21–32, 67; National Resources Committee, *Urban Planning and Land Policies* (Washington, 1939; vol. II of the Supplementary Report of the Urbanism Committee to the National Resources Committee), pp. 97–99; Adams, *Outline of Town and City Planning*, diagram opposite p. 232, and "The Planning and Subdivision of Land," pp. 265–266; Dahir, *Communities for Better Living*, pp. 189–190.

[40] Franklin D. Roosevelt, "Growing Up by Plan," *Survey*, LXVII (1932), 507.

Bringing Country to Town 71

tries.[41] With a rural rather than an urban emphasis, Franklin D. Roosevelt, even as Ebenezer Howard, wanted to marry the city to the country. He wondered "if out of this regional planning we are not going to be in a position to take the bull by the horns in the immediate future and adopt some kind of experimental work based on distribution of population."[42] According to Roosevelt, "we have 'growed like Topsy,' we must grow up by planning."[43] The publication of the *Regional Plan of New York* led Roosevelt to do some characteristic reminiscing in which he traced his thoughts on planning back to the Chicago plan of 1909, when Charles D. Norton and his uncle, Frederic A. Delano, had first talked to him about city planning: "I think from that very moment I have been interested in not the mere planning of a single city but in the larger aspects of planning. It is the way of the future."[44] Roosevelt gave the following evaluation of the planning movement which developed after 1909: "Out of this survey initiated by Mr. Norton in Chicago has developed something new; not a science, but a new understanding of problems that affect not merely bricks and mortar, subways and streets; planning that affects also the economic and social life of a community, then of a county, then of a state; perhaps the day is not far distant when planning will become a part of the national policy of this country."[45]

Like the accomplishments of Elwood Mead and others in rural planning, the work of the city planners, and particularly those interested in garden cities, provided a pattern for many of the New Deal communities. Radburn, New Jersey, was a prototype of the greenbelt cities and other suburban communities of the New Deal. Many other of the New Deal communities, and particularly the subsistence homesteads, combined ideas from both the rural and urban planners. Many of the individuals most closely connected with the garden city movement, such as Clarence Stein and Henry Wright, were to play an active role in the development of the greenbelt cities. In a larger sense, the concept of planning, as developed in the limited area of a city, necessarily had to be extended to include larger and larger

---

[41] Franklin D. Roosevelt, "A New Rural Planning," *Rural Government: The Proceedings of the Fourteenth American Country Life Conference* (Chicago, 1932), pp. 15–16.

[42] Roosevelt, "Growing Up by Plan," p. 506.   [43] *Ibid.*, p. 507.

[44] *Ibid.*, p. 483.   [45] *Ibid.*

areas. Thus many city planners became, in the New Deal, the directors of national planning agencies, Frederic A. Delano being a good example with his work in the National Resources Committee.

The technically qualified city planners, despite or because of their idealism, were concerned with isolated areas or single aspects of the whole economy. They had the needed skills for their respective tasks and frequently combined with their technical skill a wide grasp of economic and social problems; yet they were often isolated from the making of truly national policies or from the understanding of national problems. Exceptions to this were many of the members of the Regional Planning Association, who were not strictly city planners but economists, social philosophers, or reformers. As a whole, however, the complete background of the New Deal communities, which were a part of larger planning programs, cannot be discovered in its entirety in the movements either for planned land settlement or for garden cities, although much of the impetus for, and many of the policies that went into, the communities can be discovered here. The final and perhaps most important source of the New Deal communities can be discovered only in aspects of the long struggle by economists and others to get the federal government to assume a more direct responsibility for the total economy of the nation, or, in other words, in the attempts to achieve some degree of national economic planning.

IV

From Acorn to Oak

IN September, 1877, Richard T. Ely, a recent graduate of Columbia University, was greeted in Halle, Germany, the gateway to a then typical educational pilgrimage, by an awkward, rural-mannered Illinois scholar named Simon N. Patten. Both young men were in Germany to study in the famous universities. Because of the inspiration they received from the German historical school of economists, both returned to America with a thoroughgoing distaste for conventional American politics and religion, as well as for the archenemy, English classical economics.[1] In the summer of 1932 Rexford G. Tugwell, a former student of Patten and a member of the "brain trust" of Franklin D. Roosevelt, met with Milburn L. Wilson, a former student of Ely and a farm economist from Montana, to begin mapping a possible program of national agricultural planning. Tugwell was already trying to steer Roosevelt ever closer to full commitment on national economic planning. The advocacy of major planning policies by Wilson and Tugwell represented the fruition of ideas and policies advocated soon after 1877 by Ely, Patten, and a few other economic rebels. An acorn in 1877 was about to become a full-grown oak. When this occurred in the New Deal, Tugwell and Wilson, in addition to their policy-making influence in the broad fields of agricultural planning, were destined to shape and direct the community program in its most formative years.

[1] Richard T. Ely, *Ground under Our Feet* (New York, 1938), pp. 38–40, 121.

In 1885 Patten, Ely, John Bates Clark, Edmund J. James, Henry C. Adams, and other economists who were in revolt against classical economic theories joined to form the American Economic Association and to ask for a positive economic role for the state.[2] Uniting ethical zeal with what was then considered economic radicalism, they influenced the rising social gospel movement, the movement for conservation and scientific forestry, and the multiple reforms of the progressive era. They were influenced by the growth of the American philosophy of pragmatism. They became the academic fathers of such later economists as Thorstein Veblen, John R. Commons, and Tugwell. Although much of the economic philosophy of these men was reflected in various New Deal programs, it was their influence on agricultural policy that most clearly affected the New Deal communities.

As a professor of economics at the University of Wisconsin, Richard T. Ely became interested in the broad problems of land use. Through his influence Henry C. Taylor, one of his students, went to Europe to study land economics. A few years after Taylor's return, he established a Department of Agricultural Economics in the University of Wisconsin College of Agriculture in 1909.[3] Soon the students of Ely and Taylor were acknowledged experts in several fields of agricultural economics: Benjamin H. Hibbard as a student of farm tenancy and public land policies, Oliver E. Baker in land classification and population statistics, Lewis C. Gray in land-use planning, and John D. Black in the whole field of agricultural policy. In 1919 a growing number of farm economists from Wisconsin and other universities united to form the American Farm Economic Association. Springing in part from the interest created by Theodore Roosevelt's Country Life Commission, rural sociology became a recognized specialty at Wisconsin in 1911 when Taylor asked a rural minister, Charles J. Galpin, to become the first teacher in the new field. The rural sociologists founded the American Country Life Association in 1917.[4]

[2] Richard T. Ely, "Report of the Organization of the American Economic Association," *Publications of the American Economic Association,* I (March, 1886), 6.

[3] Leonard A. Salter, Jr., *A Critical Review of Research in Land Economics* (Minneapolis, 1948), pp. 7–11.

[4] Liberty Hyde Bailey, *The Country-Life Movement in the United States* (New York, 1913), pp. 7–10; Charles J. Galpin, *My Drift into Rural Sociology* (Baton

By that date the work begun by Ely and Taylor was beginning to affect national agricultural policies.

Even before 1917 William J. Spillman, head of the Office of Farm Management in the Bureau of Plant Industry of the Department of Agriculture, had studied such economic problems as land tenure, cost accounting, and farm records. In 1918 he asked Henry C. Taylor to come to Washington and help reorganize the Office of Farm Management. In 1919 Taylor, Ely, Oliver E. Baker, and Lewis C. Gray all worked on a committee which led to the creation of the Division of Land Economics in the Department of Agriculture. Under the direction of Gray, this division conducted research on land utilization and classification, on tenure problems, and on problems in land settlement and colonization.[5] In 1921 Henry C. Wallace, Secretary of Agriculture under Warren G. Harding, appointed Taylor as the head of a newly organized Bureau of Agricultural Economics. This new bureau absorbed the Division of Land Economics and included other divisions on farm management, rural sociology, marketing, and statistics. In addition to Spillman and the economists from Wisconsin, the Bureau of Agricultural Economics included on its staff at one time or another such important agricultural figures as Charles J. Brand, Howard Tolley, and Mordecai Ezekiel. In the twenties these farm economists carried out extensive research projects in land economics and formulated numerous proposals for farm relief. From their research and discussions came the domestic allotment system and the subsistence homesteads program of the New Deal.

Even as the Bureau of Agricultural Economics was being established at Washington, Richard T. Ely was motivating several private research projects in land economics. In connection with the interest in soldier settlement after World War I, two of Ely's students, Lewis C. Gray and John D. Black, completed a study on land colonization in the Lake States.[6] In 1920 Ely established at Wisconsin the Institute of Land and Public Utility Economics to co-ordinate research

---

Rouge, 1938), pp. 18–19; *Proceedings of the First National Country Life Conference* (Baltimore, 1919), pp. 1–5.

[5] Salter, *A Critical Review*, pp. 13–17.

[6] John D. Black and Lewis C. Gray, *Land Settlement and Colonization in the Great Lakes States* (U.S. Department of Agriculture Bulletin no. 1295; Washington, 1925).

in the broader fields of land economics and public utilities. Ely believed that urban and rural problems were closely related and in his institute tried to bring the land economists and city planners into a closer relationship. The institute sponsored a few major research projects, financed books, and published a journal. Ely himself became a member of the Board of Directors of the City Housing Corporation, which constructed the garden city at Radburn, New Jersey.[7] In rural planning, Ely and the institute backed the Fairway Farms experiment in Montana, which, even as Radburn, bore a close relationship to the New Deal communities.

From experience on his own farm, Henry C. Taylor conceived the idea of a company to rejuvenate farms and to help tenants become owners. By 1923 he had interested Ely and the institute, as well as the trustees of the Laura Spelman Rockefeller Foundation. While in Montana in 1923, Taylor broached the idea to Milburn L. Wilson, an old friend and former student who was then head of the Rural Economics Division of the Montana State Agricultural College. They jointly decided to make the experiment in Montana and, with the approval of the foundation and the receipt of a $100,000 loan from John D. Rockefeller at 5 per cent interest (but with no required repayment), incorporated Fairway Farms in 1924 to administer the funds. Among the nine directors of the corporation were Ely, Taylor, Wilson, Leon C. Marshall, head of the Department of Political Economy at the University of Chicago, and Chester C. Davis, then commissioner of agriculture and labor in Montana. Being on the scene, Wilson became secretary and managing director of the experiment.[8]

Wilson was a farm boy from Iowa who had taken a Bachelor of Science degree in agriculture in 1907 at Iowa State, where he met young Henry A. Wallace. After tenant farming in Nebraska, Wilson homesteaded in Montana in 1909. His farming experience in drought-stricken Montana led to his work with the agricultural college at Bozeman. Wilson became Montana's first county agricultural agent and first state director of extension work. In 1920 he came to the University of Wisconsin and took a Master of Arts degree, study-

---

[7] Richard T. Ely, "The City Housing Corporation and 'Sunnyside,'" *Journal of Land and Public Utility Economics*, II (1926), 174.

[8] M. L. Wilson, "The Fairway Farms Project," *Journal of Land and Public Utility Economics*, II (1926), 156–159.

ing land economics under Taylor and Ely and economics under John R. Commons. During the twenties he spent three summers studying philosophy at the University of Chicago under James H. Tufts and Eustace Hayden and one summer at Cornell, where he studied farm management under George F. Warren. He had both the academic background and the farming experience needed to direct Fairway Farms.

Wilson used the funds of Fairway Farms, Incorporated, to make experiments on the proper size of farms, the methods of selecting tenants and prospective owners, the most efficient equipping of farms, and the type of farming suited to a particular region.[9] By 1926 he had purchased eight farm units of sizes varying up to 2,500 acres. Prospective purchasers were given tenant-purchase contracts. After payment of all necessary expenses, such as taxes, insurance, and family living expenses, the tenant turned the remaining net income over to a trust fund. When the trust fund amounted to 25 per cent of the purchase price, a sales contract was to be executed. The carefully selected tenant was permitted five years to accumulate the 25 per cent. If he failed, his contract was to be canceled. The tenant was given supervision and financial help in bad years. Everything was planned to help the tenant farmer re-enter the national structure of freehold, one-family farms. These farms were the first experiments in regional land use and were early precedents for the tenant-rehabilitation and purchase programs of the New Deal. The experimentation indicated many of the policies that Wilson would adapt to his subsistence homesteads. Yet, despite complete mechanization on some units and an amazing degree of efficiency in production, the drought and depression combined to make the Fairway Farms a financial failure. The project was discontinued and, much later, the land was sold.

During the twenties the land economists and sociologists accepted as their province of study all the problems of land settlement, rural social advancement, land tenure, and rural planning that Elwood Mead was trying to solve with his rural colonies. But the approach of the economists was entirely different. They were more cognizant of the total economic situation, more dependent on research, and more cautious in making suggestions for action. After the agricultural

[9] *Ibid.*, p. 156.

depression began in 1921 and 1922, the Bureau of Agricultural Economics published a report on land utilization that seemed to challenge the ideas underlying Mead's program of development and colonization. In this report the economists declared that the age of an expanding agricultural plant should be in the past. In a period of agricultural surpluses, any further development of farm land (such as irrigation projects) should be slow and cautious. On the positive side they advocated the reforestation of lands unsuited to agriculture and in so doing raised the problem of resettlement for displaced farmers.[10]

In the twenties the Bureau of Agricultural Economics was drawn into the heated debates over farm relief proposals and, after the death of Henry C. Wallace in 1924, lost most of its policy-making influence. With some reluctance the farm economists and Wallace had supported a form of price fixing for agriculture, which was being defended by two private farm machinery dealers, George N. Peek and Hugh Johnson, and which was given legislative expression in the McNary-Haugen bills. The McNary-Haugen idea involved a controlled domestic market for agricultural products through a government-directed program of foreign dumping for all surplus goods. Herbert Hoover, as Secretary of Commerce under Harding and Coolidge and later as President, was opposed to any type of price supports and distrusted the farm economists, who, he believed, had too many socialistic ideas. Hoover proposed government aid to cooperative marketing associations as the best solution for the farm problem, an idea that was incorporated into his Farm Board, which was established in 1929.[11]

The farm economists continued to talk about other relief proposals, including submarginal land retirement and, after 1926, a domestic allotment system. The latter proposal was first broached by William J. Stillman, but was quickly modified and defended by John D.

[10] Salter, *A Critical Review*, pp. 18–20.

[11] Chester C. Davis, "The Development of Agricultural Policy since the End of the World War," in *Farmers in a Changing World: The Yearbook of Agriculture for 1940* (Washington, 1940), pp. 302–306; James H. Shideler, "Herbert Hoover and the Federal Farm Board Project, 1921–1925," *Mississippi Valley Historical Review*, XLII (1955–1956), 721; Arthur M. Schlesinger, Jr., *The Age of Roosevelt*, vol. I: *The Crisis of the Old Order* (Boston, 1957), pp. 105–110, 239–240.

From Acorn to Oak

Black and Milburn L. Wilson, who was dividing his time between Montana and the Department of Agriculture. Stillman's plan called for the issuance of allotment certificates covering the portion of a crop allocated for domestic use. These certificates were to be redeemable in an amount equal to the tariff rate on the product, increasing the farmers' income that much above the world price. Since all crops not covered by allotment certificates would sell at the lower competitive prices, it was hoped that farmers would not grow crops in excess of the allotments. Black modified the plan to make the allotment certificates transferable, while M. L. Wilson worked out an adaptation that included a processing tax to pay for the scheme and a plan for voluntary crop reductions by farmers.[12]

With the general depression beginning in the fall of 1929 and with the subsequent failure of the Farm Board to alleviate the plight of farmers, the Hoover administration was ready to try one of the proposals of the farm economists—land retirement. Secretary of Agriculture Arthur M. Hyde and the land-grant colleges sponsored a Land Utilization Conference which met in Chicago in 1931. Since Hoover would not even consider governmental controls over the amount produced by individual farmers, the conference may have represented an attempt to forestall moves toward the more radical domestic allotment system. The Land Utilization Conference met to consider the possibilities of reducing surpluses by retiring from productive use the many submarginal lands throughout the country. The idea had been broached by Ely much before the twenties, had been endlessly discussed by the farm economists throughout the twenties, and had been advocated by a Committee on the Bases of a Sound Land Policy, which included experts from engineering, city planning, land economics, and conservation, all of whom had been brought together in 1927 by Frederic A. Delano.[13]

The Land Utilization Conference represented the first great fruition of Ely's work in land economics. As an old man surrounded by his many former students, Ely said: "Now as I look at this program . . .

---

[12] John D. Black, *Agricultural Reform in the United States* (New York, 1929), p. 271; Daniel Roland Fusfeld, *The Economic Thought of FDR and the Origin of the New Deal* (New York, 1956), p. 196.

[13] Edward C. Banfield and Rexford G. Tugwell, "Governmental Planning at Mid-Century," *Journal of Politics*, XIII (1951), 143.

I feel that I am in the promised land."[14] Practically every facet of land planning was presented in papers by such men as Ely, Lewis C. Gray, John D. Black, M. L. Wilson, and Elwood Mead. The conference recommended a national inventory and classification of land, the licensing and regulation of land development, the curtailment of reclamation, public acquisition and retirement of submarginal lands, and a study of industrial decentralization. It resulted in the creation of the National Land Use Planning Committee, made up of agricultural leaders from the Department of Agriculture, the Federal Farm Board, the Federal Farmers Loan Board, the land-grant colleges, and the Department of the Interior. It also appointed a National Advisory and Legislative Committee on Land Use, made up of representatives of the farm organizations.

The National Land Use Planning Committee studied land uses in the Tennessee Valley, investigated the possibilities of industrial decentralization, and offered some guidance to the back-to-the-land movement of the depression. In the New Deal it was merged, along with Ickes' National Planning Board in the Public Works Administration, into the National Resources Committee, which was the first truly national planning agency.[15] Others of Ely's dreams were soon to be realized, many under the direction of his students. M. L. Wilson was to become Director of the Division of Subsistence Homesteads, the first land-use program. He borrowed most of his early staff members from the Bureau of Agricultural Economics and secured one of the country's leading rural sociologists as his assistant. Through the Civil Works Administration the Division of Subsistence Homesteads launched research projects on part-time farming in thirty-three states, marking one of the most extensive research programs in the land use ever projected. A large program of land retirement was set up under L. C. Gray in the Agricultural Adjustment Administration, but with funds from the Federal Emergency Relief Administration. These programs were moved to the Resettlement Administration in 1935, where the land planners not only purchased submarginal land but provided a planning staff for the location of resettlement communities. In the Resettlement Administration another of Ely's wishes was realized; here, city planners joined the land planners.

[14] *Proceedings, National Conference on Land Utilization, Chicago, November 19–21, 1931* (Washington, 1932), p. 126.
[15] Banfield and Tugwell, "Governmental Planning," p. 143.

Although M. L. Wilson welcomed the idea of land retirement, he believed that this would only begin to solve the farm problem. Thus, in the depression, he led the crusade for a domestic allotment system as a necessary part of a much broader, longer-range program of land-use planning. He always connected with the domestic allotment system and land retirement a program for subsistence homesteads. Wilson faced up to a problem that had been inherent, if seldom discussed, in almost all the land-utilization discussions since 1920. It was a dark ogre in back of any relief plan that involved a reduction in farm production. Land-use planning, it appeared certain, was going to displace many farm families (Wilson believed 2,000,000 people). What were they to do? With mass unemployment in the cities, industry offered no refuge. In fact, it added to the problem, as witness the back-to-the-land movement. Wilson believed that the only possible answer was industrial decentralization and small subsistence homesteads of a few acres. On this small acreage a family could grow all its food and thus be able to accept shorter hours in industry. Situated between commercial agriculture and full-time industrial employment, subsistence homesteads communities would bring about a new balance between agriculture and industry, absorbing both the industrially unemployed and the displaced farmers. There would be no limit to the absorption, for ever-shorter hours would enable more people to share in the industrial wage, while the workers' wages could be supplemented by home food production. Wilson's ideas on subsistence homesteads were adopted from his studies of existing prototypes. He was impressed particularly by the Mormon villages in Utah, with their subsistence homesteads and village industries. In addition, he was influenced by his belief that certain definite "moral and spiritual values" come from contact with the soil and with growing things and by a counterbelief that congested cities were not the best places to live.[16] Wilson himself attributes his earliest ideas on subsistence homesteads to Elwood Mead and to the Irish agrarian poet and philosopher, George Russell or "A. E." [17]

Wilson began a propaganda campaign for production controls and subsistence homesteads in 1931. He had many allies. In the East

[16] Milburn L. Wilson, *Farm Relief and Allotment Plan* (Day and Hour Series no. 2, University of Minnesota; Minneapolis, 1933), pp. 48–52.

[17] Author's conversation with M. L. Wilson on June 27, 1956.

were John D. Black and Henry I. Harriman, president of the U.S. Chamber of Commerce, who had met Wilson while visiting Montana. On a committee which Wilson set up in the West was Henry A. Wallace, son of Henry C. Wallace and publisher of a farm magazine in Iowa.[18] In a radio address in April, 1932, Wilson summarized his views, asking for a new economic philosophy for both agriculture and industry, including a system of planned land use. He asked for a termination of the homestead law, for land classification by the states, for the retirement of poor land, for lowered land taxes, for a consolidation of inefficient rural governmental units, for a domestic allotment system, and for part-time farming and industrial decentralization.[19] By letters and speeches Wilson continued his campaign, talking to "economists, writers, politicians, industrialists, farm leaders, bankers, and insurance executives."[20] Always, he began with his ideas on crop allotments and ended with subsistence homesteads.

When Wilson learned that Franklin D. Roosevelt had long been advocating industrial decentralization and rural-urban communities, Wilson reputedly said: "That's my man for President."[21] In any case, Wilson came to regard Roosevelt's efforts toward land-use planning in New York State as milestones toward a better agricultural program.[22] Governor Roosevelt, working closely with George F. Warren and the Cornell College of Agriculture, had secured a $20,000 appropriation for the beginning of a complete survey and classification of all New York's agricultural resources. Cornell agricultural economists used it to survey Tompkins County, showing the need for retiring from agriculture a large percentage of the farm land. On the basis of this survey, which was to be expanded to the whole state over a period of ten years, Roosevelt and his Agricultural Advisory Commission, which included Warren and Henry Morgenthau, Jr., formulated plans for the retirement and, in most cases, for the reforestation of

[18] Unpublished first draft of Russell Lord and Paul H. Johnstone, eds., *A Place on Earth: A Critical Appraisal of Subsistence Homesteads* (published in Washington, 1942), in Record Group 83, Records of the Bureau of Agricultural Economics, National Archives (to be cited hereafter as R.G. 83, National Archives).

[19] M. L. Wilson, "Land Utilization," Lecture no. 25 in the Economics Series of the National Advisory Council on Radio in Education (Chicago, 1932), pp. 1–8.

[20] Russell Lord, *The Wallaces of Iowa* (Boston, 1947), p. 311.

[21] *Ibid.*

[22] M. L. Wilson, "A Land-Use Program for the Federal Government," *Journal of Farm Economics*, XV (1933), 219.

all submarginal land. For the marginal farmer Roosevelt began a relief program that included tax adjustments, state aid for schools and roads, and rural electrification.[23] For the submarginal farmer who would have to be resettled, Roosevelt, as in his reaction to both the city planning and back-to-the-land movements, relied primarily on his cherished plan for a marriage of agriculture and industry as part of a broad program of regional planning. He described a new, third type of American life, which he called the "rural industrial group." This involved industrial decentralization and a new balance between town and country. With new transportation and communication facilities, Roosevelt believed that the country had advantages which could not be duplicated in the city and that industry was going to decentralize voluntarily.[24]

Roosevelt's land-use program represented a full-sized regional plan for New York State. It comprehended his interest in bettering rural life, his advocacy of public power developments, his sympathy for the work of city planners, his passionate interest in conservation and forestry, and his absorbing desire to unite city and country. It represented the most notable, concrete program reflecting Roosevelt's enthusiastic acceptance of the principle of planning and of a more positive role for the state. His willingness to accept the idea of governmental planning in the field of natural resources and public utilities paved the way for his acceptance of such other planning programs as were reflected in the Agricultural Adjustment Administration and the National Recovery Administration. Through Roosevelt, many of the ideas of the German-trained economists who founded the American Economic Association were to find expression in the national government, although Roosevelt never desired a basic change in American economic institutions. But he did believe that the government could and should control and regulate economic endeavor in such a way as to insure the general welfare.[25]

On a board sponsoring one of M. L. Wilson's radio addresses on land utilization in the spring of 1932 was Rexford G. Tugwell, then professor of economics at Columbia University. On reading the ad-

---

[23] Fusfeld, *The Economic Thought of FDR*, pp. 125–136.
[24] Franklin D. Roosevelt, "Actualities of Agricultural Planning," in Charles A. Beard, ed., *America Faces the Future* (Cambridge, Mass., 1932), pp. 326–347.
[25] Fusfeld, *The Economic Thought of FDR*, p. 251.

dress, Tugwell wrote Wilson that he admired his ideas. Shortly afterward, they met in Washington and liked each other, although on many things their ideas were not similar. Tugwell, as a member of Roosevelt's developing "brain trust," carried Wilson's ideas to him. Just a week before the Democratic Convention in the summer of 1932, Tugwell attended a meeting on agricultural problems at the University of Chicago. Here, he pressed both Wilson and Henry A. Wallace for details on the domestic allotment plan. These ideas were telephoned to Hyde Park and, in general terms, incorporated into Roosevelt's acceptance speech at Chicago. After further guidance from Wallace and Wilson, the ideas were expanded by Roosevelt in his September speech at Topeka.[26] In August, 1932, in Albany, both Wallace and Wilson met Roosevelt for the first time. Roosevelt and Wilson found themselves in a complete and satisfying agreement on subsistence homesteads, which were, to both men, the dearest part of a developing agricultural and relief program. In January, 1933, Roosevelt asked Wallace, Tugwell, and Wilson to draw plans for the reorganization of the Department of Agriculture into an instrument of national planning.[27] In his cheerfully confident inauguration speech on a gloomy March 4, 1933, Roosevelt asked that America "recognize the overbalance of population in our industrial centers and, by engaging on a national scale in a redistribution, endeavor to provide a better use of the land for those best fitted for the land." [28]

Rexford Guy Tugwell was a surprising addition to the group working for agricultural reform. In spite of his small-town background, he was primarily a representative of urban liberalism. Although keenly interested in agricultural problems, his approach to them was always different from, and less conservative than, that of the men with a farm and agricultural college background. Through Simon Patten, Tugwell had been exposed to, and inspired by, economic theories not dissimilar to those taught by Ely at Wisconsin, but without the special emphasis on land problems.

[26] Lord, *Wallaces of Iowa*, p. 322; Gertrude Almy Slichter, "Franklin D. Roosevelt and the Farm Problem, 1929–1932," *Mississippi Valley Historical Review*, XLIII (1956–1957), 247–250; Rexford G. Tugwell, *The Democratic Roosevelt* (Garden City, N.Y., 1957), pp. 232–233.

[27] Lord, *Wallaces of Iowa*, p. 323; Slichter, "Franklin D. Roosevelt and the Farm Problem, 1929–1932," p. 252 fn.

[28] Franklin D. Roosevelt, *Nothing to Fear: The Selected Addresses of Franklin D. Roosevelt, 1932–1945*, ed. by B. D. Zevin (Cambridge, Mass., 1946), p. 15.

Patten was probably the most brilliant of all the German-trained economists. After an interval of temporary blindness, he had gone to the Wharton School of Finance and Commerce at the University of Pennsylvania. Here he lived a frugal, abstemious life of thought and teaching. His fertile mind ranged over wide fields of sociology, ethics, and philosophy, but always came back to economics. More deductive in method than many of his colleagues, Patten was less involved with practical reforms than men like Ely, but made greater contributions to economic theory.[29] Convinced that English natural-law economic theories were antiquated in an age of plenty rather than scarcity, Patten urged a recognition of the implications of the new environment, an environment that contained not only a better technology but better men, or men with added skills. Economic strife was as antiquated as toil and struggle to wring sustenance from the earth. In the new environment a pleasure economy was available to all. Each man could be a working capitalist, whether his capital be money or skill. Competition was a carry-over from a pain economy, an age of scarcity. A new era of co-operation and voluntary socialization was possible, if only individuals would replace dogmatism with pragmatic judgments, or the "long view." Not state socialism, with its coercion, but the voluntary co-operation and mutual tolerance between organized groups was Patten's optimistic view of the future's possibilities. Unless dogmatism forced state action, the state would only have to register the mutual assent obtained by compromise between organized groups.[30]

Tugwell, who became "immersed" in Patten's teachings, wanted the same socialization, or collectivism, desired by Patten, but he did not share Patten's optimism about its achievement through voluntary co-operation. He clearly visualized the difficulty of change or adjustment and predicted that any planning by the state would necessitate involuntary regimentation and class conflict.[31] As an economist he became interested in the plight of agriculture even before 1929. In 1928 he advocated production controls, enforced by the federal government, as a necessary short-time relief measure, but only as a temporary

[29] Rexford G. Tugwell, "Notes on the Life and Work of Simon Nelson Patten," *Journal of Political Economy*, XXXI (1923), 173–177.

[30] Simon N. Patten, "The Reconstruction of Economic Theory," in his *Essays in Economic Theory*, ed. by R. G. Tugwell (New York, 1924), pp. 273–340.

[31] Rexford G. Tugwell, "The Preparation of a President," *Western Political Quarterly*, I (1948), 142.

measure.³² As a long-time solution he desired thorough economic planning for agriculture, with extensive social control over the individual and his use of the land. He deplored the fact that a dedicated, but what he believed to be antiquated, doctrine of individualism had prevented the expert supervision of farmers by those who knew how to improve a backward agriculture.

As a beginning in reform, Tugwell desired the reforestation of millions of acres of submarginal land, with the planned resettlement of the displaced families. He recognized that an ambitious program of governmental planning and the resultant controls would meet its most determined opposition in the farmers themselves, with their individualism, their ideas on freedom, and their vested property rights. They would probably continue to feel that they had a right to grow what they pleased or, if they so desired, to plow a furrow straight down the hillside. But since the farmers were always knocking at the door of Congress for assistance, they might be persuaded to "give the expert his chance" and do "what the expert says" in exchange for aid.³³ If so, and this idea permeated Tugwell's thoughts on the whole economy, the depression might serve a useful function. Unlike the agriculturalists, Tugwell was just as interested in other aspect of a planned economy, welcoming a system of regulation and control over business. In connection with community planning, Tugwell desired the resettlement of displaced farmers in agricultural villages. He also desired garden cities for industrial workers, but he was never enthusiastic about Roosevelt and Wilson's ideas on communities of part-time farming and industry. Tugwell, much later, described Roosevelt's strong support of subsistence homesteads as a bit of impractical agrarian sentimentality, a "Utopian notion out of the past—the idea that men are better off close to nature and working with their hands on their own acres." ³⁴

With strong administrative backing, subsistence homesteads legislation was almost a certainty in the hurried, rubber-stamp first session of the Seventy-third Congress. The strong influence of M. L. Wilson and the many people he had converted to his views, all of whom saw

---

[32] Rexford G. Tugwell, "Reflections on Farm Relief," *Political Science Quarterly*, XLIII (1928), 490–491.

[33] Rexford G. Tugwell, "Farm Relief and a Permanent Agriculture," *Annals of the American Academy*, CXLII (1929), 271–282.

[34] Tugwell, *Democratic Roosevelt*, p. 158.

subsistence homesteads as only a part of a larger land-use planning program, was merged with that of the more doctrinaire agrarians, the rural planners of the Elwood Mead variety, and the more urbanized garden city advocates. Bernarr Macfadden, who had influenced the introduction of subsistence homesteads legislation in the Seventy-second Congress in 1932, continued as a powerful propagandist and lobbyist for subsistence homesteads. Mrs. Edith Lumsden, his professional lobbyist, consulted with John D. Black, M. L. Wilson, and Elwood Mead, helping to unite various threads of interest. She also saw Senator John H. Bankhead of Alabama who, along with his brother, Representative William B. Bankhead, had been an advocate of the Mead-sponsored rural colonization scheme for the South. Both Bankheads, as well as Representative James G. Scrugham of Nevada, introduced subsistence homesteads bills into the first session of the first New Deal Congress, only to see them ignored by harried and rushed congressmen.[35] Senator Bankhead, the most powerful congressional advocate of the bills, was a Southern agrarian. He saw the back-to-the-land movement as an effective relief measure and, even more, as a means to "the restoration of that small yeoman class which has been the backbone of every great civilization." He also saw in it the hope of a new era not marred by sectionalism or by a spirit of disunity and suspicion.[36]

Senator Bankhead's first bill, which was introduced on the first day of the session, called for a loan of up to $1,000 a person to aid in the purchase of "subsistence farms." The beneficiaries of a $400,000,000 grant from the Reconstruction Finance Corporation were to be the unemployed city workers with an agricultural background or those who had moved back to the country since January 1, 1931. Local committees or any other agencies selected by the Secretary of the Interior were to locate suitable land, secure title to it, and then supervise the construction of dwellings and the purchase of livestock and equipment by the settler. After full compliance with a purchase contract, the land title was to be conferred upon the settler, who was to repay his loan over a twenty-year period at not over 4 per cent in-

[35] Russell Lord and Paul H. Johnstone, eds., *A Place on Earth: A Critical Appraisal of Subsistence Homesteads* (Washington, 1942), p. 24.
[36] John H. Bankhead, "The One Way to Permanent National Recovery," *Liberty*, X (July 22, 1933), 18.

terest. Only land already in cultivation could be purchased for subsistence homesteads, thus preventing an increased agricultural surplus.[37] Senator Bankhead's other bill, introduced on April 17, 1933, stipulated "subsistence homesteads" instead of "subsistence farms," permitted $1,500 loans, provided for competent and experienced supervisors for the settlers, gave recognition to the community or colony type of settlement, and provided for a Reconstruction Finance Corporation grant of $25,000,000.[38] The two measures in the House were very similar to Senator Bankhead's first bill. Representative Scrugham's bill permitted loans of up to $2,000 and provided for repayment over a period of forty years.[39] All four bills placed the administration of the program in the Department of the Interior, which, first with the Homestead Act of 1862 and then with Elwood Mead's work in the Bureau of Reclamation, had had the most experience with land settlement.

Since neither of the subsistence homesteads bills was acted upon by Congress, Senator Bankhead, with White House backing, was able to add an abbreviated form of his subsistence homesteads proposals to the National Industrial Recovery Act, which was enacted in May, 1933. Almost hidden as Section 208 of Title II of this tremendously significant act, the subsistence homesteads section received no discussion in the hearings or in the floor debates. As finally approved, Section 208 read:

> To provide for aiding in the redistribution of the overbalance of population in industrial centers $25,000,000 is hereby made available to the President, to be used by him through such agencies as he may establish and under such regulations as he may make, for making loans for and otherwise aiding in the purchase of subsistence homesteads. The moneys collected as repayment of said loans shall constitute a revolving fund to be administered as directed by the President for the purposes of this section.[40]

This small, generalized section of a larger act included few of the more detailed ideas of its supporters or of those reflected in former

---

[37] U.S. Senate, 73d Cong., 1st Sess., Senate bill S. 69, introduced March 10, 1933, published as an unpaged leaflet.

[38] U.S. Senate, 73d Cong., 1st Sess., Senate bill S. 1503, introduced April 17, 1933, published as an unpaged leaflet.

[39] U.S. House, 73d Cong., 1st Sess., House bill H.R. 4004, introduced March 21, 1933, published as an unpaged leaflet.

[40] United States, *Statutes at Large*, XLVII, pt. 1, 205–206.

legislative proposals or those exemplified in actual colonization projects. It did not necessarily provide for any program of colonization or for planned communities, as its funds could clearly be used in making loans to individual families for the purchase of isolated homesteads. The subsistence homesteads program was left to be worked out by individuals within an action agency and without any clear mandate from Congress as to details. The planning of the program was freely turned over to the Executive. This "blank check," so typical of the emergency legislation of 1933, would of necessity have to be written in terms of only a few of the many conflicting ideas about what subsistence homesteads should be. Eventually, the few ideas selected would have to be exposed to the often cruel test of experience. The result was to be one of the most interesting social experiments in American history.

Part Two

OF BUREAUS AND BUREAUCRATS

V

The Subsistence Homesteads Program

IN accordance with the expressed provisions of the earlier Bankhead subsistence homesteads bills, President Roosevelt designated Harold L. Ickes, Secretary of the Interior, to carry out the provisions of Section 208 (the subsistence homesteads section) of Title II of the National Industrial Recovery Act. Already, the other parts of Title II (the public works program) had been given to Ickes. Since Section 208 contained almost no guide as to how the $25,000,000 for subsistence homesteads should be spent, Ickes could have placed the program in his Public Works Administration, which was headed by Robert D. Kohn. With his experience in city planning and public housing in World War I and in the Regional Planning Association, Kohn wanted to use the funds to establish a few farm colonies and several garden cities of the Radburn type.[1]

Ickes decided to place subsistence homesteads in a separate program, and, either by letter or at a special meeting on subsistence homesteads on July 26, 1933, he sought advice from practically everyone interested in garden cities, farm colonies, or the back-to-the-land movement. He contacted Henry I. Harriman, president of the United States Chamber of Commerce, Dr. Arthur E. Morgan of the Tennessee Valley

[1] Memorandum on Subsistence Homesteads by Robert D. Kohn, July 8, 1933, Record Group 48, Records of the Office of the Secretary of the Interior, National Archives (to be cited hereafter as R.G. 48, National Archives).

Authority, John Nolen, one of America's best-known city planners, Bruce Melvin, a rural sociologist, Henry A. Wallace, Secretary of Agriculture, Elwood Mead, Bernarr Macfadden, Rexford Guy Tugwell, M. L. Wilson, and many of the farm economists. Among the different individuals suggested as possible directors of the subsistence homesteads program were Dean Thomas Cooper of the agricultural college of the University of Kentucky, Oscar L. Chapman, Assistant Secretary of the Interior, Hugh MacRae, the successful organizer of the farm colonies in North Carolina, M. L. Wilson, and Elwood Mead. In what was an all-important decision, Ickes selected M. L. Wilson for the position. By August 1, 1933, Wilson and Ickes were corresponding about policies for the new program.[2]

Wilson, who left the important Wheat Section of the Agricultural Adjustment Administration in order to direct the subsistence homesteads program, brought with him not only a well-formulated plan for subsistence homesteads but a conscious, defined social philosophy as well. An agricultural economist by profession, he was a philosopher by temperament. A mild, conciliatory individual, Wilson, along with Wallace, helped temper bureaucracy with philosophical discussions in the rapidly expanding New Deal Department of Agriculture, leading to one of the most interesting experiments in self-conscious bureaucracy in American history.[3] M. L., as he was always called, drew his philosophy from three not unrelated sources: pragmatism, cultural anthropology, and, most clearly, the institutional economics of John R. Commons. Coloring his formal beliefs was always a tinge of dust from the wide fields of Iowa and Montana, for Wilson always had a sentimental, as well as a rationalized, love for agriculture.

Wilson remained calm in a period of rapid, stirring change. He saw the need, even the necessity, of institutional changes, but he recognized and, most important, accepted the difficulty of change. He believed that adjustment was required constantly as the environment changed, but that the problems involved in adjustment were never simple. Ultimately, they were cultural problems, involving moral and philosophical issues, traditional beliefs, attitudes, customs, and institu-

[2] Henry I. Harriman to Ickes, July 22, 1933; Tennessee Valley Authority to Ickes, July 21, 1933; Chapman to Ickes, July 19, 1933; Elwood Mead to Ickes, Aug. 3, 1933; Rexford G. Tugwell to Ickes, July 21, 1933; all in R.G. 48, National Archives.

[3] Russell Lord, "M. L. Wilson, Nutritionist," *Land,* II (1942–1943), 309–312.

tions. Thus, reform could not be rapid, for it required generations instead of years, and reform measures had to be judged on how well they met the only vaguely known psychic needs of man and not on their formal perfection. Psychological and cultural insight was more important than technical competency. Reforms could not be purely economic, for adjustment involved whole cultural patterns, myths as well as facts. Associated with passing institutions were many virtues, moral values, and even religious ideals. Wilson believed that there was, in 1933, a serious maladjustment between the world of things and the world of thought, or, in more popular terms, a serious cultural lag. How to reconcile the two worlds was the problem.[4]

An attitude of good will and a rejection of absolutes were, according to Wilson, indispensable to successful adjustment to change. Wilson both believed in and practiced tolerance toward other men with varying ideas. Unlike many of the reformers of his day, he credited other people, businessmen as well as farmers, with intelligence and high intentions. Thus, he was able to include diverse individuals in his programs and even to encourage friendly controversy. He believed that bitterness, personal and class conflict, and intolerance prevented understanding and accomplishment. He deplored a tendency to blame the slowness of change on "vested interests," believing that such a tendency would lead to a personal-devil theory and to class antagonism. Just as much, he feared the results of dogmatism. A firm believer in the existence of social change as well as natural evolution, Wilson was a relativist and a pragmatist. In his view, man lives briefly and sees only a small segment of the universe. Only this small segment does he know. To adjust to this, his world, man needs new, creative thinking instead of old, exclusive doctrines. But yet the old, with its legacy of both valuable and antiquated ideas, with its "truths" and its myths, is modified only with great difficulty. Education may hold an answer, according to Wilson, but not education in the sense of a social scientist or an expert telling people the "truth," for quite likely the expert himself needs educating. Only by developing a critical sense, a broader point of view, and a creative imagination

[4] M. L. Wilson, "Beyond Economics," in *Farmers in a Changing World: The Yearbook of Agriculture, 1940* (Washington, 1940), pp. 925–927; M. L. Wilson, "Great Decisions upon Which the Future of Rural Life Will Depend," *Proceedings of the American Country Life Association, 18th Conference* (Columbus, Ohio, 1935), pp. 94–95.

does education contribute to the difficult task of adjustment. Only this type of education would permit necessary social experimentation to be carried out in a democratic atmosphere, with numerous committees and unending discussions. Only this type of education could lead to the consideration and the questioning of fundamental values. "Philosophic probing, if it is sincere and deep enough," Wilson said, "can realine our total thinking in such a way as to alter the nature of our attack upon those problems, for which immediate, calculable, and practical programs are possible." [5]

Democracy was the nearest thing to an absolute to Wilson. As a national planner advocating broad changes in American life, he was sincerely concerned over whether, in an increasingly complex economic system, with its required public controls, American society "is capable of producing a kind of supergovernmental economic and social intelligence which can function in harmony with our democratic heritage and attitude of mind." [6] But if democracy was to survive, believed Wilson, the new planning and the new governmental controls had to be built from the ground up, and on the solid rock of democratic opinion. Governments may provide the "devices whereby the rank and file may set their local problems into a national perspective, help to articulate the opinions that are formed on this basis, and finally assist in turning ideas into action." [7] But always, the planning had to spring from the people. The people plan in a democracy; they are not planned. Said Wilson: "When you try to move things faster than the awakened will and understanding of the people, it isn't good education and it isn't democracy." [8] Wilson would not depart from this. It was incorporated into the Agricultural Adjustment Administration through the principle of reliance on local committees. To Wilson, decentralized organization and local participation had to be at the heart of any lasting subsistence homesteads program.

Wilson was enough of an agrarian to deplore some of the trends of an industrial, materialistic society, but he did not make a reactionary

[5] Wilson, "Beyond Economics," pp. 924–930.

[6] M. L. Wilson, "How New Deal Agencies Are Affecting Family Life," *Journal of Home Economics*, XXVII (1935), 275.

[7] Wilson, "Beyond Economics," p. 925.

[8] M. L. Wilson, as quoted in an unpublished first draft of Russell Lord and Paul H. Johnstone, *A Place on Earth: A Critical Appraisal of Subsistence Homesteads* (published in Washington, 1942), in R.G. 83, National Archives.

appeal to past gods and past authorities. Instead, he viewed modern civilization from the viewpoint of a humanist who desired a "better life" for everyone and, because of background or philosophy, defined the "better life" in such a way that it always included some contact with the soil and the countryside. Wilson was aware of the freeing potentialities of technological improvements. He was not anti-industrial. Although he appreciated the values and the beauties of the old farm, he never joined Ralph Borsodi in a retreat from modernity. Rather, he wished to stop and look about before continuing the march onward toward more and more technology and efficiency. He desired the economic security, social stability, neighborliness, lack of social pressure, and social participation of America's agricultural past, while he believed that much of city life was unnatural, leading to frustrations, taxed nervous systems, and decreased physical vitality.[9] He believed that the trend toward urbanization, centralization, and increased commercialism was not necessary and desirable for all people and that more and more people were likely to be squeezed out of the economic system by progress. Because of economic necessity, some farmers and industrial workers would have to live on subsistence homesteads, perhaps with a subsidy from society. Apart from economic reasons, some people would aesthetically revolt against the "jazz-industrial age," choosing instead subsistence homesteads and industrial decentralization.[10] For both of those groups there could be a real gain, for "there are certain moral and spiritual values for all of us coming from this contact with the soil and from living with growing things."[11]

On August 1, 1933, Wilson outlined to Ickes his thoughts on how best to use the $25,000,000 subsistence homesteads appropriation. Because of the limited funds, Wilson advised widely distributed experimental communities as object lessons in the decentralization of industry and in the creation of a new pattern of life, with greater security and more opportunity for the constructive use of leisure time. He recommended a federal plan of administration, with decentralized

[9] M. L. Wilson, "Science and Folklore in Rural Life," in Oliver E. Baker, Ralph Borsodi, and M. L. Wilson, *Agriculture in Modern Life* (New York, 1939), pp. 242–244.
[10] Russell Lord, "M. L. Wilson: Pioneer," *Survey Graphic*, XXX (1941), 691.
[11] M. L. Wilson, *Farm Relief and Allotment Plan* (Day and Hour Series no. 2, University of Minnesota; Minneapolis, 1933), p. 50.

administration and responsibility. The communities, which were to be located near available employment, were to include four types: experimental farm colonies, subsistence gardens for city workers, colonies for stranded workers, and, primarily, homesteads for part-time industrial workers. He also desired a research program and close co-operation with the Departments of Agriculture, Commerce, and Labor, with state governments, and with agricultural colleges.[12] On August 23, 1933, the Division of Subsistence Homesteads was officially organized in the Department of the Interior. In addition to Wilson, early staff members included Clarence Pickett of the American Friends Service Committee; Dr. Carl C. Taylor, a leading rural sociologist at North Carolina State College; Bruce Melvin, a sociologist; and Roy Hendrickson, an Iowa newspaper reporter. Additional staff members were borrowed from the Bureau of Agricultural Economics.[13]

The early staff of the Division of Subsistence Homesteads was confronted with tremendous policy problems. Very few colonization schemes had succeeded in the past, and almost none had combined industry with part-time agriculture. Despite the growth of research in land utilization, there was only one current study of subsistence farming.[14] This paucity of research led to later criticism of the subsistence homesteads program,[15] but Wilson could not await the completion of any elaborate studies. With Civil Works Administration funds, the Division of Subsistence Homesteads did launch extensive research projects on part-time farming in most states, but in 1934 the Civil Works Administration funds were withdrawn before most of the projects were completed. Wilson frankly proposed to find answers and develop policies through experimentation, although he had a vast knowledge of past and existing colonization schemes.[16] He believed that past colonies had failed because of poor location, remoteness, paternalism, politics, poor settlers, or unsound promotion. He thought success possible with subsistence homesteads communities because of

[12] Memorandum from M. L. Wilson to Ickes, Aug. 1, 1933, R.G. 48, National Archives.

[13] Russell Lord and Paul H. Johnstone, *A Place on Earth: A Critical Appraisal of Subsistence Homesteads* (Washington, 1942), pp. 40–41.

[14] David Rozman, "Part-Time Farming in Massachusetts," in Massachusetts Agricultural Experiment Station, *Bulletin no. 266* (1930), pp. 104–146.

[15] Leonard A. Salter, Jr., "Research and Subsistence Homesteads," *Rural Sociology*, II (1937), 207–208.

[16] M. L. Wilson, "Place of Subsistence Homesteads in Our National Economy," *Journal of Farm Economics*, XVI (1934), 81.

Subsistence Homesteads Program 99

the developments in land-use planning, because of the movement for decentralization of industry, and because of the new tendencies in American life, such as the movement back to the land and to the suburbs.[17] Certainly the dangers and pitfalls of the program were visualized. Roy Hendrickson drew up seventy-six possible or probable mistakes. Significantly, in light of later experience, the first two of these were: poor land or inadequate water and mistaken assumptions about employment opportunities.[18]

Both a help and a hindrance in the early attempts to develop a concrete, practical program for the Division of Subsistence Homesteads were the many individuals and groups with dogmatic ideas about what subsistence homesteads should be. From some of these Wilson drew many practical ideals while mildly rejecting at least part of the doctrines behind the ideas. From Ralph Borsodi and the escapist agrarians, who wanted to retreat from modernity and industrialization, and from Hugh MacRae, who had paternalistic rural colonies in North Carolina, Wilson learned some of the practical problems of creating subsistence homesteads. Of less value were the ideas of people like Bernarr MacFadden, who felt that once the individual was out on the farm little more need be done for him. A constant problem was that of appeasing the farmers, who, despite the very diplomatic use of the word "subsistence," still feared government-sponsored competition. On the other side were the few industrialists who would have liked to use subsistence homesteads to anchor, at no expense to themselves, an ample, complacent labor force.

Less important, but more interesting, were the thousands of suggestions that came from individuals all over the country. Every new idea on community life found its way eventually to Franklin D. Roosevelt, Eleanor Roosevelt, Wilson, or the Division of Subsistence Homesteads. One person wanted to use subsistence homesteads for eugenic experiments; he planned to mix various bloodlines, such as introducing Quaker stock into an Alabama colony.[19] A dancing teacher wanted to use the subsistence homesteads appropriation to introduce Greek robes and aesthetic dancing into colonies of clumsy farmers.[20] A plan to revive

---

[17] M. L. Wilson, "New Land-Use Program: The Place of Subsistence Homesteads," *Journal of Land and Public Utility Economics*, X (1934), 3–9.
[18] Russell Lord, *The Wallaces of Iowa* (Boston, 1947), p. 426.
[19] *Ibid.*, p. 423.
[20] Unpublished first draft of Lord and Johnstone, *A Place on Earth*, R.G. 83, National Archives.

medieval craft guilds competed with the ideas of a brilliant psychologist, who couched his plans in such language that no member of the Division of Subsistence Homesteads could understand them. A persistent advocate of the "road town" finally, after weeks of fruitless promotion, plunged to his death from a window in New York City.[21] From California came an earnest advocate of dairying colonies. He brought detailed blueprints of huge dairy barns which could hold 2,000 cows each. An opening at the top ridgepole of each barn led to a secondary roof, which contained an electrical device for killing the cow flies that were sucked up to the trap. A chain of buckets carried the dead flies to manure spreaders. The electric power to circulate the chain of buckets, kill the flies, light the barn, and run the milkers was to be supplied by power-producing treadmills, operated by the exercise of twenty-four bulls (the exact number for 2,000 cows). When told that his plan was too perfect, he was almost satisfied.[22]

In formulating policies Wilson had the advice of a group of distinguished individuals who, sharing a common interest in subsistence homesteads, had voluntarily organized a National Advisory Committee on Subsistence Homesteads. On the invitation of Henry I. Harriman, United States Chamber of Commerce president, the committee held its first meeting on September 26, 1933, in order to formulate recommendations on subsistence homesteads. Attending were the following individuals: M. L. Wilson; Harold Ickes; Rexford G. Tugwell, then Undersecretary of Agriculture; Senator John H. Bankhead, father of the subsistence homesteads legislation; Hayden B. Harris, head of the Harris Trust and Savings Bank of Chicago and a strong supporter of subsistence homesteads for relief; William A. Julian, Treasurer of the United States and an advocate of industrial decentralization; Edward A. O'Neal, president of the American Farm Bureau; Louis J. Taber, master of the Grange; Bernarr Macfadden, back-to-the-lander extraordinary; Louis Brownlow, an expert in municipal government; Dr. John D. Black, an agricultural economist and friend of M. L. Wilson; Philip V. Carden, director of the Utah Experimental Station and an authority on Mormon colonies; Ralph E. Flanders, a

[21] Clarence Pickett, *For More than Bread* (Boston, 1953), pp. 50–51.
[22] Unpublished first draft of Lord and Johnstone, *A Place on Earth*, R.G. 83, National Archives.

Vermont manufacturer who employed part-time farmers; Dr. John A. Ryan, of the National Catholic Welfare Conference; Bernard G. Waring, a Philadelphia industrialist with a knowledge of conditions in the coal fields; George Soule, editor of the *New Republic* and formerly a member of Elwood Mead's commission to study colonization opportunities in the South; Meyer Jacobstein, economist, labor arbitrator, and politician; Dr. Philip Weltner, chancellor of the University System of Georgia and promoter of one of the first subsistence homesteads; William Green of the American Federation of Labor; and Dr. Clark Foreman, a Department of the Interior adviser on the economic status of the Negroes.[23] The personnel on the committee reflected the broad interest in subsistence homesteads, as well as the desire of Wilson and other staff members to develop a wide public support for their movement. Because of the divergent interest groups represented, the committee bogged down in endless discussions before issuing fifteen rather general recommendations. These followed most of Wilson's ideas in asking for experimental communities, the maximum of local responsibility, close co-operation with local and federal agencies, agricultural guidance for the homesteaders, long-term credit, and, perhaps most important, local nonprofit corporations to administer each project.[24]

Although most of the Advisory Committee's recommendations became the original policies of the Division of Subsistence Homesteads, they did not encompass the philosophy of subsistence homesteads as developed by Wilson and his assistants. Wilson's emphasis on local autonomy and co-operation with local agricultural groups, his desire to avoid class antagonism and any rapid departure from the individualistic basis of American society, his ability to reconcile differences between antagonistic groups, his wide range of friends, from industrialists to agrarians, and his great prestige among agriculturalists helped allay any fears of radicalism in the early subsistence homesteads program. Support was won from diverse groups. In many

[23] Lord and Johnstone, *A Place on Earth*, p. 42; a press release, Department of the Interior, Sept. 25, 1933, Record Group 16, Records of the Office of the Secretary of Agriculture, 1935–1937, National Archives (to be cited hereafter as R.G. 16, National Archives).

[24] U.S. Department of Labor, Bureau of Labor Statistics, "Subsistence Homestead Movement under National Recovery Act," *Monthly Labor Review*, XXXVII (1933), 1327–1328.

ways, Wilson was at his best as a liaison man and an arbitrator and not as an administrator. This early atmosphere of good feelings tended to conceal the fact that Wilson, and most of his assistants, viewed subsistence homesteads as a new frontier, as the locale for a new way of life, with new and controversial values and institutions. Even as they envisoned certain material and economic benefits from subsistence homesteads, such as better diets, security, a cushion against unemployment, a better place to raise children, a closer association with nature, less social pressures, cheaper living expenses, and a better use of leisure time, they also envisioned a new, improved man, with new attitudes and new values.[25]

The subsistence homesteads community, with its gardens and neighborhood industry, was, in Wilson's mind, an ideal to be achieved, perhaps with difficulty, for it did not fit many existing patterns and would require extensive adjustments. In some ways he shared a type of idealism that had influenced all the community builders of the past. He envisioned a new village life, with handicrafts, community activities, closer family relationships, and co-operative enterprises. He called it the "community idea."[26] It featured a retreat from extreme materialism and from a highly individualistic, competitive society to a more simple, more secure, more socially minded existence. But the average American, believed Wilson, would not readily adjust to such a village or community life. Man himself would have to change. This comes close to the heart of Wilson's thoughts and aims. He said: "Somehow, or in some way, attitudes and lives of the families who occupy these communities must be integrated so as to provide a new and different view of life and a new and different set of family values."[27] To Wilson, there would be a dual process. On one hand, there would have to be an extensive education program to help develop the attitudes necessary for an integrated community life. On the other hand, life in subsistence homesteads communities would help develop the new attitudes. Thus, he believed that co-operative institutions would develop, serving as aids to "creative community development." Perhaps his greatest hope was expressed in the follow-

[25] Wilson, "New Land-Use Program," pp. 10–12; M. L. Wilson, "Decentralization of Industry in the New Deal," *Social Forces*, XIII (1935), 597–598.
[26] Wilson, "Place of Subsistence Homesteads in Our National Economy," p. 81.
[27] Wilson, "How New Deal Agencies Are Affecting Family Life," p. 227.

Subsistence Homesteads Program

ing statement: "Co-operation will be the basis of our future society if we are to maintain our individual freedom and not bow to the force of a dictator. I believe that the subsistence homesteads community can well serve as a cradle for a new growth of the co-operative attitude." [28]

Even as policies and aims were being formulated, the Division of Subsistence Homesteads was preparing for an action program. The original five full-time employees of the division occupied three rooms in the Interior building, but were quickly swamped by a flood of correspondence. By October there were twenty-three people in the Division of Subsistence Homesteads, occupying a whole floor of the Hurley Wright Building. Almost as quickly as the $25,000,000 appropriation for subsistence homesteads was announced, letters, thousands of letters, began to pour into Washington, usually addressed to Franklin D. or Eleanor Roosevelt, both of whom had taken a great interest in the subsistence homesteads movement. Everyone wanted some of the money for himself or for his area of the country. By February, 1934, the requests for loans amounted to $4,500,000,000.[29] From these requests the Division of Subsistence Homesteads had to select the most deserving.

The largest share of the letters received by the Division of Subsistence Homesteads (all had to be answered) were personal requests for loans, despite division press releases explaining that only community settlements were planned. Other letters were from individuals or real estate promoters who wanted to unload a piece of land or from leading citizens or the Chamber of Commerce of cities, requesting a subsistence homesteads community for their area. Almost every city in the United States could prove that it most needed or most deserved a subsistence homesteads community. A few people wanted employment in the division, and thousands wanted the division to adopt their particular scheme. A few letters offered excellent advice and were individually answered (most were answered by form letters).

[28] M. L. Wilson, "The Subsistence Homesteads Program," *Proceedings of the Institute of Public Affairs, 1934,* VIII (1934), pt. i, 171–172.
[29] M. L. Wilson to B. L. Berg, Feb. 24, 1934, Record Group 96, Records of the Farmers' Home Administration (includes records of the Division of Subsistence Homesteads, the Resettlement Administration, and the Farm Security Administration), National Archives (to be cited hereafter as R.G. 96, National Archives).

Some merely disgusted the staff of the division. One man in a Michigan city asked that the division establish a colony well away from his community in order to settle there all the Negroes of his city, which, according to him, had a serious Negro problem.[30] One woman wrote a 150-page letter to Mr. and Mrs. Roosevelt, recounting a life of unbelievable misfortune and asking for money to purchase a farm.[31] One man, asking for a loan for a subsistence homestead, complained that his family was in poor health "due to the carbon monoxide poison which accumulates in New York City on a heavy day."[32] On receiving one of the standard, explanatory replies, he protested that he merely wanted money to buy "a tent and build a homestead in Florida" and was not interested in "coal-miners, negroes and starving farmers and the rest of the horseradish soup."[33] Some wrote in groups, as the following people from Arkansas: "We are 100 familys which like to buy 3000 to 5000 acres of U.S. land For to colonize in state of Arkansaw."[34] One person wrote a poem to President Roosevelt:

> Our state has thousands of acres of logged off land
> Where timber again will never stand
> Also thousands of families unemployed
> That FDR could make overjoyed.
>
> Build a nice little house and also a barn
> Put on a cow and some chickens and pigs and do no harm
> With a chance like this ten out of eleven
> Would think they were at the gate of heaven.
>
> A home is one thing we would all enjoy
> And if any one can do this you are the boy
> Now what do you think Franklin D.
> I am sure that you'll agree with me.[35]

After examining some 400 proposals that possessed some merit, Wilson announced, on October 14, 1933, that the division would concentrate on three types of colonies. First, and primarily, there

[30] Burrall G. Newman to M. L. Wilson, Feb. 20, 1934, *ibid.*
[31] Lizzie Crane to Mr. and Mrs. Roosevelt, Feb. 27, 1934, *ibid.*
[32] Samuel Bernstein to M. L. Wilson, Feb., 1934, *ibid.*
[33] Bernstein to Wilson, Feb. 22, 1934, *ibid.*
[34] K. A. M. Bergenstal to U.S. Department of Agriculture, Jan. 30, 1934, *ibid.*
[35] Dave Z. Murphy to F. D. R., Jan., 1934, *ibid.*

would be communities of part-time farmers near industrial employment. Secondly, there would be all-rural colonies for resettled submarginal farmers. Thirdly, there would be a few villages with newly decentralized industry. The last were to be the most experimental and the most controversial communities. They included the communities for stranded coal miners, which represented a continuation of Assistant Director Clarence Pickett's work as head of the American Friends Service Committee and which were of particular interest to Mrs. Roosevelt and Louis M. Howe. Wilson also announced that the communities would be constructed either by a federal corporation or by a local corporation, both of which were being planned. For the guidance of those interested in specific projects, Wilson stipulated that, to receive the division's approval, any proposal would have to have strong local backing, including the co-operation and planning aid of the state colleges of agriculture, the agricultural experiment stations, and the Extension Service.[36] At this time many local groups and committees were already formulating proposals to submit to the Division of Subsistence Homesteads.

In November, after a few projects had already been approved, the division published its first information circular, explaining the purposes and policies of the subsistence homesteads program. The circular contrasted the permanent nature of subsistence homesteads with temporary relief schemes, related the new communities to a broader program of public housing, national economic planning, and population redistribution, and stressed the experimental and demonstrational purposes of the projects.[37] The typical community was described as containing from 25 to 100 families living on individual homesteads of from one to five acres, which would accommodate an orchard, a vegetable garden, poultry, a pig, and, in some cases, a cow. Eventual ownership was promised for most colonists. The community sites were to be approved by agricultural experts, and the homestead development had to be in accordance with approved planning, architectural, and engineering practices. Houses were to be moderate in cost, but in conformity with standards of convenience,

[36] Progress Report by M. L. Wilson, Oct. 14, 1933, *ibid.*
[37] U.S. Department of the Interior, Division of Subsistence Homesteads, *General Information concerning the Purposes and Policies of the Division of Subsistence Homesteads* (Circular no. 1; Washington, Nov. 15, 1933), pp. 1–6.

durability, attractiveness, and sanitation, with essential utilities provided. The homesteaders, selected from low-income groups, were to be chosen only after an inquiry into character traits, agricultural fitness, employment prospects, and other factors. In all cases the federal funds were to be lent and not granted, with repayment over a period of thirty years at 4 per cent interest. The funds were to be lent by a Federal Subsistence Homesteads Corporation to local corporations at the community level.[38]

After an extensive study of the many legal problems involved, Secretary Ickes announced the formation of a Federal Subsistence Homesteads Corporation on December 2, 1933. Incorporated under Delaware law, the corporation was to be an action agency for the Division of Subsistence Homesteads. The stock was to be held in trust by Ickes. Shortly thereafter, subsidiary local corporations were formed for most of the prospective homestead projects. The parent corporation held the stock issued by the local corporations and thus had ultimate control over their policies. This corporate device, which had been suggested to Ickes by the Attorney General as early as August, 1933, was adopted to meet four needs: to acquire, hold, and dispose of title to land, buildings, and personal property and to enter contracts with borrowers, purchasers, and architects; to assure local administration and support; to remove the aura of paternalism and to differentiate the subsistence homesteads communities from relief projects; and, perhaps most important, to free the subsistence homesteads program from the procedural technicalities and delays that hampered the operations of a United States Government that was ill adapted to the vastly increased activities of the New Deal period.[39]

The corporate device promised to clear up some of the problems attendant upon a rather broad program of community building that had no well-defined legal basis. Section 208 clearly permitted loans for subsistence homesteads; beyond that, it gave only the general authority for "otherwise aiding." If this entailed the creation of complete communities and the governmental ownership of the land, Section 208 contained no provisions to clarify certain legal points involved. Complete communities create a large demand for local public

[38] *Ibid.*, pp. 6–12.
[39] Philip M. Glick, "The Federal Subsistence Homestead Program," *Yale Law Journal*, XLIV (1935), 1332–1335.

services, such as schools and roads. Yet federally owned property is not taxable by lesser governmental units, while the subsistence homesteads legislation made no provision for payments in lieu of taxes. At the same time the federal government was legally prevented from building schools, a function reserved to the states. This created a dilemma in respect to the local acceptance of subsistence homesteads communities. Certainly the homesteaders would not be welcome unless they paid their share of the local tax burden. In addition, the existence of state civil and criminal jurisdiction and even the right to vote were apparently endangered by federal ownership. It was feared that subsistence homesteads communities would become federal islands on the order of Indian reservations. It was hoped that the locally organized corporations would permit local taxation and local jurisdiction.[40] Later interpretations did not justify these hopes in regard to taxation.

The local corporation appeared to be an excellent device for carrying out all the local work of the Division of Subsistence Homesteads. It could borrow the money, construct the communities, and issue purchase contracts to homesteaders. Local sponsors and prominent citizens would be on its Board of Directors, insuring local interest and support. Later, when the communities were completed, the corporation could collect payments from the homesteaders and manage the community. As the homesteaders gained an equity in their homes, they would be given the stock of the corporation, making them joint owners of their own community. With its abilities to use ordinary business procedures, it could purchase land and contract for construction with much greater speed than could the government. It was really the foundation of Wilson's administrative organization.[41]

The community projects approved by the Division of Subsistence Homesteads exhibited an endless variety. The first loan was granted in October, 1933, to Ralph Borsodi's homestead project in Dayton, Ohio. Borsodi was the adviser to a Council of Social Agencies in Dayton which already had planned several small homestead communities. The ideas back of these plans combined the need for relief with Borsodi's escapist agrarianism and an emphasis on self-help. Homesteaders were to build their own homes, grow subsistence crops on a small acreage, carry on group activities, and have a common

[40] *Ibid.*, pp. 1345–1349, 1367.   [41] *Ibid.*, p. 1335.

pasture and wood lot, while receiving wages for part-time employment in Dayton. Weaving, sewing, and other family crafts were to be developed. Homesteads were to be leased to clients in a modified single-tax system.[42] A small loan of $50,000 for the first of the planned communities was all Borsodi ever received from the Division of Subsistence Homesteads. His Dayton project was the only one in which the government never owned the land. From the beginning Borsodi resisted any federal control over his project, desiring financial aid without governmental control.

The second project, also approved in October, was, by far, the most controversial and the most publicized of all the subsistence homesteads. It was a projected community of 200 family units for stranded coal miners at Reedsville, West Virginia. Growing directly from the work of Clarence Pickett and the humanitarian interest of Eleanor Roosevelt, this project, which was soon to be named Arthurdale after the name of a former owner of the estate, was the first to be developed and was the site of much open experimentation, countless mistakes, and many hard-learned lessons. It will receive detailed attention in a later chapter. In December, 1933, and January, 1934, three other stranded workers' communities were announced by the Division of Subsistence Homesteads. These were Cumberland Homesteads, near Crossville, Tennessee; Tygart Valley Homesteads, near Elkins, West Virginia; and Westmoreland Homesteads, near Greensburg, Pennsylvania. They were planned for from 250 to 300 units each and were the largest of the subsistence homesteads. They were designed for unemployed miners who had been stranded since the closing of coal mines as far back as 1920. Tygart Valley was planned in connection with a large forest area which promised some opportunity for employment. The four stranded communities presented unique and almost insurmountable problems, as well as unending embarrassment, to the Division of Subsistence Homesteads and its successor agencies. They were the only subsistence homesteads to be settled by destitute relief clients who had no opportunity for employment. Since they were planned only for part-time farming, with very small plots of ground, some type of industrial employment was essential. Either industry had to move voluntarily to these communities or the Division

[42] Ralph Borsodi, "Dayton, Ohio, Makes Social History," *Nation*, CXXXVI (1933), 447–448.

of Subsistence Homesteads had to find some method of providing economic security, else the homesteaders would remain stranded government wards, even though they lived in bright new homes. This economic problem was never solved completely.

Perhaps the most interesting community developed by the Division of Subsistence Homesteads was Jersey Homesteads near Hightstown, New Jersey. Since it was also a very controversial one, it too will be discussed in detail in a later chapter. Two hundred Jewish garment-workers in New York City banded together to establish the colony at Hightstown. Supplementing the funds authorized by the Division of Subsistence Homesteads with individual contributions of $500 each, they planned a co-operative garment factory, a co-operative farm, and consumer co-operatives. In many ways Jersey Homesteads was to be more of a garden or satellite city than a part-time farming, part-time industrial community. Because of long delays in its planning, its construction was entirely carried out by the Resettlement Administration.

M. L. Wilson and his closest advisers, all particularly interested in agricultural problems, desired to establish a few all-rural colonies to absorb submarginal farmers and to demonstrate the possibilities of organized rural communities. In this they were following the lead of Elwood Mead, who had tried to get the government to establish a few such colonies in the South. Since the University System of Georgia already had made plans for moving about 500 farmers from eroded, worn-out farms to new lands where they could practice diversified farming, the Division of Subsistence Homesteads announced its support of this plan in January, 1934. A million dollars was authorized for the project, which was named Piedmont Homesteads. Although over 11,000 acres of land were purchased, Piedmont suffered innumerable delays and legal difficulties. Only 50 homestead units were completed.

In North Carolina, Hugh MacRae, who for years had been trying to get governmental support for his type of intensively cultivated farm colonies, succeeded in getting Wilson's approval for another proposed million-dollar colony. Located in Pender County, North Carolina, and named Penderlea Homesteads, MacRae's colony was planned for 300 families who were to derive all their income from ten-acre farms. Its turbulent history will be traced in a subsequent chapter. The only other full-time farming colony, a small project, Richton Homesteads, at Richton, Mississippi, was approved in April, 1934, and actually was constructed by the Resettlement Administration. In Wisconsin a homestead community for workers in a national forest was planned by the Division of Subsistence Homesteads but later was turned over to the Forest Service. The rural projects were defended against the wrath of farmers and farming organizations on the ground that they would produce only nonsurplus crops for sale. Involved in them was an attempt to convert a few tenant farmers into landowners.

Before June 30, 1934, which marked the end of Wilson's work in the Division of Subsistence Homesteads and an important change in policies, approximately thirty-one industrial-type subsistence homesteads were announced, although of these only twenty-three were ever completed. As a whole, these were more successful and less controversial than the stranded-workers or the rural type, although much less publicized. From a financial standpoint, several of these were to prove the most successful of any of the communities constructed by the New Deal. They more nearly conformed to the intentions of the subsistence homesteads legislation and to the ideas of most of the administrators of the subsistence homesteads program. In one sense they were the only true subsistence homesteads, combining access to part-time industrial employment with an opportunity to earn a partial subsistence from the land. All of them were located within commuting distance of some type of industrial employment, in either a small or large city. Almost invariably they were small communities of from 25 to 125 units, with an average of from two to five acres to each homestead. Either as single colonies or as a related group of colonies, they were almost always sponsored by a local corporation. Beyond these similarities they offered great variations, but in most ways conformed to the following official definition of a subsistence homestead:

A subsistence homestead denotes a house and out buildings located upon a plot of land on which can be grown a large portion of the foodstuffs required by the homestead family. It signifies production for home consumption and not for commercial sale. In that it provides for subsistence alone, it carries with it the corollary that cash income must be drawn from some outside source. The central motive of the subsistence homestead program, therefore, is to demonstrate the economic value of a livelihood which combines part-time wage work and part-time gardening or farming.[43]

Over half of the completed industrial homesteads were located in three groups in the South. Five homesteads were secured for the area around Jasper and Birmingham, Alabama, perhaps because of the influence of Senator Bankhead.[44] Designed for commuting workers, they were handicapped by being too far from the larger cities. One of the proposed Alabama colonies, Cahaba, was converted into a small greenbelt city by the Resettlement Administration. The other four, Bankhead Farms, Greenwood Homesteads, Mount Olive Homesteads, and Palmerdale Homesteads, were all semirural. In Texas five garden projects of from 50 to 100 units each were developed near five cities. These were Houston Gardens near Houston, Beauxart Gardens near Beaumont, Wichita Gardens near Wichita Falls, Three Rivers Gardens near Three Rivers, and Dalworthington Gardens near Arlington. Three Rivers Gardens involved a guarantee of part-time employment by two local industrialists.[45] Four of the smallest communities, Tupelo, McComb, Hattiesburg, and Magnolia Homesteads, were constructed near Tupelo, McComb, Hattiesburg, and Meridian, Mississippi. Each of these contained from 20 to 35 units, with a combined total of only 104. Because of their small size and their proximity to their parent cities, they never became distinct communities in themselves.

Only four subsistence homesteads were completed west of the Rockies. At Phoenix a garden community for 300 families was planned, but only 25 homes were constructed. Although on plots of less than an acre, the homesteaders shared a community pasture.[46] In the suburbs of Los Angeles, two communities, El Monte and San Fernando Homesteads, were planned by local citizens of Los Angeles as demonstrations of small farm-home possibilities. Backed by the Los Angeles Chamber of Commerce and the County Planning Board, planned by local architects, and located on excellent land, they were to

[43] U.S. Department of the Interior, Division of Subsistence Homesteads, *Bulletin 1* (Washington, 1934), p. 4.
[44] For an excellent account of the Alabama colonies see Paul W. Wager, *One Foot on the Soil: A Study of Subsistence Homesteads in Alabama* (Bureau of Public Administration at the University of Alabama, 1945).
[45] Memorandum on the Texas Project, n.d., R.G. 96, National Archives.
[46] C. B. Baldwin to Paul Appleby, May 26, 1937, R.G. 16, National Archives.

become, at least from the financial standpoint, two of the most successful of the subsistence homesteads. The Los Angeles sponsors did not form a local corporation, desiring federal control because of the avowed demonstrational purposes of the model communities. Wanting a successful demonstration rather than relief, the communities were designed for skilled workers, clerks, and even retired people. The acreage of the individual homesteads was very small, being less than an acre at El Monte.[47] Another very successful homestead community was located partly within the city limits of the relatively new, planned city of Longview, Washington. Here, in an area that already contained many part-time farmers and in a region that offered ample opportunities for part-time employment in the lumbering industry, the sixty homesteads of approximately two and one-half acres each were assured of success. Longview Homesteads received enthusiastic support from the citizens of Longview and quickly became an integrated part of the larger community, being only a new and very attractive subdivision.[48]

Five subsistence homesteads were eventually completed in the north central states, although two of these, Duluth Homesteads, Duluth, Minnesota, and Lake County Homesteads, near Chicago, Illinois, were only planned by the Division of Subsistence Homesteads and actually were constructed by the Resettlement Administration. Austin Homesteads at Austin, Minnesota, was unique in being located near a one-factory town and in being sponsored by the president of that one factory, George A. Hormel of the Hormel Packing Company. Seventy per cent of the homesteaders at Austin were to be Hormel employees.[49] The fact that M. L. Wilson accepted the plans of Hormel and many other industrialists on other sponsoring committees reflected his belief in the good intentions of industrial leaders and in the necessity of co-operation from industry in setting up part-time farming, part-time industrial communities. To some critics of subsistence homesteads, particularly those representing labor, such communities as Austin were only proof of their contention that the

---

[47] Lord and Johnstone, *A Place on Earth*, pp. 97–106; U.S. Department of Labor, Bureau of Labor Statistics, "Subsistence Homesteads for Industrial and Rural Workers," *Monthly Labor Review*, XL (1935), 27.

[48] U.S. Department of Labor, Bureau of Labor Statistics, "Housing under the Resettlement Administration," *Monthly Labor Review*, XLIV (1937), 1393–1394.

[49] Lord and Johnstone, *A Place on Earth*, pp. 58–61.

Subsistence Homesteads Program

subsistence homesteads program was anchoring a new group of industrial serfs for exploitation by business. Located almost within the city of Decatur, Indiana, Decatur Homesteads, a small community of forty-eight units, was developed with the assistance of Purdue University. The homesteaders at Decatur were promised work in the local General Electric Corporation plant.[50] At Granger, Iowa, a moderately successful community was promoted by Father Luigi G. Ligutti of the Catholic Rural Life Conference for part-time coal miners of several diverse nationalities. Granger Homesteads, which had much publicity from the Catholic press, will be discussed in more detail in a later chapter.

These thirty-two communities, all planned by June, 1934, were, except two, the only subsistence homesteads ever to become completed communities, despite the fact that over fifty others were planned and, in some cases, land was purchased. One of the two other completed projects, Shenandoah Homesteads, was planned in June, 1934. It was a special-type project of seven widely scattered sections to absorb the mountain farmers who were being pushed out of the area of the Shenandoah National Park in Virginia. As such it became a political liability for the Resettlement Administration. The other project, which was barely on the planning boards in May, 1935, when the Resettlement Administration absorbed the Division of Subsistence Homesteads, was to become the first Negro subsistence homesteads community. It was located near Newport News, Virginia. At the very beginning of the subsistence homesteads program, M. L. Wilson had contemplated a loan to a community under construction by the Tennessee Valley Authority at Norris Dam.[51] The loan was not made, and Norris, Tennessee, remained in the hands of the Tennessee Valley Authority; it is the only New Deal community not within the scope of this study. Also contemplated in the earlier days, but never attempted, were some irrigation communities to be developed with the aid of the Reclamation Service.[52]

One of the crucial elements in the success of a subsistence home-

[50] Harold M. Ware and Webster Powell, "Planning for Permanent Poverty: What Subsistence Farming Really Stands For," *Harper's Magazine*, CLXX (1934–1935), 522.

[51] M. L. Wilson, Progress Report of the Division of Subsistence Homesteads, Oct. 14, 1933, R.G. 96, National Archives.

[52] Division of Subsistence Homesteads, *General Information*, p. 8.

steads community was its location, in regard to both the fertility of the soil and the availability of industrial employment. Under M. L. Wilson the Washington staff of the Division of Subsistence Homesteads did not select, except in a few cases, the location for communities. This was left to the local sponsors. But before the Division of Subsistence Homesteads would approve a loan for a local project, the site had to be fully surveyed, analyzed by soil experts, and expertly appraised. As a result, the local corporations usually called upon the state agricultural colleges and the local agricultural experiment stations for assistance in developing their detailed project plans. Much of the land appraisal was done by Federal Land Bank appraisers. Since the stranded communities grew out of the work of the American Friends Service Committee, their locations were selected by Clarence Pickett and the Division of Subsistence Homesteads, with the aid of a Committee for Soil Surveys appointed by the Department of Agriculture to assist in the subsistence homesteads program.[53]

By January, 1934, nine project sites had been laid out. Construction was under way only at Reedsville (Arthurdale) and there without even the minimum amount of planning. The early site planning was done under the direction of the local corporations. At Penderlea, John Nolen, one of America's foremost city planners, designed the all-rural village. Local architects, assisted by agricultural experts, laid out most of the communities. Construction operations, which began on many of the projects in the spring of 1934, soon came under project managers appointed by the Division of Subsistence Homesteads. House construction at Dayton, Cumberland, and Tygart Valley was originally carried out under the self-help idea, with the homesteaders building their own homes. Most of the smaller, industrial homesteads were constructed by contract. Some work on the stranded communities was done by relief labor under the supervision of project engineers.

One of the early policy problems that led to endless debate was the question of house design and size. The protagonists ranged from Macfadden, who wanted only shacks, to Mrs. Roosevelt and many of the officials of the Division of Subsistence Homesteads, who wanted

[53] M. L. Wilson to Ickes, Aug. 29, 1933, R.G. 48, National Archives; Ickes to the Acting Secretary of War, Sept. 29, 1933, *ibid.*

bathrooms and plumbing in four- or five-room houses. In general those who saw subsistence homesteads as a relief measure wanted smaller, cheaper homes than those, such as Wilson, who saw them as demonstrations of a new way of life. Both Ickes and President Roosevelt, seeking economy, wanted small, inexpensive houses with the plumbing left for the homesteader to install later.[54] Eventually Mrs. Roosevelt's ideas were accepted. With great variations, the subsistence homesteads houses never had less than four rooms and sometimes had up to six; they were constructed of durable materials and, in all but one or two cases, had bathrooms and electricity. In the North they sometimes had basements and central heating. Many of the local sponsors were fearful that the houses were going to be so expensive that the homesteaders would never be able to afford them, for the idea of a possible government subsidy was not present in the early program. This fear led, in a few cases, to attempts at extreme economy in construction and to flimsy houses which were later rebuilt. In some cases the homes were close enough to larger cities to receive city water, Decatur and Longview being good examples. In a majority of cases individual wells were used. Tygart Valley, Houston Gardens, and a few other communities had central water systems. House construction was usually of native materials, with adobe used in Phoenix Homesteads and Crab Orchard sandstone at Cumberland Homesteads. Most of the communities were of frame or cinder-block construction. In every colony certain outbuildings were provided, ranging from garages in the garden suburbs to chicken houses, cow barns, and washhouses at those with the larger acreages. Combination community buildings and schools were planned for the more isolated communities.

At the end of Wilson's directorship in June, 1934, there were no houses occupied, although fifty homes were almost completed at Arthurdale. The problem of selecting homesteaders had already begun. In some areas, as where the homesteaders were building their own homes, the selection or tentative selection was necessary very early. Wilson turned the selection duties over to the local corporations, but suggested certain procedures. He advised the appointment of local selection committees, the use of experienced investigators,

[54] Harold L. Ickes, *The Secret Diary of Harold L. Ickes*, vol. I, *The First Thousand Days, 1933–1936* (New York, 1953), pp. 227–228.

an adequate familiarization program for applicants, and the requirement of certain qualifications as to background, particularly in regard to farming experience, health, habits, stability, and financial status.[55] By June, 1934, the selection process had been federalized to the extent that local selections were approved at Washington. At that time 145 homesteaders had been definitely approved and 618 tentatively approved out of 13,934 applicants for 2,176 homesteads.[56]

The first serious impediment to the subsistence homesteads program came from Congress in February, 1934. In October, 1933, the Division of Subsistence Homesteads had hoped to complete the construction of at least a few houses at Arthurdale before the winter. Since no industry had shown any intention of establishing a factory at Arthurdale, the division sought some other means of securing employment opportunities. The Post Office Department agreed to manufacture certain postal equipment, including hardware and furniture, in a factory to be established at Arthurdale with Public Works Administration funds. The Post Office Department had been allotted $525,000 for the factory, had selected a site, and had drawn plans by February, 1934. When the plans were made public several furniture manufacturers took alarm, accusing the government of using tax funds to compete against private enterprise. Ickes argued that the factory would be used only as a yardstick to determine if the government was paying too much for its postal supplies. The argument was then transferred to Congress, with congressmen from furniture manufacturing regions leading a campaign against the proposed factory for Arthurdale. Congress had no way of preventing the Public Works Administration from allotting funds for a factory, but it could prevent any Post Office appropriations from being used in the West Virginia factory. Representative Louis Ludlow of Indiana, the congressman most incensed at the factory plan, introduced a restrictive amendment to the Post Office Department appropriation prohibiting any expenditure for the manufacture of postal supplies outside of Washington, D.C., where the Post Office Department was already in

[55] John B. Holt, *An Analysis of Methods and Criteria Used in Selecting Families for Colonization Projects* (Social Research Report no. 1, U.S. Department of Agriculture, Farm Security Administration and the Bureau of Agricultural Economics; Washington, 1937), pp. 36–37.

[56] Report of Operations Section, Division of Subsistence Homesteads, June 30, 1934, R.G. 96, National Archives.

the mailbag business. The amendment, which passed by voice vote, killed the plan for Arthurdale unless the Senate rejected the amendment.[57] Ludlow declared that the proposed plant involved the eventual destruction of private business and violated "fundamental American philosophy."[58] Representative Daniel Reed of New York pointed to former legislation preventing government competition with business, to the idle furniture factories all over the nation, and to the irresponsible bureaucrats who desired the "nationalization of industry."[59]

In the Senate an almost unnoticed move to strike out the House restriction was challenged by Senator Arthur Vandenberg of Michigan, precipitating a floor debate, with the proposed factory being defended by Senator Kenneth D. McKellar of Tennessee, chairman of the Appropriations Committee. Vandenberg declared, with some reason, that the question at issue was whether or not the federal government should "embark upon an experiment in creating industrial communities under the subsistence plan."[60] He asked if the Senate wanted the government to enter this new field of business. The most resounding "No" came from a Democrat, Senator Josiah W. Bailey of North Carolina. He believed that approval of the factory would be the beginning of a process leading to government control of all industry, to a complete bureaucracy, to the overturn of all liberties, and to the absolute subversion of free government.[61] Other Senators countered his argument by pointing to the sorry record of private enterprise in running business. One Senator asked how anyone could be put to work without competing with someone.[62] By a vote of 34 to 29 the Senate reversed the House decision and approved the factory. The House promptly refused to concur in the Senate action by an overwhelming vote of 274 to 111. The Senate could only concede after this overwhelming expression of House sentiment.[63] Thus it was determined that, although the government might build subsistence homesteads and hope for industry to come, it could not provide industry, at least not directly or openly.

This action by Congress should not be construed as an attack on subsistence homesteads. Most of the congressmen showed little fa-

[57] *C.R.*, 73d Cong., 2d Sess., 1934, pp. 1431–1432. [58] *Ibid.*, p. 1359.
[59] *Ibid.*, p. 1272.   [60] *Ibid.*, p. 2754.   [61] *Ibid.*, p. 2756.
[62] *Ibid.*, pp. 2759, 3429.   [63] *Ibid.*, pp. 3433, 3902.

miliarity with the subsistence homesteads program, and very few of them showed any animosity toward it. Many expressed sympathy for the objectives of the over-all program. The most bitter attack against subsistence homesteads came from Senator Thomas D. Schall of Minnesota, who referred to Arthurdale as the "communist project" and the "West Virginia commune." [64] On the other side, Representative Jennings Randolph from the Arthurdale District was a consistent defender of the whole subsistence homesteads program. He even tried, unsuccessfully, to get a separate bill passed to authorize the Post Office factory at Arthurdale.[65] By far the most fervent supporter of subsistence homesteads was Representative Ernest W. Marland, who envisioned subsistence homesteads communities in every county of his home state of Oklahoma. He desired an appropriation of $4,000,000,000 for subsistence homesteads, stressing that the back-to-the-land movement "must succeed, or we are all lost." [66] Before retiring to Oklahoma to run for governor and work for subsistence homesteads, Marland gave the following picture of a subsistence farm:

> A small farm with a wood lot for fuel, a pasture for cows, an orchard with hives of bees, a dozen acres or so of plow land, and a garden for berries and annual vegetable crops.
> There is always plenty on a farm such as this.
> In winter a fat hog hangs in the smokehouse and from the cellar come jellies and jams and preserves, canned fruits, and dried vegetables. In the summer there is a succession of fresh fruits from the orchard and fresh vegetables from the garden.
> There is always comfort on this farm.
> The pure air, the deep silence of the night, the healthful outdoor work, all make for sound and restful sleep.
> The house is tight against the wind and rain; wood fires keep it warm in winter, trees and vines shade it in summer. The furniture is not overstuffed, nor is it covered with tapestry, but it is made to be comfortable.[67]

When the local corporations were set up it was assumed, under advisement from the Solicitor of the Department of the Interior, that the local groups were not accountable to the General Accounting Office for expenditures and that the government was not accountable for any claims against the local corporations. This assumption was based on a past ruling in relation to the Emergency Fleet Corporation

[64] *Ibid.*, p. 7738.
[66] *Ibid.*, pp. 7353–7354.
[65] *Ibid.*, pp. 7194, 10852–10854.
[67] *Ibid.*, p. 7081.

Subsistence Homesteads Program

of World War I. The inability of the local corporations to conform to the complicated and time-consuming accounting procedures of regular government agencies was recognized. On January 3, 1934, however, President Roosevelt ruled that government corporations had to render their accounts to the General Accounting Office if not provided otherwise by law.[68] On January 11, 1934, Comptroller General John R. McCarl ruled that a Public Works Administration housing corporation had to conform to standard accounting procedures and finally, on March 15, 1934, ruled that the local subsistence homesteads corporations would have to deposit their borrowed funds with the United States Treasurer and use standard disbursing and accounting procedures.[69] This represented only the beginning of a series of adverse decisions by McCarl that restricted and at times almost blocked the work of the Division of Subsistence Homesteads. An angered Ickes described McCarl as "not only a Republican, but . . . a reactionary Republican." [70]

The decision by McCarl was not merely a legal obstacle. By requiring the same accounting procedure from the local corporations as from government agencies, McCarl nullified one of the primary purposes of the corporate device. He also made it almost impossible to use the local corporations in other than an advisory capacity. This threatened the whole policy of decentralized administration which was at the foundation of Wilson's entire program. On March 19, 1934, Wilson reluctantly outlined a new plan of administration, which entailed complete control over the local projects by the Federal Subsistence Homesteads Corporation. The project manager was to control each project, and accountants were to be assigned to each project. The local corporation would act as an advisory board, while educational and cultural activities could be aided by local co-operation.[71] Wilson would have liked to devise some legal method of continuing local control, for on the question of local planning he was most adamant. The legal staff of the division believed that there was no question that the local corporations could continue to make policy decisions.[72]

---

[68] Glick, "The Federal Subsistence Homesteads Program," pp. 1339–1384.
[69] McCarl to Ickes, March 15, 1934, R.G. 48, National Archives.
[70] Ickes, *The Secret Diary*, I, 335.
[71] Wilson to Ickes, March 19, 1934, R.G. 48, National Archives.
[72] Lord and Johnstone, *A Place on Earth*, p. 47.

The question of local versus federal control led to the first major policy and administrative change in the subsistence homesteads program. Unfortunately for the local projects, it was not the last. Ickes, despite his resentment over McCarl's interferences, had long deplored the decentralized administration of the Division of Subsistence Homesteads. Nor did he think highly of Wilson as an administrator or executive, and he disliked some of Wilson's appointees. In January, Ickes forbade any appointment at the local level, requiring all applications to be cleared through him.[73] By March he was bringing pressure on Wilson and his staff to abandon completely the decentralized administrative structure. By an order of May 12, 1934, Ickes abolished all control by the local corporations and completely federalized the subsistence homesteads program.[74] By this time there was a well-defined break between Ickes and the personnel of the Division of Subsistence Homesteads, springing from a variance in philosophy as well as from disagreements over administrative devices.

Ickes came to Washington after long experience in political reform in Chicago, a large city. Wilson was a farm leader, having dealt with farm people most of his life. This difference in background may explain their basic disagreements. Ickes tried personally to supervise all expenditures and was constantly on the watch for graft, which, to him, was lurking behind every corner. He strongly believed that authority had to go along with responsibility if efficiency and economy were to be the end results. He was sincerely worried about the possibility of competently executing the subsistence homesteads program when important policy decisions were being made by several local groups which, not having any direct financial interest in the projects, would certainly not make the type of decisions best designed for governmental economy. Ickes was a bureaucrat who, in a time when government spending was loosely controlled, kept his own administrative purse tightly locked. No scandal plagued his Public Works Administration, but Ickes believed that scandal threatened the Division of Subsistence Homesteads because of the loose way money was being spent. Since it was often impossible to have an accurate account

[73] Ickes to Wilson, Jan. 22, 1934, R.G. 48, National Archives.
[74] Unpublished first draft of Lord and Johnstone, *A Place on Earth,* R.G. 83, National Archives.

of how funds were being spent at the local level, the way seemed open for all kinds of graft and reckless inefficiency. The only solution was to centralize the administration and tighten the controls.

Wilson trusted his appointees and gave them responsibility. He characteristically remarked that Ickes could never realize that "these farmers could be trusted,"[75] for Wilson's basic philosophy and his experience both pointed to the "good will" of most men. Perhaps Ickes' experience did not. In any case Wilson was sure that other things were more vital than economy or efficiency, although he certainly desired these too. He believed that a subsistence homesteads program controlled and directed from Washington, even if efficient in the beginning, would not be democratic and, in the long run, would fail because it would involve the imposition of the foreign ideas and values of a far-off official upon the various and different values of the local area. It would mean experts from Washington, however honest and idealistic, making decisions that vitally affected the lives of other individuals who, though most concerned, had no responsibility in making the decisions. To Wilson the subsistence homesteads projects, if they were to become real communities, had to be wanted, planned, and managed by the people within the locality where they were to be constructed.[76] To him, planning had to be democratic planning.

Under the local corporations all had not been perfect, or democratic. Frequently the leading citizens on local sponsoring committees were far removed from the circumstances and problems of the homesteaders, often advocating not what the homesteaders wanted but what they wanted for the homesteaders. The danger of charitable paternalism was always present. In several cases the projects were practically controlled by one person, who had his own set ideas on what a subsistence homestead should be and heeded the wishes of neither the homesteaders, the other local citizens, nor the officials of the Division of Subsistence Homesteads.[77] This was particularly true at Dayton, Penderlea, and Jersey Homesteads. Many local corporations, working under certain assumptions about the subsistence

---

[75] Author's interview with M. L. Wilson on June 29, 1956.
[76] Lord and Johnstone, *A Place on Earth*, p. 45.
[77] Memorandum from Frederic Howe to Rexford G. Tugwell, May 17, 1935, R.G. 96, National Archives.

homesteads program or working with an ignorance about the whole program, made decisions that hurt the chances of success for individual projects. A good example was the Birmingham projects which, in order to save money on the land purchases, were located much too far from the city. In some cases the prices paid for land were too high; in other cases administrative expenses were huge. Beyond all that, a Washington representative on each local board of directors was very powerful. Since all plans had to be approved at Washington, he was often the determining factor in decisions.[78]

The one project that gave Ickes the most headaches, and the one that, more than any other, precipitated the arguments over federalization, was Arthurdale. Here the "villains" were, to Ickes, Mrs. Roosevelt and Louis M. Howe. Working as members of an Arthurdale Committee, Mrs. Roosevelt and Howe, according to Ickes, virtually took over the project, "spending money like drunken sailors."[79] Because of early mistakes and because of Mrs. Roosevelt's insistence on expensive homes, Ickes believed that each homestead was going to cost $10,000 rather than the $2,500 to $3,000 originally planned. The adverse publicity at Arthurdale plagued Ickes, who believed that popular support depended on economy.[80] He tried to remedy the situation by personal intervention, which resulted in unpleasant feelings between him and Mrs. Roosevelt. Meanwhile Wilson maintained a friendly relationship with Mrs. Roosevelt and appreciated both the humanitarian and experimental nature of her work at Arthurdale. Ickes carried his problems to President Roosevelt, who apparently sympathized with Ickes' desires for economy. All these misunderstandings helped make Wilson's time in the Department of the Interior far from pleasant. When the projects were ordered federalized, he decided to go back to the friendly environs of the Department of Agriculture as of June 30, 1934. Here he became Assistant Secretary and, later, Undersecretary of Agriculture. Leaving the Division of Subsistence Homesteads with Wilson were most of his assistants who were of an agricultural background, including Carl C. Taylor.

The federalization order dashed the plans and hopes of many local groups, leaving a legacy of bitterness at many projects.[81] Whatever

[78] Lord and Johnstone, *A Place on Earth*, p. 46.
[79] Ickes, *The Secret Diary*, I, 207.   [80] *Ibid.*, p. 162.
[81] George S. Wehrwein, "Appraisal of Resettlement," *Journal of Farm Economics*, XIX (1937), 192–193.

Subsistence Homesteads Program

the relative merits of decentralized or centralized control, the sudden shift of policy seriously prejudiced the popularity of subsistence homesteads. A few of the more doctrinaire project sponsors fought back. Borsodi, at Dayton, refused to have his project federalized and brought suit against the Federal Subsistence Homesteads Corporation for breach of contract. The Division of Subsistence Homesteads decided to honor the loan contract with Borsodi's group, allowing the project to continue under local direction. On his part, Borsodi withdrew his suit for the money already allotted for four additional homestead tracts at Dayton.[82] In his arguments, Borsodi declared that the federalized projects would now become federal islands, without voting rights or state civil and criminal jurisdiction. This fear was not justified by the experiences of the other projects. At Dayton the twenty families already on the project continued to milk their goats, work their looms, and build their own homes, while temporarily living in tents and grass huts. A disgusted Borsodi went home to New York.[83] Meanwhile the University of Georgia began withdrawing from the Piedmont project, while an angered Hugh MacRae at Penderlea appealed to President Roosevelt for a conference to settle the federalization issue. Numerous sponsors, summarily dismissed from any actual control, felt rebuffed and did not continue their support of local projects.

The federalization order left local projects more open to the criticism of newspapers. The early sentiment in local newspapers had been preponderantly favorable to subsistence homesteads, perhaps partly because they were sponsored by leading citizens. The earliest criticism, some of it very bitter, came from farm organizations and from labor spokesmen. The farmers could point to the apparent inconsistency of production controls and, at the same time, new farming colonies. Although Edward O'Neal was on the Advisory Committee for Subsistence Homesteads, the American Farm Bureau was opposing any additional subsistence homesteads communities as early as December, 1934.[84] Several critics representing the viewpoint of laborers

---

[82] Charles E. Pynchon to Ickes, June 25, 1934, R.G. 48, National Archives; Pynchon to Ebert K. Burlew, June 6, 1934, *ibid.*

[83] "Homesteading Comes A-Cropper in Dayton," *Architectural Forum*, LXI (1934), 142–143.

[84] American Farm Bureau Federation, "Editorial," *Official News Letter*, XIII (Dec. 18, 1934), 2–4.

saw subsistence homesteads as a means of "planning for permanent poverty," with the government providing cheap labor for industrialists.[85] Louis M. Hacker, a historian, feared that the "American Government, hard driven by the contradictions of its own position, may even (as in Italy and Germany) seek to build up exactly such a sheltered peasant group as a rural reactionary bloc to withstand the revolutionary demands of the organized industrial workers." [86] Attacking the whole idea of subsistence homesteads, Alvin Johnson, an economist and director of the New School for Social Research, shrewdly surmised that the "worker ought to be happier, living in his own garden, pulling weeds with his wife and children on Saturday afternoons instead of going to the movies. The family ought to be happier, but 'ought' is an obsolete word." [87] As the construction phase began, another group of critics were to have their heyday. Those who disliked the New Deal or those who opposed any type of governmental planning were to make effective use of every mistake at Arthurdale or elsewhere. This criticism began as early as August, 1934, with a *Saturday Evening Post* article which considerably embarrassed Ickes by pointing out the many foolish errors made at Arthurdale.[88]

In May, 1934, Ickes had moved Charles E. Pynchon from the Public Works Administration to the Division of Subsistence Homesteads to be business manager of the Federal Subsistence Homesteads Corporation. Ickes hoped that Pynchon, a housing expert and businessman, would get the division on a more efficient basis.[89] Upon the resignation of Wilson in June, Pynchon became the new Director, bringing with him a largely new staff and a new emphasis on the housing and administrative aspects of subsistence homesteads, although without reversing the original purposes of the program. At the time Pynchon took over the division, the administrative staff occupied three floors of the Architects Building and numbered over

[85] Ware and Powell, "Planning for Permanent Poverty," p. 515.
[86] Louis M. Hacker, "Plowing the Farmer Under," *Harper's Magazine,* CLXIX (1934), 73–74.
[87] Alvin Johnson, "Homesteads and Subsistence Homesteads," *Yale Review,* XXIV (1934–1935), 439.
[88] Wesley Stout, "The New Homesteaders," *Saturday Evening Post,* CCVII (Aug. 4, 1934), 5–7, 61–62, 64–65.
[89] Ickes, *The Secret Diary,* I, 206–207.

300 people. The total administrative expenses under Wilson had been only $225,655.29. As of June 30, 1934, funds had already been advanced to twenty-seven projects; house construction was under way on nine projects. The division had provided employment for 1,851 persons in other than administrative capacities.[90]

The federalization order required a complete organizational change in the Division of Subsistence Homesteads. Although project plans submitted by local groups were still considered, a Planning Section was established to take the lead in initiating new projects. Under its direction several new projects were in the planning stage by May, 1935, when the Division of Subsistence Homesteads was absorbed by the Resettlement Administration. A Construction Section was organized to direct the projects' physical development. An Operations Section, which controlled the administrative problems of each local project, directed the all-important project managers, who had primary responsibility for the individual projects. Since a few projects were nearly completed by October, 1934, a Community Development Section was established to guide and direct the new communities. On the unfinished projects the project managers supervised the architects, accountants, engineers, and city planners. As projects were occupied, the project managers were replaced by community managers, who were assisted by farm and home supervisors, by educational advisers, and, at Arthurdale, by several additional employees, including a project nurse.[91]

During the last months of the existence of the Division of Subsistence Homesteads, from June 30, 1934, to May 15, 1935, the principal activity was the continued construction of the communities initiated under M. L. Wilson. The federalization order often occasioned an extensive delay, either to revise project plans or to get the new administrative machinery working. Despite his high hopes for Pynchon, Ickes soon decided that, despite his good intentions, loyalty, and hard work, Pynchon was no more efficient than Wilson, since expenses remained much too high on the projects. To Ickes,

---

[90] Division of Subsistence Homesteads, Report for the End of 1934, R.G., 96, National Archives; Lord and Johnstone, *A Place on Earth*, p. 48.

[91] U.S. Department of the Interior, Division of Subsistence Homesteads, *A Homestead and a Hope* (Washington, 1935), p. 13; Pynchon to All Employees, Oct. 22, 1934, R.G. 96, National Archives; Divisional Notice no. 22, Oct. 22, 1934, *ibid.*

Pynchon seemed in a daze, unable to answer questions or grasp the details about the projects.[92]

By May, 1935, there were only 466 families living in subsistence homesteads on eleven projects. After federalization, these homesteaders had been selected by a special committee at Washington from recommendations made by local committees. Selection criteria included citizenship, children in the family (or a couple young enough to have children), physical ability to do farm work, farming experience, and an income under $1,200 a year. The last requirement was often violated in practice, with over half the homesteaders at one project having incomes in excess of $1,200.[93] In almost all cases the tendency was to select homesteaders who, both character-wise and financially, seemed most able to meet payments and to contribute to the success of the community. As the subsistence homesteads communities began filling with people, it was very obvious that they were not experiments in relief, much to the surprise of many people.

One irksome problem confronted by the Division of Subsistence Homesteads was that of land tenure. Since the single-tax ideas of Henry George, most community planners, even including the rabid agrarians, had desired some limitation on fee simple or unrestricted landownership. But just as persistently, most Americans had continued to accept fee simple ownership as an essential part of the American way of life and were either unaware of, or unconcerned about, such possible evils as speculation, high land prices, and uncontrolled exploitation of land resources. Even the limited restrictions imposed by zoning laws had been, and still are, viewed with alarm and apprehension by many Americans who, with at least a sentimental attachment to a rural past, can hardly adjust to the more necessary socialization of a close-living, urbanized present. Thus the agricultural economists and social planners were usually at odds with the broader public on this important question. Because of the avowed experimental and demonstrational nature of the subsistence homesteads communities, most officials of the Division of Subsistence Homesteads felt that, despite the expressed desire of most

[92] Ickes, *The Secret Diary*, I, 205–207.

[93] Division of Subsistence Homesteads, *A Homestead and a Hope*, pp. 15–16; An Office Record, Division of Subsistence Homesteads, dated Feb. 11, 1935, R.G. 96, National Archives; Lord and Johnstone, *A Place on Earth*, pp. 100, 164–165, 172.

homesteaders for free title to their small estates, something less than fee simple ownership would be necessary to assure the success of the experiments and also to protect the real interests of the homesteader. It seemed that free titles would quickly lead to speculation in both land and homes, especially in light of the probable increase in land values near the new communities. This would destroy the economic and aesthetic design of the communities, lead to exploitation of some homesteaders, and enrich other individuals who were not supposed to be aided by the program. Yet the homesteaders wanted the security and independence that they believed could come only with complete ownership. Moreover, Section 208 provided money for "the purchase" of subsistence homesteads. From earlier congressional debates it was evident that the members of Congress, just as much as the homesteaders, put a great value on landownership.

The Division of Subsistence Homesteads solved this dilemma by a compromise. It announced that, in all but the stranded communities, the homesteader would be permitted to purchase his own home within a thirty-year period at 3 per cent interest, without any down payment. But the homesteader could not receive title to his land until he had paid three-fourths of the purchase price and, in no case, not until after five years. This meant government control for anywhere from five to twenty-two years, yet partially appeased the proponents of fee simple. Actually, since no communities were completed when the Resettlement Administration absorbed the subsistence homesteads in May, 1935, all homesteaders were under temporary licensing agreement.[94]

From the beginning of subsistence homesteads, M. L. Wilson and others had stressed the community aspects of the program. They had consciously aimed at something more than a group of carefully engineered and designed rural houses located in a rather odd, city-rural pattern. Thus they put their greatest emphasis on the educative influence of subsistence homesteads, desiring to develop a new community life, with community or social attitudes to replace extreme individualism, with a greater emphasis on creative endeavor, such as handicrafts, with less social competition and more stability and se-

---

[94] Resettlement Administration, Division of Land Utilization, Land Use Planning Section, "Resettlement Policy and Procedure: Suggestions," manuscript in R.G. 96, National Archives, p. 73.

curity, and, capping it all, with as many as possible of the community activities organized on a co-operative rather than a competitive basis. As some of the communities neared completion, the Community Development Section assumed the task of converting a group of houses and a group of homesteaders into a community. It also had the task of developing an adequate economic life for the communities, which was a near impossibility in the stranded communities. The Community Development Section contained specialists in education, co-operation, insurance, home management, gardening, agriculture, and industry.[95] It approved the selection of settlers, educated and supervised the homesteaders in their new enterprises, provided educational services for adults and children, directed the health and welfare services, guided the social and recreational activities, and supervised and assisted in the organization of co-operatives.[96] Actually this work in community building was barely started by the time the subsistence homesteads were transferred to the Resettlement Administration, since only eleven projects were then partially completed. For this reason it may be best studied, from other than the standpoint of administrative organization, along with the similar work of the Resettlement Administration.

Federalization did not free the Division of Subsistence Homesteads from further legal entanglements. A ruling by the Solicitor of the Department of the Interior in November, 1934, stressed the fact that Section 208 specifically provided aid for the redistribution of population in industrial centers and not for resettlement of farmers.[97] This almost outlawed the all-rural colonies, since most of the homesteaders had been farmers and had not lived in industrial centers.[98] The Solicitor also cast doubt on the legality of the stranded workers' communities. These rulings meant that the subsistence homesteads program would have to be restricted to industrial communities. In February, 1935, the Comptroller General challenged the legality of nearly all the expenditures, made approximately one year earlier,

[95] Wendell Lund to Pynchon, May 13, 1935, R.G. 96, National Archives.
[96] Pynchon to All Employees, Oct. 27, 1934, *ibid.*
[97] Nathan R. Margold to Ickes, Nov. 24, 1934, R.G. 48, National Archives.
[98] Wesley Stout, "The Government Builds Fifty Houses," *Saturday Evening Post*, CCVIII (April 4, 1936), 76; Bruce L. Melvin, "Emergency and Permanent Legislation with Special Reference to the History of Subsistence Homesteads," *American Sociological Review*, I (1936), 627.

Subsistence Homesteads Program

of the local corporations, ruling that there had been no authorization for the formation of local corporations, no authority for advancing funds to them, no authority for land purchased under Section 208, and no compliance with government procedures by the local corporations. This apparently made new legislation imperative. On March 6, 1935, Representative Hampton P. Fulmer of South Carolina introduced in the House a more detailed subsistence homesteads bill, which died in committee.[99] Then on May 7, 1935, McCarl ruled that the Division of Subsistence Homesteads, not having been extended by new legislation and as a temporary part of the National Industrial Recovery Act, would automatically go out of existence on June 16, 1935, with all unexpended funds reverting to the Treasury. This meant so many uncompleted communities and unfulfilled obligations that some new authorization was imperative. Actually President Roosevelt was already formulating plans for a consolidation of several agencies into a new Resettlement Administration. Bruce Melvin, one of M. L. Wilson's earliest assistants, declared that the subsistence homesteads idea, because of a poorly written law and constant involvements with legal technicalities, did not fail but "was never tried." [100]

On May 15, 1935, fully two months before the expiration date set by McCarl, Roosevelt, by Executive Order 7041, transferred all the property and assets of the Division of Subsistence Homesteads to the newly created Resettlement Administration.[101] In order to complete the transfer, the Division of Subsistence Homesteads remained in existence until June 16, 1935, as a division of the Resettlement Administration. At the time of absorption, the Division of Subsistence Homesteads had completed 691 houses and had begun construction on 1,369 homes.[102] Many projects had developed no farther than the original land purchase. Since the Division of Subsistence Homesteads, constantly plagued by legal and administrative delays, had expended

[99] C. E. Pynchon to Ickes, Feb. 22, 1935, R.G. 48, National Archives; *C.R.*, 74th Cong., 1st Sess., 1935, p. 3066.

[100] McCarl to Ickes, May 7, 1935, and Pynchon to Ickes, May 7, 1935, R.G. 48, National Archives; Melvin, "Emergency and Permanent Legislation," p. 631.

[101] Select Committee of the House Committee on Agriculture, *Hearings on the Farm Security Administration*, 78th Cong., 1st Sess., 1943–1944, pp. 966–968.

[102] Memorandum from the Division of Subsistence Homesteads to Tugwell, May 24, 1935, R.G. 96, National Archives.

less than $8,000,000 of its $25,000,000 appropriation, its surplus funds were transferred to the Resettlement Administration for the brief two months before they were to revert to the Treasury. The executive order expressly required the Resettlement Administration to carry out the subsistence homesteads program in accordance with the original legislation.[103] This did not prevent an inevitable change in policies, which again affected the local communities.

The popular back-to-the-land and subsistence homesteads program had been born in the depths of the depression and, despite the views of its administrators in the New Deal, had been motivated largely by the hopelessness and despair of the depression. It represented a longing and a hope for that security that surely could be found at the source of life itself. But by 1935 the sense of despair and of urgency was disappearing. The powerful emotional appeal of an envisioned homestead, of gardens and handicrafts, was beginning to fade. The administration of the subsistence homesteads program had been carried out in the happy honeymoon period of the New Deal, when desperation and a sense of impending catastrophe apparently unified almost all groups and all classes in a truly national effort toward recovery. Although the enemy was not so clearly defined, or even well known, the period had many of the earmarks of a great wartime effort. But by 1935 the honeymoon was almost over. The enemies who began to emerge in the eyes or the imagination of men were not such as could demand the hostility of all Americans, for these enemies were not natural, or providential, or foreign, but human and native. A class and group consciousness was forming. The New Deal, which was becoming the champion of some individuals and groups, was believed by others to be an enemy. Beneath all the bitterness that followed this, the nearest approximation of a class struggle in American history, there was a sharp clash of ideas, ideals, values, and gods, which once again, in the easily accepted presence of manna, became seemingly more important than manna. The subsistence homesteads, in a new administrative agency, were to be shaped by a new bitterness and an increased clash of values.

[103] *Hearings on the Farm Security Administration*, p. 968.

VI

The Federal Emergency Relief Administration Communities

AS the subsistence homesteads program developed, it became limited to one type of community and to the benefit of one economic group. Although the stranded communities, which were intended to aid destitute miners, were part of the original program, they were quickly curtailed after the first four met legal and economic difficulties. The three colonies for submarginal farmers were declared illegal by the Solicitor of the Department of the Interior. The one type continued, the industrial communities, benefited only those people with an income near or over $1,200 and with the highest of character qualifications. A significant experimental program in land-use planning, in the decentralization of low-income populations, and in low-income housing, the subsistence homesteads program, as it developed, did not relieve, or profess to relieve, the immediate problems of the mass of unemployed and stranded people, both rural and urban. With all the talk of subsistence homesteads and of back-to-the-land, it was only natural that relief agencies would attempt to adapt the idea of rural-urban communities to relief problems. Thus, the Federal Emergency Relief Administration became the second New Deal agency to initiate and develop communities.

First created by the Emergency Relief Act of May 12, 1933, the Federal Emergency Relief Administration provided relief funds to the states, which distributed them through state relief organizations.

The organizer and director of state relief in Texas was Colonel Lawrence Westbrook, an engineer, agriculturalist, and politician. As a member of the state legislature from 1928 to 1932, he had been chairman of the Committee on Agriculture and had helped organize the Texas Cotton Co-operative Association. As Texas relief administrator he desired to use relief funds for permanent rehabilitation rather than for outright grants. Supporting him in this desire was a handsome, colorful Dallas architect, David Williams, who had already contemplated rural-industrial communities for the unemployed of Dallas. Plans for a test community were developed in the fall of 1933. In January, 1934, a group of former farmers, who were then on city relief rolls, moved into a section of pinewoods about 100 miles north of Houston and began constructing the Woodlake community, which was designed for 100 relief families.[1] This project was to be a model for most of the later Federal Emergency Relief Administration communities.

Woodlake was quickly constructed, with the families of the men moving into their new homes during the summer of 1934. The 100 homes of three, four, or five rooms were placed on three-acre subsistence plots, each of which also included a combination barn-garage-laundry, an orchard, a vineyard, and a chicken house. The homes, of frame or log construction, were designed by David Williams, cost about $1,500 each, and included modern baths. They were leased to destitute relief clients for three years at $180 rent a year, all payable in farm and poultry surpluses. The whole community jointly owned a 225-acre park, a school, a community house, a bathhouse, a trading post, and two co-operative farms of 600 acres each. Each family, in addition to farming the three-acre subsistence plot, was expected to participate in handicrafts and processing industries. This project, administered by a separate legal entity, the Texas Rural Communities, Incorporated, possessed some characteristics of a European village, with its outlying fields, or of a Russian co-operative farm, with its individual subsistence plots and its collectively operated fields.[2]

[1] "Rural Industrial Community Projects: Woodlake, Texas, Osceola, Arkansas, and Red House, West Virginia," *Architectural Record*, LXXVII (1935), 12.

[2] *Ibid.*; Resettlement Administration, Division of Land Utilization, Land Use Planning Section, "Resettlement Policy and Procedure: Suggestions," manuscript in R.G. 96, National Archives, pp. 35–36; Select Committee of the House Committee on Agriculture, *Hearings on the Farm Security Administration*, 78th Cong., 1st Sess., 1943–1944, p. 1107.

Meanwhile, in February, 1934, Harry Hopkins, Administrator of the Federal Emergency Relief Administration, created, by an informal administrative order, the Division of Rural Rehabilitation and Stranded Populations within the Federal Emergency Relief Administration and, for assistance in the formulation of a rural rehabilitation program, asked Lawrence Westbrook and David Williams to come to Washington. In March, Westbrook called a series of regional conferences of agricultural and civic leaders to discuss the problems of returning stranded agricultural workers to farms and of making special loans to those farmers who needed to replace work stock and equipment in order to become self-sustaining. Both Hopkins and Westbrook believed that most farmers who were then on relief could be rehabilitated and made self-sustaining for less money than was likely to be involved in continued relief grants. On March 22, 1934, Hopkins announced that all direct relief and Civil Works Administration programs carried on in rural areas would be replaced, as of April 1, 1934, by a rural rehabilitation program.[3] Since it was doubtful that the Federal Emergency Relief Administration had any legal authority to purchase other than submarginal agricultural land or to build houses (two projects contemplated by Westbrook), a member of the legal staff worked out a plan for state rural rehabilitation corporations to handle the financial operations of rehabilitation loans and of community development, both under the direction and control of the Rural Rehabilitation Division of the Federal Emergency Relief Administration.[4]

Even as the rural rehabilitation program was being developed within the Federal Emergency Relief Administration, another complementary program was initiated partly under the auspices of the Federal Emergency Relief Administration. Land-use planning, as developed by the agricultural economists, as stressed by planning agencies, and as developed in New York State by Franklin D. Roose-

[3] Lawrence Westbrook, "The Program of the Rural Rehabilitation Division of the FERA," *Journal of Farm Economics*, XVII (1935), 89–91; *Hearings on the Farm Security Administration*, pp. 862–863.

[4] Philip M. Glick, "Memorandum on Federal Governmental Agencies Involved in Land Acquisition, Administration, and Planning," in Record Group 69, Records of the Work Projects Administration and Its Predecessors (includes the Works Progress Administration, the Civil Works Administration, and the Federal Emergency Relief Administration), National Archives (to be cited hereafter as R.G. 69, National Archives).

velt, always included a retirement program for submarginal land. In the New Deal a land-purchase and land-retirement program was first initiated by the Federal Surplus Relief Corporation in early 1934, but was restricted to the purpose of reducing agricultural surpluses. In the spring of 1934 this land-purchase program was shifted to the Federal Emergency Relief Administration, where it included other than surplus-producing agricultural lands. In July, 1934, it was further broadened to include not only the purchase of such land but its conversion to some new use. The funds for the program were allotted to the Federal Emergency Relief Administration, but the technical direction was placed in other agencies. The Land Policy Section of the Division of Program Planning, Agricultural Adjustment Administration, directed about three-fourths of the program. The rest was under the National Park Service, the Bureau of Biological Survey, and the Office of Indian Affairs. One final problem, that of resettling the dislocated farmers, was placed, quite appropriately, in the newly formed Division of Rural Rehabilitation, under Lawrence Westbrook. Although very few people were resettled before the land program was switched to the Resettlement Administration in 1935, the existence of the program was further justification for the Division of Rural Rehabilitation and for a program of rural community building.[5]

The Rural Rehabilitation Division of the Federal Emergency Relief Administration was largely staffed with agricultural personnel. It maintained close contact with the Department of Agriculture, the Agricultural Adjustment Administration, and the Farm Credit Administration. Its operations were entirely in the hands of the rural rehabilitation corporations, which existed in twenty-one states by November, 1934, and in forty-five states by June, 1935. All stock of the local corporation was deposited with the Federal Relief Administrator, thus insuring federal control. On the Board of Directors of each state corporation was a regional representative of the Federal Emergency Relief Administration, the state administrator of relief, the director of the State Extension Service, a representative of the Land Policy Section of the Agricultural Adjustment Administration,

[5] Lewis C. Gray, "The Social and Economic Implications of the National Land Program," *Journal of Farm Economics*, XVIII (1936), 261–263; Resettlement Administration, Interim Report (Washington, 1936), p. 6; Franklin D. Roosevelt, *The Public Papers and Addresses of Franklin D. Roosevelt*, IV (New York, 1938), 145–147.

and three outstanding citizens.[6] The similarities between this organization and the original one set up by M. L. Wilson in the Division of Subsistence Homesteads are very obvious. The significant difference is that the rural rehabilitation corporations did not face almost insurmountable legal obstacles under the Federal Emergency Relief Act, which specified a form of decentralized administration.

Although each state corporation was supposed to formulate its own rehabilitation program, both Lawrence Westbrook and David Williams, in light of their work at Woodlake, influenced the corporations to use part of their funds in the construction of rural-industrial communities. Westbrook believed that the gravest relief problems involved the stranded workers, rural or urban, who had no prospect for employment at their present locations. Relief grants should not have to continue indefinitely. Why could not these workers be rehabilitated and resettled in organized rural communities, which they themselves could build and then purchase, repaying the government for its investment? Although these communities would be somewhat experimental, there were already several examples of farm villages in the United States. In spite of the fact that they would be more aesthetic in design and better located and would depend more on community enterprises, these new rural-industrial communities would not be materially different from older farm villages. They would not be "crack-pot economic or social panaceas"[7] and would provide guidance to the back-to-the-land movement. Westbrook hoped to see developed from 100 to 150 of these communities, with up to 1,000 families in each community.[8]

The program of the Rural Rehabilitation Division of the Federal Emergency Relief Administration differed considerably from that of the Division of Subsistence Homesteads. First, and most important, the rural-industrial communities were only a small part of the total program of the state corporations, although a part much beloved by Westbrook. In many states no communities were even planned. Most of the relief funds of the corporations were lent to individual farmers (a total of about $50,000,000 to 398,000 farmers by June,

[6] Westbrook, "The Program of the Rural Rehabilitation Division," pp. 92–93.
[7] *Ibid.*, pp. 95–100.
[8] Lawrence Westbrook, "Rural-Industrial Communities for Stranded Families," R.G. 69, National Archives, pp. 4–9.

1935 [9]), enabling them to purchase livestock, equipment, or even subsistence. A second difference was that all rural rehabilitation communities were planned for relief clients. As such they resemble only the four stranded communities of the Division of Subsistence Homesteads. The rural-industrial communities were usually constructed with much greater speed and economy than the subsistence homesteads, perhaps because of the corporate device which allowed local control and little red tape. As conceived by Westbrook and Williams, the rural-industrial communities were to have a dual economic base—there were to be co-operative farms and co-operative village industries, related either to crafts or to the processing of specialized farm products. This contrasts with the industrial decentralization desired by the Division of Subsistence Homesteads. The dependence upon processing industries or upon highly specialized types of agriculture led to small farm plots or to very small co-operative farms in relation to the number of homesteaders. When the Resettlement Administration absorbed the communities, the farm units were usually consolidated to create an adequate agricultural base, and the rural industries were often dropped. Thus, the Resettlement Administration could attribute all later economic difficulties in these communities to poor early planning. On the other hand, the community architects of the Federal Emergency Relief Administration, like David Williams, were just as certain that the communities failed because their original plans had been betrayed by unsympathetic agriculturalists in the Resettlement Administration.

One of the first rural-industrial communities, and the only one of its type, was a community at Red House, West Virginia, for stranded coal miners. Red House was very similar to the subsistence homesteads communities of Arthurdale and Tygart Valley. It too was planned in the expectation of industrial decentralization—a hope as vain at Red House as at Arthurdale. On 600 developed acres of a 2,013-acre tract, 150 cinder-block homes were constructed on plots of from three-fourths of an acre to one acre, beginning in September, 1934. The cinder blocks were made at a cost of ten cents each in a temporary plant; the lumber was fabricated in a local shop. As in almost all Federal Emergency Relief Administration communities, most of the work was done by the prospective settlers. The sturdy

[9] *Hearings on the Farm Security Administration,* p. 864.

Relief Communities

homes included three to five rooms, cellars, baths, porches, and large attics. Each homestead had a barn and a chicken pen. Unique among all New Deal communities, Red House had a gas well which supplied the fuel for the homes. As was true of almost all Federal Emergency Relief Administration communities, Red House had a general, cooperative farm.[10]

Three of the most publicized and, in the end, the most unsuccessful of the rural-industrial communities occupy an administrative history separate from all the other New Deal communities. Those three—the Dyess Colony, near Wilson, Arkansas; Pine Mountain Valley, about thirty miles from Columbus, Georgia; and Cherry Lake Farms, near Madison, Florida—were not turned over to the Resettlement Administration in 1935. Except for the Resettlement Administration's supervision of certain aspects of community management, such as settler selection, education, and special services, those communities became a part of the Works Progress Administration, therefore remaining in the hands of Hopkins and Westbrook. Not until 1939, long after all construction had been completed, were they turned over to the Farm Security Administration, the successor to the Resettlement Administration. Matanuska, Alaska, perhaps the most fascinating relief colony, was never turned over to the Farm Security Administration and will not be included in this study.[11]

The Dyess community, the largest farm colony ever developed by a public agency in the United States, was initiated in 1934 by the Arkansas Rural Rehabilitation Corporation. In the delta country, sixty miles from Memphis, Dyess contained 17,500 acres of rich but gummy cotton land which, according to original plans, was to be subdivided into 750 small, one-mule farms of approximately twenty acres each. Construction of roads and buildings began in 1934 and continued at a rapid pace, with 1,500 relief laborers at work at one time. By October, 1934, eighty-three houses were ready for occupancy. By June, 1936, approximately 500 homes were completed. No more were started, for, by then, it had been decided that the farm units were too small and

---

[10] William N. Beehler, *Relief Work and Rehabilitation: A Report of the West Virginia Relief Administration* (Charleston, 1934), pp. 69–70; "Rural Industrial Community Projects: Woodlake, Texas, Osceola, Arkansas, and Red House, West Virginia," pp. 14–15; *Rural Rehabilitation*, I (Nov. 15, 1934), mimeographed, R.G. 69, National Archives.

[11] Carl C. Taylor to Fred Bartlett, July 6, 1933, R.G. 96, National Archives.

should be consolidated. The homes were three- to five-room cottages of rather poor quality. The lumber was cut and sawed on the project, leading to a low unit cost. The houses were, for the most part, located on the individual farms, with four houses grouped at the angles of each crossroads in order to promote neighborliness. A central community center, fully five miles from some of the outlying farms, comprised 100 acres of land, thirty-two subsistence homes, a large administration building, several warehouses, a large mule barn, a theater building, a twenty-two-bed hospital, a twelve-year school for about 1,600 pupils, a seed house, a cotton gin, and a store. Subsidiary community centers developed around eight scattered Sunday schools and nine home demonstration clubs.[12]

After the completion of construction in 1936, the Dyess Colony, a $2,000,000 all-white, all-Protestant project, was operated by a local corporation under Works Progress Administration direction until it was turned over to the Farm Security Administration in 1939. During this time the colony was a financial failure. The twenty-acre units were much too small, leading to a consolidation of units and a reduction to approximately 300 homesteads. The local corporation, which operated several co-operatives, lost over $750,000 from 1937 to 1939. It operated a store, café, warehouse, craft shop, hospital, garage, cotton gin, blacksmith shop, printing press, shoeshop, and harness shop. This sorry financial record and a series of quarrels on the project led to a threatened investigation by the State of Arkansas in 1939. Dyess was hardly a welcome addition to the communities of the Farm Security Administration in 1939.[13]

One of the most idealistically planned colonies of the Federal Emergency Relief Administration was Pine Mountain Valley, near Pine Mountain, Harris County, Georgia. Planned and designed by David Williams and adjoining Franklin D. Roosevelt's Warm Springs,

---

[12] "Preliminary Report on Community Development at Dyess Colony, Arkansas," a study directed by Dr. Charles P. Loomis, submitted on Aug. 1, 1936, R.G. 96, National Archives; Hearings on the Farm Security Administration, pp. 1667–1669; "Rural Industrial Community Projects: Woodlake, Texas, Osceola, Arkansas, and Red House, West Virginia," p. 13; a notation dated Dec. 11, 1936, R.G. 16, National Archives; Lawrence Westbrook to David Lilienthal, Sept. 4, 1934, R.G. 69, National Archives.

[13] Audit Report on Dyess Colony, March 22, 1939, R.G. 69, National Archives; Floyd Sharp to Lawrence Westbrook, Feb. 25, 1939, *ibid.*

it was probably the most publicized of the Federal Emergency Relief Administration communities. Pine Mountain Valley, which was officially developed by the Georgia Rural Rehabilitation Corporation, was advertised as being "based on a new idea in planning in which the farm and the city are so amalgamated as to be one inseparable whole." [14] It was planned for some 500 former farm families on relief in Atlanta and other Georgia cities. At Pine Mountain Valley they were to thrive on specialized agriculture, such as the cultivation of scuppernong grapes, on small agricultural industries, such as canneries and hatcheries, and on manual arts and household crafts. It was to be an educational and demonstrational colony, having all the advantages of the city, with five community centers and a central water, telephone, and electrical system.[15] For the construction of this dream the Federal Emergency Relief Administration allotted $2,207,572. For demonstration purposes 12,651 acres of broken and exhausted, but basically fertile, land was purchased in a formerly prosperous valley of north central Georgia. The land was divided into 300 instead of the contemplated 500 homestead units. The community contained homes, outbuildings, a water system, a school center, seven barracks buildings, a store and warehouse, an electric power system, several storage barns, an office and administration building, an auditorium, a large canning plant, a dairy, an egg freezing plant, a hatchery, a sawmill, a vineyard, a telephone system, and a church.[16] No more complete community could be imagined. Pine Mountain Valley was a favorite project of Franklin Roosevelt, who honored the community with a speech on December 2, 1935.[17]

Pine Mountain had as unfortunate an existence as did Dyess. Like Dyess, it was operated by a locally organized community corporation under Works Progress Administration direction from 1936 to 1939. Dissension resulted in the eviction of twenty-eight families in 1936,[18] and economic problems were never solved. A large number of the units at Pine Mountain Valley were only subsistence homesteads of one to five acres, since several village industries had been planned.

[14] "Pine Mountain Valley, a Rural Industrial Community," n.d., *ibid.*
[15] *Ibid.*
[16] *Hearings on the Farm Security Administration*, pp. 1693–1694.
[17] St. Louis *Post-Dispatch*, Dec. 3, 1935.
[18] Atlanta *Georgian*, Aug. 21, 1936.

Few of the farm units, ranging from ten to forty acres, were large enough to assure economic independence apart from the processing industries. Thus, as at Dyess, several consolidations were made, reducing the number of units to 205 and leaving several surplus houses. The local corporation financed many of the farmers, losing a good proportion of the loans. The largest enterprise, the cannery, proved moderately successful, but depreciated in value. By 1943 the estimated value of Pine Mountain Valley was only approximately $1,000,000.[19]

Cherry Lake Farms in northern Florida was very similar to Pine Mountain Valley. With nearly $2,000,000 in relief funds, the Florida Rural Rehabilitation Corporation acquired 12,420 acres of sandy, nonproductive soil on which it planned to establish 500 small, ten-acre, specialized farms. Poultry and eggs, gourds, scuppernong grapes, and exotic show birds for zoos were considered possible sources of income. The project was planned for relief clients in Tampa, Miami, and Jacksonville. About one-half of the 132 completed units (as of 1943) were subsistence homesteads with four- or five-room cottages containing modern conveniences. A central water system was established for the subsistence units, which were close enough together to have common facilities. A huge administrative building dominated the community center. A co-operative association, with compulsory membership, operated a poultry farm, a store, and a gristmill. A separate handicraft co-operative completed the local industries. With poor land and few industries, Cherry Lake had little rehabilitation possibilities, although it was well placed for a winter resort. When the Farm Security Administration took over in 1939 the local corporation was practically bankrupt.[20]

Approximately twenty-two other communities, of less size or less importance, were initiated by the Federal Emergency Relief Administration. In some cases the planning had only begun in 1935, leaving all the development and much of the determination of policy to the Resettlement Administration. Besides these community projects, the local corporations also developed several resettlement projects which involved widely scattered individual farms rather than rural communities. In California the Federal Emergency Relief Administration established migratory camps for farm laborers, which was an-

[19] *Hearings on the Farm Security Administration,* pp. 1694–1700.
[20] M. D. Burrows to Leroy Peterson, Oct. 29, 1935, R.G. 96, National Archives; *Hearings on the Farm Security Administration,* pp. 1663–1664.

other responsibility turned over to the Resettlement Administration in 1935.

The Federal Emergency Relief Administration initiated ten all-rural farming colonies in the South, nine very small (as low as ten units each) farm communities in Nebraska and South Dakota, two small industrial-type communities in Minnesota and North Dakota, a farm colony in New Mexico for farmers displaced from submarginal lands, and a subsistence homestead community near Phoenix, Arizona (see the Appendix for a complete list of Federal Emergency Relief Administration communities). Almost all of these communities were actually constructed by the Resettlement Administration. The largest communities were initiated by the North Carolina Rehabilitation Corporation, which refused to surrender its assets to the Resettlement Administration in 1935. One project, Roanoke Farms, contained 294 units separated into two communities, one for the white people and one for the Negroes. In addition to these communities, the Wisconsin Rural Rehabilitation Corporation planned several homesteads for the aged, handicapped, and retired, but completed only nine homes on eight scattered plots of ground.[21]

The planning of rural-industrial communities was carried out by the state corporations, but always with the approval of the Federal Emergency Relief Administration. As in most of the subsistence homesteads communities, the site surveys were made by the state agricultural colleges and the land appraisals were made by the Federal Land Bank. The construction was usually carried out by the prospective colonists; in all cases it was done by relief labor. The houses, in those instances where the construction was completed by state corporations, were often smaller and less expensive than those constructed by the Division of Subsistence Homesteads. Several projects included some three-room homes. The selection of settlers was assigned to the social service divisions of the state relief agencies, with varying standards for different states and different projects. The settler was almost always from the relief rolls and had to express a desire for rural life.[22] Since only two projects, Woodlake and Red House, were

[21] *Hearings on the Farm Security Administration*, pp. 1037–1116.
[22] John B. Holt, *An Analysis of Methods and Criteria Used in Selecting Families for Colonization Projects* (Social Research Report no. 1, U.S. Department of Agriculture, Farm Security Administration and the Bureau of Agricultural Economics; Washington, 1937), pp. 39–44.

completed by June, 1935, most of the settlers were actually selected by the Resettlement Administration. The communities were, first of all, planned to serve a rehabilitation function, but, if rehabilitation occurred, they were to be sold to the settlers. Westbrook suggested a trial lease of one year and then sale at 3 per cent interest and twenty-year terms. The state corporations were to provide for the social, economic, recreational, and educational needs of the communities.[23]

By early 1935 a reorganization of the agencies administering the relief and land programs of the New Deal was being considered by Roosevelt and many of his advisers. As the unprecedented Emergency Relief Act of 1935, which provided an appropriation of $4,880,000,000, wended its way through Congress, the great concern of Ickes, Hopkins, and even Tugwell was how the President would use the funds and through what agencies. Some reorganization was almost certain because of the confused and overlapping administrative organization of the land program. The purchase of submarginal land was carried out by Federal Emergency Relief funds, but was administered by personnel from four other agencies. In addition, research for the program was directed by another agency, the National Resources Board. Good farm lands were being purchased by both the Rural Rehabilitation Division and the Division of Subsistence Homesteads. All this led to endless confusion.[24]

Since both the Federal Emergency Relief Administration and the Division of Subsistence Homesteads were constructing communities and since the subsistence homesteads, particularly Arthurdale, were a constant embarrassment to Ickes, Roosevelt had considered turning the subsistence homesteads program over to Hopkins as early as November, 1934. Ickes had tried to make a deal with the Department of Agriculture, by which he would turn over to Wallace his reclamation, erosion control, and subsistence homesteads programs for the Department of Agriculture's Bureaus of Roads, Forestry, and Biological Survey. By this swap Ickes hoped to be rid of subsistence homesteads and to have all the conservation activities. He then hoped to lure Tugwell from the Department of Agriculture and create for him the

[23] Westbrook, "Rural-Industrial Communities," R.G. 69, National Archives, pp. 11, 19.
[24] Gray, "The Social and Economic Implications of the National Land Program," p. 263.

Relief Communities

office of Undersecretary of the Interior, from which he could direct a co-ordinated conservation program. After Wallace declined the exchange of agencies and after Hopkins declined to accept the subsistence homesteads, Roosevelt, in February, 1935, considered placing all the community activities in a new, independent agency. When, in March, Ickes talked to Roosevelt about combining all the community building in one agency under his Assistant Secretary, Oscar Chapman, Roosevelt surprised him by announcing that Tugwell wanted to administer the subsistence homesteads program.[25]

On April 30, 1935, Franklin D. Roosevelt, by an executive order and under the very broad authority granted in the Emergency Relief Act of 1935, established the Resettlement Administration under Rexford G. Tugwell, who was also to retain his position as Undersecretary of Agriculture. The original functions of the Resettlement Administration, as detailed in the executive order, included the "resettlement of destitute or low-income families from rural and urban areas, including the establishment, maintenance, and operation, in such connection, of communities in rural and suburban areas."[26] It also provided that the Resettlement Administration continue the whole, confused submarginal land program, although with an emphasis on the developmental aspect of the acquired land (on reforestation, erosion control, flood control, and recreational development), since the relief act provided for work relief and not for a new land program. As later amended, this authority for land development included "any other useful projects," giving Tugwell almost unlimited authority in selecting projects. A third function given the Resettlement Administration was the rural rehabilitation program. The executive order granted the power to purchase land, to use eminent domain, to improve and develop land, and to sell or lease, with or without the privilege of purchasing, any land so held.[27]

On April 30 Roosevelt transferred the land program of the Federal Emergency Relief Administration to the Resettlement Administration. On May 15 he transferred the Division of Subsistence Homesteads. The Land Policy Section of the Agricultural Adjustment Administra-

---

[25] Harold L. Ickes, *The Secret Diary of Harold L. Ickes*, vol. I: *The First Thousand Days, 1933–1936* (New York, 1953), pp. 227, 250, 288, 309–310.
[26] *Hearings on the Farm Security Administration*, p. 966.
[27] *Ibid.*, pp. 966–967.

tion was moved to the Resettlement Administration on June 1, furnishing many of the personnel for a continued submarginal program. On June 30 the Rural Rehabilitation Division of the Federal Emergency Relief Administration, including the state corporations and the communities, was given to Tugwell. Although Tugwell wished to continue the state corporations as an administrative device, the Comptroller General ruled that the Resettlement Administration funds could not be granted to local corporations. Under an agreement worked out between the Resettlement Administration and most of the state corporations, thirty-seven states turned their funds over to the Resettlement Administration in 1935, with a provision that they be expended within the state that relinquished them. Eight state corporations refused to turn over their funds at that time, but later, cut off from all sources of federal support, the corporations either had to sign the agreement or become virtually defunct.[28] For a while, in those few states, a duplication of effort occurred, with both the Resettlement Administration and the state corporations administering a rehabilitation and a resettlement program.

From the Federal Emergency Relief Administration the Resettlement Administration inherited plans for approximately twenty-five communities, only two of which were totally completed. These twenty-five communities, when completed, were to contain approximately 1,814 family units. This compared with thirty-four subsistence homesteads communities containing, when completed, 3,304 family units. But it must be remembered that the three largest, if most unsuccessful, Federal Emergency Relief communities were retained by the Works Progress Administration. It is difficult to give an exact number of units for these three, since each of them went through periods of consolidation, but at one time they included over 1,000 units. These Federal Emergency Relief Administration communities were almost entirely rural farming or semifarming communities, with the most notable problem being a lack of ample acreage to assure economic success. Since the Division of Subsistence Homesteads had initiated three all-rural, all-farming communities, the Federal Emergency Relief Administration contributed no new type of community. Although co-

[28] Henry Wallace to Louis Brownlow, Feb. 3, 1937, R.G. 16, National Archives; Memorandum from the Farm Security Administration to M. L. Wilson, Nov. 19, 1937, *ibid.*

operative farms had been planned at a few subsistence homesteads communities, such as Westmoreland and Hightstown, the Federal Emergency Relief Administration was most notable for its combination of village subsistence plots with large co-operative farms.

Despite the accomplishments of the Division of Subsistence Homesteads and the Federal Emergency Relief Administration in community building over a two-year period, the Resettlement Administration inherited the task of doing more than half of the construction work on these communities, of selecting a majority of the settlers, of doing almost all the very important managerial work within the completed communities, and of selling or otherwise disposing of each community. In addition, the Resettlement Administration had the clearest mandate yet given for the initiation of new communities. In mid-1935 it seemed as if the community-building program of the New Deal had only begun.

⤳ VII ⤴

America Resettled

IN the first year and a half of the Resettlement Administration the community-building program of the New Deal reached its climax. A large administrative organization was developed, policies were determined, and an ambitious program was launched. On the other hand, planned communities became more controversial and more unpopular than ever before. By the beginning of 1937 the whole program was stabilized and ready to begin a long period of completion and liquidation. In the minds of most people the term "Resettlement Administration" was almost synonymous with the name of its first Administrator, Rexford G. Tugwell. Already one of the most controversial major figures in the New Deal, Tugwell himself, as head of the Resettlement Administration, insured that its program would also be an object of much attack and abuse. Although no more to blame for every mistake or error made by the Resettlement Administration than he was responsible for its every acknowledged accomplishment, Tugwell did do far more than anyone else to determine the policies and program of the Resettlement Administration. His early direction gave the Resettlement Administration and its successor, the Farm Security Administration, an orientation that was to remain virtually unchanged until 1943, even though Tugwell left it in December, 1936.

As a sophomore at the University of Pennsylvania, Tugwell wrote a poem in which he concluded:

> I am sick of a nation's stenches
> I am sick of propertied czars . . .
> I shall roll up my sleeves—make America over! [1]

He later may have regretted the writing of it, for it was one of many of his past writings that were used during the New Deal to show what a radical he was. An anti-Tugwell Club was formed in Chicago. Newspapers warned parents not to let children get hold of his books. By writing authoritative articles on wine drinking he roused the ire of many American churches. At one and the same time he was labeled a dangerous Red and an impractical, utterly ineffective professor. He could not be both, and actually was neither.[2] But he was different from the past run of Washington bureaucrats. To many he seemed to typify the young liberals, a completely new crop of "eager-faced, immature technicians and academicians with lean bodies and no bellies, running around hatless, acting rather breathlessly mysterious and important." [3] Only his colleagues knew the real Tugwell, for the newspapers painted a distorted view, a view which his friends recognized as "one of the most bewildering examples of a deliberately rigged and distorted public opinion in our time." [4]

Tugwell was a social scientist with the temperament of an extremely sensitive artist. Experience spoke to him in such loud tones that its lessons were overamplified, in fact were often overwhelming. World War I left him ill. The depression roused in him anger and hate and bitterness, as well as hope. Later the atomic bomb overwhelmed him with despair. Though an economist, with a matured economic philosophy, Tugwell was the eternal reformer, moved to action and even to martyrdom by his own overwhelming sensitivity and antipathy to injustice, to inhumanity, to sin. His world was peopled with devils, although his economic philosophy and his scientific training persuaded him to give them a very modern and very naturalistic identity. His attack upon them was not timid; neither was it superficial or moralistic. In another age it might have been moralistic, but his modern tools were different from those of his long-past kindred. Of Thomas Hardy, his favorite writer, Tugwell said: "But for all his large defeatist principles,

---

[1] Russell Lord, *The Wallaces of Iowa* (Boston, 1947), p. 349.
[2] *Ibid.*, p. 347; Russell Lord, "Governor Rex, a Tough Poet," *Land*, II (1942–1943), 102.
[3] Lord, *Wallaces of Iowa*, p. 352. [4] *Ibid.*, p. 459.

he lived as though he were important, as though it always mattered what he did." [5] At another time he said: "There is something wrong with any man who does not spend parts of his life serving far and fundamental causes. That is the best contribution he can afford to the immortality of his culture." [6]

Tugwell's world was peopled with heroes as well as with devils. A few men had seen through the superficiality of modern society, through the thin crust of orthodoxy and dogma which concealed injustice and exploitation. One of these men had been a kindred spirit, Thorstein Veblen; another, his teacher, Simon Patten, or "My Patten." [7] Another type of hero was his "Boss," Franklin D. Roosevelt, who was everything Tugwell was not. Extroverted, jovial, optimistic, supremely confident, Roosevelt moved and acted with sureness and with a sense of moving with tradition and with history.[8] Tugwell, the introverted intellectual, could only worship or envy Roosevelt, even while looking deeply within himself and at the world and finding no real surety and no real security. When he carefully weighed tradition he found it badly wanting. The American political and economic tradition was rooted in a far past, in rural values, in individualism and independence, in small, negative governments, in free enterprise, and in the political philosophy of Jefferson. All this needed to be replaced by collectivistic ideas, by urban values, by ideas suited to proletarian aspirations rather than to the ideas of either large or small property holders.[9] More than that, some of the puritanism and provincialism of Americans had to be replaced by a degree of sophistication. An admirer of European culture, Tugwell, dapper and urbane always, wanted Americans to develop a few social graces, an appreciation of the arts, and an enjoyment of fine food and wine.

There was little compromise in Tugwell, little readiness to accept the good will of all men, for, to him, all men did not possess good will.

[5] From Tugwell's "Meditations in Stinsford Churchyard," as quoted in Lord, *Wallaces of Iowa*, p. 351.

[6] Quoted by Russell Lord in "The Education of a Farm Reporter," *Land*, III (1943–1944), 219.

[7] Rexford G. Tugwell, *A Chronicle of Jeopardy, 1945–55* (Chicago, 1955), p. 38.

[8] Rexford G. Tugwell, *The Stricken Land: The Story of Puerto Rico* (New York, 1947), p. ix.

[9] Rexford G. Tugwell, "The Sources of New Deal Reformism," *Ethics*, LXIV (1954), 251.

He despised accommodation with evil. He was scrupulously honest and alarmingly frank. Most of Tugwell's unpopularity sprang from his inability or unwillingness to conceal revolutionary ideas in traditional terminology. He desired collectivism and called it by that name. Believing that science had made possible a new world of plenty, he believed it the duty of social scientists to forge the new social institutions for the realization by all of the value of a surplus economy. The social scientists had failed in this noble task. They had not pushed for fundamental reforms, had lacked courage, and had worked in a confined orthodoxy. A few critics and dissenters had been labeled fanatics and crushed even as the early Christian martyrs. As a result they too had failed and "the apex of the capitalist structure glittered on a broad base of dirty factories, ravaged land, and miserable slums; but even the poorest faces were turned adoringly to its light." [10]

Impeding adjustment to change, blocking a world of beauty and plenty, Tugwell held, was a hard crust of dogmatized institutions and ideas. Tugwell wanted to break the crust, to stir up fruitful thought, and, at least temporarily, to prevent a new crust from forming. He believed the depression might be justified if it helped to do just this. To him the most iniquitous institution was uncontrolled capitalism or, related to it, free enterprise, laissez-faire theories, competition, or, in his terms, any system that permitted the "ganging up" of the unscrupulous few against the many, any system that invited struggle rather than co-operation, divisiveness rather than unity, bitterness rather than tolerance. The institution of capitalism, well justified in the propaganda put out by interest groups, complemented in the political realm by negative governments, and perpetuated because of an antiquated worship of individualism, permitted the exploitation of both human and physical resources. The depression, Tugwell believed, was caused by an inequity in income distribution, leading to a lowered purchasing power on the part of too many people. There was too much scarcity in the midst of surpluses, all of which pointed to the necessity of institutional changes.

Tugwell discovered a key to reform within the very fortifications of his greatest enemy, business. Because of scientific business management, industry had developed toward more co-operation, concentration, and efficiency and toward ever less competition, all of which was good

[10] Tugwell, *A Chronicle of Jeopardy*, p. 38.

according to Tugwell. But since competition and democracy had long been believed to be Siamese twins, the trend in industry had been forced underground by misguided, rural-minded reformers who pressed for a return to more competition, less efficiency, and more struggle. The trend toward concentration had continued anyway, clandestinely at times, and the result was large noncompetitive organizations in no way under the control of public interest. The lesson of business now had to be applied to government and the whole economy. The final consolidation had to occur and the oppressive possibilities of business-operated industries had to be eliminated by the public control of industry. After all, stressed Tugwell, modern business operations were just as much clothed with public interest as were other functions traditionally reserved to government. The identity of industry and government must be recognized as a beginning to reform. He said: "When industry is government and government is industry, the dual conflict in our modern institutions will be abated." [11]

Tugwell desired an organic society, with a unity of purpose, with a co-operative and collective economy, and with a purposeful, functioning government. On the part of the people this would require a willingness to make some sacrifices, for a collective society would mean a publicly controlled economy, whether through nationalization or strict regulation of industry. It had been most nearly approached in wartime, when many controls were instituted by the government. It would mean a larger degree of regimentation, a necessity for discipline, an end to individualism as an economic concept, and the cessation of speculation. But it also could mean no violent contrasts in income and well-being, no irrational allotment of individual liberty, no unconsidered exploitation of human resources.[12] It would entail a tremendous growth of government and governmental functions, with an end to checks and balances and the spasmodic legislative process. A strong executive would have to possess a large amount of delegated power. At the heart of government would be the social scientists, the experts, the planners, who would determine the future needs and possibilities of society and who would lay out the roads of progress. More than anything else, Tugwell was a planner. He saw in a planned economy the "eventual

[11] Rexford G. Tugwell, "The Principle of Planning and the Institution of Laissez Faire," *American Economic Review,* Supplement no. 1 to vol. XXII (1932), 85–86.
[12] *Ibid.,* p. 76.

possibility of a rewarded honesty for every man which so few have now."[13]

Tugwell did not expect ideality to be just around the corner. He knew that planning implied a revolution, with new attitudes, new disciplines, revised legal structures, unaccustomed limitations on freedom, and an end of completely private business. It would, if understood, be wanted by most people, but bitterly hated by others. It would involve laying a rough hand on "sacred precedent," which Tugwell rather enjoyed doing. There would be no more profit motive. The privileged groups in society would use their whole power to resist the change, relying on all the traditional gods to win a majority to their side. Not only would business fight, but even the legislators who supposedly represented the public interest. The depression aroused Tugwell's hopes that the "interests" had been so discredited that, in the New Deal, an "organic nation, part linked intelligently with part, advancing to the fullest extent of its capacities, might be realized."[14] But his hopes were thwarted. It seemed to him that special interests, which depended on divisiveness, prevailed. Tugwell had envisioned a revolution if reform did not come, yet had hardly dared hope that certain groups would ever voluntarily or even peacefully permit the reforms so badly needed.[15]

In many ways Tugwell was a tragic figure, out of touch with the less intellectualized majority of mankind. He was a savior without a flock, constantly frustrated when most people failed to respond to his ideas. Reform was so slow, yet to Tugwell so urgent. Despite the message of deliverance he proclaimed, "stupid" Americans continued to rejoice in their old gods, in individualism and independence, refusing to welcome or even rationally consider collectivism. They continued to heed the "interests," the predators, the devils, that Tugwell identified for them. Few other intellectuals spoke out as fervently and as honestly as did Tugwell, and this made him despair. At times he relapsed into complete bitterness or questioned the whole democratic process. To him the problems were so apparent, yet he was rejected by everyone but a few liberals. Reason ought to direct the integration of society, yet it had not. Technology might prove an irresponsible and destructive

[13] *Ibid.*, pp. 85–86 fn.
[14] Tugwell, "The Sources of New Deal Reformism," p. 269.
[15] Tugwell, "The Principles of Planning," p. 92.

monster if left in the hands of capitalist adventurers. With the advent of
the atomic bomb in 1945, a somewhat mellowed Tugwell saw once
again the absolute necessity of an integrated, socially controlled society.
The whole range of his idealism and disillusionment appear in the
following remark about the advent of the atomic age:

> We now had, at once, to acknowledge that individualism, competition,
> private initiative, and production only for profit were as destructive as
> tigers loose in a circus crowd. We could only live on in our world if we
> collectivized, cooperated, produced for use, shared with one another. But,
> if we conformed to these necessities, we could live as only kings, potentates,
> and American millionaires have heretofore dared to think of living. We had,
> in other words, a choice between untold luxury for everyone and the total
> destruction of everything. And damned if I didn't half-believe that we
> would choose destruction! For I was very sore and cynical about American
> intellectuals and academicians. They had never accepted Patten, and every-
> one since who had attempted his approach had been ignored.[16]

Tugwell was somewhat of a misfit in the Department of Agriculture,
but a valuable misfit. In the presence of the agriculturalists, who often
tended toward conservatism and whose identities and sympathies were
most often with the larger farmers and the landowners, Tugwell was
not always happy in his job as Undersecretary. With the famous purge
of the urban liberals connected with the Agricultural Adjustment Administration in 1935, only the broad tolerance of Wallace kept an un-
happy Tugwell in the department. Working primarily with the older
agencies of the department, Tugwell saw more clearly than anyone
else the need for conservation and was instrumental in the creation of
the Soil Conservation Service. Even as the Agricultural Adjustment
Administration was helping the advantaged farmer, Tugwell's attention
was directed to the disadvantaged farm groups, to the tenant and to the
farm laborer, who, Tugwell believed, needed a labor union. Tugwell
was more aware of rural poverty and degraded rural labor than most
land-grant college graduates. He wanted a section in the department to
advance the welfare of the little man, or the lower one-third.[17] The
Resettlement Administration was this agency. Although it was made an
independent agency, Tugwell's position as Undersecretary assured a

[16] Tugwell, *A Chronicle of Jeopardy,* p. 24.
[17] Lord, *Wallaces of Iowa,* p. 459.

close relationship between the Resettlement Administration and the Department of Agriculture.

The Resettlement Administration was a repository for a multitude of New Deal programs. It had the task of carrying on rural relief or rehabilitation, of continuing the whole land-utilization program, and of continuing and extending the New Deal community-building program through both rural and urban resettlement. Rural rehabilitation was soon to include loans to individuals, loans to co-operatives, grants to destitute farmers, and a debt-adjustment program. An additional problem was the care of migratory workers. An editorial comment that the order creating the Resettlement Administration might better have read "To rearrange the earth and the people thereof and devote surplus time and money, if any, to a rehabilitation of the Solar System" [18] was almost appropriate. The person who wrote the following request can certainly be excused for slightly overestimating the functions of the Resettlement Administration: "May I appeal to you to help me collect five dollars which I loan to a fellow five years ago to be paid back inside 24 hours as he was getting married that day." [19]

To Tugwell the assignment of the Resettlement Administration was twofold: rehabilitation and permanent reform. For the more than a million farm families on relief the Resettlement Administration could offer security through loans and careful supervision. But the important task was reform. Tugwell believed this meant a rearrangement of America according to plan. In rural areas men were living on land that could not provide security, largely because of past mistakes in land policy.[20] This submarginal land would have to be converted to new, more satisfactory uses, such as for recreation or forest culture. Its poverty-stricken inhabitants would have to be resettled on land that could provide security. This retirement and resettlement would change the face of rural America, but it would not absorb all the surplus farm population, for fewer and fewer farmers would be needed. Some would be going to the cities, where a horrible lack of imaginative city planning had created problems in land use even more grave than those

[18] Portland, Maine, *Press-Herald*, May 24, 1936.
[19] John Bandura to Rural Resettlement, Aug. 24, 1936, R.G. 96, National Archives.
[20] Rexford G. Tugwell, "Changing Acres," *Current History*, XLIV (Sept., 1936), 58–61.

in rural areas. Both to provide a "more orderly pattern for the inevitable movement from farm to city" [21] and to provide resettlement opportunities for urban slum dwellers, suburban towns or garden cities would be constructed. Tugwell was ready to begin the unprecedented task of rearranging the physical face of America.

The first task facing Tugwell was a staggering one. Thrown together into the Resettlement Administration were the Division of Subsistence Homesteads, three sections of the Federal Emergency Relief Administration, the state rural rehabilitation corporations, the Land Policy Section of the Agricultural Adjustment Administration, and small sections of several other agencies. These inherited agencies, programs, and personnel had to be molded into a completely integrated administrative organization that could direct several distinct programs. In addition, very vital policies had be be formulated. Even as this proceeded there was to be a constant pressure for hasty accomplishments, for the Resettlement Administration was part of the emergency relief program and had legislative justification only insofar as it provided immediate work relief for the unemployed.[22] These facts should partially excuse any early mistakes made by the Resettlement Administration.

For the office of Deputy Administrator of the Resettlement Administration, Tugwell selected Dr. Will W. Alexander, a clergyman, an expert on race relations, president of Dillard University in New Orleans, and closely identified with several other Negro colleges. After the registration of Tugwell at the end of 1936, Alexander headed the Resettlement Administration and the Farm Security Administration until 1940. One of Tugwell's many assistant administrators was Calvin Benham Baldwin, who had been a Virginia railroad worker and a small businessman before coming to the Department of Agriculture as an assistant to Henry A. Wallace. He was to head the Farm Security Administration from 1940 to 1943 and, even as Alexander, was to continue Tugwell's policies. Lewis C. Gray, farm economist and former head of the Bureau of Agricultural Economics, came to the Resettlement Administration with the Land Policy Section of the Agricultural Adjustment Administration. He quite appropriately headed the land program in the Resettlement Administration, utilizing a large proportion of the person-

---

[21] Rexford G. Tugwell, "Down to Earth," *Current History*, XLIV (July, 1936), 38.

[22] Will W. Alexander, "Rural Resettlement," *Southern Review*, I (1936), 538.

nel formerly with the Bureau of Agricultural Economics. To direct rural resettlement, Tugwell selected Dr. Carl C. Taylor, rural sociologist and M. L. Wilson's early assistant in the Division of Subsistence Homesteads. Dr. Eugene E. Agger, a friend and former colleague of Tugwell's on the economics faculty of Columbia University, was given the very important task of managing the completed communities. A New Mexico lawyer and judge, Joseph L. Dailey, became the head of the rehabilitation program. John S. Lansill, a city planner, was made director of the suburban resettlement program. A lawyer in the Department of Agriculture, Lee Pressman, was borrowed to head the Resettlement Administration's legal staff. From the personnel of the many inherited agencies the Resettlement Administration selected those that were to be retained and reappointed them. Approximately 4,200 employees were thus acquired from nine different agencies, but it is noticeable that most of the top administrative positions were staffed with new appointees.[23]

In line with the previous work of the Federal Emergency Relief Administration, Tugwell set up a completely decentralized organization for most of the Resettlement Administration program, dividing the country into eleven regions and placing most of the action programs in the regional offices. Small offices were also set up in each state and in most counties. This form of organization was necessary for the rehabilitation program, which involved loans and supervision in practically every rural county in the country.[24] The suburban resettlement program, limited to the environs of a few large cities, was controlled from Washington and had no connection with the regional offices. On the other hand, the rural resettlement program was under the direction of the regional offices, but with a great deal of supervision from Washington.

The administrative organization of the Resettlement Administration was complex and much criticized. Instead of four main divisions to perform the four main tasks of the Resettlement Administration—rural relief, land utilization, rural resettlement, and suburban resettlement—Tugwell created twelve co-ordinate divisions. In addition to the four main divisions, such services as management, planning, pro-

[23] Select Committee of the House Committee on Agriculture, *Hearings on the Farm Security Administration*, 78th Cong., 1st Sess., 1943–1944, p. 1107.
[24] Tugwell to L. C. Gray, Nov. 14, 1935, R.G. 96, National Archives.

cedure, information, investigation, personnel, labor relations, business management, finance, and construction were given full divisional status.[25] Under each division there were sections, some as large and important as other divisions. This plan of organization was criticized on the grounds that it led to an overlapping of function, to higher administrative expenses, and to difficulties in allotting responsibilities. Many believed that the Resettlement Administration was overorganized. Certainly it was not set up as a temporary organization, since whole divisions were devoted to determining procedures, to publishing information, and to making investigations. The personnel of the Resettlement Administration soon numbered over 13,000.

The Rural Resettlement, Suburban Resettlement, Construction, and Management Divisions were most intimately connected with the Resettlement Administration communities. The Construction Division did all the construction for both Rural and Suburban Resettlement Divisions. Rural Resettlement approved plans for and initiated all rural communities, as well as continuing the planning of those uncompleted rural communities begun by the Division of Subsistence Homesteads and the Federal Emergency Relief Administration. Suburban Resettlement, which had very little connection with the other divisions of the Resettlement Administration, had complete control of the greenbelt cities and the uncompleted suburban-type subsistence homesteads. Management controlled completed communities, directing educational and community activities, developing economic opportunities, selecting settlers, organizing community governments, and seeing to the maintenance of the buildings in the communities. Of the other main divisions, the Land Utilization Division was primarily concerned with completing the land-use program, which involved over 9,000,000 acres of optioned or purchased land and over 200 work projects to develop new uses for the land. From the displaced persons resulting from this program came many resettlement clients. Also in the Land Utilization Division was a Land Planning Section, which acted as the Resettlement Administration's main research organization. It published a *Land Policy Circular*, studied the nation's land problems, located areas for resettlement communities, continued the research on part-time farming, and made studies that were used

[25] Tugwell to Division Directors and Section Chiefs, June 11, 1935, and Burton D. Leeley to E. E. Agger, Aug., 1936, *ibid.*

America Resettled 157

by the Suburban Resettlement Division in planning the greenbelt cities. The Rural Rehabilitation Division administered rural relief, lending millions of dollars to farmers and co-operative groups for equipment and repairs, making grants to completely destitute farmers, and adjusting the debts of farm families. Some of its loans were made available to co-operatives in resettlement communities, and many of its first clients "graduated" into rural communities.[26]

Cognizant of the problems already encountered by the subsistence homesteads and rural-industrial communities, the administrators of the Resettlement Administration attempted to formulate a completely altered program for its new communities. To assist with the formulation of policy, Tugwell and his associates had the assistance of the Land Planning Section of the Land Utilization Division, which co-operated with the Bureau of Agricultural Economics. They also were assisted by the Social Research Section which, as late as 1937, included 114 employees.[27] Frederic C. Howe, the grand old man among the reformers in the Department of Agriculture and a very close friend of Tugwell, spent six weeks abroad studying housing and rural settlement.[28] The Suburban Resettlement Division set up a Technical Research Unit which studied English housing and garden cities. In 1935 requests were sent to the Secretary of State, asking that the Consular Service provide information on foreign housing.[29] Even more important, the Resettlement Administration had the advantage of all the experience gained by the Division of Subsistence Homesteads and the Federal Emergency Relief Administration.

Like the Division of Subsistence Homesteads, the Resettlement Administration received many unsolicited recommendations for its community program. One man continuously advocated a tung-oil plantation project.[30] Another asked for experimentation in each of the following types of communities: a German suburban homestead; a Swiss chalet with its cheese industry; a French *ferme* with its wine

[26] Resettlement Administration Weekly Information Report no. 47, June 13, 1936, R.G. 96, National Archives; Resettlement Administration, *Interim Report* (Washington, 1936), pp. 8–9, 17, 23; Resettlement Administration, *First Annual Report* (Washington, 1936), pp. 10–15, 21–26, 63–64.
[27] Carl Taylor to W. W. Alexander, March 4, 1937, R.G. 16, National Archives.
[28] Memorandum on Rural Rehabilitation, n.d., *ibid.*
[29] Cordell Hull to Henry A. Wallace, June 27, 1938, R.G. 96, National Archives.
[30] William K. de Blocq to Tugwell, June 3, 1935, *ibid.*

press; a Danish co-operative dairy farm; a Russian mir with its cooperative farm; a Bavarian *Dorf* with its unusual crop rotations and its carp farm; and a forest community.[31] Gerald Geraldson, director of Brotherhood House in New York City, suggested that the Resettlement Administration construct communal households resembling monasteries, with the men housed on one floor, the women on another, and the children cared for in a single flock. The women would be free to arrange for "what ever amount of natural motherhood they may desire."[32] The whole colony would be controlled by the "One at the Top," who corresponded to a pope. All would labor according to ability. Hailing the "Doorway to a new civilization" and "communism now," Geraldson stated: "I am free to say that I regard the family as a fading social institution and see little of permanant [sic] good to be accomplished by efforts to save or re-establish it."[33]

Other advice was of more value. The Land Use Planning Section compiled an enormous report on resettlement policy and procedure, citing the history of prior settlement efforts in the United States and abroad. The report reflected the cautious approach of the land economists and advised resettlement on individual or closely grouped farms rather than in organized communities. The land economists urged every possible encouragement to co-operatives, but warned against compulsory or planned co-operation. They cautioned against any attempt to combine infant industries with farm colonies and asked for an ultimate sale price based more on an appraised value and the client's earning power than on the actual cost to the Resettlement Administration. On the difficult problem of land tenure, they wanted a permanent lease for the client unqualified for landownership, a temporary trial lease with an option of future purchase for the average client, and an extended, forty-year purchase contract for the superior client.[34]

Also advising Tugwell on policy matters was a short-lived Planning Division, whose personnel represented a distinctly nonrural background in contrast to the Land Policy Section. Its recommendations

---

[31] Dmitry M. Borodin to Tugwell, May 6, 1935, *ibid.*
[32] Gerald Geraldson to Henry A. Wallace, Nov. 24, 1936, *ibid.*
[33] *Ibid.*
[34] Resettlement Administration, Land Utilization Division, Land Use Planning Section, "Resettlement Policy and Procedure," pp. 11–62, *ibid.*

America Resettled 159

were, therefore, even less orthodox. The Planning Division set for itself the question: "What influence do we want the Resettlement Administration to have on the current and coming course of events in America?" [35] On the question of tenure in resettlement communities it suggested a long-time or permanent control over real property by the government. It advised against part-time farming as a means of raising living standards of low-income workers, stressed the small economic importance of handicrafts and the greater possibilities of co-operative enterprises, and recommended some plantation projects and completely co-operative farms as social experiments. It advised decentralization in existing industrial areas by town planning of the garden city type rather than by setting up more Arthurdales and then praying for industry to follow. It believed that tiny, remote settlements were not attractive and "should be set on wheels and moved to town." [36] Most of all, the Planning Division questioned the whole policy of loans as a means to rehabilitation, asking instead for grants and a frank subsidy to an already-overburdened group. Keith Southard, head of the Planning Division, believed that rehabilitation by loan was "a dubious insistence upon some of the pioneer virtues which are actually anti-social in this period and circumstance." He believed "rugged but ragged individualism" might yield "advantageously to the co-operative forms." These in turn could prove educational and create an up-to-date citizenship. They might "almost make Democrats out of Green Mountain Republicans." [37]

Tugwell formulated an initial community program that incorporated ideas from both the Land Planning Section and the Planning Division. Although he did not exclude a few more subsistence homesteads communities, Tugwell's main emphasis was to be on all-rural communities for farmers and garden cities for full-time industrial workers, neither depending upon a mixed agricultural and industrial economy. The ideas of Elwood Mead and Ebenezer Howard were to find their fullest expression in the Resettlement Administration. Rural resettlement projects would include both the infiltration of settlers into existing communities and the creation of new communities. Although not affirmed, the probability of some subsidy was accepted; the general

[35] Keith Southard to W. W. Alexander, Sept. 30, 1935, *ibid.*
[36] Boyd Fisher to Keith Southard, June 15, 1935, *ibid.*
[37] Keith Southard to Tugwell, Sept. 4, 1935, *ibid.*

policy of rehabilitation by loans, however, was never dropped, in fact could not have been dropped because of public opinion. Cooperative enterprises were to be a major objective of the Resettlement Administration. Tugwell, who appreciated the need for some limitation on fee simple ownership, stressed security as a better goal than ownership, recognized that some people needed continuous assistance and supervision, and asked for a long-time relationship between the government and the individual, either by a long purchase contract or by a conditioned lease. Tugwell's greatest interest was garden cities or greenbelt cities. For those he followed the well-developed ideology of the garden city movement.[38]

The Resettlement Administration was closely related to both the Extension Service of the Department of Agriculture and to the Works Progress Administration. Since the close supervision of rural relief clients and the development of agricultural plans for rural communities involved extension work, the Resettlement Administration and the Extension Service drew up a plan of co-operation.[39] This never led to a close working relationship, mainly because of conflicting philosophies. Tugwell confided to Roosevelt: "My greatest difficulty has been and will continue to be with the Extension Service which is arrogant, opinionated—and largely Republican or reactionary." [40] Later, many extension agents would ally themselves with the leadership of the Farm Bureau in a long battle against the Farm Security Administration. Underneath it all was a class difference. The Extension Service usually worked with a group of farmers different from those aided by the Resettlement Administration. The ideas and policies of Tugwell were anathema to the prosperous, individualistic, independent farming class most often represented in the Farm Bureau. To the landowner, large or small, Tugwell must have seemed the antithesis of the agrarian tradition of individualism; his collectivism was alien, radical, and dangerous.

The Resettlement Administration and the Works Progress Administration were both relief agencies with a positive emphasis on

[38] Address by Tugwell to a conference of regional directors of the Land program, June 18, 1935, and an address by Tugwell to a session of the Resettlement Administration's regional directors, Jan. 28, 1936, *ibid.*

[39] Memorandum of Understanding between the Extension Service and the Resettlement Administration, June 7, 1935, *ibid.*

[40] Tugwell to Roosevelt, Nov. 18, 1935, *ibid.*

useful work and reform; both fed from the same trough, the Emergency Relief appropriation of 1935. Moreover, the Resettlement Administration, in all its project work, was committed by law to the use of relief labor under Works Progress Administration regulations. The land-utilization projects were approved only when Works Progress Administration laborers were available. This forced relationship led to some friction and to a constant struggle for executive funds between Tugwell and Harry Hopkins. The relationship became critical in October, 1935, when the funds for land-utilization projects went to Hopkins instead of Tugwell, who had already planned the program and assembled an administrative staff. After bitter telegrams to Roosevelt and unanswered messages to Hopkins, Tugwell was given permission to supervise the program, although the money remained in the Works Progress Administration.[41] Later, labor and construction problems would cause added friction.

With personnel, an administrative organization, and a set of policies, the Resettlement Administration had to begin a rapid program of work relief. Since the unspent subsistence homesteads funds reverted to the Treasury on June 16, 1935, Roosevelt, on June 24, 1935, allotted $7,000,000 of the emergency relief appropriation to Tugwell for the completion of thirty-three subsistence homesteads communities. The inherited Rural Rehabilitation Corporation funds were available for the completion of the Federal Emergency Relief Administration communities. With the $375,511,675 committed to the Resettlement Administration from the $4,880,000,000 Emergency Relief Act, Tugwell made plans, by November, 1935, to use $31,000,000 for four approved greenbelt towns and $49,045,650 for rural resettlement projects.[42] Actually these plans and allotments were very tentative, since they were soon reduced, only to be vastly increased by later deficiency appropriations and other emergency relief acts. But they indicate the vastly enlarged scope of the Resettlement Administration as compared with the Division of Subsistence Homesteads, which spent only about $8,000,000 in its two years of operation.

Although the Resettlement Administration received funds to com-

[41] G. E. Falke to Tugwell, Oct. 2, 1935; Tugwell to F. D. Roosevelt (telegram), Sept. 28, 1935; Tugwell to Roosevelt (radiogram), Oct. 3, 1935; Falke to Tugwell (telegram), Oct. 7, 1935; all *ibid.*

[42] Tugwell to Roosevelt, Nov. 18, 1935, *ibid.;* U.S. Senate, *Resettlement Administration Program*, Document no. 213, 74th Cong., 2d Sess., 1936, p. 5.

plete only thirty-three subsistence homesteads communities, it received from the Division of Subsistence Homesteads plans for sixty-five projects, none of which were rejected until an investigation was made by a Special Plans Division. Eleven of the industrial homesteads (Bankhead Farms, Beauxart Gardens, Houston Gardens, Wichita Gardens, El Monte, Decatur, Austin, McComb, Magnolia, Tupelo, and Hattiesburg Homesteads) were near enough completion to be assigned to the Management Division. By November, 1935, their construction was completed. By December, seven other industrial homesteads (Palmerdale, Phoenix, San Fernando, Granger, and Longview Homesteads; Dalworthington and Three Rivers Gardens) were complete. These eighteen communities gave the Resettlement Administration fewer problems than any other inherited communities, since they were usually located near economic opportunities and usually had excellent settlers. Because they were in various stages of construction, usually under piecemeal contracts, the Construction Division had its problems in completing them, often finding poor accounting procedures, bad workmanship, and high maintenance costs.[43] The Resettlement Administration completed these communities according to original plans, but often added extra community facilities, such as community buildings. This, along with the use of inefficient relief labor, increased the fears of homesteaders that the sale price of their homes would be prohibitive, for it was not then clear that the sale would be based on appraised value and a consideration of the client's earning power instead of on cost.

Three other industrial homesteads (Mount Olive and Greenwood in Alabama and Lake County Homesteads in Illinois) were much longer delayed in construction. Duluth Homesteads; Cahaba, near Birmingham, Alabama; Hightstown; and the Negro community near Newport News were all completely replanned and became, except for the choice of location, Resettlement Administration communities. Since the homesteaders in the industrial communities had been promised ownership and since the local tax problem still plagued these communities, Tugwell, soon after the organization of the Resettlement Administration, announced that title to the completed subsistence homesteads communities would be turned over to co-operative home-

[43] Resettlement Administration, *Interim Report*, p. 49; Resettlement Administration, *First Annual Report*, p. 69.

stead associations made up of all the homesteaders in a community and that, through this association, the homesteaders would be issued purchase contracts. The homestead association, although conducting all business, would have to agree to Resettlement Administration supervision in order to protect the government's investment. By July, 1936, the five Texas projects and Longview Homesteads had been turned over to local associations.[44]

Shenandoah Homesteads became a special problem for the Resettlement Administration, since it was a special type of community. Because the State of Virginia was purchasing large areas of mountainous land for the Shenandoah National Park, the Division of Subsistence Homesteads had undertaken a resettlement project for the displaced hill people. As planned there were to be seven different groups of approximately twenty homesteads each, located on small tracts both to the east and west of the Shenandoah chain. As the Resettlement Administration proceeded with the construction of these seven small communities, a furor arose. Many of the mountaineers did not choose to be resettled and, in the hands of newspapermen, became martyrs to government planning and autocracy. Letters such as the following from thirty-one mountaineers contained political dynamite: "Don't beleave in mooven these famileys out of there homes in the Park era. . . . We all beleave in letting thes mountain people stay wher tha are at as long as tha are not in the way." [45] It was useless for the Resettlement Administration to protest that it was the State of Virginia that was forcing the moves and that it had been another agency that had planned the project.

The whole problem at Shenandoah became aggravated when Virginia's Senator Harry F. Byrd began a long campaign against the Resettlement Administration, incensed by what he interpreted as a stench coming from gross inefficiency and Russian communism. He estimated that the cost of the Shenandoah project would reach $1,520,219, that the houses would cost from $6,000 to $8,000 each, and that they would involve an impossibly high rent for the simple

[44] House Agricultural Subcommittee of the Committee on Appropriations, *Hearings on the Agricultural Department Appropriation Bill for 1938*, 75th Cong., 1st Sess., 1937, p. 1311.

[45] Will Bailey and Thirty Others to the Resettlement Administration, Oct. 8, 1936, R.G. 96, National Archives.

mountain folk. As the first homes were completed, he avowed that a contractor would have built them for $900 whereas they cost $8,000. He decried the purchase of high-priced furniture to give to the world's best furniture makers and asked the reason for constructing costly community buildings for these people. He described the whole project as "a permanent monument to a waste and extravagance such as has never before been known in a civilized country."[46] He was even more angry when the Resettlement Administration started to carry out a plan to have a village-type agriculture and a co-operative farm at one of the tracts. Byrd described it as being similar to Russia and against all the habits, experiences, and traditions of the homesteaders. The plan was changed by the Resettlement Administration.[47] As completed, some groups of homes at Shenandoah, with only four rooms and without baths and running water, cost as low as $1,518.19. The high cost of some of the first units, which Byrd accurately described, was caused by some expensive wells that were condemned and by the very modern fixtures in the homes. The final audit of Shenandoah showed an average unit cost of $6,357 for the 172 units, and this included every single expense, including the cost of the land, roads, and management.[48]

The four stranded subsistence homesteads communities, Arthurdale, Westmoreland, Tygart Valley, and Cumberland, were the real problem children of the Resettlement Administration, even as they had been of the Division of Subsistence Homesteads. Since the Resettlement Administration had inherited them, they were now even less loved. Although Arthurdale came to the Resettlement Administration with a long history of expensive experimentation, it was the lack of economic justification that was to plague the Resettlement Administration, since Tugwell was not averse to some expensive experimentation of his own. The Resettlement Administration soon learned the forgetfulness of mankind, for the stranded communities were identified with Tugwell and became his mistakes, even though Tugwell constantly reiterated that they were established "on a theory in which none of

[46] Washington *Star*, May 27, 1937; correspondence between Byrd and Henry A. Wallace in *C.R.*, 75th Cong., 1st Sess., 1937, pp. 7964–7967.
[47] *C.R.* 75th Cong., 1st Sess., 1937, pp. 7964–7967.
[48] Department of Agriculture, Farm Security Administration, "Shenandoah Homesteads: Final Report of Project Costs to June 30, 1939," R.G. 96, National Archives.

America Resettled 165

us believed." [49] He had always believed fallacious the idea that industry, particularly in a time of depression, would decentralize voluntarily, particularly to isolated mountain communities. But since the Resettlement Administration had the stranded communities, Tugwell decided to make the best of a sorry fate. He assigned them directly to the Washington office of the Management Division in order to spare the regional offices any embarrassment.

The economic problems of the four stranded communities went to the Economic Development Section of Management. The situation on the four projects was not encouraging. At Westmoreland only 40 per cent of the heads of families had outside employment. Beyond the food produced on their subsistence plots, the rest were dependent upon construction work at the project or on the co-operative farm.[50] At Arthurdale there was a limited amount of construction work, some employment in a co-operative furniture factory, and prospects for employment in a vacuum-cleaner factory, which was finally opened in June, 1936. At Tygart Valley there was a co-operative farm, some limited possibilities of employment in the lumber industry, but primarily work on the completion of the project. At Cumberland most of the families were living in barns while enjoying what was to them lucrative relief wages as they constructed their own homes. Beyond that there was only the rather large subsistence plots of unfertile plateau soil or a benevolent government between them and acute destitution. Three methods were adopted by the Resettlement Administration to relieve the situation for the four projects. In some cases additional land was purchased and added to the co-operative farms. In all cases the construction was not rushed to completion at these projects, allowing the homesteaders a longer period of employment. But primarily the Resettlement Administration relied on co-operative enterprises to benefit the communities. Both consumers' and producers' co-operatives were organized and aided by ample loans. They became fascinating experiments in co-operation, but never solved the economic problems. Tugwell rejoiced at the use of co-operatives, defied the enemies of these experiments who stood around "with bared teeth,"

[49] Rexford G. Tugwell, "Cooperation and Resettlement," *Current History*, XLV (Feb., 1937), 74.
[50] J. O. Walker to Edwin G. Arnold, April 9, 1937, R.G. 96, National Archives; Resettlement Administration, *First Annual Report*, p. 55.

and rejoiced that the government was finally organizing the sheep instead of aiding the wolves.[51]

Of the Federal Emergency Relief Administration communities inherited by the Resettlement Administration, only two, Woodlake and Red House, were enough completed to be assigned to the Management Division. Red House was to suffer the same economic ills as the stranded subsistence homesteads. Woodlake was the first completed all-rural colony in the New Deal. It, along with the other uncompleted Federal Emergency Relief Administration communities—practically all rural and many no farther advanced than land purchase—became almost indistinguishable from the all-rural communities initiated by the Resettlement Administration. The same could be said for the three all-rural subsistence homesteads, which were replanned and completed as Resettlement Administration communities. In many cases the Resettlement Administration, in its inherited rural colonies, vastly increased the acreage planned for the individual units, since the Resettlement Administration's emphasis was usually upon a complete farming economy.

Except for some of the inherited rural communities which were easily made to conform to the Resettlement Administration's new policies in community building, the inherited communities were often considered a burden and a liability pushed upon the Resettlement Administration by other agencies. Their many problems could be blamed on other men. But not so the communities planned and initiated by the Resettlement Administration. These were the favored children of Tugwell and his assistants. Most favored were the garden cities or greenbelt towns. They had been projected in the early New Deal days and were closest to Tugwell's heart. Just after the creation of the Resettlement Administration, Tugwell had charted a program for the Suburban Resettlement Division which included twenty-five suburban communities.[52] Limited appropriations and a court decision lowered to three the number actually constructed, but these three communities—Greenbelt, Maryland; Greenhills, Ohio; and Greendale,

---

[51] Resettlement Administration, Weekly Information Report no. 49, June 27, 1936, R.G. 96, National Archives; New Brunswick, N.J., *Daily Home News*, May 9, 1936; Tugwell, "Cooperation and Resettlement," p. 75.

[52] Jonathan Mitchell, "Low-Cost Paradise," *New Republic*, LXXXIV (1935), 152–155; Tugwell to Harry Hopkins, July 18, 1935, R.C. 96, National Archives.

America Resettled

Wisconsin—were by far the largest and most important constructed by the New Deal. They were so different from a majority of the other communities that they represent an almost isolated aspect of the Resettlement Administration. Based on world-wide influence, the greenbelt cities, next to the Tennessee Valley Authority, were probably the most influential creations of the New Deal. As such they will be given extended treatment in a subsequent chapter.

Beyond the three greenbelt cities, the Suburban Resettlement Division so altered the plans of two of the subsistence homesteads communities that they became suburban housing developments with many similarities to the greenbelt cities. The Suburban Resettlement Division also initiated one suburban project which did not strictly follow the garden city pattern. At Newport News the subsistence homesteads community for Negroes was converted into a small Negro housing development of 159 units, surrounded by a greenbelt of farms and gardens. Near Birmingham the Resettlement Administration inherited from the Division of Subsistence Homesteads a tract of undeveloped, slag-covered land at Trussville, Alabama. On this the Resettlement Administration began the construction of the small garden city of Cahaba, which was planned for 400 units, although only 287 were completed. Planned as a small town, Cahaba had a central water system, a sewage system, streets and sidewalks, a recreational area, a complete trading center, and a community building and auditorium. The homes were on lots of one-half to three-fourths acres, which permitted individual gardens. A similar community was planned and initiated near Ironwood, Michigan, by the Resettlement Administration. Of 400 planned homesteads only 132 were developed, each containing five-eighths acres of land. Ironwood included a community farm, a canning plant, a small town hall, and a park. Each of these three suburban projects was planned for leasing rather than for sale.[53]

The largest number of Resettlement Administration communities were of the agricultural type. The Rural Resettlement Division initiated over 100 rural projects, about 32 of which could be classified as communities, although the selection is very arbitrary, since the Resettlement Administration resettled some families on individual, scattered farms, settled others on contiguous tracts of land and pro-

[53] Resettlement Administration, *First Annual Report*, p. 72.

vided them community facilities, and placed some in well-established rural communities. Thus only part of the projects were complete communities. In only two or three cases was the European village plan tried. In this type of community the houses were grouped together, with the fields lying at a distance. The rural projects of a community type were predominantly in the South. Although planned and the development initiated by the Resettlement Administration, they were almost always completed by the Farm Security Administration, some as late as the beginning of World War II. Invariably they were designed for a full-time agricultural economy, with no reliance upon industrial decentralization. They were planned as demonstrations of a better type of rural life as well as for the rehabilitation of the settlers. Prerequisites of all the rural communities included good land, economically adequate farms, an emphasis on home production, adequate buildings for health and demonstrational purposes, modern conveniences, complete supervision, and co-operative production.[54]

Though exhibiting individual differences, a majority of the farm colonies were similar enough to be characterized collectively. A typical one would be in the South. It would contain about 100 individual farm units, inhabited by either white or Negro tenants, but not by both. Each farm unit would contain from 40 to 100 acres. The house, constructed in 1937 or 1938, would be of light frame construction, with from three to five rooms and, in a majority of cases in the South, without plumbing. The farm and home practices would be closely supervised by the Resettlement Administration or its successor, the Farm Security Administration. Until 1940 the tenure would always be by lease, with rent payments usually based on a varying percentage of the annual crop production. The community would contain certain public facilities, such as a school, a community building, a co-operative cotton gin, and a warehouse. In all cases it would include from one to over a dozen co-operative enterprises, operated by a co-operative association sponsored and heavily financed by the government. (See Appendix for a complete list of Resettlement Administration communities.)

Of particular interest are those rural communities which were not planned in conformity with the existing agricultural pattern. At Lake Dick, Arkansas, a 4,529-acre tract was made into a large co-operative

[54] *Ibid.*, pp. 33–37.

America Resettled

plantation. A village of sixty houses was constructed on the shore of a beautiful lake. Each unit contained a two-acre plot for gardens. The village had a central water supply, a community building, a co-operative cotton gin, a co-operative general store, and the many buildings needed for housing and processing the livestock and crops. The farm land was leased to an association of all the villagers, who co-operatively owned the livestock and farmed the land.[55] The individual farmers, carefully checked by timekeepers, received wages for their work and shared in any profits made by the co-operative at the end of the year. Lake Dick very much resembled a day-labor plantation, except for the profit sharing. The association took the place of a landlord, and the government, by lending money to the association, replaced the local bank or merchant. Lake Dick began full operations in 1938 and was never a success. A large number of the tenants disliked the co-operative system. Only twenty-six units were occupied in 1941.[56] The Resettlement Administration defended this arrangement as a demonstration of new methods and as a school for inexperienced farmers. At Casa Grande Farms in Arizona the Resettlement Administration established a very similar project which contained a village of sixty adobe houses and a large irrigated co-operative dairy and beef farm, all operated collectively.[57]

In 1936 and 1937 the Resettlement Administration purchased a large sugar-cane plantation in Terrebonne Parish, Louisiana, and converted it into a collective farm of seventy-one families. The homes were located on six-acre subsistence tracts, making a modified village. At Terrebonne a 2,800-acre collective farm was devoted to sugar cane, truck crops, and livestock. The farm was leased to the co-operative association for 99 years.[58] The principle of the co-operative farm, already used to a limited extent by the Division of Subsistence Homesteads and to a much greater extent by the Federal Emergency Relief Administration, was adapted to all or parts of about a dozen other rural resettlement projects, but without the village plan for the homes. The ninety-nine-year lease or a forty-year lease was used

[55] *Hearings on the Farm Security Administration,* p. 1043.
[56] House Agricultural Subcommittee of the Committee on Appropriations, *Hearings on Agricultural Department Appropriation Bill for 1943,* pt. II, 77th Cong., 2d Sess., 1942, pp. 241–242, 246, 248.
[57] *Hearings on the Farm Security Administration,* pp. 1038, 1043.
[58] *Ibid.,* pp. 1063–1064.

on several Resettlement Administration and Federal Emergency Relief Administration communities, usually in connection with a co-operative association. The village form of agriculture, the collective farming enterprises, and the long-term leases were the most important departures from traditional American agriculture and the ones most criticized. The co-operative plantation, such as Terrebonne, was defended as being more in keeping with the Southern plantation style of agriculture than were individual farms, particularly for a certain untrained class of tenants. The lease system was in line with the thinking of many land economists.

Except for the greenbelt cities, all plans for communities were submitted to the Resettlement Administration at Washington from the regional offices. By April, 1936, the regions had submitted 196 projects for final planning and approval by Tugwell. These early plans were the nucleus of almost all the communities initiated by the Resettlement Administration.[59] All community construction was directed by the Construction Division. Employing up to 3,000 men on each project, the division was committed to the use of relief labor except for certain skilled tasks that were performed by people selected by the United States Employment Service.[60] As much as was possible under Works Progress Administration commitments, the Resettlement Administration used its own clients in construction work. In all cases it paid prevailing regional wages and, as a whole, maintained an enviable relationship with labor, receiving commendations from William Green of the American Federation of Labor and from John L. Lewis of the United Mine Workers.[61]

The first year of the Resettlement Administration was one of forced haste and expensive experimentation in construction. The most obvious result was extremely expensive housing. Tugwell, who believed that housing methods had lagged far behind the efficiency exhibited in other fields of endeavor, was determined to find new, mass-production techniques for the Resettlement Administration. His first experiment was in concrete-slab construction, which involved one immensely heavy prefabricated slab of concrete for each side and for the roof

[59] Resettlement Administration, *Interim Report,* pp. 14–15.
[60] Resettlement Administration, *First Annual Report,* pp. 69–70.
[61] U.S. Senate, *Resettlement Administration Program,* Document no. 213, 74th Cong., 2d Sess., 1936, pp. 19–21.

of a house, all to be quickly placed in position by heavy machinery. This method was planned for the greenbelt cities and was first experimented with at Jersey Homesteads, where a portable factory was constructed at a cost of approximately $225,000. Many of the slabs cracked and the experiment failed, with the Resettlement Administration being threatened with patent suits.[62] Another much-publicized but less expensive experiment was tried at Mount Olive Homesteads near Birmingham, where rammed earth was used in the construction of seven houses. This type of construction, though providing almost perfect insulation with its seventeen-inch earthen walls, involved much less expense for materials (mostly a mixture of soils) but much more expense for labor, since the earth had to be packed between forms by hand labor. In the long run it was feared that the seven houses at Mount Olive would not stand up to the windy, rainy climate. But in 1958 they were still standing and were considered among the most attractive homes at Mount Olive. Later, under the Farm Security Administration, experiments were made in all-steel and in cotton-duck construction. The most valuable experimentation was in rapid prefabrication of rural, frame-constructed homes, which later led to much-lowered construction costs.[63]

Another factor contributing to the high cost of the early construction was the high standards maintained. An administrative order of September 23, 1935, required all houses to contain inside toilets, baths, and electric wiring. Unless specified otherwise, furniture was also to be supplied by the Resettlement Administration.[64] Both the high standards and the experimentation were ended by early 1937, after the resignation of Tugwell and the absorption of the Resettlement Administration into the Department of Agriculture. A conference of Resettlement Administration and Department of Agriculture officials in April, 1937, decided on the future use of standard house designs only. They also decided to limit the cost of houses to $1,200 in the South and to $2,100 in the North, a difference dictated by climate.

[62] New York *Post*, Oct. 17, 1935; Washington *Herald*, Dec. 22, 1935.

[63] New York *Herald Tribune*, April 12, 1937; "Cotton and Mud Go into Houses: Government's Effort to Use Native Materials in Low-Cost Rural Housing," *Business Week*, Oct. 28, 1939, pp. 20–21; Department of Agriculture, Farm Security Administration, *Report of the Administrator of the FSA, 1940* (Washington, 1940), p. 17.

[64] Adrian Dornbush to Grace E. Falke, Nov. 27, 1935, R.G. 96, National Archives.

In most cases this meant the elimination of baths in the South and the construction of smaller homes. By 1939 only 800 houses in the South, out of approximately 2,445, had baths. On one community project the average house cost reached a low of $825. This was made possible by the elimination of all purely decorative features, by a reduction in the number of gables, beams, and rafters, and by using standard designs which permitted precutting and prefabrication at small portable sawmills.[65]

The original Resettlement Administration house designs, approved by farm management experts and structural engineers, were further perfected during construction operations. Plans were changed as many as thirty times, with resultant savings of up to $400 per home. All the designs and improved techniques were turned over to private builders and the public in 1938. The continuous work of the Division of Subsistence Homesteads, the Resettlement Administration, and the Farm Security Administration in rural home design represented an innovation in American architecture. Formerly rural homes, insofar as they had any design, had been modeled on urban homes or on impractical designs from the past. The resettlement program marked a beginning in functional rural architecture. It also represented the first beginning in rural public housing. Will W. Alexander, Administrator of the Farm Security Administration, said that "if we could house all our low-income farm families with the same standards the Danes use for their hogs, we would be a long step ahead." In order to do this he stressed the necessity of accepting a government subsidy for rural housing even as it had already been accepted for urban housing.[66]

The Construction Division of the Resettlement Administration procured all its supplies through the Procurement Division of the Treasury. In September, 1936, this Procurement Division investigated the Resettlement Administration projects, finding construction costs from 33 to 50 per cent higher than by private contract under open-market conditions.[67] This naturally led to much adverse criticism of the Re-

[65] Memorandum for the Secretary of Agriculture, April 14, 1937, *ibid.;* "Cotton and Mud," p. 20; Department of Agriculture, Farm Security Administration, *Report of the Administrator of the FSA, 1938* (Washington, 1938), pp. 18–19.

[66] Will W. Alexander, "A Review of the Farm Security Administration's Housing Activities," *Housing Yearbook, 1939* (Chicago: National Association of Housing Officials, 1939), pp. 141–143, 149–150.

[67] Henry A. Wallace to F. D. Roosevelt, March 19, 1937, R.G. 16, National Archives.

settlement Administration. It was also an accurate estimate. A comparison of the unit construction costs of homes practically completed by the Division of Subsistence Homesteads under the contract system and those completely constructed by the Resettlement Administration indicates this high cost. The unit costs of homes constructed by the Division of Subsistence Homesteads ran from $1,916 at Houston Gardens to $3,013 at Decatur. The unit costs on Resettlement Administration construction varied from $5,223 at Newport News to $8,827 at Lake County Homesteads.[68] Some critics blamed the high cost on poor planning and poor engineering, as well as on costly experimentation. The Resettlement Administration blamed it on the use of relief labor and on the necessity of conforming to Works Progress Administration regulations, which, according to the Resettlement Administration, made any co-ordination between the planning and construction divisions impossible.[69]

Legal and congressional obstacles plagued the Resettlement Administration even as they had the Division of Subsistence Homesteads. Funds for a vacuum-cleaner factory at Arthurdale were temporarily frozen by Comptroller General John R. McCarl, and several congressmen tried to prevent furniture production by the local co-operatives at several different projects.[70] But the most serious obstacle placed before the Resettlement Administration came from the courts. One of the greenbelt cities, Greenbrook, New Jersey, was planned for an area near Bound Brook in Franklin Township, where the local citizens were well aware of some of the mistakes already made at Jersey Homesteads. As the Resettlement Administration proceeded to take options on the land for Greenbrook, a group of citizens in Franklin Township filed an injunction against the Resettlement Administration in December, 1935, on the grounds that the whole Emergency Relief Act of 1935 was unconstitutional, that the order creating the Resettlement Administration was not under the scope of any United States statute or law, that the proposed community was not for the general welfare or the common defense, and that the Resettlement Administration was exercising powers reserved for the states.[71] The

[68] House Agricultural Subcommittee of the Committee on Appropriations, *Hearings on the Agricultural Department Appropriation Bill for 1938*, pp. 1303–1304.
[69] C. D. Kinswon to M. L. Wilson, July 20, 1937, R.G. 16, National Archives.
[70] C.R., 74th Cong., 1st Sess., 1935, pp. 14383–14384, 14418.
[71] New Brunswick, N.J., *Daily Home News*, Dec. 11, 1935.

local citizens objected to the loss of tax revenue, since the Resettlement Administration could pay no taxes, to the location of the project, to the type of architecture planned (they feared the concrete-slab construction tried at Jersey Homesteads), to the low class of people they believed would live in the project, and to the purchase of such a large amount of land (needed for a greenbelt).[72]

When the first injunction was denied, the citizens of Franklin Township filed a new one in January in Washington, D.C., against Tugwell himself, retaining Spencer Gordon and Dean Acheson as their attorneys. After charges of bribery against Resettlement Administration officials had added new heat to the controversy, the Court of Appeals of the District of Columbia rendered a decision on May 18, 1936, that seemed to doom the whole Resettlement Administration, as well as the other relief agencies. The court ruled, first of all, that the whole Emergency Relief Act of 1935 was unconstitutional, since in it Congress unlawfully delegated legislative powers to the President by not specifying the actual programs which would be financed by the appropriation under the act. To the court this was "delegation running riot."[73] The Resettlement Administration program was declared in opposition to state rights, since there was no constitutional power for the government to regulate housing or to resettle populations. The court further ruled that the Emergency Relief Act of 1935, even though unconstitutional, did not in "a word or syllable" authorize a policy of resettling destitute or low-income families or of establishing model communities.[74]

The court decision evoked joy in the hearts of all the enemies of Tugwell and the Resettlement Administration. For a few days it seemed as if the decision might doom the Resettlement Administration to the same fate as the Agricultural Adjustment Administration and the National Recovery Administration. One editor exulted that "when the Court of Appeals of the District of Columbia said home building is not a public function, it pretty closely expressed the will

[72] New Brunswick, N.J., *Times,* Nov. 17, 1935.

[73] "Franklin Township vs. Tugwell," in *Federal Reporter* (2d ser., Cases Argued and Determined in the United States Circuit Courts of Appeal, the United States Court of Appeals for the District of Columbia, and the United States Court of Customs and Patent Appeals, St. Paul, 1937), LXXXV, 209.

[74] *Ibid.,* pp. 219–220; "Editorial," *Literary Digest,* CXXI (May 30, 1936), 10.

and desire and thought of the plain people of the nation." [75] On May 19, 1936, one day after the decision, the Attorney General ruled that the decision, despite its sweeping language, applied only to the Greenbrook project, the only one included in the injunction. Tugwell himself withheld comment pending an appeal to the Supreme Court, but stressed the fact that other construction would proceed. The only result of the decision was that the Greenbrook project was discontinued. During the time allowed for an appeal to the Supreme Court, the other greenbelt cities were pushed toward completion. The Resettlement Administration had wisely decided not to risk an appeal to the higher court, but rather surrendered the one project and, perhaps, salvaged the rest of its program. An ironic ending to the Greenbrook story came on July 9, 1936, with the death of Henry Wright, who had been coplanner of Radburn, New Jersey, and who, working for the Resettlement Administration, had lovingly designed his last garden city for the doomed Greenbrook site.[76]

One of the principal reasons for the Greenbrook trouble was the inability of the Resettlement Administration to make payments in lieu of taxes. On the recommendation of Resettlement Administration officials, a corrective bill was introduced in the House by Representative William B. Bankhead of Alabama on May 27, 1936, nine days after the court decision. It not only permitted the Resettlement Administration to make payments to local governments in lieu of taxes but definitely established the state's political, civil, and criminal jurisdiction over Resettlement Administration projects. Complemented by a similar bill in the Senate, the Bankhead bill became law on June 20, 1936, without serious opposition, since it was modeled on similar legislation passed for the Public Works Administration.[77]

In February, 1936, a series of four articles entitled "Utopia Unlimited" appeared in the Washington *Post*. Written by a staff writer, Felix Brunner, this series was a revelation to many people, including some congressmen, and was reprinted in newspapers all over the country. Although Tugwell and many of his individual projects, such

[75] Grand Rapids, Mich., *Herald,* May 25, 1936.
[76] New York *Times,* July 9, 1936.
[77] *C.R.,* 74th Cong., 2d Sess., 1936, pp. 8145, 10596–10597; House Subcommittee of the Committee on Ways and Means, *Hearings on H.R. 12876, Payments in Lieu of Taxes on Resettlement Projects,* 74th Cong., 2d Sess., 1936, pp. 1–2.

as Greenbelt, Maryland, had received much publicity, mainly of a derisive sort, the over-all work of the Resettlement Administration was ill understood. Combining an accurate statement of facts with subtle insinuations, Brunner described what he, perhaps correctly, considered the most far-flung experiment in government paternalism in American history. He pointed out that the executive order creating the Resettlement Administration gave Tugwell unlimited powers. He stressed the immensity and irresponsibility of the Resettlement Administration, correctly listing the number of people in its employ at 13,045. He conveyed an emotional repugnance by the use of such words as "campus houses," "communistic," and "utopian," but the kernel of his attack was his insistence upon the impossibility of limiting or controlling the actions of the Resettlement Administration. It had not been created by Congress. Its too numerous employees were not under civil service. Its huge and expensive program was not the considered objectives of the people or of Congress, but of a few planners, such as Tugwell, who were not responsible to the people's desires and who had radical ideas about "making America over." [78]

Brunner's attack probably isolated the basic weakness of the Resettlement Administration and the one that eventually doomed much of its program. Many aspects of the resettlement program were not based on wide public support, despite the Information Division's attempts to maintain good public relations. Tugwell believed in broad, delegated executive powers which would permit the wide leeway needed by planners and experts. He was disdainful of congressmen, who, to him, all too often failed to represent the best interests of the people they were supposed to serve. He also doubted the efficiency of the slow legislative process, particularly in times of emergency. Thus Tugwell, with his broad authority under the executive order, set up a large administration and initiated an ambitious program without any clear mandate from Congress. The Resettlement Administration was itself legislator and executor. Many of the policy decisions made by the Resettlement Administration staff would never have found majority support in Congress. Tugwell probably realized this. Yet he felt that his staff, much more than Congress, with its con-

[78] Felix Brunner, "Utopia Unlimited," Washington *Post*, Feb. 10, 11, 12, 13, 1936.

flicting interests, knew what the lower third of rural and urban America needed. Thus he set out, in a limited sense, to make America over. He knew it needed remaking, whether it wanted it or not. But just when he had barely begun the task, he began to face opposition from the courts, from the public, and from Congress. As the emergency lessened, Congress once again became jealous of its legislative and policy-making authority and wanted it back. This, in the eyes of many congressmen, meant eventual retribution to an upstart like Tugwell, particularly if Tugwell made some mistakes. Tugwell may have been more nearly right than anyone else. He may have correctly identified his opposition as the instruments of special interests. But, in any case, his program was doomed unless it found favor with a majority of congressmen, for Congress controlled the purse strings.

The most vulnerable aspect of the Resettlement Administration was its communities, regardless of whether they were inherited or initiated by the Resettlement Administration. Congressional disfavor had first appeared in connection with the Post Office venture at Arthurdale, and many congressmen continued to view with alarm any attempts to create industries for the homesteaders. The huge expense of constructing the individual communities provided ammunition for congressmen like Byrd of Virginia. The revelation of Brunner opened the whole administrative organization of the Resettlement Administration to congressional criticism. Representative Roy O. Woodruff of Michigan compared the Resettlement Administration with the Passamaquoddy and shelter-belt projects. He had received a letter from a disgruntled Resettlement Administration official which purported to prove that the Resettlement Administration paid $2,000,000 a month in payrolls to glorified relief clients who were creating a bureaucratic empire for themselves, that 894 men in the Management Division managed nothing, that the Construction Division spent $30,000 a day to build no more than ten houses a month, and that 16,000 employees represented a government within a government. Woodruff, like many other congressmen, blamed the mistakes made at the Matanuska, Alaska, project by the Works Progress Administration on the Resettlement Administration and defined the Resettlement Administration philosophy as one maintaining that, "by shifting people around from where they are to where Dr. Tugwell thinks they ought to be, somehow in the process the subjects of his experimentation will realize the 'more abundant life.' "[79] Woodruff also erroneously stated that Tugwell spent $13,000 in administration for every $2,500 of aid given to the needy. This accusation was similar to many others that tended to identify the Resettlement Administration's activities only with its communities. For example, many people could, and did, point to Tugwell's 13,500 employees in 1936 and then to the less than 4,000 clients in the completed communities, thereby completely ignoring the vast rehabilitation program which required the largest number of personnel and distributed the largest share of the funds. But the critics of the Resettlement Administration did have one factual point of criticism. To May, 1936, the end of its first full year of operation, the Resettlement Administration spent or obligated $205,000,000. Of this $23,000,000 went for administrative expenses, or more than 10 per cent, which was not an enviable record. The large administrative costs were defended by the Resettlement Administration officials as necessary to initiate a new and complicated program.[80]

Senator W. Warren Barbour of New Jersey became one of the most consistent critics of the Resettlement Administration, particularly because of mistakes made at Jersey Homesteads. At the time of the legal snarl over the Greenbrook project, he led a campaign in the Senate for a congressional investigation of Tugwell's agency. On March 11, 1936, he introduced a resolution which called for an investigation of the nature and extent of the Resettlement Administration's expenditures, the nature and extent of its projects already undertaken and the advisability of future projects, the effect of projects on state and local taxing units and on real estate values, the extent to which such projects benefited labor, and the circumstances relating to the selection of tenants and purchasers, as well as the effect on these people selected. Although this resolution was tabled by a vote of 32 to 30, Barbour continued his attack. Using arguments supplied by Felix Brunner, he emphasized the enormous size of the Resettlement Administration, with its sixteen divisions, its twenty-seven buildings, its own telephone exchange, and its large personnel. He particularly stressed its irresponsibility to Congress. To enable Congress to obtain the inside information on such a large program existing

[79] *C.R.*, 74th Cong., 2d Sess., 1936, pp. 6110–6111.
[80] *Hearings on Payments in Lieu of Taxes*, pp. 6–7.

without law, Barbour secured the acceptance of a resolution asking, not for a congressional investigation, but for the Resettlement Administration to provide the Senate with a full account of its work. Tugwell already had the report about ready and submitted it on May 12, 1936.[81]

The Resettlement Administration had congressional friends as well as enemies. Its rehabilitation programs were widely praised. Representative Fred H. Hildebrandt of South Dakota praised Tugwell and asked why not "make America over." He believed it was needed.[82] Representative Maury Maverick of Texas, who knew Tugwell personally, sympathized with him, since he believed that Tugwell had received more unjust criticism than any other person in Washington. He declared that Tugwell was not a "wild man from Moscow" and that he had tackled an unappreciated and tremendously difficult task in forming a new organization to handle four separate and tough jobs. He also defended the administrative organization of the Resettlement Administration, which, according to Maverick, followed civil service salary scales and was just a step below the Tennessee Valley Authority in efficiency.[83] In the Senate, Robert La Follette declared that history would judge the Resettlement Administration favorably, even though fun had been "poked at this program of resettlement by those too stupid or too blind to care about the future." [84]

In May, 1936, the Senate, in debating a deficiency appropriation bill, defeated by a vote of 38 to 28 an Appropriations Committee amendment to the Resettlement Administration section of the appropriation which substituted "loans" for "rural rehabilitation." [85] This defeated what was clearly an early attempt to limit the Resettlement Administration's activities to loans. The 1936 deficiency appropriation did not continue the Resettlement Administration's right to purchase land, although this right, granted by Roosevelt under the 1935 relief act, continued until 1937.[86] These expressions of congressional displeasure were contemporaneous with the court opinion about the Greenbrook project. As a result the Resettlement Administration,

[81] C.R., 74th Cong., 2d Sess., 1936, pp. 3547, 6194, 6264–6267, 7141. The report was contained in U.S. Senate, *Resettlement Administration Program*, Document no. 213, 74th Cong., 2d Sess., 1936.
[82] C.R., 74th Cong., 2d Sess., 1936, p. 3716. [83] *Ibid.*, pp. 4068–4070.
[84] *Ibid.*, pp. 8184–8185, 8187. [85] *Ibid.*, pp. 8184–8185, 8202.
[86] *Hearings on the Agricultural Appropriation Bill for 1938*, p. 1191.

in September, 1936, announced the curtailment of its community program to projects already planned, which, in light of the large number in the planning and early construction stages, meant very little except that no more project plans would be accepted from the regional offices.[87] Both Tugwell personally and the resettlement communities were objects of attack in the election of 1936. As early as March, 1936, the Republican National Committee had declared that the Resettlement Administration was setting up communist farms.[88]

By election time it was rumored that the Resettlement Administration would soon be absorbed by the Department of Agriculture. Tugwell, already planning his resignation from government service, desired a more permanent status for his Resettlement Administration and had been urging Roosevelt to place it in the Department of Agriculture, a move that would have been in line with Roosevelt's desire to consolidate many of the New Deal agencies. On the other hand, many Department of Agriculture officials were fearful of the move, seeing a possibility of another feud between the right and left wings within the department. Wallace was definitely undecided whether or not to accept and continue the resettlement program. In November, Roosevelt, following up many of Tugwell's suggestions about tenure and tenancy and in recognition of a tenant-purchase bill already introduced into Congress by Senator John H. Bankhead, appointed a special committee on farm tenancy to make a national study of the problem. Wallace and Tugwell were both on the committee, Wallace as chairman. Just after the announcement of the formation of the committee, Wallace and Tugwell left for an important tour of the South, both to inspect the Resettlement Administration program and to study the tenancy situation. It was Wallace's first trip to the area and proved to be a very educational one. Wallace was visibly stirred by some of the poverty and exploitation. Long before the trip was over, he was completely convinced of the need for a continued Resettlement Administration. He announced that the Resettlement Administration, which had done a "really marvelous job," would probably become a part of the permanent program of the Department of Agriculture. This was a notable victory for Tugwell.[89]

[87] Washington *Post,* Sept. 2, 1936.
[88] New York *Herald Tribune,* March 31, 1936.
[89] New York *Times,* Nov. 14, 1936, p. 3; Nov. 18, p. 1; Nov. 26, p. 36.

Meanwhile, just as the tour began, Tugwell announced his intention of retiring from government service in order—of all things for an avowed enemy of business—to join two of his friends, Charles W. Taussig and Adolf A. Berle, Jr., in the molasses business. Tugwell then gave only personal reasons for his resignation, although there was much speculation in Washington about the old feud within the Department of Agriculture between liberals and conservatives, about Tugwell's seemingly indiscreet statements in the recent political campaign, and about his long-time role as "whipping boy" in the Department of Agriculture and even for the whole New Deal. Years later Tugwell hinted that it was really Roosevelt who desired his resignation, not for personal reasons but for political expediency.[90] In any case, Tugwell left as a friend. His resignation from both the Resettlement Administration and the Department of Agriculture became effective on December 31, 1936, at which time his beloved Resettlement Administration, by an executive order, became part of the Department of Agriculture. Dr. Will W. Alexander became Tugwell's handpicked successor as Administrator of the Resettlement Administration. One colleague aptly remarked that the Department of Agriculture "was a somewhat duller but more peaceful place with Tugwell gone."[91]

After its transfer to the Department of Agriculture, the Resettlement Administration's community-building program was slowly revised. A greater emphasis was placed on the infiltration type of resettlement. Experimentation in construction was replaced by standard designs. It was decided that construction efforts would be centered on the completion of projects already under way. Planning activities gave place to community-management problems, with the Management Division absorbing the Rural Resettlement and Special Skills Divisions. This conformed to the expressed desire of the Senate, which almost (by a vote of 36 to 42) deducted $14,000,000 from the 1937 Resettlement Administration appropriation in order to show its desire to have all old projects completed before new ones were started. The Senate also threatened to remove $1,000,000 from the appropriation for administrative expenses of the Resettlement Administration in order

---

[90] Rexford G. Tugwell, *The Democratic Roosevelt* (Garden City, N.Y., 1957), p. 547.

[91] New York *Times*, Nov. 19, 1936, p. 1, and Nov. 26, 1936, p. 36; Lord, *Wallaces of Iowa*, p. 462.

to show its disapproval of administrative expenses that often ran as high as 18 per cent of the total budget and its displeasure at high construction costs, which sometimes totaled as much as $14,750 for each homestead unit. With the 1937 appropriation, the Resettlement Administration had received $536,000,000 since its inception. This provoked Representative Robert F. Rich of Pennsylvania to call it the most costly experimentation in American history, approaching a "national scandal." [92]

In the New Deal the lowly tenant farmer became the subject of a nation's attention. The problem of tenancy, more than any other, united urban liberals and Jeffersonian purists, for both could agree on the seriousness of the malady if not on the remedy for it. As early as 1935 a bill involving an appropriation of $1,000,000,000 for tenant purchase passed in the Senate, only to die in the House. In 1936 Roosevelt appointed his special Presidential Committee on Farm Tenancy, which included, in addition to Wallace and Tugwell, many of America's foremost agricultural leaders.[93] The committee made a gloomy report in February, 1937. Two out of every five farmers in the United States were tenants; fully one-half of all farmers were insecure in their tenure. The submerged groups of farmers were losing incentive, and an old American ideal was rapidly passing. Rigid class lines were forming as the normal democratic processes broke down in rural areas. Only the assumption of responsibility by the federal government could reverse the trend.[94]

As an answer to the problem of tenancy and rural insecurity, the committee endorsed the beginning work of the Resettlement Administration, but asked for an expanded organization within the Department of Agriculture to be called the Farm Security Administration. The new agency would continue land retirement, resettlement, and rehabilitation, but would also purchase land and sell it to qualified tenants under long purchase terms. Sale would only follow a trial lease, and no title would be granted until after the first twenty years of a forty-year purchase contract. Repayment would be based on crop yields. As experiments, it recommended some government

[92] *C.R.*, 75th Cong., 1st Sess., 1937, pp. 637, 678, 681, 687, 6819–6820.

[93] "Report of the President's Committee on Farm Tenancy," in U.S. House of Representatives, *Activities of the Farm Security Administration*, Report no. 1430, 78th Cong., 2d Sess., 1944, pp. 89–90.

[94] *Ibid.*, pp. 70–75.

leasing of land and a few collective farms. But in the main it asked for ultimate fee simple ownership of family-sized individual farms, whose basic economic disadvantages could be overcome by co-operative ownership of heavy machinery and breeding stock. To retard speculation in land it recommended a capital-gains tax on any profit made on land for the first three years after purchase.[95]

In Congress the best eloquence of the politicians was called upon to defend the small farmer and home ownership. Representative William B. Bankhead of Alabama went to great lengths to picture the desperate plight of the farm tenant, of a "desolate, hopeless, dejected man, working some other man's property, pillaging it, despoiling its rich resources by virtue of the fact that it is not his." Then, after a fitting quotation from "The Man with the Hoe," he asked: "Do you own a farm, do you own a lot in the city, have you fee-simple title to your own property? Subconsciously the satisfaction is great to go out on your own acres, on your own land, put your feet down upon it, look up into the sky and say this, thank God, this little bit is mine." Now Congress had an opportunity to allow tenants to "put off the sackcloth and ashes that they have worn for so many years with an inferiority complex and stand up and look into the face of the sun and their Creator and say, 'By the generous grace of a sympathetic Government I am being given another opportunity to prove "the mettle of my pasture." ' "[96]

Actually, despite its obvious concern, Congress showed no inclination to enact the far-reaching reforms and experiments advocated by the Committee on Farm Tenancy. In 1937, Senator John H. Bankhead of Alabama introduced a bill to alleviate tenancy through land purchase by a federal corporation which, in turn, was to lease or sell land to tenants under a supervised program. In the House, Representative Marvin Jones of Texas introduced a comprehensive farm tenancy bill which provided for direct land-purchase loans to tenant farmers and, in addition, continued, in a limited form, the rehabilitation and submarginal-land programs of the Resettlement Administration, although the resettlement communities were repudiated.[97] The members of the House, including Marvin Jones, were very fearful of bureaucratic centralization and thus tried to eliminate any supervisory

[95] *Ibid.*, pp. 76–82.   [96] *C.R.*, 75th Cong., 1st Sess., 1937, p. 6453.
[97] *Ibid.*, pp. 6433–6435, 6663–6665.

program in connection with tenant purchase. In fact, they specifically forbade land purchase by the Department of Agriculture in connection with the program. The Senate, more nearly following the recommendations of the Committee on Farm Tenancy and less fearful of bureaucracy, desired a governmental agency, somewhat like the Resettlement Administration, to purchase land and supervise the tenant purchasers, thus lessening failures and eliminating speculation. The Senate bill passed by voice vote, the House bill by a vote of 308 to 25, illustrating the near unanimity of approval. In conference the major provisions of the House bill were adopted, since the House conferees were bound by their colleagues to stand firm for direct loans to tenants. The Senate's desire for supervision and protection was embodied in a five-year prohibition against sale on the part of a tenant purchaser. The combined bill, now named the Bankhead-Jones Farm Tenant Act, passed both houses of Congress by voice vote in July, 1937. It provided for a Farmers' Home Corporation which was to lend money to a limited number of tenant farmers selected by county committees. The program was to be administered by the Secretary of Agriculture, who was authorized to lend $10,000,000 the first year, $25,000,000 the second, and $50,000,000 thereafter.[98]

The tenant-purchase program authorized by the Bankhead-Jones Act had a close relationship to the Resettlement Administration program. It dealt with the lowly class of farmers and continued a limited tenant-purchase program already tried by the Resettlement Administration in the South. Included in the Bankhead-Jones Act were sections which gave the first specific congressional mandate for aspects of the Resettlement Administration program. Special provisions continued the rehabilitation and land-purchase programs, although no money was appropriated for rehabilitation. A small but important section defined the congressional attitude toward the resettlement communities and the land-development projects. The Secretary of Agriculture was authorized to continue to perform such functions vested in him by executive orders as "shall be necessary *only for the completion* [italics mine] and administration of those resettlement projects, rural rehabilitation projects for resettlement purposes, and land development and land utilization projects." [99] At last Congress

[98] *Ibid.*, pp. 6582, 6762, 6853, 7133–7144.   [99] *Ibid.*, p. 7135.

America Resettled 185

had spoken, and clearly. It had repudiated any further experimentation in community building.

On September 1, 1937, Henry A. Wallace, following the recommendations of the committee on tenancy as much as or more than the Bankhead-Jones Act, established the Farm Security Administration to carry out the tenant-purchase program. The authorized Farmers' Home Corporation was established, as Congress had provided, but became only a legal fiction. The Farm Security Administration absorbed the Resettlement Administration or, in actuality, was the Resettlement Administration under a new name, for the personnel remained unchanged. At the same time the Land Utilization Division of the Resettlement Administration was returned to its old home, the Bureau of Agricultural Economics. The Farm Security Administration continued the resettlement communities without any major changes in policy. By this time the communities were a minor part of the farm security program, but an ever more embarrassing part because of their increasing unpopularity in Congress.

By June, 1937, the Resettlement Administration had completed the construction of only thirty-eight communities, while eighty-four projects, including communities and scattered farms, were under construction. Only 4,441 families were in residence.[100] As mentioned before, the Farm Security Administration completed all this construction. In doing this it often added more land to projects. Although the community program was already in an eclipse, heading toward completion rather than expansion, the all-important task of managing the completed communities had only well begun. The tremendous task of disposing of the completed communities, of "getting the government out of the real estate business," was still far in the future. But Tugwell's Resettlement Administration, born in a burst of idealism and enthusiasm, was no more. America remained largely unchanged, but not quite.

---

[100] Department of Agriculture, Resettlement Administration, *Report of the Administrator of the Resettlement Administration, 1937* (The second annual report of the Resettlement Administration; Washingon, 1937), pp. 14–15.

⊁ VIII ⊀

The Community as a Locale for a New Society

WHEN a simple farmer, wide-eyed with wonder and expectancy, or a hardened, cynical, suspicious coal miner, so inured to hardship and struggle as to expect only more of the same, moved into a glittering new subsistence homesteads or resettlement community, he was entering a social show window. Willingly or unwillingly, knowingly or unknowingly, he was a human mannequin in a great exhibit, for the many architects of the New Deal communities, despite varying philosophies, were all striving to create, within the conducive environment of their planned villages, a new society, with altered values and new institutions. The new society would, of course, be a "better" society, with "better" necessarily defined by the architects themselves. The communities, always on exhibit, were to demonstrate and advertise the new society to the rest of mankind. Planned by social scientists, financed by the vast resources of the government, they were to be visual signposts pointing to the future. But a community is made up of people, and people are not so easily molded to a new pattern. The social planners realized this and devoted much time and effort to turning a physical reality, land and streets and houses, into a true community, with an enlightened and co-operative people.

The community building actually began before the modern homesteaders moved into their new homes, for the decisive element in the

Locale for a New Society

success of the new community was the people selected as settlers. In order to screen the large number of applicants for homesteads, the Resettlement Administration set up a much more elaborate selection organization than had the Division of Subsistence Homesteads. In the area near each project or group of projects the Resettlement Administration sent a regional chief of family selection, who was assisted by senior and junior family-selection specialists, all trained and experienced social workers. Utilizing field invesitgators and the best casework procedure, the social worker thoroughly investigated each applicant. References were required; the applicants were visited by social workers, and questionnaires covering every aspect of the applicant's life were carefully filled out. Before final selection the applicant often had to undergo a physical examination. This thorough investigation provoked criticism, for some people alleged that the Resettlement Administration was violating civil rights in so intimately exploring the private affairs of its clients. Among the varying criteria used for selection were age, health, economic stability, character, and number of children in the family.[1]

One selection criterion was, of course, that the family selected be from a low-income group. For the suburban projects the Resettlement Administration tried to maintain an upper salary limit of $1,600. The rural clients, almost always from an even lower economic level, were either refugees from land-retirement projects, deserving tenant farmers, successful rehabilitation clients, or young people desiring to enter farming. Since the rigid screening system seemed likely to insure an industrious and intelligent group of homesteaders, many people claimed that the communities could prove very little about a better way of life, for the clients were of such caliber that they would be successful in an environment that gave them any opportunities at all. Actually the Resettlement Administration clients were not as exceptional as the screening process would indicate. Even though the most obvious undesirables were excluded, many homesteaders lacked industry and some contentious ones gave the Resettlement Administra-

[1] John B. Holt, *An Analysis of Methods and Criteria Used in Selecting Families for Colonization Projects* (Social Research Report no. 1 of the United States Department of Agriculture, Farm Security Administration and the Bureau of Agricultural Economics; Washington, 1937), pp. 44–50; Paul W. Wager, *One Foot on the Soil: A Study of Subsistence Homesteads in Alabama* (Bureau of Public Administration at the University of Alabama, 1945), p. 40.

tion nothing but trouble. A survey of resettlement communities disclosed an average family of 5.2 people, with the average husband aged 37.3 and the wife 33.3. The average educational attainment of the husband was 7.2 grades, of the wife 8.1 grades.[2]

When a resettlement client moved into a new community, sometimes from a share cropper's hut or a tenement house in a slum district, he was moving into a new world, with a standard of living heretofore hardly dreamed of by anyone in his economic status. His new home had often cost as high as $5,000 or $6,000; his farm or subsistence plot and the outbuildings had cost up to $4,000 more. If he were in a suburban community or greenbelt city the streets, sewage disposal plants, water systems, and community facilities had cost equally as much. Even granting that all those facilities were turned over to the homesteader without any cost or any obligation for repayment—and they were not—the settler was still left in a situation that required a larger income than in the past. Taxes were higher; maintenance was increased; an electric bill, perhaps a phone bill, and probably a larger heating bill were added to his expenses. This new standard of living, beyond the fact that it required tremendous social adjustments on the part of many homesteaders, raised the problem of possible economic failure. Was there any reason to hope that a group of Alabama Negro tenants, suddenly placed in new homes at Gee's Bend community, would be able to enjoy their new status by farming their same old cotton farms? What magic ingredient could be added to a small group of family-sized farms and immediately double or even triple their earning power? Whatever the magic was, it had to be supplied by the Resettlement Administration.

The problem of economic opportunities plagued the whole New Deal community program. As mentioned before, the stranded communities were planned without a sufficient economic base and suffered thereafter because of this lack. The suburban communities, and particularly the greenbelt cities, were located near enough to industrial employment to eliminate any employment problems, but the low-income families could not repay the government for its investment in what turned out to be rather expensive housing. They could, and

[2] Calvin B. Baldwin, "Farm Security Administration's Sixth Year in Rural Housing," *Housing Yearbook, 1941* (Chicago: National Association of Housing Officials, 1941), pp. 262–263.

Locale for a New Society

did, afford to live in and maintain their new communities. The industrial-type subsistence homesteads, located between industry and agriculture, were ideally situated for economical living, but not unless the subsistence plots were intensively utilized. This placed on the Resettlement Administration the task of educating the homesteaders in gardening and home production. The all-rural communities, planned for full-time agriculture, were really testing grounds for American small-farm agriculture. They were to indicate, in many cases, that either the standard of living set by the Resettlement Administration was higher than a family-based agriculture could support in the years from 1936 to 1941 or that the Resettlement Administration and the Farm Security Administration, in the planning and supervision of projects, caused economic failure, for most of the rural projects did not provide a net profit during these years, let alone permit any repayment to the government.

The magic ingredients that the Resettlement Administration proposed to add to the rural and semirural communities were two: co-operation and expert supervision. It was felt that a group of small farmers, or even a group of subsistence farmers, could reap the economic benefits of a large, highly efficient commercial farm by more socialization or by co-operation. For example, heavy machinery, utterly impractical for one small farmer, could be owned by the farmers of a whole community. Procurement of supplies, processing of products, and marketing could be done co-operatively and, therefore, with all the efficiency of a large commercial farm. The vast efforts in co-operative endeavors will be considered in later paragraphs.

The Resettlement Administration's whole rehabilitation and rural resettlement program was keyed to the extensive supervision of its clients. For the subsistence homesteads communities this meant home economists to teach canning and food processing and agricultural advisers to teach gardening and small, subsistence farming. On the all-rural projects it meant that farm and home experts were responsible for the whole economy of the project. Working from the Economic Development Section of the Management Division, at least one home economist was placed in each major community.[3] A farm management expert was present in every rural or semirural community. Each

[3] Rena B. Maycock, "Home Economic Work in the Resettlement Administration," *Journal of Home Economics*, XXVIII (1936), 560–561.

family on a rural project was required to work out complete farm and home plans for each crop year and to keep itemized records. Under the guidance of experts, the farmers planned for the home production of foods, for diversified crop and livestock programs for market production, and for practices promoting soil fertility. These plans were detailed, often including itemized budgets of all expenditures for the year. Beginning in 1937 the homesteaders in rural communities were allowed to receive government loans for their yearly needs.[4] In the South this put the Resettlement Administration in the position of the landlords and furnishing merchants of the past. Since the crops were a lien on the loan, the loan itself became an instrument for rigidly enforcing the home and farm plans prepared by the supervisory personnel. On some projects the project manager or farm adviser had joint bank accounts with the individual homesteaders, which meant that the penniless homesteader, dependent upon the government loan which had been placed in the bank for him, could not spend a penny without his supervisor's approval and signature. This close supervision led to the criticism that the Resettlement Administration or Farm Security Administration was destroying all initiative through paternalism. The Resettlement Administration early defended supervision as a means of increasing initiative through economic independence and of educating the less capable farmers.[5]

The task of a farm adviser was not an easy one. Although an expert, he was not able to work miracles, such as bringing rains when they were needed or raising farm prices to the level of 1919. Perhaps his problems are best revealed in the following unguarded reflections of a Resettlement Administration official who was attempting to devise farm plans for a new project in Michigan, but who was very fearful that a practical farm program would never repay the high building costs of the community:

Many times have I completed this vicious circle the past year. Although it is possible to prove most anything by figures my conscience is not so heavily seared but what I can see lurking behind the trees in these plans the grimacing outlines of old man weather, the always questionable management

[4] U.S. Department of Agriculture, Farm Security Administration, *Report of the Administrator of the FSA, 1940* (Washington, 1940), pp. 4–5; Resettlement Administration, "Management News," Feb. 15, 1937, mimeographed, R.G. 96, National Archives.

[5] Resettlement Administration, *First Annual Report* (Washington, 1936), p. 38.

efficiency of some of our clients, the minimum standards of living, the hazard in harnessing the human factor in a harmonious life on some of the socialized or semi-socialized plans for our project. Less foreboding than the above I see future goblins waiting for their opportunity to save mankind with their utopias. In this group are the sociologists with the guinea pig complexes, the town planners and the engineers with an earnest desire to build their monuments before death and the architects and landscape architects with their esthetic tastes so necessary to their profession. Old man red tape and old lady bureaucracy are flirting in the shadows but seem little disturbed about our present plan or my dream. They realize they will exact their pound of flesh on any plan we present.[6]

Several communities were provided with special educational facilities. In almost every community some educational activities were sponsored by the managing agencies. On the adult level the work of the home and farm supervisors, of co-operative specialists, of local extension and vocational agriculture teachers, and of specialists in handicrafts and skills represented forms of education. For the children, most isolated or large communities included project schools. Beginning under the Division of Subsistence Homesteads, a special experiment in vocational and progressive education was carried out at Arthurdale in specially constructed school buildings and under the sponsorship of several of America's leading educators, including John Dewey. The educational facilities at Arthurdale, for both adults and children, formed the center of the community activities. The Division of Subsistence Homesteads and the Resettlement Administration, in the rural and subsistence homesteads projects, erected thirty-two combination school and community buildings, nine school buildings, and twelve teachers' homes.[7] Each of the greenbelt cities had combination schools and community buildings. Although, with the exception of a short period at Arthurdale, these schools were public and operated by local governments, the Resettlement Administration exerted an influence on their operation, not only by owning the building but in helping to select teachers. In at least one community a part-time Resettlement Administration employee was also principal of the combined project and county school.

[6] Merton L. Wright to A. C. Lytle, Dec. 24, 1936, R.G. 16, National Archives.
[7] F. C. Howe to Rexford G. Tugwell, May 17, 1935, R.G. 96, National Archives; U.S. Department of Agriculture, Farm Security Administration, *Report of the Administrator of FSA, 1938* (Washington, 1938), p. 17.

A new society requires a new education. In the thirties the new type of education was progressive education, which seemed ideally suited for the transition from a competitive to a co-operative society. Dr. Morris R. Mitchell, a former member of the Advisory Committee of the Progressive Education Association, was appointed Chief Educational Specialist of the Resettlement Administration.[8] The result was that progressive education was introduced into several project schools, usually with the assistance and approval of county school superintendents or the state colleges of education. As an example of a typical progressive school, the daily schedule at the Pine Mountain Valley school included group work along developed lines of interest and outdoor activity in the morning, an hour of academic drill after a very early lunch, and then a discussion of the day's work and the planning of the next day's program. Before disbanding at 1:05 P.M. for informal activity, the children usually elected to sing a few songs.[9]

This aspect of a new society, like several others, was not always well received by the homesteaders. At Penderlea a young principal, just out of Teachers College, Columbia University, attempted to establish as the "center of the homestead community," an "experimental progressive school," which departed in "its every unit from the standard school curriculum and class division." In the midst of a rural community which had no former association "with this educational tradition," his "enthusiasm for the educational ideas in which he was trained appear to have led him from time to time to present his views more vigorously and in a light more advanced than was acceptable to a proportion of the patrons of the school." [10] Despite the wishes of the Resettlement Administration, he was dismissed by the county. At Cherry Lake Farms the new education proved hard to inaugurate, even for the children, but an enterprising teacher "took hold of a query about the dairy," which led her and her pupils into a fascinating "exploration around the dairy." They also visited the construction of a community building and were "having the time of their life," according to a visitor.[11]

In 1938 the rural communities of the Farm Security Administration

---

[8] W. W. Alexander to Erwin H. Sasman, Jan. 7, 1937, R.G. 96, National Archives.
[9] Plan of Operation for Pine Mountain Valley School, 1935, *ibid.*
[10] Memorandum from George Mitchell to R. S. Ryan, May 3, 1938, *ibid.*
[11] A report by C. B. Loomis, Jan. 31, 1936, *ibid.*

included fifty-eight community or combined community and school buildings. These community buildings became a near must for any community. They were the locale for meetings of co-operative associations, clubs, social groups, parent-teacher associations, and religious groups; they were used for dances, weekly movies, plays, lectures, and recreation. They indicated the social planners' desires to influence not only the economic and educational life of its community clients, but their social life as well. One of the primary wishes of many of the people connected with the communities was that communities foster neighborliness, co-operation, and group activity. A mark of success in a community was the number of social organizations, preferably of an educational variety. One of the principal arguments for communities rather than individual settlement was the belief that the individualistic American farmers, so long isolated on their farmsteads, lacked the social advantages of city dwellers or of European farmers. The planners believed that community activities could enrich the life of the farmer. The community buildings were criticized because they seemed to be attempts to isolate and separate the communities from the area in which they were located or because they indicated an attempt to tell people how to organize their social life when no expert had the right to do this. In many communities the community building was either not wanted or seldom used. At Austin Homesteads the homesteaders, who organized their social life around activities in the nearby town, did not want their community building and, rather than maintain it, considered giving it to the city of Austin.[12]

One of the most interesting aspects of the New Deal communities was the fervent attempt to revive handicrafts, such as weaving, woodworking, and metalwork. In the early days of the Division of Subsistence Homesteads, many people, including M. L. Wilson, Eleanor Roosevelt, and Clarence Pickett, believed that a revival of these handicrafts could provide part of the income of subsistence farmers, could invoke a community spirit, and could lead to a restored pride in workmanship, a pride that seemed so lacking in assembly-line America. The impetus to crafts came from the work of the American Friends Service Committee in the coal-mining areas. Even before

---

[12] Russell Lord and Paul H. Johnstone, eds., *A Place on Earth: A Critical Appraisal of Subsistence Homesteads* (Washington, 1942), pp. 61, 195.

the subsistence homesteads program began, a group of miners near Morgantown, West Virginia, had established a Mountaineer Craftsmen's Co-operative Association for chair manufacturing, cabinetwork, weaving, pewter ware, and metalwork.[13] With the construction of Arthurdale the association moved to a new factory provided for it by the Division of Subsistence Homesteads. From an economic standpoint the Arthurdale venture, which provided employment for several men and women, was more successful than handicraft industries on other projects.

As the subsistence homesteads communities were completed, the women were encouraged and instructed in weaving. The Quakers continued to assist in the program, with a couple accepting a homestead at Arthurdale for the express purpose of teaching weaving. With the creation of the Resettlement Administration a Special Skills Division was organized to carry on, among other duties, the handicraft program. Probably for the first time in history, government employees traveled about the country with titles such as Associate Adviser in Weaving or Assistant Adviser in Woodworking. Surveys were made of stones, clays, sands, and tools. In Region I, which included New England and the area as far south as Maryland, a routine survey of arts and crafts among resettlement clients became, under a regional enthusiast, a survey by questionnaire of every artist and craftsman in the region. Tugwell, recognizing that this went far beyond the scope of the Resettlement Administration, tried to halt the survey but could not until several cubic feet of records were accumulated.[14]

Under the handicraft program looms were set up in most communities. Since the program did not usually yield appreciable economic returns, it was continued largely as a recreational or aesthetic program. Although the Special Skills Division was disbanded soon after the Resettlement Administration went to the Department of Agriculture, a limited number of enthusiastic employees continued the handicraft program, traveling from community to community, loom to loom. As late as 1940, in the "Monthly Report on Weaving," a fieldworker reported a trip of project women to Gatlinburg, Ten-

---

[13] Clarence E. Pickett, *For More than Bread* (Boston, 1953), pp. 32–35.
[14] Grace E. Falke to George S. Mitchell, Sept. 19, 1936, R.G. 96, National Archives; Grace E. Falke to Dorothy M. Beck, Sept. 25, 1936, *ibid.;* Tugwell to D. M. Beck, n.d., *ibid.*

Locale for a New Society

nessee, to observe the craft manufacturing there. One devoted teacher of weaving had only two women come to her class on a cold winter's day. When one of the two women had the initiative to suggest a name for the small group of two, the instructoress exclaimed in an ecstasy of joy: "To hear that come from them and not me was truly delightful!!"[15] Of such enthusiasm was the whole handicraft program forged. In 1942 only three lone, traveling instructors continued the program.[16]

The Special Skills Division, organized in August, 1935, was also responsible for much of the recreation and cultural needs of the community. It was to furnish teachers in the fields of fine and applied arts and, more than that, was to produce paintings, sculpture, and other art material for the communities. It was housed in a single unit that contained workshops and laboratories. Much of its time was required for administrative duties, such as work with publications and exhibits, but its enthusiastic director, Adrian J. Dornbush, was most interested in providing special services for the projects. Under his organization there were the following units: landscaping, music, sculpture, painting, ceramics, dramatics, weaving, wood- and metalwork, research, records, furniture design, and general services. Included on his staff were Mary La Follette, daughter of Robert La Follette; Elizabeth Hofflin, interior planning expert on the faculty of Columbia University; Henry La Cognina, an Italian woodworking specialist; and Otto Wester, a metal designer who had sculptured with Norman Bel Geddes.[17]

Dornbush's greatest difficulties were in securing sufficient money to carry out his program and in establishing any clear jurisdiction for his division. He was particularly interested in rural and folk music and wanted to set up a special program to gather and record folk music, but could not secure funds. Jurisdictionally he was threatened by Rural Resettlement, which made furniture, by the Education and Training Section, which was inclined to teach in the field of art, and by the Economic Development Section, which, in encouraging economic developments, often included needlework and handicrafts. On

---

[15] Susan R. Christian, "Monthly Report on Weaving," Nov., 1940, *ibid.*

[16] Doris M. Porter to Mason Barr, Aug. 15, 1942, *ibid.*

[17] Adrian J. Dornbush to Allen Eston, Aug. 12, 1935, and Dornbush to Units and Section Heads, Oct. 13, 1936, *ibid.*

the other hand, Dornbush balked at including "the fattening of calves" as either an art or a craft.[18]

In the creation of the new society the Special Skills Division had a large share of the responsibility. It designed most of the "simple and substantial" furniture and set up demonstration houses at each project in order to show the homesteaders the best arrangements and to impress visitors to the projects. It advised the architects and engineers on house designs, decorative sculpture, flagpoles, and the playground. It planned the curtains, rugs, and upholstery for the homes. Its painters provided murals for community houses and recorded in paintings the progress of the different projects. The following "inspiring" paintings were made during the construction of Greenbelt, Maryland, for later display in the completed town: "Pouring Concrete," "Constructing Sewers," "Concrete Mixer," and "Shovel at Work." [19] Mary La Follette directed a dramatic program, scouring the country in order to collect a library of rural plays. A playwright, Margaret Valiant, wrote a play, "New Wine," which was first produced in resettlement communities and which, while receiving many favorable comments, was described as "good propaganda" for the Resettlement Administration. Yet much of the program had to be carried out with the assistance of other agencies. Since the Works Progress Administration directed the large Federal Arts Project, Henry A. Wallace personally asked Hopkins for the use of Works Progress Administration artists for decorating the Resettlement Administration's public and community buildings. Dornbush had a written agreement from the Works Progress Administration Recreational Division to provide personnel to resettlement communities whenever possible. The Federal Theatre and Music Division also agreed to co-operate with the Resettlement Administration. The Civilian Conservation Corps constructed looms and benches.[20]

In the attempt to create a new society, each of the sponsoring agencies devoted special attention to health and medicine. But since the new society was to be based on the community rather than the

---

[18] Dornbush to Grace E. Falke, Nov. 27, 1935, and Dornbush to E. E. Agger, Oct. 17, 1935, *ibid.*

[19] Dornbush to John Lansill, Feb. 9, 1937, *ibid.*

[20] William P. Farnsworth to Dorthea T. Lynch, Sept. 22, 1936, *ibid.;* Wallace to Hopkins, April 6, 1937, R.G. 16, National Archives; Dornbush to Major John O. Walker, June 23, 1937, R.G. 96, National Archives.

Locale for a New Society 197

individual, there had to be significant alterations in medical practices. Dr. William E. Zeuch, Co-operative Specialist in the Division of Subsistence Homesteads, suggested the establishment of co-operative infirmaries on large projects as the first step toward socialized medicine.[21] At Arthurdale the Division of Subsistence Homesteads paid the wages of a community nurse, and the American Friends Service Committee supported a project physician. At Dyess Colony, Arkansas, the Federal Emergency Relief Administration constructed a full-sized hospital which was operated by a co-operative association.

On the establishment of the Resettlement Administration a Public Health Section was created, with a medical officer borrowed from the United States Public Health Service at its head. It immediately correlated the construction program with state and local health ordinances and tried to insure sanitary sewage disposal, safe drinking water, and decent housing. On approval from the legal section, it attempted to place in each community project a public health nurse who, if possible, worked with the county health departments. It also recommended that small health centers, with offices for physicians and nurses, be included in plans for all future projects. In completed projects existing buildings or homes were used for medical clinics. The Resettlement Administration and the Farm Security Administration constructed fourteen health centers in their communities.[22]

The main problem faced by the Resettlement Administration medical personnel was how to provide adequate medical and dental care for fees that its low-income clients could afford to pay. This was a problem not only in the projects but for the whole rehabilitation program. Obviously health was an important element both in rehabilitation and in the ability of a client to repay his loan. A plan emerged in 1936. Co-operative medical associations were set up both in projects and in rural counties all over the country, always with the approval of local and state medical societies. The Resettlement Administration acted as an intermediary, drawing up a set of memoranda with state medical societies and lending money to the locally organized co-operatives. This was the first time the government had supported

---

[21] William E. Zeuch to Leroy Peterson, Aug. 2, 1935, R.G. 96, National Archives.
[22] Resettlement Administration, *First Annual Report*, pp. 93–94; Farm Security Administration, *Annual Report of the Administrator of FSA, 1938*, p. 17.

group medicine. Under the typical plan, the homesteader or rehabilitation client paid a monthly fee of approximately two dollars into a group fund. For this payment he received all his medical services. In a few cases similar dental associations were formed. Where the association included the rehabilitation clients for a whole county, any co-operating physician could be utilized by the Resettlement Administration client. The physicians were permitted to set their own fees without any type of interference from the Resettlement Administration. In the communities, where there were usually clinics and either part-time or full-time physicians, the members of the community medical association had to pay slightly higher fees and received better service. They could attend regular clinics or, in emergencies, call their doctor to their homes. Since the project physician was paid a set salary, the community association could assess set fees, whereas county associations often had to raise their fees because of deficiencies in funds. By 1941 over 100,000 families were included in the Farm Security Administration medical program.[23]

The group medical program was considered a success in most instances. There were reported cases of abuse by both doctors and patients, and a minority of county associations were disbanded after a year or two of operation, but as a whole the program expanded each year. The Resettlement Administration was backed in its experiments in this new field by the Rosenwald Foundation and the Twentieth Century Fund.[24] The most surprising thing was the way that the Resettlement Administration was able to win the support of rural doctors and local medical societies, despite years of propaganda by the American Medical Association against the dangers of socialized medicine. One reason for the local support was the plight of rural doctors, who, by this plan, were better assured of collecting their much-needed fees. The opposition came mainly from city specialists who were less familiar with the program or the need for it.[25] Dr. Ralph C. Williams, director of the medical program, was

[23] Richard Hellman, "The Farmers Try Group Medicine," *Harper's Magazine*, CLXXXII (1940–1941), 72–78; Dr. Ralph C. Williams to W. W. Alexander, Dec. 30, 1936, R.G. 16, National Archives; Memorandum for Arthur Chew, Oct. 9, 1941, R.G. 96, National Archives.

[24] Samuel Lubell and Walter Everett, "Rehearsal for State Medicine," *Saturday Evening Post*, CCXI (Dec. 17, 1938), 23, 62–65; Resettlement Administration, *First Annual Report*, p. 94.

[25] Hellman, "The Farmers Try Group Medicine," p. 77.

Locale for a New Society
199

responsible for an excellent selling job, but even he became involved in some controversies. In North Dakota the Resettlement Administration tried a state-wide group plan which was declared to have "extremely dangerous implication" by a writer in the *Journal of the American Medical Association*, leading to a long correspondence and controversy between him and Williams. In Wisconsin the state legislature defeated a bill to permit medical co-operatives in the state by a vote of 63 to 27, bringing a great "hurrah" from Senator F. Ryan Duffy. But, despite some criticism, the editor of the *Journal of the American Medical Association* and several leading physicians endorsed the Farm Security Administration medical program in 1943.[26]

Potentially, one of the most cohesive influences in a community is its religious life. Yet on this subject the Resettlement Administration had to be scrupulously neutral. Rigidly adhering to the separation of Church and State, it left all religious activities to the people on the projects. To an inquiring minister, the Resettlement Administration officials courteously expressed concern over the religious life of its clients and "naturally favored it being carried on on community lines as much as possible," but stressed its inability to encourage or discourage religious activities. Resettlement Administration personnel could not help to organize local religious services, but could attend religious services in project churches. The homesteaders were allowed to hold religious meetings in the community buildings and were permitted to build churches on the projects if they were willing to clear their building plans with Resettlement Administration planners. When the citizens of Penderlea actually planned a church, the Farm Security Administration laid down rather rigid rules. They could proceed at once if twenty-five families signed a written request for a lease on a piece of land. With the approval of a two-year lease, the families could begin construction only if they had 75 per cent of the construction costs in cash and had had their plans approved by the Farm Security Administration.[27]

In one aspect the contemplated new society of the community builders had to remain very much like the old society, despite the

[26] Olin West to R. C. Williams, Dec. 11, 1936, R.G. 96, National Archives; Senator F. Ryan Duffy to W. W. Alexander, July 26, 1937, *ibid.*; C.R., 78th Cong., 1st Sess., 1943, Appendix, pp. 1897–1898.

[27] J. O. Walker to Rev. C. Edwin Brown, Aug. 12, 1936, R.G. 96, National Archives; Memorandum for J. O. Walker, July 26, 1937, *ibid.*; J. O. Walker to George S. Mitchell, March 3, 1938, *ibid.*

wishes to the contrary. Racial segregation remained. From the very beginning the Division of Subsistence Homesteads invited Negroes to its council tables. Bruce Melvin headed a special section on Negroes, Mexicans, and Indians. Negro technicians were employed. In January, 1934, Eleanor Roosevelt invited a group of Negro leaders to the White House to discuss the problem of segregation in the subsistence homesteads program, enlisting their support and creating a better understanding of the problems.[28] In March, 1935, a conference in the Division of Subsistence Homesteads led to the decision that Negroes should participate equally with whites, with at least 10 per cent of the homesteaders being Negroes. But it also decided that, although no homestead in the project book should limit homesteaders as to race, homesteaders would, in practice, have to be selected "according to the sociological pattern of the community, at all times interpreting the facts as liberally as feasible, keeping in mind the success of the project." [29] In actuality this meant segregated projects, with some agitation from Negroes. Funds allotted for Indian projects were turned over to a special agency created within the Department of the Interior.

Although the Department of the Interior and the Division of Subsistence Homesteads yielded to popular opinion on the segregation issue, they did make real efforts to construct several all-Negro projects. Thirty Negro communities were considered, plans were drawn for fifteen, and applications by sponsors were received for four. Yet, in 1935, out of thirty-one projects under construction, not one was for Negroes. On the basis of population there should have been at least three Negro communities; on the basis of housing need and agricultural background, many more. As a result of this record the Division of Subsistence Homesteads announced that no more white homesteads would be constructed until the Negroes shared equally.[30] This commitment led to the initiation of the Newport News or Aberdeen Gardens project just as the Resettlement Administration absorbed the Division of Subsistence Homesteads. When

[28] Pickett, *For More than Bread*, p. 49.
[29] Memorandum, Division of Subsistence Homesteads, March 20, 1935, R.G. 96, National Archives.
[30] Division of Subsistence Homesteads, "Colored Projects," n.d., *ibid.*; Memorandum, Division of Subsistence Homesteads, March 20, 1935, *ibid.*

Locale for a New Society

opened on November 28, 1936, Aberdeen Gardens was the first completed Negro community of the New Deal. Aided by Hampton Institute, it was constructed by Negro technicians and laborers. To avoid racial clashes a greenbelt of farm land was provided.[31]

The early failure to provide Negro projects was summed up by the Division of Subsistence Homesteads as follows: "The fact remains that numerous protests on the part of white citizens against colored project locations have been one of the major contributing causes of failure."[32] When Ralph Borsodi was planning a Negro project near Dayton, 1,100 citizens from three townships petitioned him and the Division of Subsistence Homesteads not to construct such a project, since it would allegedly mean Negroes in white schools, Negro children playing with white children, and a depreciation of property values.[33] When a Negro project was planned for Indianapolis, Representative Louis Ludlow, the congressman from the area, received numerous complaints and made a protest against the proposed project to the Division of Subsistence Homesteads. Definite obstructionism in Indianapolis prevented the acquisition of any suitable site. Even the Newport News project was completed in spite of violent protests by local citizens and by Representative Schuyler O. Bland of Virginia.[34]

The Federal Emergency Relief Administration projects included some communities that were developed for Negroes and one community, Roanoke Farms, which was planned for both whites and Negroes. The Resettlement Administration, although never breaking with local patterns of segregation, was abundantly fair in its allocation of rural projects. Negroes, particularly in the South, shared equally in both rehabilitation and resettlement programs. Several communities and scattered farms projects were for Negroes. At least one project was for Indians in North Carolina. The migrant labor camps were particularly designed for Mexicans. Except for Aberdeen

---

[31] Resettlement Administration, Management News, Feb. 15, 1937, *ibid.*

[32] Division of Subsistence Homesteads, "Colored Projects," n.d., *ibid.*

[33] Citizens of Harrison, Jefferson, and Madison Townships to Ralph Borsodi, April 2, 1934, *ibid.*

[34] C. E. Pynchon to William E. Zeuch, Feb. 4, 1935, and Joseph H. B. Evans to W. W. Alexander, July 5, 1935, *ibid.;* S. O. Bland to W. W. Alexander, Feb. 22, 1937, Wallace to S. O. Bland, March 17, 1937, and D. L. Sanders to the Resettlement Administration, Feb. 25, 1937, R.G. 16, National Archives.

Gardens, the limited suburban resettlement program did not include any Negro communities. One of the most interesting compliments on the biracial program of the Farm Security Administration came from the Board of Supervisors of Bolivar County, Mississippi, who commended the Farm Security Administration for selecting clients of "the White and Negro races," for employing "White and Negro supervisors," and for selling and leasing farms to "both the White and Colored Races." [35]

Perhaps the most tragic story connected with any project came from the Cahaba community (Trussville), near Birmingham, Alabama. Many Negro families lived on the plot of ground purchased but never developed by the Division of Subsistence Homesteads. Although warned to evacuate the site, the Negroes, now admittedly squatters, lived on, since nothing happened. Then one morning the Resettlement Administration, deciding to go on with the project, gave the Negroes one week to move from the area. As reported, the "women folks knowed hardly what to do and we just went to cryen and cryen." [36] They were forced out and, perhaps for sanitary reasons, their homes were burned. The forty displaced Negro families moved to forty acres of worthless land on Sandstone Ridge, where they lived in shacks and shanties, carrying their water from the valley, while white tenants moved into the beautiful new homes constructed on their old homesites.[37]

The real key to the new society was to be co-operation. The whole history of the New Deal communities could be related to the idea of co-operation, which was to replace competition and extreme individualism. From M. L. Wilson, who saw co-operation as the only means of retaining democratic institutions, to Tugwell, whose desire for a collectivized, co-operative society was almost a religion, the architects of the New Deal communities were attempting to develop co-operation as the new institution best suited for the modern environment. No more concerted public effort was ever made in the United States to develop co-operatives of all kinds. Voluntary, democratic co-operation was to be the alternative to the economic insecurity and chaos of an individualistic, capitalistic past and to the

[35] Resolution of the Board of Supervisors, Bolivar County, n.d., R.G. 96, National Archives.
[36] "The Forty Families," n.d., R.G. 83, National Archives. [37] Ibid.

involuntary, totalitarian collectivism of both fascism and communism. But apparently most of the social scientists were at least partially aware of the hold that individualistic institutions had on the average American and of the unpredictable difficulties involved in creating the new, co-operative society.

In the dark depression days of 1933 several self-help co-operatives were established throughout the country by the Division of Self-Help Co-operation in the Federal Emergency Relief Administration. In November, 1933, M. L. Wilson and Jacob Baker, who headed the self-help program, jointly decided that subsistence homesteads would develop several talents needed in self-help and, if Ralph Borsodi's experiences were a criterion, would develop co-operative enterprises and industries. At this time they were thinking particularly about handicrafts and, perhaps, some truck farming. As the subsistence homesteads communities were constructed, four of them, the stranded communities, received loans totaling $46,400 from the Division of Self-Help Co-operation for the establishment of co-operative activities.[38] The same idea of self-help permeated the Federal Emergency Relief Administration community program, with several of the communities being constructed by the co-operative work of the homesteaders. The co-operative idea was further reflected in the many co-operative farms. It reached its fullest expression in the Division of Subsistence Homestead's plans for an all co-operative community at Jersey Homesteads, where every economic activity was to be controlled by co-operatives. The Division of Subsistence Homesteads acquired Dr. William E. Zeuch as a special adviser on co-operation. He was an enthusiast, desiring many fully co-operative communities. He believed that the transition from a "competitive to a co-operative society" could not be achieved "on a voluntary, democratic basis." Because of the "hangovers of competitive-conditioned behavior patterns," he believed that arbitrary power in the new co-operatives had to be voluntarily delegated to experienced, efficient, honest, and wise managers.[39]

Since most of the community management was left to the Reset-

[38] M. L. Wilson and Joseph Baker to Ickes, Nov. 3, 1933, R.G. 96, National Archives; Charles S. Gaines, Jr., to Edward Stone, Oct. 3, 1935, *ibid.*

[39] Dr. William E. Zeuch, "Problems of Co-operative Communities," *Co-operative Self Help*, I (May, 1934), Mimeographed, pp. 16–17, *ibid.*

tlement Administration and the Farm Security Administration, it was these agencies that put the co-operative idea to a thousand practical, or impractical, uses. Tugwell believed that co-operatives could teach the fallacy of individualism and competition. He declared that co-operation was the easiest, most natural thing in the world.[40] In the earliest days of the Resettlement Administration he secured the authority to make loans to co-operative associations as part of the rehabilitation program. Most of these loans, contrary to past government lending policies, went to producers' co-operatives, including many on the community projects. Tugwell deplored the almost entire emphasis in the past on consumers' co-operatives, declaring that if the government credit agencies were "socially minded" producer co-operatives might arise. Tugwell advocated co-operation as a practical need and not as a religious crusade, as it almost had been under the Rochdale Movement. He refused to subscribe to the dogmatic views of existing co-operative movements and rejoiced at being able to use government funds to break "large cracks in orthodoxy." Only on one point did the Resettlement Administration force conformity to orthodox co-operative theology. It required that all its co-operatives include in their by laws a provision that each member should have only one vote.[41]

A Co-operative Unit was established in the Economic Development Section of the Resettlement Administration. The unit included an executive, several co-operative specialists, and co-operative managers on many projects. The Economic Development Section drew up recommended charters and bylaws, application forms for loans and grants, and the administrative procedure for making loans to co-operatives. As early as October, 1935, the first loans were made to the co-operative associations at Arthurdale and Red House for a general store and agricultural activities. Under the Resettlement Administration most of the early co-operatives established were for the production or processing of agricultural products, for consumer services, or for medical care, since a ruling by the Comptroller General

[40] Rexford G. Tugwell, "Cooperation and Resettlement," *Current History*, XLV (Feb., 1937), 75.

[41] Robert Straus to Leroy Peterson, Aug. 9, 1935, R.G. 96, National Archives; Leroy Peterson to Thomas Holland, Nov. 6, 1936, *ibid.*; Tugwell, "Cooperation and Resettlement," pp. 71–72, 75–76; Resettlement Administration, "Guide for Planning Community and Co-operative Activities," n.d., R.G. 96, National Archives.

Locale for a New Society

in 1936 prevented loans for productive co-operatives not associated with agriculture, a ruling later amended for the stranded communities. As soon as a community was completed, it usually went through a period of rapid co-operative organization, with an unbelievably large number of co-operative activities carried on at some projects. Many co-operative associations carried on ten or twelve different programs. Among the services, facilities, and activities organized on co-operative lines in the various communities were the following: farms, pastures, dairies, wood lots, greenhouses, rock quarries, poultry enterprises, hog breeding, cattle breeding, lime crushing, canneries, barbershops, cobble shops, feed grinding, gristmills, handicraft industries, orchards, vineyards, factories, tearooms, inns, restaurants, hospitals, potato-drying houses, garages, filling stations, medical associations, blacksmith shops, warehouses, cane mills, farm equipment, cotton gins, coal mines, seed houses, hatcheries, sawmills, freezing plants, and even a burial association. As a result of too much early enthusiasm and extravagance, many uneconomical co-operatives had to be liquidated at a great loss. An alarmingly large number failed because of poor management, resentment of government control, lack of understanding of the co-operative idea, nonbusinesslike practices, factionalism in the associations, and outside competition or opposition. The medical co-operatives were probably the most successful.[42]

The Resettlement Administration realized that the project clients would not be able to operate successful co-operatives without supervision and education. As a result it initiated a program of co-operative education, utilizing reading materials and lectures given by a field force of co-operative specialists. In some projects adult study groups met as often as three times a month for lectures, group study, and forums. In many colonies youth leagues met once a month to explore the co-operative field. A youth conference on co-operation was held at Westmoreland for co-operative league members from several projects. Guides to co-operative activity were mimeographed and distributed to the projects. Beyond all this the co-operative associations were very closely supervised either by the community manager or, in the case of the largest associations, by co-operative managers

---

[42] Leroy Peterson to E. E. Agger, Oct. 30, 1935, R.G. 96, National Archives; Irving J. Levy to Walter E. Packard, Oct. 26, 1936, *ibid.*; Howard Gordon to C. B. Baldwin, April 3, 1941, *ibid.*

employed by the Resettlement Administration. One of the things that often hurt the co-operatives was the people's resentment at not having enough voice in what was publicized as "their" co-operative. In defense of this supervision, it can be pointed out that the co-operatives were entirely financed by government loans.[43]

Although co-operation was desired as a substitute for individual enterprise, in many projects co-operative enterprises became almost entirely a matter of economic necessity rather than of ideological desirability. Since Congress had forbidden government factories on community projects and since the Comptroller General refused to allow the Resettlement Administration to use government funds directly to subsidize private industries on the projects, the co-operative associations were used as the only remaining device to bring employment to the economically stranded communities. The Economic Development Section of the Resettlement Administration began making plans for co-operatively owned manufacturing plants at the stranded communities in 1935. Budgets were prepared, the work of the Tennessee Valley Authority in industrial decentralization was studied, and marketing agreements were made with Sears, Roebuck and Company. These plans had to be abandoned because of a ruling by Comptroller General McCarl preventing the use of Resettlement Administration funds for subsidizing private industry.[44]

From 1935 through 1937 the Resettlement Administration attempted to raise the economic status of the stranded communities by establishing various nonindustrial co-operatives. At Cumberland Homesteads, for example, a tremendous $550,000 loan to the Co-operative Association in December, 1936, was used to establish a sorghum plant and a cannery and to operate a project coal mine, all of which failed because of inexperience, crop failures, labor union troubles, lack of markets, and a pocket instead of an expected vein of coal. At Tygart Valley a loan of $400,000 in January, 1936, was partly used for a stone quarry, a potato-curing house, the co-operative farm, warehouses, consumer stores, and a filling station. At Red House, Arthurdale, and Westmoreland similar loans were used for farms, dairies, canneries, and other services. But none of these co-operatives

[43] Leroy Peterson to E. E. Agger, June 29, 1936, *ibid.*; Leroy Peterson to Thomas Holland, Nov. 6, 1936, *ibid.*; Report from Region IV, Resettlement Administration, Dec., 1936, *ibid.*

[44] E. E. Agger to R. G. Tugwell, n.d., *ibid.*

Locale for a New Society

erased the economic problems of the projects, partly because of management failures, but even more because they were limited to such a small economic base. The consumer co-operatives, no matter how successful, could provide employment to only a few project members, since they were service rather than productive enterprises. The co-operative farms and related activities, such as the canneries, were not large enough to employ more than a few of the settlers, since none of the stranded projects had been planned with enough acreage for commercial agriculture. The great need remained for some type of industry.[45]

On June 21, 1937, the Resettlement Administration, after clearance from the Comptroller General, went ahead with plans that had been frustrated by legal snarls since 1935. On that date M. L. Wilson, then Undersecretary of Agriculture, announced several loan agreements with co-operative associations on stranded projects for the establishment of industrial enterprises.[46] These loans, plus later ones, were used to establish a wood dimension mill at Tygart Valley, a tractor assembly plant at Arthurdale, a pants factory at Westmoreland, and hosiery mills at Cumberland Homesteads, Skyline Farms, Penderlea Homesteads, Bankhead Farms, and Red House. A total of $4,328,000 was lent to the co-operative associations for investment in plants and in early operating expenses. In each case the co-operative association worked out a managerial agreement with a private industry; the Farm Security Administration, as the financing agent, was a party to the agreement and, in reality, the major party. At Tygart Valley the co-operative association leased its industrial assets to a fictitious corporation which, in turn, entered an agreement with the Gamble Sales Dimension Company of Louisville. This company, which furnished plant management and sales services for a flat fee plus a percentage of the net profit, was protected against any serious losses, since all the investment was made, indirectly, by the government. An almost identical procedure was followed at Westmoreland, where the Washington Sales Corporation supplied the managerial and sales personnel for the pants factory. At Arthurdale the tractor

[45] Lord and Johnstone, A Place on Earth, pp. 88–91; Select Committee of the House Committee on Agriculture, *Hearings on the Farm Security Administration*, 78th Cong., 1st Sess., 1943–1944, p. 1756.

[46] Memorandum for the Secretary of Agriculture, Oct. 22, 1937, R.G. 16, National Archives.

plant was managed by American Co-operatives, Incorporated, which provided managerial services free of charge. In September, 1938, the Farm Security Administration and the other five associations entered a management agreement with the Dexdale Hosiery Mills of Pennsylvania to operate and manage the five hosiery mills. The Dexdale Company received a share of the annual earnings but no guaranteed fee.[47]

The co-operatives' venture into private industry was successful in only one respect—it provided, at least for a few years, jobs and a degree of economic security to the occupants of the projects. But to the co-operative associations, to the government, and even to the private industries involved, the enterprises were financial failures. From inception to December 31, 1942, the five hosiery mills had suffered a net loss of $63,982.44 and, with one small exception, had repaid none of the principal invested by the government. The mill at Cumberland Homesteads had shown a small profit and had made a token repayment. The woodworking plant at Tygart Valley had lost $190,816 by the beginning of 1943 and, by 1944, was being sued because of its inability to repay its loan. The pants factory at Westmoreland lost, through 1942, approximately $213,292 and, on October 1, 1943, was leased directly to the Washington Sales Corporation. After operating for only one year, the Arthurdale tractor assembly plant closed with a loss of $106,380.21.[48] The hosiery mills, operating in the finest factories in the South, were seriously hurt by the wartime scarcity of nylon and the forced conversion to rayon. An experienced textile expert investigated the Penderlea factory and concluded: "In all of my experience in hosiery I have never seen a greater waste of money or a mill more badly managed, and cannot by the greatest stretch of imagination think of anyone who would be so careless in manufacturing if they had to use their own money." [49] By 1944 the hosiery mills were being readied for sale.

[47] U.S. Department of Agriculture, Farm Security Administration, *Report of the Administrator of the FSA, 1939* (Washington, 1939), p. 22; House Agricultural Subcommittee of the Committee on Appropriations, *Hearings on the Agricultural Department Appropriation Bill for 1941*, 76th Cong., 3d Sess., 1940, pp. 973–977; *Hearings on the Farm Security Administration*, pp. 1749–1760.

[48] U.S. National Housing Agency, *Third Annual Report, January 1 to December 31, 1944* (Washington, 1945), p. 214; *Hearings on the Farm Security Administration*, pp. 1748–1763.

[49] *Hearings on the Farm Security Administration*, p. 1763.

Locale for a New Society

The industrial plants made the Farm Security Administration even more vulnerable to criticism from a Congress which was becoming more and more hostile to all the reform programs of the New Deal. To Congress the co-operative associations were ruses to enable the Farm Security Administration to get around the prohibition of government factories on the projects. By furnishing all the money, through the associations, the Farm Security Administration was defying the expressed intent of Congress. More than that it was, in essence, granting subsidies and favors to selected private industries. The Farm Security Administration appropriation for the fiscal year 1944 prohibited any further loans to co-operative associations, thus impairing the whole co-operative program of the Farm Security Administration. At the time the prohibition went into effect (July 1, 1943), the Resettlement Administration and the Farm Security Administration had lent over $7,000,000 to 446 co-operative associations. After 1943 the Farm Security Administration continued to supervise the existing co-operatives.[50]

The co-operative associations were supposed to serve one other purpose. While a project remained under direct government management, about the only place the homesteaders could have a voice in managing their own community was in "their" co-operatives, where they were all assured one equal vote. Even when the first communities were turned over to the homesteaders, ownership and management were placed, not in the individuals, but in co-operative homestead associations. In both cases the co-operative device was intended to be, and in many cases probably was, an education in democratic processes and in the problems of group organization. Yet in neither case was there completely free individual participation. The Farm Security Administration, with its large investment at stake, was afraid to turn the co-operative associations over to the inexperienced people of a community. Thus their participation in their co-operatives was often a mere formality, with either the project manager or a co-operative manager making all the important decisions. Even the homestead associations had to sign a managerial agreement with the

[50] House Agricultural Subcommittee of the Committee on Appropriations, *Hearings on the Agricultural Department Appropriation Bill for 1945*, pt. II, 78th Cong., 2d Sess., 1944, p. 989; U.S. Department of Agriculture, Farm Security Administration, *Postwar Developments in Farm Security*, Annual Report of the Farm Security Administration for 1945–1946 (Washington, 1946), pp. 16–17.

Farm Security Administration, thus assuring a continued control or supervision of community activities.

The furthest extension of the co-operative idea was in those projects where practically all economic activity was organized along co-operative lines. These included the industrial community at Hightstown and the co-operative farm colonies. One group of farm colonies included the three communities (Lake Dick, Casa Grande, and Terrebonne) so designed that co-operative farming was almost necessitated, since the farm lands surrounded farm villages which included only subsistence plots. In another type the Farm Security Administration leased a large plot of ground, usually for ninety-nine years, to a group of families organized into a co-operative association. These associations usually leased only a part of a community project, with Scuppernong Farms in North Carolina including two such co-operatives. These completely co-operative farms represented an expansion of the same co-operative ideas that were applied to the partly co-operative projects. From a practical standpoint it was believed that only group activities and co-operative devices could give the small farmer the productive efficiency needed if he were to survive the competition of large commercial farmers. From a social and personal standpoint, they were to bring the joys of social participation, the ability to work together, the economic security of an organized group, and a new set of social rather than individual goals and values. Many of the co-operative farms were planned as a continuation of the plantation tradition in the South. They were usually planned for the class of farmers that were most incapable of carrying on successful individual farming operations.

The co-operative farms represented an almost complete break with free enterprise. One tenant facetiously remarked that he owned only his chickens and his children.[51] From a standpoint of physical organization, the co-operative farm colonies were closely related to the communal colonies of America's past. The Farm Security Administration sent representatives to study and to prepare a report on the Amana colonies in Iowa, one of the few remaining examples of colonies founded around a religious ideal. The co-operative farm colonies were also very similar to the Delta Co-operative Farm which Sherwood Eddy had just recently established in Mississippi. The Farm Security Ad-

[51] Oren Stephens, "FSA Fights for Its Life," *Harper's Magazine*, CLXXXVI (1942–1943), 482–483.

ministration had agreed to provide some aid to Delta. Yet the government colonies, such as Lake Dick, had to be peopled with American farmers, who had a deeply ingrained sense of individualism and no cohesive ideology.[52]

The co-operative farms were economic and, apparently, social failures. First of all they suffered from the same problems of many of the other rural projects. All the fine homes and facilities on such a project as Lake Dick could not be paid for by the plantation income. At Lake Dick, the purest example of a collective farm, the acreage was not large enough to support sixty families. Only when the population was reduced to thirty-five families did the farm actually pay a profit for one brief year. But the largest problem was the nature of the people involved. Many of them were ready to live in a co-operative colony when, in the depression, it offered them the only security they could find. But once on the project, a settler often disliked depending upon his less capable neighbor. His central goal soon became a farm of his own, where he could be free and independent. In five years the turnover at Lake Dick was 400 per cent. The co-operative farm there was disbanded in 1942, and the plantation rented to Negro tenants on a share-crop basis.[53] At Casa Grande, Arizona, the farm director resigned in 1939, calling the project a Russian co-operative. This same accusation was widely voiced and was, perhaps, inevitable, in view of the physical similarities between the Russian collective farms and the Farm Security Administration co-operative colonies; but, since all the resettlement clients voluntarily resided on the co-operative projects and left at will, the accusation was very unfair. At Casa Grande the settlers said that the only thing communistic about their project was "our dictator and he's resigned." [54]

The new society was a goal of the social and economic planners. Their work at the project level was in furtherance of this goal. But, as has been indicated before, the new society, as a reality, was very difficult to achieve. Much of the detailed social planning had been untried before in this country and may have been rewarding in even its negative results. The avowed experimental nature of the communities probably

---

[52] Carl H. Monseen to J. O. Walker, Feb. 3, 1938, R.G. 96, National Archives; Lewis E. Long to Sam H. Franklin, n.d., *ibid.*

[53] Stephens, "FSA Fights for Its Life," pp. 482–483.

[54] "Farm Troubles: Co-operative and Ex-Director Call Each Other Communists," *Newsweek*, XIII (Jan. 16, 1939), 40–41.

endangered their early success. It is problematical what the homesteaders at such publicized places as Arthurdale must have felt when they read that their government had, in the past, sponsored experimental stations for the breeding of plants and animals and now was spending money for experimental communities. Some of the communities aroused almost as much critical curiosity as nudist colonies or the early Oneida. This made the settlers feel as though they were on exhibit and prevented the communities from being accepted into the larger community. They remained islands, visited by "sociological souvenir hunters" who could ask the "most personal and intimate" questions.[55]

Too often the homesteaders were overly idealistic in their expectations about their new homes and, when disappointed at the reality, became bitter toward the government. Almost always the early homesteaders were enthusiastic, feeling that they were modern pioneers. Part of the Tygard Valley Song illustrates this:

> In nineteen thirty-five
> We began to arrive
> From empty mine and wasted timber-line
> And farms that no longer could thrive
> Back to the plow and the land
> By the sweat of our brow and our hand,
> To build from the start
> With faith in our heart
> As shoulder to shoulder we stand.[56]

But once on the project, things usually went wrong. Policies were changed at Washington, and the homesteaders felt cheated. The large expenses in construction often aroused fears of such high purchase prices that the homesteader could never afford them. More than anything else, the long delay in granting purchase contracts led to dissatisfaction. Always there was the ever-present reality of personal clashes. Some community managers were disliked. The same Tygart Valley homesteaders who sang the enthusiastic song all went on a strike in 1937 over the appointment of a manager, leading to a great

---

[55] William E. Brooks, "Arthurdale—A New Chance," *Atlantic Monthly*, CLV (1935), 203; Millard M. Rice, "Footnote on Arthurdale," *Harper's Magazine*, CLXXX (1939–1940), 418.

[56] Russell Lord, *Wallaces of Iowa* (Boston, 1947), p. 425.

Locale for a New Society

deal of excitement and lasting bitterness.[57] At Cumberland Homesteads the whole community went on a rent strike that lasted for almost a year because they thought that the government was going to cheat them out of some work credits. On project after project factions arose around strong leaders or around favorite community managers. In several projects dissident homesteaders had to be evicted, leaving their remaining friends dissatisfied. Yet, by 1942, in the subsistence homesteads projects retained by the Farm Security Administration, there had been a turnover of only 18 per cent, and much of this because of new employment.[58] Even though the new communities were not at all like heaven, they apparently were better than anything else available.

People usually dislike rapid change and feel resentment toward anyone who tries to reform or even to educate them. The farmer on the rural project disliked the college expert who told him how to farm. To many the close supervision and rigid limitations on individual initiative were galling. The endless investigations and inspections were also resented. News reporters and sociologists joined the frequent inspectors from Washington in asking about things that the homesteader often considered only his own business. When three different investigators visited Westmoreland on three successive days, the Washington office received an urgent request that investigators be sent together in groups rather than one a day, for they were disrupting normal activities.[59] Even the work of the Special Skills Section in bringing culture and recreation was not always welcomed by the settlers. Some special recordings sent to Penderlea for a special gathering were returned with a request for hillbilly music, which the homesteaders preferred. At Westmoreland the educational director suggested that special-skills people be sent only at the request of the Education and Training Section in order "that we do not burden the communities with more advantages than they can absorb at one time." [60] Not even a small community can be built in a day.

[57] M. L. Wilson to Eleanor Roosevelt, Aug. 25, 1937, R.G. 16, National Archives.
[58] Report on Subsistence Homesteads, 1942, R.G. 96, National Archives.
[59] Agnes King Inglis to E. E. Agger, Sept. 26, 1935, *ibid.* [60] *Ibid.*

❧ IX ❦

The Old Society Reasserts Its Claims

THE Resettlement Administration and the Farm Security Administration faced almost insurmountable difficulties in experimentally creating a new society within the bounds of their new communities, perhaps largely because of the individualistic nature of their clients. They faced an even more difficult task in maintaining the major features of this new society in the midst of the old society, which, with returning prosperity, was regaining much of its past popularity. The attempt to preserve the distinguishing attributes of the New Deal communities is bound up in the long controversy over their disposition and in the wartime struggle of the Farm Security Administration to maintain its very existence in the face of almost overwhelming opposition. In the course of these controversies the communities, once so loved and cherished by their planners and creators, became, in the minds of many congressmen, disreputable, heretical, and exceedingly wasteful symbols of misguided idealism or even of ideological treason.

In many of the subsistence homesteads and rural rehabilitation communities, the Resettlement Administration inherited definite commitments to eventual homeownership. The Resettlement Administration decided to honor all these commitments, but at the same time wanted to preserve the aims and objectives of the communities.[1] In January,

---
[1] Edward Stone to E. E. Agger, Nov. 7, 1935, R.G. 96, National Archives.

Old Society Reasserts Claims

1936, Tugwell secured Roosevelt's approval of a plan to turn the completed subsistence homesteads communities over to local, co-operative homestead associations made up of the homesteaders residing in the communities. The association would hold title to the land, issue purchase or lease contracts to individual homesteaders, select future settlers, collect all payments, maintain the property, and make all tax and insurance payments. In most cases the association would sell the individual homesteads by means of a long purchase contract, running for forty years at 3 per cent interest. Included in monthly payments would be fees for management, repairs and upkeep, taxes, and a reserve fund. The co-operative property would be surrendered to co-operative associations, whose membership would be open to all homesteaders. The homestead association, before accepting title to the property, would have to sign a management contract with the Resettlement Administration, giving that agency or its successors the right to supervise the management of the community until it was completely liquidated at the end of forty years.[2] This method of disposition seemed certain to solve local tax problems, to give the homesteader the satisfaction of working toward eventual ownership, to insure community control over all land use for forty years, and to guarantee the continued supervision and direction of community life by the Resettlement Administration.

Before conveying the communities to homestead associations, the Resettlement Administration decided to adopt a sale policy based on the ability of homesteaders to pay, on a reasonable appraisal of the project, and, only lastly, on the original cost to the government. In no case was the sale price of an individual homestead to exceed 25 per cent of the client's income, the appraisal figure, or the original cost to the government. Yet, despite this, Tugwell predicted that there would "be no serious gap between the evaluation of the property for conveyance and its cost."[3] This proved to be a tragically false prediction.

In 1936 and 1937, thirteen communities (Houston, Beauxart, Dalworthington, Three Rivers, and Wichita Gardens in Texas, El Monte and San Fernando Homesteads in California, Longview Homesteads

[2] Policy Statement signed by Tugwell and approved by President Roosevelt, Jan. 18, 1936, *ibid.;* U.S. Senate, *Resettlement Administration Program,* Document no. 213, 74th Cong., 2d Sess., 1936, pp. 23–24.

[3] U.S. Senate, *Resettlement Administration Program,* Document no. 213, 74th Cong., 1st Sess., 1928, p. 23.

in Washington, Decatur Homesteads in Indiana, Hattiesburg, Magnolia, and Tupelo Homesteads in Mississippi, and Phoenix Homesteads in Arizona) were transferred to homestead associations.[4] These were all industrial homesteads and included the most prosperous and successful of all the New Deal communities. The individual homesteader in the conveyed communities had an opportunity, if he wished, to enter a forty-year purchase contract for his homestead. If he later decided to move, he was required to offer his homestead to the association, which could repossess it by paying him the equivalent of his accumulated equity. This purchase contract was known as tenure "A." For those not desiring to purchase a homestead, a tenure "B" or lease contract was used, with the cost of the monthly lease based on the same considerations as the sale price. When a new homesteader moved into a community, the association usually required a year's trial period under lease before granting a purchase contract. If a purchaser defaulted on payments, he could use his accumulated equity to pay rent on a tenure "B" contract, remaining on the project until his equity was exhausted.[5]

Since the conveyance price usually fell well below the original cost, the transference of whole communities to homestead associations invited new accusations of financial irresponsibility on the part of the community agencies. El Monte and San Fernando Homesteads, alone among the subsistence homesteads communities, sold at a price equal to cost, and Longview almost broke even. On the other hand, Dalworthington Gardens, which cost $325,712.35, was sold for $150,000, and Hattiesburg Homesteads, which cost $75,648.78, was sold for $49,720. The first twelve communities sold to homestead associations cost $2,102,762.44 and sold for $1,700,232, or for about 81 per cent of their cost.[6] In view of the community facilities, such as roads and schools, which are usually provided by local governments and not as the direct expense of the purchaser of a home, this record was satisfactory, or even excellent. But these communities, built by contract under the Division of Subsistence Homesteads, were by far the most inexpensive ones. Even as they were transferred, surveys at Arthurdale

[4] Edward Stone to Earle P. Zack, July 6, 1938, R.G. 96, National Archives.
[5] U.S. Senate, *Resettlement Administration Program*, pp. 23–24.
[6] Select Committee of the House Committee on Agriculture, *Hearings on the Farm Security Administration*, 78th Cong., 1st Sess., 1943–1944, pp. 1118–1119.

Old Society Reasserts Claims

indicated a probable sale price of only 21.3 per cent of cost, and the probable sale price of Jersey Homesteads, which cost $3,402,382.27, was estimated at only $924,022, or 27.1 per cent of the investment. For twenty-six homestead projects the estimated liquidation price was 43.1 per cent of cost, meaning a government subsidy of 56.9 per cent.[7]

Only one project (Bankhead Farms in Alabama) was conveyed to a homestead association between 1937 and 1942, and one project (Tupelo Homesteads) was turned over to the National Park Service as part of the Natchez Trace Parkway. In 1942 the last associations were formed at Austin, Duluth, Granger, Mount Olive, Palmerdale, and Greenwood Homesteads, making a total of nineteen. Under congressional pressure to dispose of all the communities as quickly as possible, the Farm Security Administration, in 1942, began plans for conveying several other communities that had been retained because of economic difficulties, since at some projects the monthly income of homesteaders was hardly sufficient to pay local taxes. On these projects the homesteaders had continued to pay monthly rents while awaiting a chance to purchase their homes. Three communities, Cumberland, McComb, and Lake County Homesteads, were opened for sale to individual homesteaders, with the Farm Security Administration retaining title until the fulfillment of the forty-year purchase contracts. The greenbelt towns and Ironwood, Cahaba, and Aberdeen Gardens were all being prepared for conveyance to special leasing associations.[8]

Of the homestead projects conveyed to associations only two, Magnolia and Hattiesburg in Mississippi, completely defaulted in their payments. On fifteen other projects the cumulative delinquency was only 0.9 per cent from 1936 to May 1, 1940. There had been a 35.9 per cent turnover, but mainly among tenure "B" clients. On the nonconveyed projects there was only an 18 per cent turnover, with new employment constituting the most important reason. The temporary licensing agreements averaged only $16.99 a month. To February 28, 1941, there had been a delinquency of only 3.9 per cent on the monthly rentals.[9] With a consolidation of all New Deal housing agencies in

[7] Enclosure, H. W. Truesdell to E. G. Arnold, May 28, 1937, R.G. 96, National Archives.

[8] *Hearings on the Farm Security Administration*, p. 1032; "Disposition of Projects," n.d., R.G. 96, National Archives; a memorandum for J. O. Walker, March 16, 1941, *ibid.*

[9] "Report on Subsistence Homesteads," n.d., R.G. 96, National Archives.

1942, Roosevelt, by an executive order dated October 1, 1942, transferred all the Farm Security housing in which the family did not earn its principal income from farming to the Federal Public Housing Authority in the National Housing Agency.[10] This took from the Farm Security Administration all the homestead associations and all the nonrural colonies, plus several undeveloped subsistence homesteads plots. Transferred to the new agency were twenty-eight subsistence homesteads communities, the three greenbelt cities, one suburban resettlement project, and two Federal Emergency Relief Administration communities. The Farm Security Administration retained twenty-six Federal Emergency Relief Administration rural communities, three rural subsistence homesteads communities, and all the rural resettlement communities.

For the rural communities Tugwell early decided on a temporary policy of leasing, with purchase details to be worked out later. Some of the inherited rural communities were first leased for a set monthly or yearly cash rent, but at Woodlake the Federal Emergency Relief Administration had initiated a system of payment in kind. In 1937, carrying this idea further, the Resettlement Administration adopted a "D" type lease for some of its co-operative farms. This lease, which was later extended to most of the rural colonies, resembled the traditional share-cropping system, with rentals based on a set percentage of the crops. In 1938 a lease and purchase contract was readied, featuring a variable payment plan based on production and the ability of the client to pay. Yet, until 1940, the Farm Security Administration did not issue a single purchase contract in its rural colonies, arguing that the tenants were still under trial leases to determine their qualifications for landownership. In 1940, under congressional pressure, the Farm Security Administration began issuing these lease and purchase agreements in most of its nonco-operative type rural colonies. By 1942 approximately 2,586 units in either the rural communities or the scattered farms had been sold to individuals.[11]

[10] House Agricultural Subcommittee of the Committee on Appropriations, *Hearings on the Agricultural Department Appropriation Bill for 1944*, 78th Cong., 1st Sess., 1943, pp. 988–991.

[11] U.S. Department of Agriculture, Farm Security Administration, *Report of the Administrator of the FSA, 1938* (Washington, 1938), pp. 21–22; House Agricultural Subcommittee of the Committee on Appropriations, *Hearings on the Agricultural Appropriation Bill for 1941*, 76th Cong., 3d Sess., 1940, p. 970, and *Hearings*

The lease and purchase contract was really a promise of future sale. The farmer agreed on a certain price for his homestead, with the first one-fourth of this price to be paid by a designated percentage of the cash income from his crops. The percentage could be changed by each alteration of his well-supervised farm and home plan. Title and all rights to the land remained in the Farm Security Administration. The government pledged that, when the variable payments beyond interest, insurance, and taxes had amounted to one-fourth of the purchase price, the purchaser would be granted a quitclaim deed conveying the property to him, but with all the mineral rights reserved to the government. At that time the purchaser would execute a promissory note, agreeing to pay the balance of the purchase price within forty years at 3 per cent interest. He also had to execute a mortgage as security for the indebtedness. The note and mortgage were to be "in such form, and contain such conditions and covenants, consistent with the provisions of this contract, as the Government may prescribe, including a provision prohibiting the sale, lease or other disposition of the property without the consent of the Government." [12] Although this contract promised a deed after the indefinite period required for an accumulation of the first 25 per cent of the purchase price, it left the client completely under Farm Security Administration supervision for this indefinite period and, after the issuance of the deed, under whatever controls and restrictions the Farm Security Administration might insert into the mortgage.[13] The client could not hope for complete control of his land until a minimum of forty-one years from the time he entered the original agreement, and only then if he were so fortunate as to accumulate the first 25 per cent of the purchase price in one year. This long waiting period followed, in many cases, the five years or more that the client had already been on the project as a tenant. Few adult men could really look forward to full ownership within their lifetime. Even if they did live until the complete fulfillment of their contract, they still did not own the mineral rights. This contract insured Tugwell's desire for a long relationship between

---

on the Agricultural Appropriation Bill for 1942, pt. II, 77th Cong., 1st Sess., 1941, pp. 112–118, 258–259.

[12] *Hearings on the Farm Security Administration*, p. 90, see also pp. 86–90.

[13] Farm Security Administration Instruction 555.5, Oct., 1942, R.G. 96, National Archives.

the government and individual. It also insured the physical plan of the community against early alteration.

Even as the Farm Security Administration began to dispose of its rural colonies, its whole program was under attack. The fight over the abolition of the Farm Security Administration was one of the most bitter domestic issues during World War II. It was a fight that was related to congressional opposition to the whole New Deal reform program. This particular fight had been shaping up ever since the Farm Security Administration was created in September, 1937, presumably to carry out the provisions of the Bankhead-Jones Farm Tenant Act. The Bankhead-Jones Act not only set up the new tenant-purchase program but provided for a rehabilitation program and for the completion of the resettlement communities. The intent of Congress was relatively clear. The Farm Security Administration could continue the rehabilitation program but only by securing an appropriation under the Bankhead-Jones Act. It could complete the existing resettlement communities but could not begin new ones. In fact, the Bankhead-Jones Act did not grant the authority to purchase land. What actually occurred, however, is that the Resettlement Administration received a new name, added the tenant-purchase program to its already large repertory of activities, and continued very much as it had before the Bankhead-Jones measure. It continued to secure its rehabilitation funds from relief appropriations and to administer them according to executive orders rather than the provisions of the Bankhead-Jones Act. It not only completed resettlement communities but added extra land to many of them. It was the Farm Security Administration that initiated many of the experiments in co-operative farming and all the experiments with ninety-nine-year leases. The Farm Security Administration was slow in making even the initial steps toward liquidating the community projects and, when it did so in 1940, affixed such terms as would insure a continued government interest in the projects for over fifty years.

With no authority to purchase land for additional community projects, the Farm Security Administration, beginning in 1938, formed land-leasing and land-purchasing associations to which it lent rehabilitation funds. These associations, composed of families who could not qualify for regular community projects, used their loans to lease or, in four cases, to purchase large tracts of land for subleasing to individual members. This group rehabilitation led to the creation of about thirty-five close settlements that differed from other New Deal communities only insofar as the Farm Security Administration did not actually itself make any of the improvements or construct any community facilities. But its funds were used. These associations were a means of continuing, in essence, the land-purchase and community-building programs of the old Resettlement Administration. The Farm Security Administration officials believed that the associations offered security of tenure, higher living standards, savings through co-operative activity, education in co-operative ideas, simplified Farm Security Administration supervision, larger bargaining powers with landlords, and better rental terms.[14] In the beginning days of World War II the Farm Security Administration temporarily expanded this land-leasing and land-purchase program by administering a relocation program for people displaced by war preparations. To do this the Farm Security Administration formed relocation corporations which began the purchasing of large tracts of land until a ruling of the Comptroller General stopped the practice. These programs, even if strictly legal, seemed to be against the spirit and intent of the Bankhead-Jones Act.

Both the Farm Security Administration program and its personnel were such as to gain many enemies. The Farm Security Administration, inheritor of Tugwell's distinct class feelings, was a militant defender of the small farmer and laborer. It constantly stressed the lack of economic and social justice for the small farmers who had no real stake in the American democracy, contrasting them with the large farmers who were becoming more and more separated from those at the bottom.[15] At a time when industrial labor was receiving many gains, the Farm Security Administration almost became a labor union for small farmers, tenants, and farm laborers. The leaders in the Farm Security Administration were enthusiastically devoted to their task of helping the exploited farm classes. Their over-all philosophy tended to be collectivist, with a distrust of the ideas of the capitalists and of the kindred ideas of the middle-class farmers. Ideological and economic

---

[14] Senate Agricultural Subcommittee of the Committee on Appropriations, *Hearings on Agricultural Department Appropriation Bill for 1944*, 78th Cong., 1st Sess., 1943, pp. 742–744.

[15] U.S. Department of Agriculture, Farm Security Administration, *Report of the Administrator of the FSA, 1941* (Washington, 1941), pp. 1–2; Grant McConnell, *The Decline of Agrarian Democracy* (Berkeley, 1953), pp. 89–93.

differences led to controversy in Congress and throughout the country.

The Farm Security Administration aided the lowest and most helpless class of farmers, from the migrant laborers in California to Southern sharecroppers. But the cotton plantations, the truck farms, and the large orchards were dependent upon these very same cheap laborers and croppers that the Farm Security Administration was aiding through rehabilitation loans or resettlement opportunities. At the same time the loans and support to local co-operatives often threatened the profits of private processors and retailers. Thus those who feared competition or who were about to lose their cheap labor were naturally opposed to the Farm Security Administration. Many commercial farmers, aided by the Farm Bureau and by many extension agents, became the most bitter opponents of the Farm Security Administration. The Farm Security Administration, during World War II, controlled the placement of migrant farm laborers and exacted such strict conditions on wages, hours, sanitation, and housing as to anger the many plantation owners who much preferred to treat their laborers as they had in the past. Most vulnerable because of its sorry financial record in many of the resettlement projects and because of its collective-farming experiments, the Farm Security Administration was accused of useless extravagance and of harboring communist ideas. On the other side, the Farm Security Administration was defended by many of its clients, by the labor unions, and by the National Farmers' Union. These groups pointed accusing fingers at the "economic royalists" who wished to hold the low-income farmers in a system of peonage.

The controversy soon became one of emotion and of bitterness, with some people believing that the attack on the Farm Security Administration was in the interest of saving American freedom, whereas others believed that it meant the beginning of a return to slavery or to an acceptance of a form of "Fascism." [16] For example, a Farm Bureau report on the Farm Security Administration urged that the farm program for low-income families be placed in a new agency in order to "save the low-income farmer from political exploitation and save American agriculture from collectivism and Government land-

---

[16] Alfred W. Griswold, *Farming and Democracy* (New Haven, 1952), p. 170; Oren Stephens, "FSA Fights for Its Life," *Harper's Magazine*, CLXXXVI (1942–1943), 479–480; "Pillar of Democracy: The Meaning of the Fight Against the FSA," *Commonweal*, XXXIX (1943–1944), 225–228.

lordism," and Ray P. Chase, a Minnesota attorney and former congressman, argued that the Farm Security Administration was using taxpayers' money "to destroy American business" while its leaders "preach the doctrine of Communism but lack the courage to carry a card." [17] On the other side, the legislative representative of the National Farmers' Union, Russell Smith, was firmly convinced that "the Farm Security idea is a good idea, indeed, that it is an idea basic to the attainment of complete democracy in this country." [18] In a prepared report the Emergency Committee for Food Production declared that the opposition to the Farm Security Administration arose because it "had begun to wreck the dream of factory farmers for a rural serfdom and agricultural monopoly." Thus, the efforts to kill the Farm Security Administration, according to the report, "strike at the heart of democracy itself and must be opposed by the people of America." [19]

The Farm Security Administration first faced serious congressional criticism over the liquidation of the community projects which, though only a small aspect of the whole farm security program, were always at the center of any controversy, probably because they were the most embarrassing part of the Farm Security Administration's activities. As early as 1938, the first year after the creation of the Farm Security Administration, Congress explicitly appropriated money for the "liquidation and management" of the resettlement projects. But no appreciable liquidation occurred. In debates over another appropriation in 1939, Will W. Alexander, Administrator of the Farm Security Administration, was called an "off-color politician" by Representative Edward E. Cox of Georgia.[20] Representative Guy L. Moser of Pennsylvania declared that the old Resettlement Administration had pounced upon the Bankhead-Jones Act like a vulture, while "wandering minstrels and scavengers" continued to infest farm communities with "gratuitous advice by childless women who never kept house themselves." [21] In 1939 Congress refused to allot further funds for the completion of communities and, in 1940, cut off all loans to new co-operatives.[22] By

[17] *Hearings on the Farm Security Administration*, pp. 802, 1867.
[18] *Ibid.*, p. 1495.   [19] *Ibid.*, p. 1507.
[20] *C.R.*, 76th Cong., 1st Sess., 1939, p. 3456; *ibid.*, 77th Cong., 2d Sess., 1942, p. 4304.
[21] *Ibid.*, 76th Cong., 1st Sess., 1939, p. 3457.
[22] House Committee on Appropriations, *Appropriations for Work Relief, Relief, and for Loans and Grants for Public Works Projects, Fiscal Year 1940*, Report

1941 Representative Harold D. Cooley of North Carolina was seeking authority for a full congressional investigation of the Farm Security Administration.[23]

The real struggle over the Farm Security Administration began in 1942. In that year the Farm Bureau officially went on record against the Farm Security Administration, and the Farm Bureau head, Edward O'Neal, testified against it in the Appropriations Committeee hearings. Two Southern senators, Harry F. Byrd and Kenneth D. McKellar, both of whom opposed the extravagance and the collectivist experiments of the Farm Security Administration, led the Senate attack. McKellar bluntly stated of the Farm Security Administration's Administrator: "I think Mr. Baldwin is a Communist."[24] Byrd, who used lengthy statistics to prove the extravagance of the Farm Security Administration, attacked its paternalism, its defiance of Congress, and its failure to liquidate the communities. He believed the homestead associations were ruses to conceal continued governmental control.[25] In the House, Representative Malcolm C. Tarver of Georgia, chairman of the House Committee on Agriculture, belabored the Farm Security Administration for its collective farms and stated that further retention of the community projects would place the Farm Security Administration in open defiance of Congress.[26] As a result of this attack, Congress forbade further expenditures for collective farms, land purchase, and migratory camps and requested a rapid liquidation of all remaining communities.[27]

In the early part of 1943 Representative Cooley finally secured the passage of a resolution calling for a complete investigation of the Farm Security Administration. He justified the investigation on the basis that the original Resettlement Administration was created with the broadest power ever conferred upon a United States Government agency, that

---

no. 833, 76th Cong., 1st Sess., 1939, p. 16; U.S. House of Representatives, *Activities of the Farm Security Administration*, Report no. 1430, 78th Cong., 2d Sess., 1944, p. 50.

[23] *C.R.*, 77th Cong., 1st Sess., 1941, p. 9458.

[24] *Ibid.*, 77th Cong., 2d Sess., 1942, pp. 2029, 4283.   [25] *Ibid.*, p. 4306.

[27] House Agricultural Subcommittee of the Committee on Appropriations, *Hearings on the Agricultural Department Appropriation Bill for 1943*, pt. II, pp. 197–198, 255–259.

[27] House Agricultural Subcommittee of the Comitee on Appropriations, *Hearings on the Agricultural Department Appropriation Bill for 1944*, p. 992; U.S. House of Representatives, *Activities of the Farm Security Administration*, p. 51; *C.R.*, 77th Cong., 2d Sess., p. 2427.

Old Society Reasserts Claims

the Farm Security Administration had largely ignored the Bankhead-Jones Act, that the existence of collective farms and ninety-nine-year leases threatened the traditional land policy of the United States, and that the land-leasing and land-purchasing associations were means of evading congressional restrictions on land purchase. Cooley stressed the fact that, with the sudden accretion of federal activity, the Congress did not have the time or the ability to be fully advised on all federal agencies, and this apparently had permitted the Farm Security Administration to violate congressional intentions.[28]

Representative Cooley headed the select committee which thoroughly investigated every aspect of the Farm Security Administration. The lengthy investigation aroused fear among Farm Security Administration supporters that Cooley maliciously desired the death of their agency. The American Federation of Labor, the Congress of Industrial Organizations, the National Farmers' Union, the National Council of Churches, the National Catholic Welfare Council, and President Roosevelt all came out in support of the Farm Security Administration. On the other hand, the Farm Bureau and organized business groups, both of which opposed the Farm Security Administration and wanted it abolished, found no sure ally in Cooley, who sincerely believed in aid to the small farmer and who wished the tenant-purchase and rehabilitation programs to be continued. Based on his published statements in the thorough and extensive hearings of 1943 and 1944, Cooley, a Southern Democrat, was very sympathetic to the aspirations of the small farmers and particularly to their desires to achieve homeownership and economic independence. He hated the idea of bureaucracy and was especially angry at the Farm Security Administration for its defiance of Congress. He was strongly individualistic, believing in the traditional land policies and in governmental thrift. He disliked extensive paternalism and was against any tendency toward collectivism. But at the same time he distrusted the motives of the large farmers and of businessmen in opposing the Farm Security Administration, seeing behind their opposition a good bit of self-interest.

The congressional hearings revolved around the committee members' attack upon the extravagance, the philosophy, and the community-building activities of the Farm Security Administration and the countering defense of the officials of the Farm Security Administration, which

[28] *C.R.*, 78th Cong., 1st Sess., 1943, pp. 2185–2186, 2192, 2194.

was based upon the merit of the rehabilitation and tenant-purchase programs. The committee members tended to blame most of the community projects on Tugwell. They even tried to connect these projects and his collectivist philosophy with his pre-New Deal trip to Russia.[29] Involved in their attack was a distrust of intellectuals and theorists, who lacked a "hard-boiled" understanding of people. The congressmen believed that Ph.D.'s too often evolved "these theories the average man may not be able to quite formulate and set in motion."[30] The committee members were astounded at the financial loss on some of the projects, at the close supervision, at the attempts to insure a lengthy control over the communities by the government, and at the amount of industry sponsored on the projects. Cooley was constantly angered to learn the extent to which the Farm Security Administration had departed from congressional intentions, avowing that the Farm Security Administration officials "have been doing too much thinking for themselves and have not been following the policies laid down by Congress."[31]

The most telling criticisms were leveled at the collective farms and the long leases. These were the most obvious breaks with the old society and the ones most disliked by the congressmen. Representative John W. Flannigan, Jr., of Virginia, a member of the committee, said: "It looks to me that a studied effort has been made . . . to finally abolish fee ownership of land in this country." He declared fee simple ownership to be "one of the fundamentals in the establishment of this country" and tried desperately to place responsibility for the "un-American scheme of getting around fee simple ownership."[32] Cooley believed the issue of vital importance "because it involves a great principle; it goes deep into the traditional land policy of this country."[33] Through it all Calvin B. Baldwin, Administrator of the Farm Security Administration, was a rather ineffective, overly submissive, and evasive witness. He refused to defend the community and co-operative projects, admitting that none of them "should be continued."[34] The whole Farm Security Administration controversy came at a time when the Roosevelt Administration, busily devoted to the task of winning a war, was

---

[29] *Hearings on the Farm Security Administration*, p. 279.
[30] *Ibid.*, pp. 185, 269.   [31] *Ibid.*, pp. 36–39, 44, 493–495.
[32] *Ibid.*, pp. 20–21, 55.   [33] *Ibid.*, p. 21.   [34] *Ibid.*, p. 455.

not willing to take a strong stand in support of the Farm Security Administration program at the risk of offending a conservative Congress. The embarrassing communities and other aspects of the Farm Security Administration were sacrificed without a really strong effort in their defense.

In its final report the Cooley Committee indicted the Farm Security Administration on several counts. It was accused of starting collective farms, stretching executive orders, disobeying the intent of the Bankhead-Jones Act, using ninety-nine-year leases to prevent instead of encourage landownership, colonizing, regimenting, and too closely supervising its clients by regulating every detail in their lives, uprooting families, deceiving clients with false promises of ownership and a "promised land" in a community, granting loans to unqualified borrowers, obeying the President's Committee on Farm Tenancy rather than Congress, backing industrial enterprises in competition with private business, and permitting an enlarged and inefficient administrative organization.[35] But despite this, the Cooley Committee recommended that the tenant-purchase and rehabilitation programs be continued in a new agency, a Farmers' Home Corporation, which would absorb both the Farm Security Administration and the Farm Credit Administration. A bill to this effect was introduced into Congress.

The Farmers' Home Corporation bill, which was first introduced in 1944 and, after much delay, eventually enacted in 1946, abolished the Farm Security Administration. It provided for a Farmers' Home Corporation to regulate tenant-purchase and rehabilitation loans. After six months for study, the corporation was to liquidate the remaining resettlement projects. It was to have only eighteen months to dispose of all this property. Further loans to co-operative associations were strictly forbidden.[36] The new corporation was to have no authority to purchase land and no basis for paternalistic supervision, and it was required to render annual accounts to Congress. The undeveloped subsistence homesteads property turned over to the Federal Public

[35] U.S. House of Representatives, *Activities of the Farm Security Administration*, pp. 1–19.
[36] House Committee on Agriculture, *Hearings on Farmers' Home Corporation Act of 1944*, 78th Cong., 2d Sess., 1944, pp. 1–9.

Housing Authority was to be repossessed and immediately sold. The most unfair criticism of the Farm Security Administration was contained in the minority report on the Farmers' Home Corporation Act. Tugwell was falsely accused of filling his agency with "thousands of utopian planners who were 'hell bent' on remaking the United States into a Communist State." They argued that the Cooley Committee had "uncovered hundreds of communistic projects." [37]

Even as the Cooley Committee debated the eventual fate of the Farm Security Administration, the various communities were benefiting from the wartime boom. In many of the projects the wages of homesteaders soared above earlier limitations. Even the stranded communities became more prosperous, with many of the coal mines reopening. The Farm Security Administration was unsuccessful in an attempt at procuring decentralized defense industry for some of the projects, but this did not mean any shortage of jobs. As prosperity returned to the homesteaders, there was an increasing tendency to neglect the subsistence plots, either leaving them idle, leasing them, or hiring laborers to work them.

The Cooley investigation led to many changes in the Farm Security Administration. In 1943 the lease and purchase contracts were replaced by quitclaim deeds with approximately the same restrictions and the same variable payment plan already being used in the tenant-purchase program. In the same year the House Appropriations Committee seriously considered turning the Farm Security Administration loans over to the Farm Credit Administration and its supervisory activities over to the Extension Service as a method of getting rid of its distrusted leadership and philosophy.[38] Baldwin, much harassed from all sides, was hindered in his liquidation of projects by a requirement of the Solicitor of the Department of Agriculture that the projects be sold in such a manner as to help in the rehabilitation of needy families, since the original appropriations had been made for this purpose. This prevented an open-auction method of disposition. Baldwin himself was reluctant to dispose of the projects at such a

---

[37] U.S. House of Representatives, *Farmers' Home Corporation Act of 1944*, Report no. 1747, 78th Cong., 2d Sess., 1944, pp. 2–3, 56.

[38] *Hearings on the Farm Security Administration*, pp. 289–291; Senate Agricultural Subcommittee of the Committee on Appropriations, *Hearings on Agricultural Department Appropriation Bill for 1944*, pp. 264–266.

rate as to harm or dispossess the homesteaders or to cause the government any greater loss than absolutely necessary. But despite these feelings, he promised in February, 1943, to be rid of the co-operative projects by June 30, 1943, which proved to be an impossibility.[39]

In November, 1943, Baldwin and his assistant, George S. Mitchell, resigned from the Farm Security Administration to join Sidney Hillman in the Congress of Industrial Organizations' Political Action Committee, lending some ammunition to the conservative attack on the radicalism of the Farm Security Administration. Baldwin was replaced by a former North Carolina congressman, Frank Hancock, who immediately appointed a new staff and secured the confidence of Congress. This change in leadership really marked the end of the Resettlement Administration and the Farm Security Administration programs as initiated by Tugwell and continued by his successors. It meant that Congress had, at last, gained control over the policies of the Farm Security Administration. It meant that experimentation and broad attempts at institutional reform were ended. Hancock himself signified, at least in the eyes of Congress, a shift from idealism to practicality, from extravagance to economy, from dangerous radicalism to safe moderation. He immediately reduced the personnel of the Farm Security Administration and began studying methods for disposing of the resettlement projects.

Hancock found that many of the former sales of homesteads to project clients were merely paper transactions, since the clients were already so deeply in debt to the Farm Security Administration that they could never pay out. He slowed the process of sales temporarily in order to place the liquidation on a sounder basis, incurring some wrath from Congress. By June 30, 1944, only 3,045 deeds had been granted on over 9,000 units. Eight co-operative associations were still in existence, with one refusing to cancel its ninety-nine-year lease, much to the embarrassment of the Farm Security Administration. Then the sales began at a rapid pace. As of January 1, 1945, only 2,016 units were unsold; as of June 30, 1945, only 1,434 units. The units were sold, if possible, at fair market values to low-income fam-

---

[39] House Agricultural Subcommittee of the Committee on Appropriations, *Hearings on the Agricultural Department Appropriation Bill for 1944*, pp. 1036, 1088, and *Hearings on the Agricultural Department Appropriation Bill for 1945*, p. 989; *Hearings on the Farm Security Administration*, p. 450.

ilies who met Bankhead-Jones standards. None were sold to people who had more debts than assets, and this eliminated many of the old homesteaders who had waited expectantly for a chance to purchase their homes. All units not salable to low-income clients were sold at public auction after a newspaper announcement.[40]

The liquidation of the rural projects, even though carried out at a time of inflated land values, resulted in a tremendous loss to the government. On many projects the liquidation price was only approximately one-fourth of the total cost. Out of 8,945 units costing $70,775,970.42, the Farm Security Administration sold 7,276 units for only $29,245,446.59. At this same rate the total units would have sold for $35,953,755.08, or almost exactly one-half of cost. As examples, the average unit sale price on sixty-six units at Penderlea was $3,110, whereas each unit cost $11,633. Eighty-eight units at Gee's Bend sold for an average of $1,400, whereas they cost an average of over $4,000.[41] These high unit costs included the many community facilities which were not included in the sale prices. They also included all the losses incurred by the use of relief labor.

In 1946, with the passage of the Farmers' Home Corporation Act, the Farm Security Administration was abolished and its functions transferred to a new agency, the Farmers' Home Administration, on November 1, 1946. This new agency had specific authorizations and instructions for the disposition of the few remaining homestead units. By April, 1947, only 290 units remained unsold, and this led Representative Everett M. Dirksen of Illinois to remark that, at last, "it appears that in the year ahead there is some likelihood of finally closing out Mr. Tugwell's lovely dream in the field of resettlement." [42] By February, 1948, the last units were sold, but Tugwell's dream was

[40] House Agricultural Subcommittee of the Committee on Appropriations, *Hearings on the Agricultural Department Appropriation Bill for 1945*, pp. 197, 966, and *Hearings on the Agricultural Department Appropriation Bill for 1946*, pt. II, 79th Cong., 1st Sess., 1945, pp. 516–517, 525–527, 564; U.S. Department of Agriculture, War Food Administration, Farm Security Administration, *The Annual Report of the FSA, 1943–1944* (Washington, 1944), p. 14.

[41] House Agricultural Subcommittee of the Committee on Appropriations, *Hearings on the Agricultural Department Appropriation Bill for 1947*, 79th Cong., 2d Sess., 1946, pp. 1411–1419.

[42] House Agricultural Subcommittee of the Committee on Appropriations, *Hearings on the Agricultural Department Appropriation Bill for 1948*, pt. I, 80th Cong., 1st Sess., 1947, pp. 1467–1468.

Old Society Reasserts Claims 231

far from an end.[43] Dirksen had forgotten about the greenbelt cities and the subsistence homesteads communities, which were still retained by the Federal Public Housing Authority.

Under the Federal Public Housing Authority the nonfarming communities were liquidated as quickly as possible. Most of the supervisory activities of the Farm Security Administration were dropped, and the Federal Public Housing Authority was only a creditor agency for the nineteen homestead associations. Since many individuals had forty-year purchase contracts, Congress, in 1944, passed a law providing that, on proffering the full payment of the purchase price, the homesteader had to receive a deed for his property, regardless of the lapse of time since he had purchased it. It also required a quitclaim deed with no reservations, conditions, or restrictions whatsoever.[44] The Federal Public Housing Authority immediately began to issue deeds for those who wanted to complete their payments and, at the same time, granted releases from the mortgage lien to the homestead associations concerned. Congressional intent even prevented the Federal Public Housing Authority from utilizing deed restrictions in order to avoid speculation, resale, commercial building, or added dwellings. This left no government control over the communities and ended all social experimentation. The communities were thrown open to real estate speculators unless the citizens themselves, without government backing, took steps to ward them off through voluntary restrictions or zoning laws. Even the mineral rights were restored to the homesteaders as quickly as possible.[45]

In 1944 the Federal Public Housing Authority sold two homestead associations, at Hattiesburg and Meridian, directly to the individual homesteaders because of continuous delinquencies on the part of the associations. In the same year Three Rivers Gardens was foreclosed and declared surplus property when it defaulted in its payments. The Tygart Valley Co-operative Association was sued for not keeping up

[43] House Agricultural Subcommittee of the Committee on Appropriations, *Hearings on the Agricultural Department Appropriation Bill for 1949*, pt. II, 80th Cong., 2d Sess., 1948, p. 387.

[44] *C.R.*, 78th Cong., 1st Sess., 1943, p. 1418; *ibid.*, 78th Cong., 2d Sess., 1944, p. 6477.

[45] Paul W. Wager, *One Foot on the Soil: A Study of Subsistence Homesteads in Alabama* (Bureau of Public Administration at the University of Alabama, 1945), pp. 146–148.

its payments on its loans, and four co-operative stores were sold on other projects.[46] The Farm Security Administration had been accused of coddling its clients; no such accusation could be leveled against the Federal Public Housing Authority. Everything was businesslike now.

At the end of World War II the Federal Public Housing Authority rushed its liquidation program. The hosiery mills at three projects were sold for $1,200,000, or 83 per cent of cost. On December 1, 1945, Westmoreland was sold to an association of its residents, insuring community control at this project. At least a few individual units had been sold on all but six projects, and 189 clear deeds had been granted to individuals on the homestead association projects.[47] In 1946 four homestead associations secured private financing and paid off their loans in full. Of 1,960 unsold units in the nonconveyed subsistence homesteads communities, over 1,000 units were sold in 1946. In selling, all former commitments were honored, with clients on four projects receiving credit for rentals paid under the temporary licensing agreements. If no sales commitments had been made by the Farm Security Administration or predecessor agencies, the units were sold at fair market value and, if possible, to the resident homesteaders. The terms of sale required a 25 per cent down payment and the remainder over twenty years. If possible, common utilities were sold to associations organized by the homesteaders.[48]

In 1947 the remaining subsistence homesteads units and the three greenbelt cities became the responsibility of the Public Housing Administration in the newly formed Housing and Home Finance Agency. By the end of 1947 only 431 units in the subsistence homesteads projects were unsold. By the end of 1948 they had been reduced to thirty. These represented units that had been sold to individuals by the Farm Security Administration under forty-year purchase terms. Under the contract and later legislation the government retained title until the final payment was made, at any time up to the forty years al-

[46] U.S. National Housing Agency, *Third Annual Report of the National Housing Agency, January 1 to December 31, 1944* (Washington, 1945), p. 214.

[47] U.S. National Housing Agency, *Fourth Annual Report of the National Housing Agency, January 1 to December 31, 1945*, pt. IV (Washington, 1946), pp. 60–61.

[48] U.S. National Housing Agency, *Fifth Annual Report of the National Housing Agency, January 1 to December 31, 1946* (Washington, 1947), pp. 256–257.

lowed. Most purchasers of this type had paid in full or, under encouragement from the Public Housing Administration, had secured other financing in order to fulfill the contract and receive title. The thirty mentioned had not done that and continued their payments under their old contract. By 1952 these thirty units had been reduced to eleven.[49] But for all practical purposes the liquidation of the subsistence homesteads projects was completed in 1948. At that time only the greenbelt towns remained in government ownership. Their liquidation will be discussed in a subsequent chapter.

The finale to the story of the New Deal communities was written in an age ever farther removed from the insecurity and intellectual volatility of the depression. It was written in terms of reaction. The idealism and reforming zeal of the architects of the communities and the new society were repudiated. The revolution was over. The old society, slightly revamped, was again embraced, at least for a while. Traditional gods once again possessed men's minds and claimed their loyalties. Experimental communities became, except for their odd designs, ordinary communities. Most people soon forgot that Dyess, Arkansas, or Cahaba, Alabama, had been part of a large social experiment. Even Arthurdale and Hightstown, once so controversial, were remembered only because of the controversy. But a few people remembered, remembered well. They were the homesteaders, the living clay in the great exhibit. To them Cahaba and Dyess and Arthurdale represented not only an experiment but their homes. To them the story of the New Deal communities was really a story of one community, their community. Thus, beyond ideas, policies, administrators, bureaus, the story of the New Deal communities was really many varying stories—one for each individual community.

[49] U.S. Housing and Home Finance Agency, *First Annual Report, 1947*, pt. IV (Washington, 1948), p. 21, *Second Annual Report, 1948* (Washington, 1949), p. 321, and *Sixth Annual Report, 1952*, pt. IV (Washington, 1953), p. 431.

Part Three

OF INDIVIDUAL COMMUNITIES

X

Arthurdale—An Experimental Community

ON a cold night in early November, 1933, Clarence Pickett, executive secretary of the American Friends Service Committee and Assistant Administrator of the Division of Subsistence Homesteads, Louis M. Howe, confidential secretary to Franklin D. Roosevelt, and Mrs. Franklin D. Roosevelt entrained at Washington, D.C., for Fairmont, West Virginia. The next morning they were escorted by some American Friends Service Committee workers to the site of the old Arthur mansion at Reedsville, halfway between Fairmont and Morgantown. Here everything was confusion, for the first work on the first subsistence homesteads community was already under way. Mrs. Roosevelt and Louis Howe came with promises of rapid accomplishment; they met with architects, engineers, prospective builders, educational leaders, ministers, and planning officials. Before the day was over, Howe, in a burst of enthusiasm, placed a telephone order for fifty prefabricated cottages to be delivered to the homestead site within two weeks. Howe inspired the prospective homesteaders with assurances that, by Christmas, the first homestead cottages would be ready for occupancy. Clarence Pickett later wrote: "What one saw on that November day was the turning point in American concepts of public responsibility for suffering of citizens, wherever they might live and whatever might be their circumstances."[1] Many other people, looking back to that November day, saw only the first and most serious mistake in a long series of mistakes at Arthurdale.

The origin of Arthurdale, as many other of the subsistence homesteads communities, had predated the passage of the subsistence homesteads legislation. In 1931 the American Friends Service Committee began a program of child feeding in the bituminous coal fields; it grew, by 1932, into a broader rehabilitation program, with subsistence gardening and handicrafts. The worst conditions in the coal-mine areas were in West Virginia, where many mines had been virtually closed since 1920. Scott's Run, a term applied both to a creek near Morgantown and to the mining settlements clustered close to its bank, became a symbol for the worst poverty and degradation of the company towns. Thus it was in the Scott's Run or Morgantown area that the Friends attempted their most extensive rehabilitation program. The committee, under the direction of Clarence Pickett, received help in its rehabilitation program from a Council of Social Agencies in Morgantown and from officials of West Virginia University, also located in Morgantown. Even as the subsistence homesteads program was being born in Washington, these groups in Morgantown had prepared a prospectus for a Co-operative Self-Help Association, which was to settle stranded miners on subsistence farms throughout the state. The College of Agriculture at West Virginia University made a survey of available lands, and public-spirited citizens were asked to contribute to a $50,000 budget for the homestead efforts.[2] Among the local promoters of subsistence farming, the old Richard M. Arthur estate near Morgantown was much in mind as a possible site for subsistence farmsteads. This farm of approximately 1,200 acres had been used as an experimental farm by the College of Agriculture and contained fertile land. The estate, which was about to revert to the state for unpaid taxes, had been purchased in 1903 by Arthur, a Philadelphia merchant, from the Fairfax family, which had owned the farm since the Revolution. The area reputedly had been surveyed by George Washington.

In the summer of 1933, as plans for subsistence homesteads were developed at Morgantown, Clarence Pickett interested Mrs. Roosevelt

---

[1] Clarence E. Pickett, *For More than Bread* (Boston, 1953), p. 47.

[2] Millard Milburn Rice, "Footnote on Arthurdale," *Harper's Magazine*, CLXXX (1939–1940), 411–413.

in the plight of the miners and brought her to visit the Scott's Run area. Mrs. Roosevelt immediately became an enthusiastic supporter of the rehabilitation and subsistence homesteads program of the Friends. When the Division of Subsistence Homesteads was organized in August, Pickett became Assistant Administrator and headed the program for stranded miners. This, plus Mrs. Roosevelt's enthusiastic backing, insured a project somewhere in the Morgantown area. On October 12, 1933, Ickes announced approval of plans for a project at Morgantown. Already the Division of Subsistence Homesteads had purchased the Arthur estate, which was surveyed by the College of Agriculture of West Virginia University and by the United States Department of Agriculture. The local sponsors, including university officials and the members of the Morgantown Council of Social Agencies, early submitted plans for a homestead community on the higher grounds of the estate, with community gardens in the low-lying meadows. This plan was rejected by the Division of Subsistence Homesteads, which required the subsistence plots to be connected with the homes. The accepted plans called for 200 five-acre homestead plots, a community school, and a co-operative store. It was hoped that the first homesteads could be completed in the fall of 1933, possibly even by Thanksgiving. Bushrod Grimes, a university extension agent and leader of the sponsors at the university, became the first project manager.[3]

In the fall of 1933 Arthurdale was a great dream, which somehow never became a complete reality. The dream involved a transition from hell to heaven for a group of stranded miners. From their huts clinging to a hillside above Scott's Run, from their lack of sanitary facilities, from the midst of malnutrition, disease, alcoholism, crime, delinquency, and high mortality, a fortunate few were to escape to pretty white homes, situated on small plats of farm land, surrounded by lawns, flowers, orchards, and fields. They were to enjoy regular meals, not through the bitter bread of charity, but through the food produced by their own hands. They were to have cows, poultry, root cellars, preserve closets, and plenty of air and sunshine. In their new com-

[3] Pickett, *For More than Bread*, p. 45; Wesley Stout, "The New Homesteaders," *Saturday Evening Post*, CCVII (Aug. 4, 1934), 62; Blair Bolles, "Resettling America," *American Mercury*, XXXIX (1936), 342; Henry I. Harriman, "A New Pattern for Industrial America," New York *Times*, Sept. 23, 1934, sec. 6, pp. 4–5; Millard Milburn Rice, "The Fuller Life at Reedsville," *Nation's Business*, XXIV (May, 1936), 25.

munity they could "face to the sky instead of to the earth, to watch the long summer wane, and the color come on the mountains, and the snow fall and pass, and the redbud turn the hills to new splendor and the dogwood fleck them with white, instead of being shut away among the slag pile down in one of the 'hollows.'"[4] They were to have part-time employment in a government-sponsored Post Office factory, were to govern themselves through a town meeting, and were to find other sources of employment and a constructive use of leisure time in multiple handicrafts. The community was to point the way to a new way of life, not just for the miners but for all America. It was to show the way to a solution of the problems of stranded populations, was to promote industrial decentralization, and was to show what social and economic planning might accomplish if given a chance.

Yet, with all the dreams, there was very little co-ordinated planning for the community that was later to be called Arthurdale (it was at first known as the Reedsville Experimental Community). As at most of the subsistence homesteads communities, the ideas of the local sponsors did not always meet the approval of the Division of Subsistence Homesteads. This was to be expected and, in most cases, led merely to delays in securing approval of project plans. At Arthurdale another element complicated any attempt at formalized administration. Mrs. Roosevelt adopted Arthurdale as her own special project and became a sort of godmother to the miners of Scott's Run. Sharing her interest were Louis Howe and even President Roosevelt, although the latter was too busy to take an active part in the development of Arthurdale. Not so Howe, Mrs. Roosevelt, and many of her humanitarian-minded friends. They occupied an indefinite, semiofficial position that brought Ickes, the administrator par excellence, to a point of near desperation. Although not employees of the Division of Subsistence Homesteads, Mrs. Roosevelt and Howe made many of the important decisions and determined much of the policy at Arthurdale. Mrs. Roosevelt selected or approved most of the important personnel employed. The situation became one of administrative confusion, with Mrs. Roosevelt's humanitarian impulses often running counter to the administrative policies of the Division of Subsistence Homesteads. Embarrassment followed embarrassment as far as the Division of Subsistence Home-

[4] William E. Brooks, "Arthurdale—A New Chance," *Atlantic Monthly*, CLV (1935), 197.

Arthurdale

steads was concerned, although M. L. Wilson was much more tolerant of the situation than was Ickes.

On the same day that Howe placed his telephone order for fifty prefabricated houses at a cost of $48,600, he also telephoned the War Department and asked for fifty mattresses, fifty pillows, and sufficient blankets and pillow cases, all to be delivered to Arthurdale by Monday, November 6. The War Department had no authority to turn this equipment over to another agency, but since Howe presumably spoke for the Commander in Chief they complied, listing the request as an emergency requirement and later demanding an accounting from a surprised Ickes.[5] At about the same time Mrs. Roosevelt's secretary presented an expense account to the Division of Subsistence Homesteads for one of Mrs. Roosevelt's early trips to Arthurdale, throwing the Department of the Interior into a quandary, since they had no authority to pay for her transportation.[6] This was the only such request ever received from Mrs. Roosevelt and was probably made by her secretary without her knowledge, but it did show the problems occasioned by her sincere but unofficial endeavors. Actually Mrs. Roosevelt unselfishly spent thousands of dollars of her own money at Arthurdale.

From November, 1933, to July, 1934, the history of Arthurdale was bound up in the long-deferred completion of the first fifty homes. As Howe's prefabricated cottages arrived, they proved utterly worthless for the intended use. The houses, ten by forty feet in size, were made of Oregon cedar frames, cedar siding, and, for the interior, building paper and fiberboard. Intended for vacation use, they were not at all suited for the cold winters at Arthurdale. Nevertheless they were bolted together and placed on prepared foundations. In January, Mrs. Roosevelt selected an architect from New York to come to Arthurdale and supervise the alteration of the prefabs. This marked the beginning of outside control and direction at the project, although the local sponsors remained loyal to the project despite their having less and less voice in its direction. At Arthurdale new foundations were constructed and three sides of the prefabs pulled out and expanded. The basements remained a maze of foundations, while the walls of the prefab section of each house remained extrathin. As drastically revised and finally

[5] Oscar L. Chapman to Ickes, Nov. 17, 1933, R.G. 48, National Archives.
[6] H. M. Gilliam to Ebert K. Burlew, n.d., *ibid.*

completed in July, 1934, the first fifty homes included either four, five, or six rooms, basements, and baths.[7]

The first fifty homes were constructed by relief labor, with prospective homesteaders among those employed. The houses included copper plumbing, oversized air furnaces to heat the thin prefabs, and water from individual wells. Each home had an individual septic tank and, to protect the bacterial action of the tank from grease, a $37.50 grease trap that, because of the high cost, became one of the many famous follies of Arthurdale. Each homestead plot had a barn. The community buildings were grouped around a town square. They included an old Presbyterian church that was moved to the project and converted into a pretty community building, although its sides were knocked out to accommodate a barbershop, forge, and furniture shop. A building originally planned for a power plant was converted into an administration building. The old Arthur mansion was used as an early headquarters and as a meeting place.

Not only did Mrs. Roosevelt select the architect to redesign the prefabricated homes, but she also helped plan the interior design and furniture for the homes which, after all the confusion and expense, were neat, pretty, and well landscaped on completion. Assisting Mrs. Roosevelt was Miss Nancy Cook, who had operated a small co-operative furniture plant with Mrs. Roosevelt at Hyde Park. Mrs. Roosevelt excused Howe's mistake in ordering the prefabricated homes and the resultant expense in redesigning them as a necessary part of a beginning experiment. She regarded Arthurdale as a social laboratory, where experimentation could be carried on in house types, use of electricity, and use of government factories and in a new type of rural education. She deplored a tendency on the part of Ickes and others to use the subsistence homesteads appropriation to place as many people as possible in inexpensive homes provided with only the bare necessities. She wanted Arthurdale to be an exhibit of a new way of life, visited by 50,000 to 100,000 people each year. She desired a national research center in subsistence homesteading at West Virginia University, since Arthurdale would be the first project of its kind in the world and, as an experiment, would rival Radburn, New Jersey, in its importance. Be-

---

[7] Farm Security Administration, "Arthurdale: Final Report of Project Costs to June 30, 1939," in R.G. 96, National Archives; Stout, "The New Homesteaders," pp. 5–6.

yond all that it would be the focal point for the regional planning and development of the Upper Monongahela valley. As such an experiment any early mistakes or excessive costs were justified.[8]

Mrs. Roosevelt's expensive plans for Arthurdale plagued Ickes. He felt that the first fifty homes appeared "a good deal like a joke" and had difficulties in restraining the expenditures of Mrs. Roosevelt's architect and the countless other planners and architects. At the same time a businesslike project manager appointed by Ickes was opposed by Mrs. Roosevelt and eventually forced out of his job. Mrs. Roosevelt publicly announced that the excessive costs of the Howe houses would be written off as an experiment and would "not be borne" by the homesteaders.[9] This came as a surprise to Ickes and again led to embarrassment, since it opened the way for new criticism of the subsistence homesteads program. Meanwhile Howe was constantly interfering with the plans of the Division of Subsistence Homesteads. He had a scheme for an experimental power plant at Arthurdale which was to be used as a yardstick to measure private-power prices. All the experts consulted by the Division of Subsistence Homesteads said such a plant would cost at least $50,000 and would provide no saving, but Howe was never satisfied, arguing that the cost would not have exceeded $15,000. Howe, although occupying no official position in the Division of Subsistence Homesteads, was chairman of the Electrical Committee for Arthurdale, one of the committees staffed by Arthurdale sponsors. He was vexed to learn that the first homes did not contain refrigerators. He wrote Pynchon: "God alone knows how refrigerators came to be eliminated. . . . Nothing was to be done without reference to me." Howe threatened to have the man fired who was responsible for the electrical service since, as he claimed, President Roosevelt wished all the electrical work done under his (Howe's) supervision. He also stated that Mrs. Roosevelt was very disappointed, since she had been selecting refrigerators for some time.[10]

Mrs. Roosevelt and Nancy Cook, who was employed by the Division of Subsistence Homesteads as a specialist, supervised the internal ap-

[8] Mrs. Franklin D. Roosevelt to M. L. Wilson, March 26, 1934, R.G. 48, National Archives.

[9] Ickes, *Secret Diary*, I, 150–152; C. E. Pynchon to Oscar Chapman, Oct. 4, 1934, R.G. 48, National Archives.

[10] Pynchon to Burlew, Oct. 17, 1934, R.G. 48, National Archives; Louis Howe to Pynchon, July 24, 1934, *ibid.*

pointments of the new homes. Furniture was provided by the Mountaineer Craftsmen's Co-operative Association, which was the handicraft group founded by the American Friends Service Committee and which was later supported by the Civil Works Administration. This co-operative group, which later moved into shops at Arthurdale, constructed beautiful maple furniture for the project at no cost to the Division of Subsistence Homesteads (but at a cost to the Civil Works Administration). The furniture included not only major items, but linens, curtains, and tapestries. By June two model homes were completed and decorated for the benefit of visitors and photographers. The landscaping was perfect down to the smallest item. Wild grapevines were procured from a nearby wood and carefully twined around trellises. One reporter discovered that rhododendron were hauled sixty miles at an expense of several hundred dollars in order to impress visitors. By this time Arthurdale was so well publicized and so much on exhibit that the Division of Subsistence Homesteads felt bound to make it as perfect as possible. The wishes of the homesteaders or the self-help ideas of the local sponsors had to take second place to the desire to make a favorable impression on the visiting public.[11]

The first fifty homesteaders were selected as early as December, 1933, when they moved to the project as workers. Although from among the stranded miners, they represented a select group, despite Mrs. Roosevelt's wishes to settle a representative group. The prospective homesteaders were selected only after physical examinations, an interview with a social worker, and the completion of an eight-page questionnaire. Education, physical fitness, attitudes, ambitions, and agricultural abilities were all considered. West Virginia University assisted in the selection process, basing the selection partially on such practical farming tests as seed selection and animal judging.[12] A critic of the rigid requirements for settlers complained: "Probably there are a lot of 'poor risks' out on Scott's Run. Probably their bellies are just as hungry as those of the good risks." [13]

[11] Stout, "The New Homesteaders," pp. 6–7; Rice, "Footnote on Arthurdale," p. 414.
[12] U.S. Department of Labor, Bureau of Labor Statistics, "Subsistence-Homestead Movement under National Recovery Act," *Monthly Labor Review*, XXXVII (1933), 1329; Mary Meek Atkeson, "Too Many Hopes," *Country Gentleman*, CV (Dec., 1935), 38.
[13] T. R. Carskadon, "Hull House in the Hills," *New Republic*, LXXIX (1934), 313.

Because of delays in construction the prospective homesteaders at Arthurdale saw their long-awaited day of moving constantly postponed, from Christmas to March to May to June and even July. Nevertheless, on February 26, 1934, M. L. Wilson formally presented an uncompleted Arthurdale to the homesteaders during a driving snowstorm. Also present and speaking was Representative Jennings Randolph, who accepted for the homesteaders and excused the delay and early mistakes as inevitable in a new undertaking. On June 7, 1934, Arthurdale celebrated its formal opening, although the fifty homes were hardly finished and were not yet occupied. Speaking at the opening was Mrs. Roosevelt, who also conversed with the homesteaders in the Arthur mansion. Among the important guests in the large crowd were Bernard Baruch and Mrs. Harold Ickes. Mrs. Roosevelt was anxious to secure Baruch's support for some educational experimentation. The grateful homesteaders, already blessed by the fruits of labor and a bountiful soil if not by completed homes, presented Mrs. Roosevelt with a big bunch of onions and radishes.[14]

By July 15, 1934, forty-three of the first fifty homes were occupied. Construction of 150 more was already planned. Ickes reported that the average unit cost of the first houses and outbuildings was $4,880, which was much above earlier plans for something like $2,500 but much below the estimates of several critics, who had envisioned a cost of up to $10,000. Ickes' report was probably based only upon the expenses of the Division of Subsistence Homesteads and excluded costs attributable to other agencies, such as the Civil Works Administration. The final accounting at Arthurdale showed an average cost of $16,377 for each family unit, which included all expenditures for community facilities and for management. The actual cost of the homes and outbuildings averaged $8,665, but this average included forty larger and more expensive houses constructed later by the Resettlement Administration. The first homesteader at Arthurdale was an unmarried mechanical engineer who had worked for the Friends and who homesteaded in order to teach woodworking to the miners. He planned to have his mother and father live with him.[15]

From July, 1934, to May, 1935, when the Resettlement Administra-

---

[14] Stout, "The New Homesteaders," p. 65; New York *Times,* June 8, 1934, p. 6.
[15] New York *Times,* July 15, 1934, sec. 2, p. 12; Farm Security Administration, "Arthurdale: Final Report of Project Costs," R.G. 96, National Archives; Stout, "The New Homesteaders," p. 7.

tion inherited the subsistence homesteads, the activity at Arthurdale centered on the construction of seventy-five additional homes and on the educational plans of Mrs. Roosevelt. The new houses did not suffer from the same waste and haste as the first fifty. Like the first ones, they were located on subsistence plots of from two to five acres, but were of combined concrete-block and frame construction. Only six had basements. They were one and one-half story buildings, with hardwood floors, brass fixtures, paneled walls, and furnaces. Although they also had individual wells, they, unlike the first fifty, had a central sewage disposal system. These homes were reported to resemble an expensive suburban housing project except for their unique spacing.[16] In January, 1935, the Division of Subsistence Homesteads allotted an added $900,-000 to Arthurdale for the new houses and the school buildings. It also admitted a loss of $500,000, which it frankly attributed to experimentation and errors in judgment. Not explained was the fact that the largest error in judgment was made by Howe in ordering the fifty prefabricated houses. The costs were again defended by Mrs. Roosevelt and also by her ally at Arthurdale, Bernard Baruch.[17]

In the very first plans for Arthurdale a school was contemplated, since the community was to be relatively isolated and since the added school population would have been an impossible burden on the local school system, which gained no increase in tax receipts from the untaxable homestead property. As early as January, 1934, Mrs. Roosevelt took over the direction of the educational plans for Arthurdale and, working both within and without the Division of Subsistence Homesteads, eventually made Arthurdale the site of an ambitious experiment in progressive education. By January, 1934, Mrs. Roosevelt had contacted Miss Elsie Clapp of the famed Ballard Memorial School near Louisville, Kentucky, asking her to direct the Arthurdale school program. By June she and Miss Clapp had formulated some very ambitious plans. The school at Arthurdale was to consist of several units and was to employ up to twenty-one faculty members, all for a community of no more than 200 families. The projected cost was approximately $163,800, much above the subsistence homesteads budget. As a result Mrs. Roosevelt used her own money to pay Miss Clapp's salary and

[16] Farm Security Administration, "Arthurdale: Final Report of Project Costs," R.G. 96, National Archives; Rice, "The Fuller Life at Reedsville," p. 26.
[17] New York *Times*, Jan. 18, 1935, p. 25; Jan. 24, 1935, p. 14; Jan. 29, 1935, p. 23.

Arthurdale

successfully appealed to Bernard Baruch and others for part of the funds for the school. Their advisers included John Dewey, Dean William Russell of Teachers College, Columbia University, Fred J. Kelly of the United States Office of Education, and, later, Eugene E. Agger of the Resettlement Administration. The Department of Education at West Virginia University joined in the planning and was responsible for the plans covering the school buildings. In the fall of 1934 Miss Clapp began the first school year with classes in the Arthur mansion and in the community building. Six new school buildings were under construction.[18]

The six school buildings at Arthurdale were a cause of much criticism. The buildings, which were completed in 1936, were constructed in a row. There were an administration building, a gymnasium, a nursery school, a primary department, an elementary school, and a high school, all costing $253,102.96.[19] The buildings were planned for adults as well as children, with the gymnasium and auditorium being used for most of the community activities. Miss Clapp, who had degrees from Vassar, Barnard, and Columbia, lived in a specially constructed house and directed the unusual school program, which was to begin before a child was born and was to continue throughout his life. Pre- and postnatal instruction was given by the project nurse and doctor. By the age of two or three the child graduated into a special nursery which was directed by the former head of the Harriet Johnson Nursery School in New York City. In terms of both equipment and results the Arthurdale nursery became a widely known model. Here the small children used wooden blocks constructed in the shop of the high school and learned self-expression through creative painting. Since by agreement with state and county school boards, the elementary and secondary schools were permitted to teach a "new economic and social freedom," the elementary grades were based on example, discussion, and actual work rather than on formal teaching, which was completely excluded along with set examinations. The high school, which emphasized vocational and shop work, had only forty-seven members the first year and for a time failed to secure accreditation in the West Virginia school system.

---

[18] M. L. Wilson to Ickes, Jan. 27, 1934, R.G. 48, National Archives; Pynchon to Ickes, June 20, 1934, *ibid.*; Pickett, *For More than Bread*, pp. 57–59.

[19] Farm Security Administration, "Arthurdale: Final Report of Project Costs," R.G. 96, National Archives.

Miss Clapp believed in the development of natural instincts and a positive outlook. She summarized as follows: "We remove mental and physical impediments and graft on the things that help. Negative thoughts and attitudes do not flourish here. This is virgin soil and tomorrow is another day." [20]

The progressive school at Arthurdale was turned over to the Preston County school system after two years of private operation. At that time much of the experimentation ended, for many of the parents had been fearful that their children were not getting as good an education as children in "regular" schools. Thus the dreams of the private sponsors were not realized for long, although the nursery school was popular with parents and was continued with subsidies from the private sponsors. Clarence Pickett, a member of Mrs. Roosevelt's educational committee, decided that "the enthusiasm of a few people who had thought deeply and dreamed long about the possibilities of the right kind of education led in this case to commitments which assumed more experimental-mindedness among the homesteaders than had yet developed." But he also concluded that "none of us who took part in the experiment has any regrets at the amount of energy we put into it." [21]

Closely connected with the educational program were the health services. Arthurdale eventually contained a small health center (a converted house), with two beds, two doctors, and a nurse. The nurse was paid by the Resettlement Administration, and, in the beginning, the physician was furnished by the American Friends Service Committee. Later a medical co-operative was inaugurated, with monthly dues of one dollar for those using the project physicians.[22]

When the Resettlement Administration inherited Arthurdale in May, 1935, only 125 homes were completed or near completion. Five of the school buildings were almost completed. This construction was left under the supervision of a New York architect who had worked on a contract basis for the Division of Subsistence Homesteads. The Resettlement Administration, in order to offer longer employment opportunities to homesteaders, deferred the construction by limiting employment to 402 workers each month. Moreover, despite past failures

[20] Charles E. Pynchon, "School as Social Center," New York *Times*, May 5, 1935, sec. 9, p. 23.
[21] Pickett, *For More than Bread*, pp. 58–59, 62.
[22] Rice, "Footnote on Arthurdale," pp. 416–417; R. C. Williams to W. W. Alexander, Jan. 8, 1937, R.G. 16, National Archives.

and gloomy prospects for employment, the Resettlement Administration added a third group of forty homes to the project. These, the most expensive homes of all, were of locally quarried stone veneer over frame construction. Each consisted of six rooms and the best of conveniences. On the project as a whole, which now included 165 homesteads, the Resettlement Administration added 108 root cellars and 56 storage houses. When thirty-six individual wells in the low-lying areas had to be abandoned because of contamination, the Resettlement Administration provided a central water system for these homes and for the community center. The school had its own water system and fireplugs.[23] Mrs. Roosevelt continued her interest in Arthurdale and exerted her influence by frequent trips and through a Committee on Arthurdale, which included Mrs. Henry Morgenthau, Jr., and Clarence Pickett. Pickett was retained by the Resettlement Administration as a consultant, as was Miss Nancy Cook.

Arthurdale, because of the many admitted mistakes and the conflicting groups trying to make policy, was a boon for New Deal critics, amply rewarding the cynical or the hostile with exhibits of waste and stupidity. On the other hand, the many people sympathetic with the aims of Arthurdale were more likely to judge it on the intentions of its sponsors and thus overlook some of the unpleasant realities of Arthurdale as a fact. For those sympathetic ones the idea of an experiment was always useful in explaining away early mistakes and excessive expenses. Others saw the end result at Arthurdale and were impressed, since the completed Arthurdale was a beautiful village, with pretty new homes, a neat community center, and productive gardens and farms. The following impression may have been shared by a majority of casual visitors:

The place is beautiful on Sundays. Little white homes, chattering visitors, mountain scenery of the Allegheny Plateau. Visitors admire the hand-made furniture that Mrs. Roosevelt selected, and listen with awe to the plans for the school, the church, and the community center. They think it is wonderful the way all the homesteaders are going to have an opportunity to learn handicrafts. They'll learn to make furniture and weave mats and rugs just like those in the model homes. It all sounds so cozy and "early American." The homes are like little corners of Arcady.[24]

[23] Resettlement Administration, *First Annual Report* (Washington, 1936), pp. 75–76.
[24] Carskadon, "Hull House in the Hills," p. 314.

Other people came looking only for the mistakes, and of course they found them. In August, 1934, the *Saturday Evening Post* published an exposé on Arthurdale that set the pattern for all later attacks, while causing acute embarrassment to the Division of Subsistence Homesteads, since the article, although very slanted, was factually irrefutable on most points. Soon the inanities of Arthurdale were well known, in fact were so well known that the whole story of Arthurdale was completely distorted. Much that was done at Arthurdale was pictured as something resembling a joke, and the whole subsistence homesteads program, by generalization, was subjected to ridicule. The following inanities became classics, bandied about for years by reporters and always worth a laugh: the basements with countless foundations; the paper-thin walls of Howe's "famous fifty"; the expensive grease traps; the copper plumbing which, according to one report, was ruined by the homesteaders' driving nails into the floor; the wells that became contaminated; the pumps that froze; the six school buildings for only 400 children; the leaking roofs; the high school that was not accredited; the fifty halters purchased for fifty cows that never arrived; the eight wells which were never used because of a change in plans; the barn foundations that were placed too close to the houses and then covered with soil; the dead wild grapevines wound on trellises; the imported rhododendron in an area rich with rhododendron; and the estimated cost of over $10,000 per home when a new two-story brick dwelling and a thirty-five-acre farm in the same area were selling for $5,000.[25]

Since Arthurdale was the most publicized of the subsistence homesteads communities, since it was the first New Deal community to be initiated, and since it was an avowed experiment and demonstration in government planning, it perhaps was inevitable that it would become a symbol of the whole subsistence homesteads program and, in critical hands, of all government planning and experimentation, despite the fact that Arthurdale suffered most from a lack of detailed planning. The first congressional displeasure centered on Arthurdale and the contemplated Post Office factory. From then on Arthurdale was always brought into any discussion of New Deal communities, always serving as a convenient example to use in attacking the whole program. When the American Liberty League condemned all New Deal experimentation, it quite naturally used Arthurdale as an example of "what

[25] Stout, "The New Homesteaders," pp. 6–7; Bolles, "Resettling America," pp. 343–344; Rice, "The Fuller Life at Arthurdale," p. 27.

happens when misguided zealots obtain access to the public Treasury." [26] For that reason the inanities of Arthurdale, even though minor and overexploited, had great importance in the realm of anti-New Deal propaganda.

The greatest problem at Arthurdale, from completion of the first fifty homes until World War II, was the lack of opportunities for employment, a problem shared by each of the other stranded communities. The earliest plans for Arthurdale contemplated some newly decentralized industry to supplement the subsistence farming and the handicraft work. Even as the construction began, the plans for industry appeared solved by the announcement about a contemplated Post Office factory, but, as already recounted, this plan was blocked by Congress. Thus, until 1936, the only sources of industrial employment at Arthurdale were in the handicraft shops of the Mountaineer Craftsmen's Co-operative Association, which was located in the community center. The loom, the forge, and the furniture factory gave continuous employment to some eleven or twelve craftsmen. Meanwhile, most of the men found employment in the continuing construction program, either on the new homes or the school buildings. The subsistence plots, though providing garden crops and permitting hogs, chickens, and a cow, never replaced the need for a cash income.

In 1934 Mrs. Roosevelt took the employment problem at Arthurdale to Gerard Swope of the General Electric Company. He promised to operate a vacuum-cleaner assembly plant at Arthurdale. The Division of Subsistence Homesteads drew up an agreement with a General Electric affiliate, the Electric Vacuum Cleaner Company of Cleveland, and began the construction of a factory near the railroad that cut through the northern section of the Arthur estate. The factory was to be leased to the company for five to ten years, and homesteaders were to travel to Cleveland for training. Completed in October, 1935, the factory had to remain idle. The contemplated operation was blocked by a ruling of the Comptroller General which forbade the use of Resettlement Administration funds for the support of private industry. In January, 1936, the Resettlement Administration lent the Arthurdale Association, a co-operative made up of homesteaders, $12,804.47 to enable it to purchase the factory from the government. After this paper transaction, the factory was finally opened on June 23, 1936. The Electric Vacuum Cleaner Company leased the factory from the

[26] New York *Times*, Oct. 28, 1935, p. 2.

association at a set monthly rental. Only homesteaders had preference in employment. In 1936 the factory gave employment to approximately thirty homesteaders, with a minimum wage of forty cents an hour for men. Yet, in one year, the enterprise was a financial failure, and the company canceled its lease. The Arthurdale Association had to begin bargaining with other companies in the hope of finding a new occupant for the factory.[27]

Several nonindustrial enterprises at Arthurdale were also unsuccessful or nearly so. In 1934 the Arthurdale Association purchased 442 acres of extra farm land. On this, plus about 100 acres already on the project, the association established a co-operative dairy and crop farm. Despite thirty-three purebred Jersey cattle, this co-operative venture lost money, probably because it paid industrial rates for farm work. In 1939 the farm was leased to two homesteaders and, in private operation, returned a profit for a few years. A poultry farm was operated co-operatively from 1936 to 1939, when it was turned over to private enterprise because of heavy losses. In January, 1936, the association, using a loan from the Resettlement Administration, opened a co-operative store which gave employment to four homesteaders. Despite reports of excessively high prices during its early years, the store managed to survive until the project was liquidated. Besides the store, the association operated a gristmill that was never successful and a gasoline station that was ruined by the war. It also operated a barbershop and a tearoom. In 1936 one of the more publicized ventures at Arthurdale was planned. The old, sturdy Arthur mansion was torn down and replaced, at a cost of nearly $28,000, by a modern inn of comparable size. The inn suffered from the wartime restrictions on travel and was leased to an airplane company. These agricultural and retail co-operatives could provide employment for only approximately thirty-two people, many of whom were women, girls, or young boys.[28]

In 1937 the Phillips-Jones Corporation occupied the vacated vacuum-

---

[27] Pynchon to Ickes, Aug. 21, 1934, R.G. 48, National Archives; Committee for Economic Recovery, Resettled Communities Committee, *Arthurdale: A Partial Pattern for the New American Way of Life,* a report prepared for President Franklin D. Roosevelt (n.p., Jan., 1937), pp. 19–20; New York *Times,* April 27, 1936, p. 40.

[28] Committee for Economic Recovery, *Arthurdale,* pp. 5, 15–18; Rice, "Footnote on Arthurdale," p. 416; *C.R.,* 76th Cong., 1st Sess., 1939, pp. 3861–3862; "Eden Liquidated; Arthurdale Plants Sold; Tenants Buying Homes," *Business Week* (July 27, 1946), pp. 22, 26; Resettlement Administration Weekly Information Report no. 38, April 13, 1936, R.G. 96, National Archives.

cleaner factory and began a collar factory. It manufactured and cut shirts in a Pennsylvania factory and then sent them to Arthurdale for final assembly, employing up to sixty homesteaders during its brief tenancy. It closed its plant allegedly because of labor troubles in Pennsylvania, leaving Arthurdale with an empty factory once again.[29] In April, 1939, the most ambitious industrial enterprise yet attempted at Arthurdale began operations. With a loan of $325,000 from the Farm Security Administration, the Arthurdale Co-operative Association formed an Arthurdale Farm Equipment Corporation and constructed a tractor assembly plant, which was managed by the American Co-operatives, Incorporated. This was one of the eight major industries financed by the Farm Security Administration and was contemporaneous with the five hosiery mills at other projects. The venture at Arthurdale was the largest financial failure of them all, losing $106,380.21 in one year while employing only approximately twenty-five homesteaders. The factory assembled hybrid tractors by using parts purchased from various tractor companies, but never found a large enough market for its product to sustain operations.[30] It closed in April, 1940, after also assembling a few Rust Brothers cotton pickers. At the time it closed, only one industry remained at Arthurdale. The Mountaineer Craftsmen's Co-operative Association continued to produce handicrafts and had adopted mass-production methods in a new furniture factory (the third factory for Arthurdale). Since it could offer employment to only a few homesteaders, the situation in 1940 remained desperate, despite all the efforts of the Farm Security Administration and the local co-operative associations.

With the increasing prosperity of 1941, Mrs. Roosevelt and her Committee on Arthurdale succeeded in getting the best industry thus far for Arthurdale. The Brunswick Radio and Television Company of New York agreed to establish a radio cabinet factory in one of the Arthurdale factories, thereby utilizing the woodworking ability of many of the homesteaders. In 1942 it was employing approximately 100 people and was a financial success until wartime scarcities forced it to close. By this time employment was no longer a problem at Arthurdale, for with the coming of the war the mines reopened. Even more important, the furniture factory, the old vacuum-cleaner factory, and

[29] Rice, "Footnote on Arthurdale," p. 415.
[30] Select Committee of the House Committee on Agriculture, Hearings on the Farm Security Administration, 78th Cong., 1st Sess., 1943–1944, pp. 1759–1760.

the tractor assembly plant, plus the inn, were all leased by the Hoover Aircraft Corporation for manufacturing defense materials. Suddenly there were too many jobs and too few homesteaders.[31]

As a completed village, Arthurdale included 165 homes and related outbuildings situated on their plots of from two to five acres. The community center included the large community building, the forge, the co-operative store, barbershop, weaving room, furniture-display room, the administrative building, and the filling station. On a hillside was the inn. In addition, there were the six school buildings, the three factories, the health center, the gristmill, and the farms. This all cost, by 1943, the large sum of $2,744,724.09, or $15,635 for each homestead.[32] Yet, even by 1940, the average income of each Arthurdale family was only $467 a year.[33] Thus, even though the government could never expect to sell the homesteads at cost, it also could not sell the homes to the homesteaders at anything near the existing value. To have sold the homes to the homesteaders according to their ability to pay would have necessitated a virtual gift on the part of the government. Therefore, the homesteads were rented, with any future sale depending upon increased economic opportunities, which never came until the war.

From 1936 there were plans for turning Arthurdale over to a homestead association as soon as there was full employment. But as one enterprise after another failed, the homesteaders practically lost hope of ownership. A homestead association was formed but never received title to the homesteads. Meanwhile the homesteaders had to make rent payments from their limited incomes. As early as 1936, Bernard Baruch took the lead in advocating lenient terms for the homesteaders, since they had been given unfulfilled promises of employment and ownership. He asked: "Does anybody still think that any homesteader can make a living for himself and his family on a five-acre lot?" [34] The government heeded such pleas. By 1940 the average monthly rent at Arthurdale was only $9.99.

Even though without employment or substantial incomes, the homesteaders at Arthurdale were well cared for. They had model homes, a

---

[31] J. M. G. to Mason Barr, July 26, 1941, R.G. 96, National Archives; "Eden Liquidated," p. 25; *Hearings on the Farm Security Administration*, p. 1760.

[32] *Hearings on the Farm Security Administration*, p. 1119.

[33] House Agricultural Subcommittee of the Committee on Appropriations, *Hearings on the Agricultural Department Appropriation Bill for 1941*, 76th Cong., 3d Sess., 1940, pp. 974–975.

[34] Franklin D. Roosevelt to Tugwell, May 6, 1936, R.G. 16, National Archives.

model school, excellent recreational facilities, and a governmental landlord that was never harsh. They also enjoyed, or suffered, a nationwide notoriety. No other community of its size was so publicized in newspapers all over the country. No other community was visited so frequently by the President's wife. Nowhere else did the First Lady so often join in the local square dancing in the school gymnasium. At no other small community did the President of the United States deliver the high school commencement address, as did President Roosevelt at Arthurdale in 1938 (Mrs. Roosevelt attended and spoke at each commencement from 1936 through 1941). Yet all the publicity and the constant stream of visitors had its drawbacks. One mountaineer was reported to have exclaimed: "Got so a man couldn't set down to his sow belly and turnip greens without some stranger peeking in at the window or walking in to ask fool questions." [35]

In 1942, after employment increased, Arthurdale was readied for sale to individual homesteaders rather than to a homestead association. The first sales were based on income and a fair evaluation, with no down payment required. Some houses sold for as low as $750, and the Farm Security Administration frankly estimated that all the homesteads would sell for only $175,000, less than 7 per cent of the total cost of the community or less than 13 per cent of the total costs of the homesteads exclusive of all community and public facilities.[36] Just as the sales were commenced, Arthurdale was transferred to the Federal Public Housing Authority, which soon raised the prices on the homesteads not already contracted for sale. By 1946 only fifty-five homes remained unsold, and those were valued at up to $6,000 each; liquidation was completed in the next two years. On June 15, 1946, the inn and three factories, no longer used for war materials, were sold to the Belfort Corporation of Baltimore for the manufacture of kitchen cabinets and furniture. They sold for $105,000.[37] With the final liquidation, the government at last relinquished one of the most embarrassing experiments in its history.

[35] "Eden Liquidated," p. 29.
[36] House Agricultural Subcommittee of the Committee on Appropriations, *Hearings on the Agricultural Appropriation Bill for 1943*, 77th Cong., 2d Sess., 1942, pp. 224–225; *Hearings on the Farm Security Administration*, p. 1119; Farm Security Administration, "Arthurdale: Final Report of Project Costs," R.G. 96, National Archives.
[37] "Eden Liquidated," pp. 22, 29.

≯ XI ≮

Jersey Homesteads—A Triple Co-operative

IT is a long way from Scott's Run to the Jewish garment district of Manhattan, long not so much in terms of miles as of cultural differences. But in both areas the depression led to hardship and to concerted efforts at colonization upon the land, although the background of Jersey Homesteads was entirely different from that of Arthurdale. In contrast to the brief, depression-born subsistence homesteads movement in West Virginia, the all co-operative Jewish colony in New Jersey was the culmination of a long history of Jewish agricultural and industrial colonization in the United States that reached back beyond 1881. In the past efforts of Jewish immigrants to go onto the land and in the long and little-known efforts of Jewish leaders to develop a strong Jewish agricultural community are contained almost all the roots of Jersey Homesteads. In fact, almost the total program of the Division of Subsistence Homesteads and the Resettlement Administration had been anticipated by the work of Jewish organizations in colonization, part-time farming, decentralization of industry, rehabilitation, and social engineering.

Because of numerous restrictions on landownership and constant persecutions and migrations, the ancient Jew, a nomadic herder or a farmer, became, by 1800, almost exclusively a city dweller. Seven colonies of Jews in South Russia in 1804 represented the first modern attempt of Jews to become farmers. In 1825 an ambitious Jewish refugee colony was planned for Grand Island in the Niagara River, but never proceeded beyond land purchase. Beginning in 1837, a small Jewish colony of twelve families in Ulster County, New York, survived for five years. Other ambitious back-to-the-land schemes, but no real accomplishment, culminated in the formation of a Jewish Agricultural Society in 1856, which never went farther than elaborate planning for colonies. After the assassination of Alexander II of Russia in 1881, a series of pogroms and restrictive laws forced thousands of Jews to emigrate to the United States and other countries. Among the intelligentsia of these emigrants was an organized agrarian group, Am Olam, which, beginning in 1881, established several abortive and a few lasting farm colonies in the United States. A number of these featured collectivist plans; all were founded without previous farming experience, without adequate guidance, and without sufficient funds. The first settlement was at Sicily Island, Louisiana, with others following in Arkansas, Kansas, Colorado, South Dakota, and New Jersey. Only the New Jersey colonies survived.[1]

Alliance, the first of the New Jersey colonies and the first permanent Jewish agricultural colony in the United States, was founded in 1882 by about twenty-five Jewish immigrants from Russia. Aided by a newly formed Hebrew Emigrant Aid Society, they purchased 1,100 acres of land, divided it into fifteen-acre plots, and established small factories. The Hebrew Emigrant Aid Society searched the West for farms for those other Jews determined to go onto the land, but, as the stream of immigration temporarily slowed, soon went out of existence, leaving a Jewish author, Michael Heilprin, as the father of several later colonies. In this first great spurt of Jewish colonization, lasting from 1881 to 1888, enduring colonies were started in South New Jersey at Norma, Brotmanville, Rosenhayn, Carmel, Garten Road, and Alliance. The Jewish people, with their distinct communal proclivities and without any real experience in agriculture, chose the colony or community method of agricultural settlement. They also, even in the first settlements, introduced factories into their farm villages. Mean-

[1] Jewish Agricultural Society, *Jews in American Agriculture: The History of Farming by Jews in the United States* (New York, 1954), pp. 8, 16, 19, 23–26; Philip Reuben Goldstein, *Social Aspects of the Jewish Colonies of South Jersey* (New York, 1921), p. 12; Gabriel Davidson, *Our Jewish Farmers and the Story of the Jewish Agricultural Society* (New York, 1943), pp. 194–249.

while an overwhelming majority of the Jewish immigrants settled in the large cities and became needleworkers.²

When the heavy Jewish migration resumed by 1890, a wealthy European industrialist and Jew, Baron Maurice de Hirsch, became so interested in the plight of the Russian Jews that he endowed a Jewish Colonization Society which, from its European headquarters, aided in the colonization of Jews in several countries. In 1891 Baron de Hirsch also contributed $2,400,000 to be used exclusively for the aid of Jewish emigrants to the United States. Of this sum, $240,000 was specifically designated for farm colonies, since Hirsch was a convinced agrarian. The executors of the Baron de Hirsch fund (American Jewish leaders) appointed an agricultural and industrial committee which early decided that any new colonies should be both agricultural and industrial. Meanwhile the South Jersey colonies were adopted and aided by the committee, which also made loans to individual Jews who wished to enter agriculture. For its first major endeavor the committee considered establishing either a suburban-type colony at Hightstown, New Jersey, or a predominantly agricultural colony in southern New Jersey. The latter plan was adopted, while a Jewish colony at Hightstown had to await the New Deal.³

To develop their first farm colony the trustees of the Baron de Hirsch fund founded a colonization corporation which purchased 5,300 acres near Vineland, New Jersey, and, in 1892, began the development of what was to become the Woodbine colony. Sixty families were selected for the farms, with each being required to contribute some small sum as down payment. The land was divided into three parts—a central town, an encircling area divided into fifteen-acre farmsteads, and, at the outskirts, a circle of pasture land. In the first year sixty-four farmhouses, valued at $600 each, were constructed by the corporation, and twenty-five town houses were constructed at a cost of from $850 to $1,300 each. The first factory, a cloak company, was opened during the first year, and, everything seeming well under way, all aid from the Baron de Hirsch fund ceased. This led to a strike on the

² Goldstein, *Social Aspects of the Jewish Colonies*, pp. 13–17; Samuel Joseph, *History of the Baron de Hirsch Fund—The Americanization of the Jewish Immigrant* (Philadelphia, 1935), pp. 5, 8–9; William Kirsch, *The Jew and the Land* (American Association for Agricultural Legislation, Bulletin no. 7; Madison, Wis., 1920), p. 12.

³ Joseph, *History of the Baron de Hirsch Fund*, pp. 11–22, 24, 32–34, 48–50.

Jersey Homesteads

part of the farmers, who found poor soil and who lacked experience in farming. They had received a house, a cow stable, money for cows and chickens, farm implements, seeds, and fruit trees. For three years they were obligated for an annual payment of only fifty dollars, but by the end of twelve years were to have paid the full cost of the farm, receiving fee simple ownership at an estimated cost of only $1,100. After the strike the leases were modified, and the colony entered a long period of supervision and direction from the trustees of the Baron de Hirsch fund, who suddenly discovered the magnitude of the undertaking at Woodbine. Woodbine, planned as a beginning of the reconstruction of Jewish life in America, was the last such colony attempted. The trustees of the fund spent years of effort in securing adequate, subsidized industry for Woodbine, presaging the efforts of the Resettlement Administration at Arthurdale and elsewhere. Although the first Jewish agricultural school was established at Woodbine, the colony became an industrial village with only a few farms surrounding it. By 1900 the population of Woodbine was 1,400.[4]

The efforts of the trustees of the Baron de Hirsch fund to establish Woodbine, to aid the older Jewish colonies, and to establish individual farmers led to the formation of the Jewish Agricultural and Industrial Aid Society (since renamed the Jewish Agricultural Society) in 1900 and to more experimentation. The original purposes of the society included the "removal of those working in crowded metropolitan sections to agricultural and industrial districts," the granting of loans to artisans seeking suburban homes, the decentralization of industry, and the encouragement of co-operatives. In the first few years the society devoted much of its efforts to unsuccessful attempts at decentralizing industry, especially in connection with several of the New Jersey colonies. It also attempted to found a few new colonies in the West, but failed each time. By 1909 the society became orientated toward a lasting policy of aiding individual Jewish farmers. It continued to direct the settlement of individual back-to-the-landers, but depended upon individual farms in community groups rather than on organized colonies. It published a farm magazine in Yiddish, initiated an itinerant supervisory program that predated the United States Extension Service, organized the first rural co-operative credit unions in America, formed local Jewish farm federations which experimented in

[4] *Ibid.*, pp. 52–56, 89.

group purchasing, organized test farms, made short-term rehabilitation loans, carried out the first work in rural sanitation in the United States, and, in the New Jersey colonies, conducted evening schools, established libraries, built community halls, and supervised recreation. In fact, the Jewish Agricultural Society, directed by many of America's best-known Jewish leaders, became a miniature Resettlement Administration. From only 200 to 400 families in 1900, the Jewish farm population grew to approximately 5,000 families in 1910 and, by 1930, to approximately 16,000 families. The work of the Jewish Agricultural Society was intended to prove false the long-standing and bitterly resented allegation that Jews did not make good farmers. In this it succeeded.[5]

By 1924 the Jewish Agricultural Society was seriously considering part-time farming as a transitory step for Jewish urbanites who eventually desired to be farmers. From this came plans for agro-industrial communities, one of the earlier precedents for subsistence homesteads. In 1926 an agro-industrial settlement was started at Bound Brook, New Jersey, by Jewish families who were advised and assisted by the Jewish Agricultural Society. By 1929 forty families were living on four- to fourteen-acre tracts and commuting to their city jobs. In 1929 the Jewish Agricultural Society decided to initiate a second such community. It purchased a tract near New Brunswick, New Jersey, where it intended eventually to settle about twenty-five families on five- to seven-acre plots. Cautiously beginning the experiment, it constructed nine four- and five-room houses which the settlers helped plan. The first homesteaders contributed about one-fourth the value of their homesteads as a down payment. Although further expansion was curtailed because of the depression, the society continued to believe that the idea was sound and welcomed the support given to a very similar idea by Franklin D. Roosevelt in 1931 in his early advocacy of subsistence homesteads.[6]

In the back-to-the-land movement of the depression the Jewish Agricultural Society was swamped with applications for aid in locating

[5] *Ibid.*, pp. 120–121, 129; Goldstein, *Social Aspects of the Jewish Colonies*, pp. 25–28; Davidson, *Our Jewish Farmers*, pp. 19, 24, 29, 36, 75; Jewish Agricultural Society, *Jews in American Agriculture*, pp. 35, 38–41.

[6] Jewish Agricultural Society, *Annual Report, 1929* (New York, [1930]), pp. 8–10; *Annual Report, 1930* (New York, [1931]), pp. 10–12; *Annual Report, 1931* (New York, [1932]), p. 10.

and buying farms, but was handicapped by a lack of funds. Yet its long work in directing farm settlement, in granting farm credit, and in part-time farming quickly became a part of the New Deal program. One of its members. Henry Morgenthau, Jr., became the first director of the Farm Credit Administration. In New York City the back-to-the-land idea captured the minds of many Jewish leaders and of many idle garmentworkers. Against the cautious advice of the Jewish Agricultural Society, several ill-conceived farm colonies were attempted, including the short-lived Sunrise Community in Michigan. This movement also led to Jersey Homesteads, which, because of its collective features, was viewed hopefully but with some skepticism by the Jewish Agricultural Society, since many former such colonies had failed. If Jersey Homesteads had followed the pattern of the other, less-collectivized industrial homesteads, it would have been a direct extension of the two agro-industrial communities of the Jewish Agricultural Society.

Benjamin Brown, the immediate father of Jersey Homesteads, was a Jewish emigrant from the Ukraine. Coming to the United States in 1901 at the age of sixteen, he worked his way through college and became an enthusiastic organizer of rural co-operatives, beginning with the Central Utah Poultry Exchange in 1919. By 1925 he was managing a distribution organization in New York City which served several Western farm co-operatives and had an annual business of $12,000,000. As a complement to his enthusiasm for farm co-operatives, Brown had long desired to establish co-operative agricultural and industrial colonies for the Jewish needleworkers of New York City. In 1928 Brown was a member of a delegation of Americans which traveled to Russia to help in the organization of a distribution system in Biro-Bidjan, the all-Jewish colony in the Soviet Union. Also on the trip was M. L. Wilson, who sympathized with Brown's desire to remove the garmentworkers to the country.[7]

Many Jews saw the country as a means to escape the criticism so often leveled against the Jews because of their concentration in urban areas and because of their participation in highly competitive commercial and financial occupations. Thus, in June, 1933, leaders of three Jewish labor bodies, the Workmen's Circle, the United Hebrew Trades,

---

[7] George Weller, "Land of Milk and Honey," *Literary Digest*, CXXIV (Aug. 14, 1937), 14; Ralph F. Armstrong, "Four-Million Dollar Village," *Saturday Evening Post*, CCX (Feb. 5, 1938), 7, 34.

and the National Jewish Workers' Alliance, were willing to meet in a conference in New York City to study Benjamin Brown's back-to-the-land proposals. The conference resulted in the formation of the Provisional Commission for Jewish Farm Settlements in the United States, with Brown as chairman. The commission, which in addition to support from labor organizations included among its members Rabbi Stephen S. Wise, Isador Lubin, Chief of the Bureau of Labor Statistics, and, later, Albert Einstein, planned to give form and direction to the back-to-the-land movement. Jersey Homesteads, which became its first effort, was planned as the first of a series of similar colonies, although no others were ever actually attempted.[8]

With the announcement of the subsistence homesteads program, Benjamin Brown and his commission applied for a loan of $500,000 from M. L. Wilson and the Division of Subsistence Homesteads. The plan proposed by Brown was for a colony of 200 skilled Jewish needleworkers, who were to become self-sustaining through subsistence farming combined with seasonal employment in a co-operative garment factory. Small individual homestead plots were to be supplemented by a community truck garden, dairy, and poultry plant, all operated co-operatively. Completing the circle of co-operative activities was to be a community store to sell the community-produced products. The cost of such a colony, including the factory, was estimated at $600,000, with $100,000 to be provided by the 200 homesteaders, who were to contribute $500 each. After investigation, the Division of Subsistence Homesteads approved Brown's plans and granted him the loan in December, 1933. Under the early policies, Brown and his commission became the Board of Directors of a Jersey Homesteads Corporation, which was authorized to develop the colony with a minimum of government supervision. Brown had already determined on a 1,200-acre tract of fertile land about five miles from Hightstown, New Jersey, and proceeded to buy it for $96,000 in December. In January, Max Blitzer, a former assistant to the president of William and Mary College, was appointed project manager by the local corporation. The first announcement of the project resulted in 800 ap-

[8] New York *Times*, Jan. 7, 1934, sec. 9, p. 12; "Milk and Honey: Jewish Needle-Workers Move into Highstown Project," *Literary Digest*, CXXI (June 20, 1936), 32–33.

plicants for homesteads, despite the $500 down payment. Jersey Homesteads seemed well under way.[9]

As soon as Benjamin Brown and Max Blitzer began to try to turn their plans for Jersey Homesteads into a reality, troubles multiplied. First of all, Brown failed to maintain the support of all the original sponsors, particularly those representing labor and charity groups. Brown was also foiled in his early plans to build homes for $2,000 or less, since National Recovery Administration codes had raised prices. Plans to import inexpensive cattle from drought areas were thwarted by New Jersey laws. Then, in May, the whole subsistence homesteads program was federalized, removing all actual control from Brown, even though Blitzer was retained as project manager. Shortly thereafter M. L. Wilson, Brown's friend, resigned from the Division of Subsistence Homesteads.

After the newly centralized Division of Subsistence Homesteads had reviewed the plans for Jersey Homesteads, another $327,000 was authorized for the project, and by the fall of 1934 construction operations were under way. Then a new obstacle intervened. Brown's original plan, from which he would never deviate, called for a private manufacturer to operate the garment factory until the homesteaders were settled and could organize their own co-operative. As a result Brown and Blitzer began negotiating with private concerns, only to face the determined hostility of powerful David Dubinsky, head of the International Ladies' Garment Workers' Union. Dubinsky opposed the subsidized removal of a factory and jobs from the already-harassed workers of New York City. Since Dubinsky remained adamant, despite attacks in the Jewish press and pleas from Einstein and others, the Division of Subsistence Homesteads, with no guarantee of an adequate economic base and with no desire for another stranded community, decided to suspend all operations at Hightstown. Thus was the situation stalemated when the Resettlement Administration and Tugwell took over in May, 1935.[10]

[9] Russell Lord and Paul H. Johnstone, *A Place on Earth: A Critical Appraisal of Subsistence Homesteads* (Washington, 1942), pp. 137–140; Armstrong, "Four-Million Dollar Village," p. 34; Lawrence Lucey, "A Cooperative Town," *Commonweal*, XXV (Dec. 18, 1936), 210.

[10] Lord and Johnstone, *A Place on Earth*, pp. 140–142; Armstrong, "Four-Million Dollar Village," p. 34.

At the time the Resettlement Administration took over Jersey Homesteads, 120 families had already been tentatively selected as homesteaders, $170,000 had been spent, some land had been cleared, the cleared land was being cropped by the New Jersey Rural Rehabilitation Corporation, and one well had been dug. The 120 homesteaders were carefully screened individuals who, since they contributed $500 of their own money, never regarded themselves as recipients of special government aid. The families had been selected by the sponsors, with final approval by an official of the Division of Subsistence Homesteads. Beyond the possession of $500, they had to be union members in good standing, to be sufficiently skilled in their needle trades to give assurance of economic success, to have some understanding of cooperative endeavor, and to have a family which showed evidence of good home management. The homesteaders, accustomed to organizing in unions or other groups to enforce their demands, desperately searching for security and a higher level of living, and blindly trusting in the leadership of Brown, were determined that the government complete the original plans for their colony. With the delays and the reluctance on the part of the government, the homesteaders, ably backed by their sponsors and numerous Jewish groups, began a long and perfectly united struggle to force the government to continue with the construction of Jersey Homesteads. With the delay in the spring of 1935, the Division of Subsistence Homesteads was besieged with letters, demands for action, and petitions from mass meetings. The homesteaders could cite the real sacrifices they had made to raise $500 and the jobs they had relinquished because of their prospective moves to new homes.[11]

The Resettlement Administration early decided to continue Jersey Homesteads, although administration officials considered expanding it into a larger housing project of the greenbelt type. Construction work was resumed in August, 1935. Blitzer remained as project manager, while Brown continued the negotiations with Dubinsky. But once again the project was plagued with difficulties, since the arguments between Brown and Dubinsky became more bitter than ever, with little prospect for a compromise. A ruling in September by the Comptroller General seemed to outlaw any factory not connected with agricultural pro-

[11] Armstrong, "Four-Million Dollar Village," p. 34; Lord and Johnstone, *A Place on Earth*, pp. 146–147.

duction. In November the factory plan was temporarily dropped by the Resettlement Administration, and Blitzer was dismissed. It was rumored that the project would be discontinued or that it would not include the Jewish homesteaders. In any case all construction ceased. On November 26, 1935, the Resettlement Administration announced that Jersey Homesteads would be completed, but that all responsibility for the project, including the factory negotiations, would be assumed by the Resettlement Administration.[12] This left no assurance that the original plans would be followed. Brown was practically excluded from the project, and the homesteaders were indignant. Fortunately, the Resettlement Administration was able to secure Dubinsky's approval for a garment factory at Hightstown, provided it was operated co-operatively from the very beginning. With this plan in view, the homesteaders organized a Workers' Aim Association for the operation of the factory, and the Resettlement Administration announced that it would go on with the original plans.

The first two years at Jersey Homesteads were years of controversy; the two years of construction were years of extravagance. Tugwell, interested in developing new, inexpensive methods of prefabricating houses, used Jersey Homesteads as an experiment. In the fall of 1935 approximately $200,000 was spent in erecting factories to manufacture concrete slabs for the sides and roofs of the homes. Yet when the first such construction was attempted, the walls collapsed. The whole process was abandoned. The concrete slabs were actually used for roofs, and the factory was used to manufacture concrete blocks until it was discovered that they cost about three times as much as those purchased from private manufacturers. This and other early mistakes led to an unpopular order to exclude all visitors from the construction area and to the posting of guards at the entrances.

In January, 1936, the Resettlement Administration began an accelerated construction program at Hightstown. Even though the construction was delayed by procedural snags and Works Progress Administration labor regulations, the factory was completed by May, and several homes were well under way. By July, 1936, the first seven of the flat-roofed bungalows were occupied. Most of the other 193 homes were completed by January, 1937. As finally completed, the town

[12] New York *Times,* Aug. 1, 1935, p. 25, Aug. 4, 1935, p. 7, and Aug. 6, 1935, p. 19; Lord and Johnstone, *A Place on Earth,* p. 145.

section of Jersey Homesteads contained 200 white, concrete-block homes of from five to seven rooms, located on small homestead plots of approximately one acre. The homes, although not beautiful from the outside, included modern baths, oil furnaces which air-conditioned the homes in summer, and electric refrigerators. Each homestead had a combination garage and workshop. The town contained the garment factory, a modern sewage disposal plant, a water tank and water lines, a town hall, which also contained a day nursery and library, a combination elementary school and community building, a co-operative store and butcher shop, a clothing store, a tearoom, and a medical clinic.[13]

Jersey Homesteads was the only New Deal community to be settled by a completely homogeneous population with strong religious ties. From the beginning the homesteaders were a cohesive and enthusiastic group. Almost all of foreign extraction, inured to persecution in Russia or other foreign lands, they had practically been forced into the garment industry on arriving in America, since almost a third were illiterate, since they arrived with less funds than any other major immigrant group, and since, in most cases, they were skilled only in the needle trades because of occupational limitations imposed upon them in Russia. In the garment districts of New York City they had not always found the economic security for which they longed. The opportunity for a homestead in the country, with their own people as neighbors, seemed to be a second migration, away from an insecure, chaotic, and highly competitive world to a modern promised land. They were all as eager as children to get into their new homes. As early as May 17, 1936, the homesteaders and friends picnicked on the grounds of the uncompleted project, disappointed only because no important Resettlement Administration official attended.[14]

The first moving day at Jersey Homesteads was on July 10, 1936, when seven families arrived after dark. Their fifty-mile trip from New York City was delayed by a bridge that was out and by the loss of three trucks in heavy traffic. Elaborate opening ceremonies had to be canceled, and the homesteaders unloaded in the face of a thunderstorm, delayed by a publicity director who insisted on recording the

[13] Lucey, "A Cooperative Town," pp. 210–212; Armstrong, "Four-Million Dollar Village," p. 6; New York *Times*, June 14, 1936, sec. 12, pp. 1, 8.
[14] New York *Times*, May 18, 1936, p. 6.

event on a newsreel. With the completion of the project, visitors were allowed, with approximately 5,000 inspecting the project on July 12. The first settlers were soon greeted by the "doers of good" or the "eager helpers and amiable zanies," depending on the point of view, that represented the Special Skills Division of the Resettlement Administration. There were lectures on preserving, co-operation, and drama and, to a group of frugal Jews, on the necessity for economy. On the day of moving an interior decorator came from Washington with a load of furniture and set up a model cottage, despite the fact that homesteaders were on the way from New York to move into every completed home. On her departure a van came to the house and unceremoniously removed the model furniture and placed it in storage. Soon after the first homesteads were occupied, a large surprise package arrived—a huge modernistic statue depicting a woman at a sewing machine.[15]

The central idea back of Jersey Homesteads was co-operation. M. L. Wilson stated that the "pattern of the community itself will be as co-operative as it is possible to make it," a sentiment that was in line with the ideas of Benjamin Brown.[16] Jersey Homesteads was planned as the first triple co-operative in the new world, with co-operative stores, farm, and factory. Except for homeownership and garden production, every aspect of Hightstown was to be co-operative. According to early plans, approximately 40 homesteaders were to work the farms and service the stores, while 160 were to work in the factory. Admittedly, the garment factory was the key to the economic success of the community. But with an aggressive and well-knit band of homesteaders, it appeared that Jersey Homesteads would surely be one community where co-operative or group activities would succeed.

As the first homesteads were completed in the summer of 1936, Benjamin Brown was under pressure from the homesteaders to get the factory under way, since many of the homesteaders had suffered hardship because of having to hold themselves in readiness for moving to a colony that seemed ever-longer delayed in construction. The factory building was dedicated in an elaborate ceremony on August 2, 1936. Nearly 2,000 people were present, observing the optimism of the home-

[15] New York *Times*, July 11, 1936, p. 31, and July 13, 1936, p. 31; Armstrong, "Four-Million Dollar Village," pp. 38–39.

[16] M. L. Wilson to Murray C. Lincoln, Dec. 31, 1936, R.G. 16, National Archives.

steaders, who marched into the factory to the music of "Stars and Stripes Forever." They received a congratulatory telegram from Tugwell and sang their co-operative association theme, composed by Mr. and Mrs. Benjamin Brown:

> Production, co-operation,
> Freedom for every nation,
> Here, there and everywhere,
> This is our claim:
> Workers' Aim, Workers' Aim.

The factory building was 100 feet by 220 feet, mostly all windows, air-conditioned, and declared to be the most modern in the East. Present at the dedication were union officials, sales organization executives, fashion models, and an orchestra. Large orders for coats were announced. Benjamin Brown, who presided at the dedication, defended Jersey Homesteads against charges of communism, declaring instead that it was "common sense-ism" and in line with the Constitution and the American way. The trade name of the factory product was to be "Tripod," standing for the triple co-operative foundation of the colony. Brown said: "On this tripod we will not only bring back craftmanship and pride of achievement, together with security, but we will bring back prosperity based on abundance and not on curtailment." [17]

Despite the auspicious opening of the factory, it failed in its first year of operation, with Brown blaming the government and the government inclined to place the blame on the homesteaders. Brown became committed to a summer opening of the factory because of Resettlement Administration promises to have the homes finished by July. Yet, in August, only eight homesteads were completed, even as factory orders were being received. Plans to settle homesteaders in pup tents pending completion of their homes were rejected by the Resettlement Administration, which feared the adverse publicity. As a result many of the family heads came to Hightstown and found lodging in local homes, thus managing to keep the factory going. By December the $60,000 contributed by the 120 approved homesteaders was exhausted, and orders for coats had not been large enough for a profit.

[17] Washington *Star*, Sept. 8, 1936; New York *Times*, Aug. 2, 1936, pt. 2, p. 2; Lucey, "A Cooperative Town," p. 211.

Jersey Homesteads

Brown, who led a delegation of homesteaders to Washington, accused the government of a breach of faith in not having completed the house construction as scheduled, thus preventing the success of the factory. Although the Resettlement Administration felt that the failure of the factory was due to poor management, it was keenly embarrassed by the lags in construction. This was particularly true of the Family Selection Section, which had readied the homesteaders for moving without knowing of the delay by the Construction Division. Several homesteaders faced acute hardship as a result. Therefore the Resettlement Administration granted Brown a loan of $50,000 for the further operation of the factory.[18]

The second factory season opened in January, 1937. Since the Resettlement Administration had completed the homes, any further losses could not be attributed to a lack of ready labor, although Brown could claim that the nonfulfillment of orders the first year had permanently ruined the market for the factory's products. The second factory season ended by Easter, with no further operating funds. Brown's appeal for a new loan from the Resettlement Administration (now part of the Department of Agriculture) was rejected. Brown accused the government of bad faith and raised $50,000 himself, forming the Tripod Coat and Suit, Incorporated, to design, promote, and distribute the garments. The factory products were to be sold through farm co-operative outlets throughout the country. The Tripod products were distributed by seven trucks, each of which carried complete lines of coats, plus racks and mirrors. One truck reported sales of $1,000 in one day. But by May, 1938, Tripod suspended operations for lack of funds. Appealing to the Farm Security Administration, Brown finally received a loan of $150,000, with stipulations intended to prevent reckless expenditures or overproduction. Almost unbelievably, these funds were exhausted in less than a year. The Farm Security Administration had to admit the complete failure of the co-operative factory and adamantly refused to grant Brown any further aid.[19]

Long before the final failure of the factory in April, 1939, the housing shortage at Jersey Homesteads had become a housing surplus. Even

---

[18] Armstrong, "Four-Million Dollar Village," p. 38; J. O. Walker to E. E. Agger, Oct. 9, 1936, R.G. 96, National Archives.
[19] Lord and Johnstone, *A Place on Earth*, pp. 150–151.

though the 200 homes were completed, the Resettlement Administration was unwilling to move more families into the colony than the economic opportunities warranted. In addition, no tenants could be found who were willing to contribute $500 to a factory that was an obvious failure. In February, 1938, ninety-six homes were vacant, with the Resettlement Administration threatening to lease them to nonparticipating tenants, and this it later did. Jersey Homesteads never contained more than 120 participating Jewish families.[20]

The Jersey Homesteads agricultural asociation was organized in the summer of 1936, with ninety-seven homesteaders joining. The farm co-operative had $16,000 profit from the New Jersey Rural Rehabilitation Corporation, which had leased the farm land for the first year, and two loans from the Resettlement Administration totaling $133,692. The general farm of 412 acres was operated by seven experienced farmers who had been selected as homesteaders for that purpose. They received a regular salary of twenty-five dollars a week from the agricultural association. By raising truck crops for the market, the farm made a profit of $17,000 in 1936, only to lose money consistently in the following years. In the spring of 1937 a poultry unit was started, and a nearby dairy farm was purchased in the fall of 1937. Contrary to Brown's expectations, the three farm units never provided employment for more than thirteen people on the project, and these were the professional farmers. The factory workers, used to indoor work and union wages, were not willing to supplement their earnings by farm work, even in periods of unemployment. As a result transient Negro laborers were employed in busy seasons. Of the three units, only the poultry plant managed to make any profits. After lasting only a year and losing $15,000, the dairy farm was leased to an outside co-operative.[21]

The third leg of the co-operative tripod, the consumer outlets, was slightly stronger than the factory and farms. The clothing store was doomed with the factory, but the grocery and meat market had periods of limited prosperity, while the small tearoom managed to survive, albeit with inadequate stock and facilities. The three co-operatives at Jersey Homesteads were each controlled by a Board of Directors

[20] New York *Times*, Feb. 7, 1938, p. 2; Sept. 24, 1938, p. 19.
[21] Weller, "Land of Milk and Honey," p. 13; Lord and Johnstone, *A Place on Earth*, pp. 152–154.

elected by the members. Each of the co-operatives was represented in a community council, which approved all new members admitted to the community. Each member of the co-operatives had one vote and was to share equally in any dividends. The homesteaders entered into the co-operatives with great enthusiasm, making co-operation almost a religion. They even formed a co-operative political party, which elected their first mayor. Yet enthusiasm was not enough.[22]

The co-operative factory lost money because of an inexperienced manager, because of production in excess of orders, because of an overly ambitious line of goods, and because of high labor costs and inefficient production. Even though many of the homesteaders felt that the failure was the fault of the government, they would have been more realistic if they had placed the blame on themselves and their own attitudes. Habituated to highly competitive endeavor, they were frankly seeking more wages and a better job for themselves rather than a new way of life. Co-operation meant benefits to the exclusion of sacrifices. Thus, in the case of the farm units, the homesteaders, except for the farmers, were primarily interested in what they could get from the farms. They wanted lowered prices for farm products but were unwilling to work for the lower farm wages. Eventually the nonfarmers in the agricultural association secured control of the Board of Directors and tried to run the farms for their own benefit. Even the homesteaders' cohesiveness sometimes hindered, for their attitude was one of "you protect me and I will protect you." Thus inefficient workers were retained. A clerk in the co-operative store, when dismissed, picketed the store the next day, and not a customer passed him. He was rehired, since all business had ceased.[23]

Although a co-operative economy at Jersey Homesteads failed, a second objective of the original sponsors—the successful decentralization of a seasonal industry—was not necessarily proved impractical, since decentralized clothing factories were successful in nearby towns. Just after the failure of the co-operative factory in 1939, a private company leased the factory building from the co-operative association, but remained only a short time. The homesteaders, used to the

---

[22] Lord and Johnstone, *A Place on Earth*, pp. 152–154; Harold V. Knight, "Jersey Homesteads, Co-operative Outpost," *Christian Century*, LV (Feb. 2, 1938), 142; Armstrong, "Four-Million Dollar Village," p. 7.

[23] Lord and Johnstone, *A Place on Earth*, pp. 148, 152–153, 155.

excellent positions and high wages they had given themselves, made such high wage demands that the private concern withdrew after a short period of bitter controversy. In October, 1939, the Farm Security Administration forced the co-operative association to sell the factory at auction, since its loans were still unpaid. The government bid in the factory and most of the fixtures, netting only $1,811 on the items released. After remaining idle a year, the factory was rented for five years to Kartiganer and Company of Manhattan for the manufacturing of women's hats. By that time many of the homesteaders had secured jobs in nearby cities, although in 1941 about 100 homesteaders, from 40 families, were working in the hat factory, which proved moderately successful.[24]

Another objective of Jersey Homesteads was subsistence agriculture on the small homestead plots. When first on their homesteads most of the settlers were enthusiastically interested in vegetable gardens. Experts from the New Jersey Agricultural Experiment Station gave lectures on gardening, and the farm co-operative offered to plow and sow each garden for ten dollars. Many of the homesteaders quickly lost their early interest. Eight families never made use of their garden plot at all, and thirty-eight families almost exclusively raised flowers. These families claimed that gardening did not pay when proper charges were made for their own labor, which, in spite of periods of unemployment, they felt should be amply rewarded. On the other hand, about sixty-five homesteaders took pride in their vegetable gardens, some as sources of food, many as hobbies.[25]

One objective of Jersey Homesteads was fulfilled even beyond expectations. From the first occupancy, Jersey Homesteads was a true community, with a cohesive, socially active citizenry. The first moving into homes was a community affair. Through the long wait for the completion of the homesteads and during what the settlers believed was a long struggle to get the government to fulfill its obligations, the homesteaders had developed a close bond of kinship. In the community everyone knew everyone else, and house doors were never locked. Though quick to criticize the government and its policies, the homesteaders were proud of their new homes and very happy

[24] *Ibid.*, p. 156; New York *Times*, Oct. 28, 1939, p. 17, Oct. 31, 1939, p. 23, and Nov. 1, 1939, p. 26; "Back to Capitalism," *Time*, XXXV (April 22, 1940), 87–88.
[25] Lord and Johnstone, *A Place on Earth*, pp. 157–158.

about the opportunities offered by the community. Numerous social organizations were quickly organized; in fact, the community was almost overorganized, with some meeting occurring almost every night. In 1939 there were only three adult members of the original homesteaders who did not belong to one or another of the community organizations. There was a dramatic club, a junior league, a sewing circle, a baseball club, and a regular cultural evening. In spite of the lack of steady employment, none of the homesteaders wanted to return to New York City. When economic necessity forced homesteaders to move, they always mourned the loss of friends and the pleasant social life. Jersey Homesteads, as much as any other New Deal community, was a well-defined social organism, with a character and a soul all its own.

Although the homesteaders desired, more than anything else, to own their own homes, Jersey Homesteads remained under government leases until the final liquidation by the Public Housing Authority. The rentals were very low, averaging from about $12 to $16 per month. Although Jersey Homesteads had a community manager appointed by the Resettlement Administration, it always exhibited more local control than most of the other communities. The influence of the original sponsors remained very important, with the homesteaders surrendering all authority to such leaders as Benjamin Brown. The group meetings of the homesteaders were dominated by those leaders, who often deliberately defied government officials. Unique among the subsistence homesteads projects, Jersey Homesteads was incorporated in 1937 as a borough, with its own town government. The first mayor, Philip Goldstein, practically became a permanent official, serving many years without a salary.[26]

Jersey Homesteads, even as Arthurdale, was a focal point for anti-New Deal criticism. Its controversial career invited critics, while its co-operative pattern aroused conservatives to an attack upon the ideas back of the community. Much of the early controversy was heightened by the actions of the homesteads and their leaders, who were quick to accuse the government of bad faith and who never hesitated to publicize their complaints or their wishes. The fact that many of the homesteaders had emigrated from Russia, that 90 per

[26] *Ibid.*, pp. 158–159; Armstrong, "Four-Million Dollar Village," p. 7; New York *Herald Tribune*, June 8, 1937; New York *Times*, July 13, 1941, p. 28.

cent of them were foreign-born, that Brown himself was born in Russia and had co-operated with the Soviet Government in 1928, was ammunition for the most unethical critics. The Philadelphia *Inquirer* complained that "the American taxpayer is putting up $1,800,000 to erect a model of a Russian Soviet Commune half way between New York and Philadelphia." According to the same editorial, "200 carefully selected families, headed by a Russian-born little Stalin, will be running their 'co-operative.'" [27] To counteract criticism of this sort, the homesteaders had Fourth of July celebrations, sang patriotic songs, attended Americanization classes, and tried to point out the difference between co-operation and communism.

The most convincing attacks on Jersey Homesteads were directed at the high costs, the mistakes in construction, and the failure of the co-operatives. The homesteaders and sponsors aided part of this attack by constantly expressing their fears that the project cost was going to be so high that they could never repay the government. On July 4, 1936, as the costs and criticism mounted under the Resettlement Administration construction program, Rabbi Wise, a loyal sponsor, stated: "We will pay back the government every red cent that it has invested in this enterprise, even if it takes the rest of our lives and the lives of our children." [28] This very quickly became a manifest impossibility, and not by the fault of the homesteaders, who surely were not expected to pay for the inefficient relief labor or for the $200,000 concrete-slab factory. The failure of the concrete-slab method, the lockout of visitors at the construction site, the drab appearance that was so widely belived would mark the slab-type homes, the loss of local tax revenue, and the enormous cost, all influenced Senator Warren Barbour of New Jersey to introduce his Senate resolution requiring a full, and what was hoped would be an embarrassing, report from the Resettlement Administration.

Many of the New Deal communities were disliked, for one reason or another, by the older inhabitants in the surrounding areas. This local hostility was very marked at Jersey Homesteads. The type of architecture, the extravagance, and the character and nature of the expected homesteaders were all assailed by local or, at least, by New

[27] Philadelphia *Inquirer*, May 7, 1936.
[28] In Lucey, "A Cooperative Town," p. 210.

Jersey critics. It was the mistakes at Jersey Homesteads that influenced the citizens of Bound Brook to enter their successful injunction against the greenbelt city of Greenbrook and thereby almost block the whole Resettlement Administration program. In fact, a Hearst newspaper reporter circulated a petition in the town of Hightstown requesting a similar injunction against Jersey Homesteads.[29]

It was the cost of Jersey Homesteads, more than that of any other project, that gave Senator Harry F. Byrd grounds for attacking the extravagance of the Farm Security Administration. Byrd's attack materially contributed to the final abolition of the Farm Security Administration. Using information allegedly secured from the General Accounting Office, Byrd placed the price of Jersey Homesteads at over $4,000,000. The final account by the Farm Security Administration listed the total cost as $3,402,382.27, or about $16,516 per unit if divided equally among each of the 206 homesteads (both in town and on the farms).[30] If it is considered that only 120 families ever shared in the numerous community facilities, the total unit cost for some of the participating homesteads was over $20,000. Of course much of the money was poured into the operation of the factory, into experiments in construction, and into the wages of highly inefficient relief laborers. But, in any case, there was no question in the mind of anyone, including the officials of the Resettlement Administration, that the total cost of Jersey Homesteads represented at least three times its actual value. In fact, as early as 1937, the Resettlement Administration estimated that Jersey Homesteads could be liquidated for only 27.9 per cent of cost.[31]

In one sense the end of the Jersey Homesteads experiment began in September, 1938, when the Farm Security Administration, finally realizing that the economic opportunities at Jersey Homesteads were not sufficient to attract any more Jewish garmentworkers (at $500 a family), began renting seventy-five homes to nonparticipating families from the local area. In 1940 the farm, poultry plant, and crops were auctioned, with the government bidding in most of the property. After having lost money for four years, the farm co-operative was abolished.

[29] Weller, "Land of Milk and Honey," p. 12.
[30] Select Committee of the House Committee on Agriculture, *Hearings on the Farm Security Administration*, 78th Cong., 1st Sess., 1943–1944, p. 1118.
[31] H. W. Truesdell to E. G. Arnold, May 28, 1937, R.G. 96, National Archives.

With the factory already in private hands, the co-operative community was at an end.[32]

One thing could not be liquidated—the community itself, for it involved more than economics. In July, 1941, the 102 remaining Jewish homesteaders celebrated their fifth anniversary at Jersey Homesteads. Some were commuting to other cities for work; others were employed in their old factory; all were happy with their homes and homestead plots. Mayor Philip Goldstein, deploring the fact that the homesteaders still rented their homes, asked for a homestead association for Jersey Homesteads. Such an association had been tentatively approved by the Farm Security Administration as early as July 15, 1940, but in 1942, before it was ever put into effect, Jersey Homesteads was transferred to the Federal Public Housing Authority.[33] This agency and its successor, the Public Housing Administration, completed the liquidation of the government's investment in Jersey Homesteads by selling the homes to individuals after the end of World War II. After liquidation, the homesteaders decided to change the name of their community to Roosevelt, New Jersey. Jersey Homesteads, long associated with controversy and extravagance, disappeared from the map. Roosevelt, New Jersey, a name symbolic of a better future in its very newness, was also an indication of the homesteaders' gratefulness to a recently deceased hero.

[32] New York *Times,* Sept. 24, 1938, p. 19; Oct. 31, 1939, p. 23; July 3, 1940, p. 19.

[33] *Ibid.,* July 13, 1941, p. 28; Memorandum for J. O. Walker, March 16, 1941, R.G. 96, National Archives.

❧ XII ❦

Penderlea Homesteads—Something Less than a Rural Paradise

ARTHURDALE, in addition to being the first and most experimental of the New Deal communities, was also representative of a particular type of community, the stranded workers' community. Jersey Homesteads was the only fully co-operative industrial community, but in many ways represented the difficulties encountered in the completely co-operative rural communities, such as Lake Dick and Casa Grande. Less well known by the public, but actually comprising over two-thirds of the completed communities, were the all-rural farm communities and the industrial-type subsistence homesteads communities. The hopes and dreams, the trials and tribulations that characterized the former can be observed in the first of the farm communities, Penderlea Homesteads in Pender County, North Carolina.

The approval of plans for Penderlea by the Division of Subsistence Homesteads in November, 1933, simply marked the beginning of another ambitious community project by Hugh MacRae, who started the construction of his first organized rural community in 1905. MacRae, frequently mentioned in earlier chapters, was an engineer and businessman who graduated from the Massachusetts Institute of Technology in 1885. In the next twenty years he amassed a sizable fortune in the railroad and public utilities business in the area of his home at Wilmington, North Carolina. MacRae imbibed freely of the positivistic optimism of the turn of the century. He envisioned unending progress through science and the adaptation of experts to all fields of endeavor. As a wealthy capitalist, he defended the right, even the duty, of individuals to amass wealth, but at the same time he believed that humanitarianism was the only acceptable goal of either wealth or science. He wanted the idea of public service and public morality so to capture the business world that wealth would be shared voluntarily for the common good. Philanthrophy, not taxation, was the desirable means to social progress.[1]

Even before 1900 MacRae had decided to use part of his wealth to initiate farm colonies as demonstrations of a new type of highly diversified Southern agriculture and of the social possibilities of farm communities. Beginning in 1905 he optioned approximately 453,000 acres of uncleared, undrained land north of Wilmington and formed a company to colonize it. From these options he purchased almost 200,000 acres, including the future site of Penderlea. After soil analyses and a survey by fourteen engineers, MacRae plotted the sites of several future colonies. The street systems and drainage were planned, and the land was divided into ten-acre farms. MacRae then sent an agent to the West to procure colonists. When he failed to find enough Americans interested in the ten-acre, uncleared plots, MacRae turned to Europe. His agent sought immigrants in Italy, Poland, England, Holland, Greece, and Germany. By 1908, when MacRae revealed his work to the public, 800 colonists were in residence in six colonies. The largest colony, St. Helena, included only Italians. A small colony of Greeks at Marathon was soon replaced by Poles. The Dutch settled at Van Eden. A few English bachelors formed a short-lived colony named Artesia, and the Germans settled New Berlin. The most successful colony was at Castle Hayne, where American colonists were joined by several immigrants of various nationalities.[2]

In establishing his colonies MacRae had no precedents to follow.

[1] Hugh MacRae, "Vitalizing the Nation and Conserving Human Units through the Development of Agricultural Communities," *Annals of the American Academy*, LXIII (1916), 278; Senate Committee on Agriculture and Forestry, *Hearings on S. 1800, To Create the Farm Tenant Homes Corporation*, 74th Cong., 1st Sess., 1935, p. 50.

[2] *Hearings on S. 1800*, p. 61; Edmund de S. Brunner, *Immigrant Farmers and Their Children* (New York, 1929), p. 141; "Farm Colonies near Wilmington, N.C.," *Carolinas*, I (March, 1933), 3; Robert W. Vincent, "Successful Immigrants in the South: The Difficult Problem Solved by the Business-like Efforts of One Man," *World's Work*, XVII (1908), 10908–10909.

Elwood Mead had not yet returned to America from Australia with his well-defined colonization scheme. As a result MacRae varied his methods from colony to colony and learned from his mistakes. The Italians at St. Helena, the largest colony, received extensive supervision from the colonization company, which even constructed their homes. At other colonies the company did very little development. MacRae established an experimental farm on the poorest ground for the benefit of all the colonists. He also furnished the early colonists with implements, transportation facilities, and a marketing service and paid the colonists for the wood they cut in clearing their ten acres. A superintendent was provided for each colony. The colonists were to pay for their farms through intensive truck farming, receiving clear deeds except for a provision to keep the land from ever passing into the hands of Negroes. From early failures, such as the quick departure of the English bachelors, MacRae decided that only married men would make good colonists, that the land should be cleared and even planted before settlement, and that, on the other hand, no houses should be built by the company. The essentials to success seemed to be cheap land, ample credit, scientific planning in advance, careful selection of settlers, expert guidance, co-operative activity, and a sociable community life.[3]

Castle Hayne, the mixed colony, became the most successful and, in MacRae's eyes, the most perfect demonstration of a foolproof method of colonization. The colony was based on an intensive, all-year cultivation of diversified truck crops by about forty colonists, with a few prosperous settlers extending their original ten acres to twenty or even thirty. MacRae urged the colonists to invest their profits in industrial securities rather than in more land, since he believed it possible to make a complete living on a very few acres of ground. At Castle Hayne, as at all the MacRae colonies, the settlers grew their own subsistence and joined in co-operative endeavors. MacRae believed that the success of the colonists was a demonstration to the whole South of the advantages of a diversified rather than a one-crop agriculture. He desired up to ten such colonies in each Southern state.[4]

[3] Vincent, "Successful Immigrants," pp. 10909–10910; Brunner, *Immigrant Farmers*, pp. 142–144; Felice Ferrero, "A New St. Helena," *Survey*, XXIII (1909), 174.

[4] *Hearings on S. 1800*, p. 50; Brunner, *Immigrant Farmers*, pp. 147–151; "Farm Colonies near Wilmington, N.C.," pp. 3–4.

In the early twenties the work of Elwood Mead in the California farm colonies and the growing popularity of the English garden city idea contributed to a vastly increased interest in organized community planning, leading, on one hand, to such suburban experiments as Radburn, New Jersey, and, on the other, to a long but unsuccessful attempt to create numerous farm colonies both in the South and over the whole nation. As living examples of such colonies, MacRae's work in North Carolina took on a national significance. In 1923 he and many of the world's outstanding city planners, conservationists, and irrigationists, including John Nolen, Thomas Adams, Sir Raymond Unwin, Gifford Pinchot, and Elwood Mead, joined in the formation of the Farm City Corporation of America. The corporation planned to lay out and build a farm city that would combine the advantages of town and country. The funds were to come from private investors, who would eventually gain a profit when the settlers had repaid the purchase price. The corporation desired 8,000 acres of fertile land for its first city. The farm city was to include a community center, an area for industry, subsistence homesteads around the community center, and outlying farms of increasing sizes. John Nolen and an associate planner, Philip W. Foster, actually sketched a farm-city plan for a site near the MacRae colonies. This unused plan of 1923 was very similar to the one that Nolen later used for Penderlea.[5]

Unfortunately for MacRae's dreams, private investments were not forthcoming for the proposed farm city. As a result he joined with Elwood Mead in advocating government-supported demonstration farm communities for the South. When Mead secured congressional approval for the survey of possible sites for these colonies, the MacRae colonies were much studied and were cited as examples of successful colonization. Since none of the legislative measures to establish a colonization program was passed by Congress, the farm-city idea had to await the New Deal and the subsistence homesteads program. MacRae was early considered for the position of Administrator of the Division of Subsistence Homesteads and, in November, 1933, fairly easily secured the approval of the division for a $1,000,000 farm colony on part of his land in Pender County. This, the first approved farm

[5] George H. Gall, "Making Farm Life Profitable and Pleasant," *National Real Estate Journal*, XXIV (May 21, 1923), 29–32.

colony, was intended to solve the problems of stranded and submarginal farmers and of landless tenant farmers.[6]

More than any other colony, Penderlea's conception and early direction were influenced by one man—MacRae. Under the early, decentralized plan of administration, MacRae was, very naturally, appointed project manager by the local corporation. The corporation's Board of Directors included Frank Fritts, general counsel of the Federal Subsistence Homesteads Corporation and a member of the faculty at Princeton; Carl C. Taylor, formerly dean of the Graduate School at North Carolina State College, vice-president of the American Country Life Association, and an assistant to M. L. Wilson in the Division of Subsistence Homesteads; and John Nolen, at that time president of the International Federation of Town and Country Planning, a teacher in the School of City Planning at Harvard, and a consultant to the Division of Subsistence Homesteads. As a first step, the local corporation purchased 4,550 acres of land from MacRae for $7.10 an acre. The Department of Agriculture assisted in surveys and soil analyses, the State of North Carolina agreed to furnish roads, and Pender County agreed to provide a school. John Nolen, already familiar with the area, planned a community for 300 farm families.[7]

MacRae's plan for Penderlea was based on his experience with his own colonies. He believed the ten-acre plots large enough to provide subsistence and a cash income to be used by the homesteader to purchase his homestead. The Division of Subsistence Homesteads was building the homes, there was plenty of wood for fuel, the state provided roads and education, and the planned community would assure satisfactory social conditions. What more was needed? The most carefully planned of all the rural colonies, Penderlea was laid out around a central community center. With the land already forested, the houses and roadsides were to remain shaded. The creek and drainage areas were also to remain forested and were to be used as parks. Most of the small, ten-acre farm plots faced on a road in front and a forest belt and creek or ditch in the rear (see Figure 1). The local corporation selected the early homesteaders from among local

[6] Gordon Van Schaack, "Penderlea Homesteads: The Development of a Subsistence Homesteads Project," *Landscape Architecture*, XV (1934–1935), 76.
[7] News Item, Jan. 16, 1934, R.G. 96, National Archives; News Release, n.d., *ibid.*

farmers, basing their selection on farming skills as well as on need. MacRae believed that the early selectees were among the "most skilled people" in the world.[8]

MacRae personally directed Penderlea only until May, 1934, at which time all the subsistence homesteads projects were federalized. Although he remained a short while longer as a federal employee, MacRae's influence soon waned. When his plans for Penderlea were altered, his accomplishments became a matter of angry controversy. Since only twenty acres of the purchased land was cleared, MacRae had used transient labor and rented machinery to clear approximately 1,500 acres. He had also supervised the construction of sixteen miles of roads and of ten frame houses. He had spent $18,000 of federal funds for a transient labor camp and $24,000 to establish an experimental farm, a fixture he had found necessary on his older colonies. During his management he spent $325,000 of the $1,000,000 loan. According to MacRae, all 300 homes would have been completed by March, 1935, if the project had remained under local control.[9]

MacRae, who only with misgivings accepted the idea of government financing for rural colonies, completely revolted at the idea of government control. He felt that he had a personal authorization from the President to build a community which would revolutionize rural life. As a result, he appealed to President Roosevelt after the federalization order, asking for a special hearing to determine the best type of administrative organization for subsistence homesteads. This brought a scathing reply from Ickes: "I can not see that it is feasible to hold special hearings with project managers for each project before making such administrative changes as we deem desirable." [10] Later MacRae, chafing under the federal control of his beloved project, wanted to invite Roosevelt, the governor of North Carolina, and newspaper reporters to visit Penderlea and see the progress, or lack of it. This was directly against the wishes of Ickes and Pynchon, who feared embarrassment for the Division of Subsistence Homesteads, since all was not well at Penderlea.[11] By this time MacRae was positive that

[8] Van Schaack, "Penderlea Homesteads," pp. 78–80; *Hearings on S. 1800*, p. 64.
[9] C. E. Pynchon to Oscar Chapman, Jan. 17, 1935, R.G. 48, National Archives; *Hearings on S. 1800*, p. 67.
[10] Ickes to MacRae, May 2, 1934, R.G. 48, National Archives.
[11] Pynchon to MacRae, Nov. 15, 1934, *ibid.*

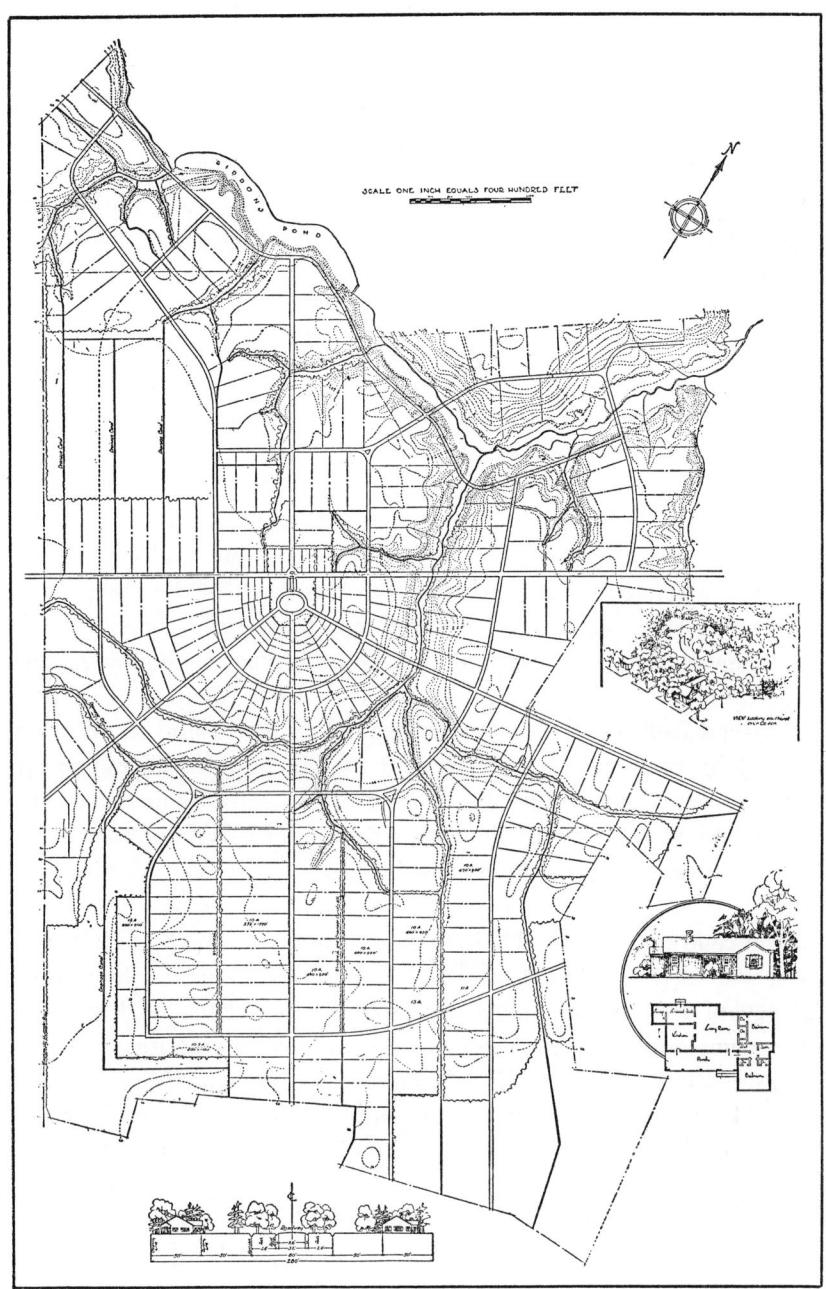

Figure 1. Penderlea Homesteads, Pender County, North Carolina. From *Landscape Architecture*, XV (Jan., 1937), 77.

the new directors of the subsistence homesteads program had betrayed his Penderlea. He blamed the government for all the later mistakes, even as the Division of Subsistence Homesteads attributed most of the mistakes to early planning errors on the part of MacRae.

The charges against MacRae were that he picked poor, undrained, sour soil that could never repay the cost of clearing, that he was careless with his expenditures, and that his ten-acre plots were much too small to support profitable farming operations. MacRae argued that he could prove that any family with sincere purpose and brains could make a complete living on two acres of ground. He described Penderlea as the "best-laid-out rural community in America" on "as productive land as you can get in the United States." He said he "personally would be willing to underwrite the success of every farm in that colony and see that the Government got back every dollar." MacRae placed the responsibility for all failures at Penderlea on an unsympathetic, centralized, urbanized management in the Division of Subsistence Homesteads, which could not "build rural communities." He believed that Penderlea, under the centralized administration, was only of value in showing how not to build a community.[12] MacRae turned from Penderlea to unsuccessful efforts to find support for a privately sponsored "Family Homesteads, Incorporated," and to attempts to get administrative backing and loans for a limited-dividend corporation which was to develop colonies near Wilmington. MacRae, now an old man, never saw his dream of more colonies fulfilled.[13]

After centralization, the Division of Subsistence Homesteads initiated farm management studies at Penderlea which indicated the insufficiency of the ten-acre plots. Accordingly the plans for Penderlea were completely revised, with the new plans calling for only 150 homestead units of approximately twenty acres each. A contract was let for sixty-five houses, and some outbuildings were completed by May, 1935, when the Resettlement Administration inherited Penderlea.[14]

By December 15, 1935, the Resettlement Administration had completed plans for 142 units of twenty acres each at Penderlea. With a

[12] *Hearings on S. 1800*, pp. 50, 63, 65, 67.
[13] MacRae to M. L. Wilson, Sept. 30, 1935, R.G. 96, National Archives; M. L. Wilson to Franklin D. Roosevelt, Aug. 31, 1937, R.G. 16, National Archives.
[14] Pynchon to Oscar Chapman, Jan. 17, 1935, R.G. 48, National Archives.

work force of up to 1,800 relief laborers, the Resettlement Administration completed the 142 homes, plus barns, hog houses, poultry houses, wells, and pump houses by September, 1936. The houses were of one story without basements, had four to six rooms, contained baths and screened porches, and were heated by fireplaces. Almost one-half of the construction budget was expended on further land clearing. Although this clearing provided relief employment, it was so expensive ($195,635 for 2,403 acres) that the value of the land was hardly sufficient to cover the cost of clearing.[15]

In 1936 and 1937 the Resettlement Administration purchased additional land at Penderlea, enlarging the project to 9,833 acres. As the first 142 homes were completed, the Resettlement Administration began planning for another 158 units of thirty acres each as an addition to the original community designed by Nolen. Actually, only fifty additional units were ever added, these being completed in 1938. Meanwhile the community center was developed, with its thirty-one-room, consolidated county school, which contained a community library, craft, music, and band rooms, a special auditorium, a large gymnasium, a social and home economics building, a shop, and a school-bus garage. Also in the community center were the administration building, the community building, a health clinic, a home for teachers, a potato-curing house, a cane-syrup mill, a cannery, a cooperative store, a large warehouse, a gristmill, a grading house, and a furniture shop. The furniture shop not only provided furniture for the Penderlea homes, but for some of the other projects. Most of the community construction was completed by June, 1938.[16]

With the exception of four or five early homesteaders in the homes completed by MacRae, the first group of homesteaders moved into Penderlea in the fall of 1936. They occupied their twenty-acre farms and almost immediately came under the supervision of farm and home management experts. The early homesteaders, who were chosen from rehabilitation clients and submarginal farmers, had to sub-

[15] Resettlement Administration, *First Annual Report* (Washington, 1936), p. 77; Resettlement Administration, "Houses," *Architectural Forum*, LXVI (1937), 490–491; C. B. Baldwin to Paul Appleby, Nov. 10, 1939, R.G. 16, National Archives.

[16] Select Committee of the House Committee on Agriculture, *Hearings on the Farm Security Administration*, 78th Cong., 1st Sess., 1943–1944, p. 601; Approved Budget Estimate, n.d., R.G. 96, National Archives; Memorandum on Penderlea Homesteads, n.d., *ibid.*; Monthly Report of the Resettlement Administration from 1937 through 1940, *ibid.*

mit to a medical examination before occupancy. They were furnished with livestock, seed, feed, fertilizer, and subsistence, for all of which they executed personal notes. These notes later led to complete confusion, since many of the bewildered homesteaders were unsure of how much they owed the government. The farms were supposed to provide subsistence, to support soil-improvement crops, and to allow a cash income from marketable truck crops. In actuality the lack of a large local market for truck crops led to the growing of such cash crops as tobacco.[17]

By January, 1937, only 112 families were occupying the 142 completed homesteads. The remaining houses filled very slowly, with seventeen houses still vacant in September. By April, 1938, as the extra fifty homes were being completed, only 141 families were in residence. Many of these families depended upon construction work for an income. A few of the farmers learned skilled trades in connection with the construction work and consequently felt so much above the status of farmers that they employed others to work their farms. But when construction ended in 1938, farming was the only recourse. The homesteaders, who came to Penderlea expecting to purchase their own homes, had to submit to the variable-payment, trial-type leases and detailed, closely supervised farm and home plans. Their income was closely budgeted, with their furnishing loans from the Farm Security Administration being disbursed only through a joint banking account with the community manager. As a result of delinquencies on loan payments, one-sixth of the homestead families were forced to leave, or voluntarily left, the project in 1939. Because of economic failures or complete dissatisfaction with government policies, there was a turnover of over 100 per cent by 1943.[18]

The large school at Penderlea was a consolidated county school, drawing part of its children from areas adjacent to Penderlea. The Resettlement Administration subsidized the school by furnishing the building and by contributing $1,400 a year to the principal's salary. The first principal of the school was selected by the Resettlement Ad-

[17] W. M. Healey to C. B. Faris, April 19, 1938, R.G. 96, National Archives; C. B. Faris to George S. Mitchell, Feb. 15, 1938, *ibid.*

[18] Monthly Report of the Resettlement Administration, May, 1938, *ibid.;* Harold D. Lasswell, "Resettlement Communities: A Study of the Problems of Personalizing Administration," n.d., p. 17, *ibid.; Hearings on the Farm Security Administration,* pp. 602–603.

ministration to begin an "experimental progressive" program, with the approval of the county school superintendent. Such practical courses as shop, forge work, diesel and automotive mechanics, and metalwork were stressed. Whether because of too much enthusiasm on the part of the young principal, because of a natural conservatism on the part of local parents, both on and off the project, or, as one Farm Security Administration investigator concluded, because of enmity between the school officials and the project manager, resulting in the latter's efforts to discredit the school in the eyes of the homesteaders and to stir up sentiment against progressive education, the aroused parents, working through a local school committee, fired the principal at the end of his first year and secured a more traditional school for the community.[19]

As at all rural communities, the great problem at Penderlea was how to devise farm plans that would permit the homesteaders not only to maintain their new level of living but also allow them to purchase their homesteads. To meet this problem the Resettlement Administration, in addition to close supervision, initiated several cooperative enterprises. In June and July, 1937, the Penderlea Mutual Association was formed as a stock company under North Carolina law. It received a loan of $30,670 from the Resettlement Administration, using the money to operate several consumer and processing cooperatives, such as the gristmill, the store, the warehouse, the potato-curing house, the vegetable-grading and packing shed, the cane-syrup mill, the community cannery, and a filling station. The co-operative facilities were later owned by a second co-operative, the Penderlea Farms Homestead Association, which borrowed a total of $813,100 from the Farm Security Administration, mostly for a hosiery mill. Of this sum none was repaid by 1943, when the first steps were made toward the liquidation of Penderlea. By 1943 the Mutual Association, the operating co-operative, had repaid only $7,459.78 of its small loan.[20]

Many of the co-operative facilities were seldom used, including the warehouse, cannery, and vegetable-grading shed. Others were misused. In 1938 the co-operative association was reprimanded by the regional office for not answering any correspondence, sending no

[19] George Mitchell to Harriett H. Robson, Jan. 19, 1938, R.G. 96, National Archives; Lasswell, "Resettlement Communities," pp. 76–77.

[20] Robert W. Strange to Mastin G. White, May 28, 1937, R.G. 96, National Archives; A Report on the Condition of Co-operatives, April, 1943, *ibid.*

minutes of meetings for four months, submitting no prescribed forms, continuing to grant credit despite positive orders to the contrary, not writing down purchase orders, keeping no records on any of the enterprises, not recording toll telephone calls, and frequently repairing the gristmill at the expense of the co-operative rather than forcing the dealer to make the repairs free of cost.[21]

Since practically every one of the homesteaders was getting farther and farther in debt to the government year by year, Penderlea was selected in 1938 as the site of one of the five hosiery mills financed by the Farm Security Administration. Utilizing a loan of $750,000, the Penderlea Farms Homestead Association constructed one of the best hosiery mills in the South and entered into a managerial agreement with the Dexdale Hosiery Mills. The managing company did not receive any fee for management above salaries and a set percentage of profits. The mill began operation with silk, but soon had to convert to nylon at a heavy cost for new equipment. Then World War II forced another change to rayon, with even the amount of rayon strictly limited by the War Production Board. Wartime also brought a labor shortage, with homesteaders seeking lucrative defense jobs at Wilmington and elsewhere. Only in 1941 did the mill meet its operating expenses. Through 1942 it had lost only $19,549.77, but had deferred all rent and interest payments to the Farm Security Administration. It provided jobs for up to 100 people, many of whom were not homesteaders. By 1943 the Dexdale Mills company was recommending a cessation of operations and the liquidation of the mill property. An investigation by an experienced hosiery manufacturer revealed managerial inefficiency and disinterest on the part of the Dexdale company.[22]

Because of the large turnover and low morale, the Farm Security Administration sent a sociologist to Penderlea in 1940 to study the whole problem of personalizing administration. This study resulted in a most intimate and authentic report on social conditions in a rural colony. The investigator found that the poor morale resulted in part from the disillusionment inevitably following the overly high expectations that the homesteaders had brought with them to the

[21] C. B. Faris to W. H. Robbins, Nov. 15, 1938, *ibid.*
[22] Report on Hosiery Mill, n.d., *ibid.; Hearings on the Farm Security Administration,* pp. 1748–1750, 1762–1763.

new project. They had expected Penderlea to provide them with a profitable farm, marketing outlets, an immediate opportunity to begin gaining an equity toward the purchase price of their farm, a perfect community life with no feuds, factions, or favorites, and co-operative stores with low prices and high dividends. They were disappointed on almost every count and on none more so than in their constant frustration in awaiting a purchase contract. The most clear goal of the homesteaders was ownership, whereas new farming skills, better farm and home management, co-operative and community participation, and social and cultural pursuits were vague goals without any real meaning to most of the homesteaders. As annual lease followed annual lease, the homesteaders became apprehensive over what they would have to pay for their farms. They puzzled over whether the government would ever really permit them to buy or, if permitted to purchase, whether they would receive clear titles.[23]

The homesteaders at Penderlea had expected a friendly, consistent policy on the part of the government, but had found inconsistency, conflicts, ambivalence, and, always, delays. Actually the homesteaders had very little understanding of government processes. Chance remarks by a government clerk became, in the eyes of the homesteaders, either a binding promise or the beginning of a spreading rumor. Furthering the misunderstandings were the frequent changes in administration, from MacRae to a centralized Division of Subsistence Homesteads to the Resettlement Administration and then to the Farm Security Administration. Each change brought new personnel and new policies. Inevitably earlier commitments were sometimes forgotten or ignored, leaving a legacy of ill will. The homesteaders also became disillusioned with government-sponsored enterprises. The packing shed aroused great hopes, only to end in disuse. The co-operatives did not have lower prices and never paid dividends. Since the government made policies for the co-operatives, the homesteaders believed that the government had the responsibility to make them pay a profit. Even "their" community building was kept locked by the management most of the time, being opened only for scheduled dances on Saturday night.[24]

The homesteader, rather than finding economic security, was constantly frightened by his insecurity. He was afraid to repair his home

[23] Lasswell, "Resettlement Communities," pp. 3–5, 9, 13.   [24] *Ibid.*, pp. 3–7.

and farm for fear the government might not justly evaluate the repairs in the final sale price. Since his annual lease was a "trial lease," the homesteader felt that he was on his "good behavior," leading to tension on one hand and to open subservience on the other. The homesteader never considered his financial obligations to the government as similar to private debts. He believed that the government should deal more gently with him and even perhaps write off part of his obligation. Thus he always paid his private debts and postponed his government obligations. When the government did deal more strictly with him, the homesteader tended to blame the local officials.[25]

The homesteaders at Penderlea resented their lack of participation in community government. They felt that the project manager and other officials dictated all policy. Very rarely were the homesteaders consulted on policy decisions. If the project manager wished to speak with a settler, he did not visit the homesteader but rather summoned him to appear at his office at a certain hour. Even in the co-operative associations the actual decisions were made by representatives of the government, and an independent, homesteader-controlled farmers' organization met only furtively, fearing Farm Security Administration disapproval. In justification of the government officials, it should be made clear that the homesteaders lacked even an elemental knowledge of parliamentary procedure and tended toward factionalism in their community alignments. Only an experienced official could have led a profitable discussion in their associational meetings.[26]

At Penderlea certain forms of social discrimination also irked the homesteaders. Many accusations of favoritism were leveled against the project manager, who personally recommended (the equivalent of selection) people for employment in the hosiery mill. The manager, a college graduate and former extension agent, lived in town and commuted to the project each day. He and his staff often organized "oyster roasts" and other social affairs, holding them forty miles from the project and inviting only the schoolteachers. He seldom attended homestead functions, such as movies and dances. His paternal attitude toward the homesteaders was reflected in the following reported statement: "These people are just like children and you have to treat them

[25] *Ibid.*, pp. 10, 16–18.   [26] *Ibid.*, pp. 14–15, 22–25, 34–35.

Penderlea Homesteads

that way."[27] On the other hand, some lesser project officials, who showed a sincere interest in and a close identification with the homesteaders, were well loved. At first the homesteaders were resented by the local farmers, who were probably jealous over the good homes and other benefits bestowed upon the people in the colony. This outside opposition was lessened by contacts at school, local dances, and youth meetings.[28]

Incentives for effort at Penderlea tended to vanish along with the loss of faith in the earlier goals and promises. The strongest incentive for maintaining payments on loans—social pressure—was completely lacking, since almost every family was delinquent. Furthermore, the widespread resentment against the government was not conducive to high morale. Most resented was the invasion of privacy resulting from the joint banking accounts, the detailed farm and home plans, the frequent advice, the multiple forms to fill, the record keeping, the inspections by visiting officials, and the fearful submission to questioning of all types by both government officials and academic researchers. According to the homesteaders, one man went around asking people how many pairs of underwear they had. One wife even stated that "one of the hardest things to get used to here on the project is the conveniences."[29] A schoolboy on the project composed the following verse which indicates some of the resentment:

> On the farm we have busted pumps
> And lots of trouble burning stumps,
> While white-collared big shots hang around
> To show the farmer how to tend the ground.[30]

By the end of 1942 the Farm Security Administration was forced to make one final alteration at Penderlea. At this time the number of farm units was reduced from 192 to 109 larger units, leaving 82 surplus houses which were rented to defense workers. To find operators for even this number of units the Farm Security Administration had to import fifty farmers from the mountains of western North Carolina in 1943. By this time 159 tenants had moved away from Penderlea, mostly from 1939 through 1942. They all left owing the government money, in amounts varying from $47 to $3,240 and averaging over

[27] *Ibid.*, pp. 12, 22, 26, 31.
[28] *Ibid.*, pp. 31–33, 38.
[29] *Ibid.*, pp. 36–37, 40–42, 72.
[30] *Ibid.*, p. 63.

$1,000. The new homesteaders of 1943 each received operating loans of from $300 to $800. The old homesteaders, three of whom had been on the project since 1935, were, except in two cases, in debt to the government for amounts up to $5,031. Yet, for the first time, the project was on a sound economic basis, with many homesteaders making splendid progress, aided by wartime prices. In most cases the farmers had assets that more than covered their debts. As a result of this beginning prosperity, the first farming units (nine) were sold to homesteaders in March, 1943, at $3,020 each.[31]

The major criticism of Penderlea was its cost. By 1943 the government had expended $2,277,685.60 at Penderlea, or nearly $11,000 for each completed family unit. In defense of this large figure, the Farm Security Administration pointed to the amount spent by the cooperative association, the cost of the community facilities, and the unused reserve land. Subtracting those items, it estimated the real cost of each homestead to be only $7,990. As if to prove the perversity of statistics, the congressional critics of Penderlea added to the costs of Penderlea the amount obviously lost on loans to homesteaders, the amount expended in direct relief grants, the loss in maintenance and operation, and, most important, the amount of interest the government had to pay on the borrowed funds invested in Penderlea. This raised the total cost to $3,107,122. Since there remained only 109 operating units, this made a unit cost of $28,506. Counting the approximate $2,000 owed by each homesteader to the government and also adding the interest he should have been paying on his loans, the total amount each homesteader owed the government, according to critics, was not $7,990 but approximately $35,000. Comparable farms in the area were selling for about $3,000.[32]

By December 31, 1944, only forty-eight homesteads had been sold at Penderlea, these at an average price of only $3,354. Also sold was the hosiery mill, at a good price of $604,000. By June, 30, 1945, sixty-six homesteads had been liquidated at an average price of $3,110.[33] The other homesteads were sold in the next two years, during which

[31] *Hearings on the Farm Security Administration,* pp. 601–603, 605–609, 1089.
[32] *Ibid.,* pp. 489, 609–610.
[33] House Agricultural Subcommittee of the Committee on Appropriations, *Hearings on Agricultural Department Appropriation Bill for 1946,* pt. II, 79th Cong., 1st Sess., 1945, pp. 519, 535, and *Hearings on Agricultural Department Appropriation Bill for 1947,* 79th Cong., 2d Sess., 1946, p. 1414.

time the Farm Security Administration was absorbed by the Farmers' Home Administration. Because of the rapid turnover at Penderlea, very few of the original homesteaders were still on the project at the time of liquidation. The difficulties at Penderlea, both in terms of economic insecurity and project management, were all too often duplicated at other farming colonies. But Penderlea was unique in two ways: it was the first farm colony and, per capita, it was the most expensive.

❧ XIII ❦

Granger Homesteads—An Escape from Modernity

FROM the inception of the subsistence homesteads program through the Resettlement Administration and the Farm Security Administration, the community program of the New Deal moved ever farther away from the ideological presuppositions of most of the back-to-the-land adherents and especially from the explicit, doctrinaire philosophy of the distributist school of agrarians. Although the ever-pervasive idea of the superiority of family-based agriculture was largely adhered to, and even though fee simple ownership was seriously challenged in only a limited number of projects, the leaders in the community-building program were not at all sympathetic with the strong emphasis on individualism and the ever-present distrust of government that characterized the agrarians. As a result of this ideological divergence, Ralph Borsodi, the most dogmatic of distributists, quit his project at Dayton in disgust over governmental policies. At Penderlea a less dogmatic agrarian, Hugh MacRae, soon resigned from the directorship of his special project. Only in the case of Granger Homesteads in Iowa did the agrarian, distributist school of thought remain important in the actual development of a New Deal community. This was through the work of one man, Father Luigi G. Ligutti, a member of and later head of the National Catholic Rural Life Conference and one of the most influential of American agrarians and distributists.

From M. L. Wilson through Tugwell, Alexander, and Baldwin, the leaders of the community program were at one in accepting the industrial revolution and its effects on both city and country. They all, with varying types of reactions, disclaimed any divine or absolute sanctity for various political, economic, and social institutions that had survived from a nonindustrial past and had seemingly proved insufficient for modern man. They all desired new, better-suited institutions which, in most cases, they wished to achieve through the instrumentality of the federal government. M. L. Wilson was unique in emphasizing the necessity of, and the difficulty in, reconciling the past with the present and in exhibiting a profound sympathy for, and a sentimental attachment to, many of the values and many of the institutions of an older America. He was particularly anxious that reforms be thoroughly democratic in execution and, in the end, enhance democracy. Tugwell was bitter in his repudiation of past institutions and values and most enthusiastic and thoroughgoing in his reforms. Tradition suffered at his hands, and in the hands of his successors.

To the distributist agrarians, one of the most reactionary groups in America, industrialism was the great enemy of mankind. Modern man, enslaved by the machine and the centralized factory, could find salvation only in a return to a decentralized economic system which would permit each man access to wealth-producing property. State socialism, or bureaucratic collectivism, simply represented another type of slavery, whatever its doubtful economic benefits. Thus, the distributists erected as an economic ideal the agrarian nation of small farmers envisioned by Jefferson. As a whole, the agrarians were authoritarian and moralistic. Institutions, such as private property, were sacred either because ordained by God, because of a revered tradition, or because they fulfilled an ethical purpose in man's life. Yet, separated from a concept of moral responsibility, such institutions could be corrupted by selfish individuals, such as had been the case with modern capitalism, which the distributists denounced as immoral and vulgar. Their reaction to modern society was really one of moral and aesthetic repugnance, springing from an absolutist concept of man and the natural world. Reform did not mean, in fact could not mean, new institutions, since the traditional institutions were firmly rooted in reality. Reform could mean only moral reform, a renewed sense of responsibility, a faithful return to traditional ideals, a purification of corrupted institutions. Such personalized reform had to spring directly from individuals, working perhaps in small, localized groups. Large, centralized governments could and should provide the necessary means to this reform; they must not direct or control the reformation.

Besides being the one project that accurately reflected the distributist influence, Granger Homesteads was also one of the most successful of the New Deal communities. Arthurdale, Jersey Homesteads, and Penderlea, although the most publicized of the communities, were also the ones that suffered the most delays, exhibited the most mistakes, and cost the most money. To judge all the communities by these three would be most unfair. Some of the industrial homesteads, a group of which Granger was a part, were constructed with little delay and few errors. Many, such as Longview and El Monte, repaid or nearly repaid the government's investment. Others, and notably Granger, fulfilled most of the objectives of the subsistence homesteads program, even though they did not liquidate at or near cost.

Father Ligutti came to Granger, Iowa, a farm village of about 300 inhabitants, in 1926 to take over the pastorate of the local Catholic church. Granger was located in a coal-mining area north of Des Moines. Several hundred miners worked in nine local coal mines, living in five different mining camps, with sordid, dismal four-room houses, no churches, poor schools, and no areas for recreation. During the depression the miners, at best, worked only during the winter months, receiving relief payments for the rest of the year. Ligutti, a member of the Catholic Rural Life Conference and a convinced back-to-the-lander, was very anxious to move the miners onto the land as part-time farmers, but had no means to do this until the organization of the Division of Subsistence Homesteads. The Granger area then seemed ideally suited for a homestead project. In addition to the needy miners, who had the required part-time employment, there was plenty of good Iowa farm land, a village with community facilities, and, very important, the nearby Iowa State College, which could lend advice and assistance. In September, 1933, Ligutti got in touch with the Division of Subsistence Homesteads about a project for the Granger area.[1]

[1] "Soil Defeats Poverty, No. 19—Granger Homesteads, Granger, Iowa," *Scholastic*, XXXIX (Nov. 10, 1941), 14; Luigi G. Ligutti, "The Story of the Granger

Ligutti's original plan was for a part-time farming community, which would accommodate fifty families on five-acre garden plots, all near the churches and schools of Granger. He desired a careful selection of settlers from among those employed part time and wanted to limit the cost of each homestead to $2,000. On November 27, 1933, Ligutti consulted with the president and other officials of Iowa State College, receiving promises of aid. He also received wide public support from the Catholic Church, labor leaders, coal companies, and even the Iowa legislature. Local sponsors, in addition to Ligutti, included an editor, a banker, an attorney, and a physician, all Protestants. On December 13, 1933, a detailed plan for the project was submitted to the Division of Subsistence Homesteads in accordance with early policies in the division. The plan was tentatively approved in February, 1934, with the Iowa State College making the land surveys of a carefully selected tract of land about one-fourth of a mile from Granger. This tract of approximately 225 acres was visited by Carl C. Taylor of the Division of Subsistence Homesteads and was appraised by the Federal Land Bank. Final approval for the project was secured on March 4, 1934, with a promise of a $100,000 loan. The loan request, which was soon raised to $125,000, was approved on July 16, 1934.[2]

In conformity with the early policies of the Division of Subsistence Homesteads, as well as with the personal views of Ligutti, a local homesteads corporation was formed in March, 1934. This local corporation planned to allow the homesteaders to construct their own homes under the self-help idea, but almost as soon as the corporation was formed it had to accept more supervision from Washington. A memorandum of April 1, 1934, limited the corporation to guidance and supervision, with the real direction being placed in a project manager, who was appointed on May 1, 1934. Complete centralization later in May ended all the authority on the part of the local corporation. This federalization, although stripping Ligutti and his friends of any official status, did not result in any serious conflict between the Division of

---

Homesteads," *Iowa Bureau Farmer*, II (Feb., 1938), 7; Raymond P. Duggan, *A Federal Resettlement Project—Granger Homesteads* (Washington, 1937), pp. 21, 35; Russell Lord and Paul H. Johnstone, *A Place on Earth: A Critical Appraisal of Subsistence Homesteads* (Washington, 1942), pp. 106–107.

[2] Duggan, *A Federal Resettlement Project*, pp. 31–32, 35–39, 41–43; W. C. Taylor, "Priest Directs Allotment Plan: Colony in Iowa Coal Town," *Christian Century*, LI (1934), 568.

Subsistence Homesteads and the local sponsors. Ligutti continued to exert a tremendous influence on project management and later became the godfather of the homesteaders. The Division of Subsistence Homesteads continued to seek his advice and welcome his support. Yet Ligutti deplored the centralization, seeing in it many dangers, such as unwarranted interference from Washington and an unprecedented interference by the government in the private affairs of citizens. He expressed his view of the role of the state as follows: "Indeed it is a familiar and well-tested axiom that a government governs best which governs least. It is the duty of the State to provide sufficient means to its citizens in order that they, by diligent application, may secure for themselves temporal prosperity." [3]

The development of Granger Homesteads was not without mistakes, but was certainly less eventful than most of the other projects. The topographical surveys were made by Iowa State College, with the 224 acres of land being divided into fifty homestead plots of from 2.32 to 8.65 acres. The final purchase of the land was long delayed, since the early appraisal had not included one small section and had to be redone, as had to be the original survey. Meanwhile the county had agreed to furnish roads; this necessitated a decision from the Attorney General, which was not received until September, 1934. Finally, one owner refused to sell until October. The final purchase price was $27,365.99, or approximately $122.00 an acre. One other problem delayed construction. The Division of Subsistence Homesteads originally planned to construct prefabricated, one-story homes, but ran into the determined opposition of the local sponsors, who insisted on full basements to satisfy the desires of the homesteaders. The end result of the controversy was an increase in the original loan to $175,000 in order to cover the added cost of basements. After the receipt of several bids, the actual contract for the construction of the fifty homes was let on January 24, 1935, for $86,130, plus an extra $1,125 for the installation of plumbing.[4]

The construction at Granger was rapid. With approximately 200 laborers employed, the wood-frame homes were completed by Octo-

[3] Duggan, *A Federal Resettlement Project*, pp. 41–44; Luigi G. Ligutti and John C. Rawe, *Rural Roads to Security: America's Third Struggle for Freedom* (Milwaukee, 1940), pp. 173–174.

[4] Duggan, *A Federal Resettlement Project*, pp. 89–94, 97–99; Pynchon to Ickes, Dec. 28, 1934, and Feb. 5, 1935, R.G. 48, National Archives.

ber, 1935. The homes had from four to six rooms, with the five- and six-room homes including a second floor. All had full basements which contained the hot-air furnaces and the hot-water tanks. The homesteader had his choice of either a barn or a combination garage and poultry house. Only twelve chose the barn. The outbuildings cost $11,760. Water for each house was supplied by individual wells and electric pumps, which were housed in small pump houses. The pumps froze the first year and had to be placed lower in the ground. Delay over electric supply forced the homesteaders to wait until December 15, 1935, before moving into their new homes.[5]

The homesteaders at Granger were first selected by a local committee, headed by Ligutti, and then eventually approved by the Division of Subsistence Homesteads. The Department of Economics and Sociology at Iowa State prepared a questionnaire and application blank for the committee and furnished a social worker for the personal interviews. Later, new forms were supplied by the Division of Subsistence Homesteads. Despite the forms, however, selection was largely based on the personal knowledge of the applicants by Ligutti and others on the committee, rather than on arbitrary criteria. Several of the applications approved at the local level were refused acceptance at Washington, in some cases because of incomes in excess of $1,500.[6]

Forty-one of the fifty family heads selected were miners or mine clerks. The others included a farmer, a bookkeeper, a barber, a bricklayer, a mechanic, a carpenter, a railroad brakeman, and a streetcar operator. All were employed part time, with yearly incomes ranging from $600 to $1,720. Most significantly, they represented several nationalities. Eighteen families were Italian, eleven were Croatian, and at least one each was Austrian, Lettish, Lithuanian, Slovakian, Irish, Dutch, English, and American. Thirty-three families were Catholic. In many cases the families were large, ranging up to thirteen members. Altogether there were 252 people. The homesteaders were enthusiastic about the project, a majority applying for a homestead in order to achieve homeownership.[7]

The objective of Granger Homesteads was the improvement of both

---

[5] Duggan, *A Federal Resettlement Project*, pp. 93–94, 101, 104–105.
[6] *Ibid.*, pp. 41–49; Lord and Johnstone, *A Place on Earth*, p. 108.
[7] Lord and Johnstone, *A Place on Earth*, p. 107; Ligutti, "The Story of the Granger Homesteads," p. 7; Duggan, *A Federal Resettlement Project*, pp. 53–72.

the economic and social conditions of the homesteaders. This was to be accomplished by teaching husbandry and subsistence farming, by forming group endeavors in order to encourage thrift, good management, and co-operation, and by organizing formal and informal social organizations to develop a consciousness of community. All these objectives were at least partially realized, none more so than subsistence agriculture. Part-time farming at Granger was probably more successful than in any other project. The large families, the good soil, the inherent love of the land present in many of the Europeans, the lack of industrial employment during the summer growing season, and the competent advice from Ligutti, Iowa State College, and the project manager were all contributing factors in the success. In the first year of occupancy the homestead plots yielded an estimated $1,190 worth of vegetables and $2,485 worth of field crops. Every homesteader had a garden, eighteen already had one or more cows, seven families had hogs, and thirty-nine had poultry. By 1939 the average annual value of garden crops per family was $300. By then the orchards were beginning to produce and biodynamic compost heaps were being tried. At the end of 1940 the homesteaders owned 36 cows and 195 hogs, and in that year the women canned 40,000 quarts of food. By 1941 there were 65 cows and 350 hogs. No one was on relief after 1935.[8]

Much of the credit for molding diverse families and nationalities into a close-knit community at Granger belonged to Father Ligutti. He preached to the homesteaders on Sunday, taught them in the parochial schools on weekdays, lectured them on co-operation, attended their meetings, visited their homes, and guarded their morals. For different ideological reasons, Ligutti and the other members of the Catholic Rural Life Conference put as much stress on the community and on co-operation as did Tugwell and other leaders in the Resettlement Administration. Whereas economic necessity and social need justified government support for co-operatives in the eyes of Tugwell, Ligutti viewed co-operation not only as a possible economic boon but as a moral compulsion. To him co-operation was almost synonymous with unselfishness. He said: "We consider willingness to

[8] Lord and Johnstone, *A Place on Earth*, pp. 108–110; Duggan, *A Federal Resettlement Project*, pp. 108–112; Edward Skillin, Jr., "Granger Homesteads," *Commonweal*, XXXII (1940), 94–95; C. Edward Wolf, "Granger's Fifth Birthday," *ibid.*, XXXIII (1941), 348; "Soil Defeats Poverty," p. 14.

help, Christian charity, and the golden rule as essentials for individual success or for the community advancement. The above are essentials. The people must regard themselves as the main spokes in the wheel of success or failure."[9] Much of Ligutti's view of the community, and even more the views of some of his colleagues, harked back to the corporate society of the Middle Ages, before the acquisitive rationale of capitalism had captured men's minds. To Ligutti, property and human industry had no moral justification apart from use or need and were sinful if directed toward mere accumulation as an end in itself. Co-operation resulting from individual obedience to a God-given moral law may be very different from co-operation based on a frank acceptance of utilitarian ends and on the use of the leveling power of government, but, in any case, it too is co-operation. In their mutual hatred of capitalism and their mutual desire for co-operative institutions, Tugwell and Ligutti could unite.

Co-operative organization at Granger was less ambitious, but more successful, than at most other projects. The largest co-operative was the one for buying, selling, and manufacturing. It permitted savings in the purchase of seed, feed, and fertilizer and promoted the economical sale of canned goods. In 1939 its members borrowed a modest $800 from the Farm Security Administration for a cannery. A second co-operative owned some heavy farm machinery which was used by all the homesteaders. Perhaps most successful was the credit union, which made small loans available to the homesteaders for the purchase of livestock and other necessities. The financial success of these co-operatives may have resulted from their slow, conservative growth based on acceptance and real need.[10]

A socially integrated community at Granger had to be achieved in the face of obvious divisions and cliques based on kinship, differing nationalities, native languages, and old-world customs. Many of the homesteaders spoke little English, and some of the housewives lived in the basements, decorating their first floor with needlework, photographs, and bric-a-brac in typical European fashion. The social cleavage was slowly broken down by adult classes, attendance at lectures by Iowa State experts, co-operative organization, attendance at the Catholic Church, attendance by the children at the local parish school,

[9] Ligutti and Rawe, *Rural Roads to Security*, p. 153.
[10] Lord and Johnstone, *A Place on Earth*, pp. 110–111.

and community athletics. Most of the community guidance was left to Ligutti and the community manager, although in 1939 the Farm Security Administration contributed a new community center, which gave the homesteaders a meeting place. Perhaps the most important social event of the year at Granger Homesteads was the annual fair in August. Here the homesteaders all co-operated, displaying farm products and craftwork, hearing speeches, and watching athletic events and folk dances performed in old-world costumes.[11]

The educational and handicraft activities at Granger Homesteads were largely under the direction of Ligutti and were centered in the local Catholic school, which was in the nearby village of Granger. Ligutti advocated a new type of homestead school where there could be training in religious motivation for the new way of life, in problems of property, liberty, and democracy, in co-operation, in health, education, and recreation, in scientific farming methods, and in home production. He practically converted his parochial school into just such an experiment. The boys from the homesteads learned arts and crafts in the school shop, while the girls learned to knit, weave, sew, and care for children as a preparation for "Home Life on the Land." According to Ligutti, "women have been so constituted by God that they lose much unless home life is their ideal." When Ligutti left Granger in 1941 to become executive secretary of the National Catholic Rural Life Conference, his successor in the parish, Father John J. Gorman, continued the unique educational program.[12]

One objective of Ligutti, the other local sponsors, and the homesteaders—homeownership—was long unfulfilled. The homesteaders were under Temporary licensing agreements until 1942, when a local homestead association (the last one formed by the Farm Security Administration) assumed title to the project and made purchase contracts with the homesteaders. The delay was caused by constantly worsening economic conditions in the low-grade Iowa coal mines. Year by year the Granger family heads found less and less employment until a wartime boom relieved the employment problem. The tempo-

[11] Duggan, *A Federal Resettlement Project*, pp. 140–145; Lord and Johnstone, *A Place on Earth*, pp. 111–112.
[12] Ligutti and Rawe, *Rural Roads to Security*, p. 114; Ligutti, "The Story of the Granger Homesteads," p. 8.

rary licensing agreements averaged $15.73 a month, with considerable delinquency resulting in seasons of unemployment. The economic conditions at Granger provoked a desire either for a factory at the homesteads or for a co-operative farm, which, very naturally, was advocated by Ligutti. Neither plan was implemented, although land for the farm was appraised.[13]

Granger Homesteads was most extensively publicized through the Catholic press and thus was believed by many people to be the nearest thing to Utopia imaginable. In Des Moines and surrounding areas of Iowa the project evoked the usual curiosity, with many people visiting the project, especially at fair time. The villagers in Granger were more hostile to the project, partly because of jealousy toward the homesteaders, partly because the project did not lead to a large increase in local business, and also because they believed that the government was coddling the homesteaders. The homesteaders themselves were often apprehensive about economic opportunities and about their lack of ownership, but liked their homes, as a whole kept them in good repair, and seemed to appreciate the opportunities given them by the government.[14]

Granger Homesteads cost the government approximately $216,189.87, or about $4,324 per homestead unit. The cost probably very closely approximated the value of the homesteads in 1942, although they were sold to the homestead association for just less than $100,000, which was based on the ability of the homesteaders to pay. Just after transference to the homestead association, Granger Homesteads was turned over to the Federal Public Housing Authority for the collection of payments on the purchase contract. With wartime prosperity the homesteaders made less and less use of their subsistence plots for truck crops, partly because of a lack of time. Instead they increased the field crops and the number of farm animals. The original community plan was protected by deed restrictions. As time passed, the local hostility slowly lessened. In 1956 approximately thirty-five of the original families were still on the project. The co-operatives were inactive with the exception of the credit union.[15] The following evaluation of Granger, made in 1942, is probably still appropriate:

[13] Lord and Johnstone, *A Place on Earth*, pp. 113–116. [14] *Ibid.*, p. 117.
[15] Letter to author from Father John J. Gorman, Nov. 5, 1956.

Granger Homesteads is no Utopia nor will it ever be. In all the idealistic planning of the subsistence-homesteads program there was no thought of making gifts, there was only the thought of providing opportunities. At Granger, these opportunities can be realized only through a program of hard work, education, and self-denial. Eighty percent of the original families at the end of 6 years are still pursuing such a program, in the hope and belief of eventual security for themselves and their descendents. With the program admittedly an experiment, only the objectives were defined. Methods and procedures were to be worked out as necessity arose. At Granger, the methods have been sound and the objectives are gradually being attained. Six years is not a long time in which to effect great changes in patterns of human behavior.[16]

[16] Lord and Johnstone, *A Place on Earth*, p. 118.

⚘ XIV ⚘

The Greenbelt Towns

IN the greenbelt towns the community idea was applied to urban planning and led to the three largest, most ambitious, and most significant communities of the New Deal. The greenbelt towns remain the grandest monuments of Rexford G. Tugwell's work in the Resettlement Administration. In world-wide influence they rank high among New Deal accomplishments; in the field of public works they were hardly excelled, even by the Tennessee Valley Authority, in imagination, in breaking with precedents, and in broad social objectives. They represented, and still do represent, the most daring, original, and ambitious experiments in public housing in the history of the United States. Although only three of approximately 100 New Deal communities, the greenbelt towns absorbed over one-third of the total cost and nearly one-fourth of the total settlers of the whole community program.

The three completed greenbelt cities represented the culmination of the garden city movement in America. They remain the nearest American approximation of Ebenezer Howard's garden city idea and were the direct successors of the housing and planning experiment by garden city exponents at Radburn, New Jersey. They combined the principal ideas of Howard with the new, automobile-inspired planning techniques first attempted at Radburn. The two planners of Radburn, Clarence Stein and Henry Wright, both participated in the Resettlement Administration program. Tugwell, although acknowledging the debt to Howard and the English garden city movement, emphasized the fact that the greenbelt idea also came from a study of contemporary population movements which showed a steady growth in the periphery of cities. He believed that the suburban movement, then a new, unexploited frontier, gave the best chance ever offered for the governmental planning of a favorable working and living environment. Past opportunities for federal planning had been ignored, with urban slums and rural poverty the results. This new area offered a last chance. Tugwell believed that there should be 3,000 greenbelt cities instead of only three.[1]

Most of the arguments for garden cities were used in defending the greenbelt towns. They were officially described as "demonstrations of the combined advantages of country and city life for low-income rural and industrial families."[2] They were to be the means for escaping the sprawling, ugly cities, with their high land costs, speculation and antiquated street patterns. For the farmers in the greenbelt, the new towns were to bring markets, an end to the economic ills of bad distribution, and relief from social and cultural starvation. They were to demonstrate a new type of community planning and a better land use in suburban areas. They were to demonstrate in practice the soundness of the garden city idea and were to provide low-rent housing in healthful surroundings for low-income families. Beyond these long-range objectives, they were to provide immediate work relief for the unemployed in the area of three large cities and were, through the use of building materials, indirectly to stimulate employment throughout the country.[3]

The greenbelt city, as conceived by Tugwell, was to be a complete community of a limited size, encircled by a greenbelt of farms, owned collectively, well planned, close to employment, in a pleasant setting,

[1] Rexford G. Tugwell, "New Frontier: The Story of Resettlement," Chicago *Sunday Times*, April 19, 1936, and "The Meaning of the Greenbelt Towns," *New Republic*, XC (1937), 43.

[2] U.S. Senate, *Resettlement Administration Program*, Document no. 213, 74th Cong., 2d Sess., 1936, p. 7.

[3] Albert Mayer, "Greenbelt Towns: What and Why," *American City*, LI (May, 1936), 59; U.S. Department of Agriculture, Farm Security Administration, "Greenbelt Communities," a pamphlet (Washington, 1938), p. 1; Clarence Stein, *Toward New Towns for America* (Liverpool, 1951), p. 101; Data compiled by W. C. Moore, Aug. 19, 1935, R.G. 96, National Archives.

with an abundance of light, air, and space, with safety assured for the children, with common utilities, with gardens, and with schools and playgrounds. Since the subsistence feature of the other suburban communities was not emphasized in the greenbelt cities and since they were planned as full cities, with eventual populations of up to 10,000, they were more directly related to the urban housing programs than any other communities. Yet they represented a special kind of housing. They were planned as the type of community housing best designed to place land, houses, and people together in a way to strengthen the foundations of the whole economic and social structure of society. The greenbelt towns differed from Public Works Administration and other public housing in being outside cities; in occupying extensive sites; in having farms, gardens, forests, and wildlife; in their distinctive rural accent; in being for agricultural workers as well as for industrial workers; and, most important, in being complete community developments, with streets, public utilities, schools, parks—in fact, completely new towns.[4]

A provision for greenbelt towns was included in the executive order creating the Resettlement Administration. They had long been a topic of interest with both Tugwell and Roosevelt. As soon as the Resettlement Administration was organized, plans for the greenbelt cities were pushed more assiduously than any other aspect of the resettlement program. The Suburban Resettlement Division studied the economic background of 100 cities in the United States, learning the rate of population growth, the numbers employed in industry, wages paid, population trends after 1900, volume of manufacturing, and the diversity of industries and occupations. From these 100 cities, twenty-five were picked for further study. In July, 1935, an ambitious and enthusiastic Tugwell envisioned greenbelt towns for all twenty-five of these cities, but he never received nearly the appropriation desired. As a result these twenty-five cities were visited by industrial engineers, who studied the outskirts for greenbelt sites and tested the attitudes of the local citizens. In September, Roosevelt approved eight greenbelt projects involving a cost of $68,000,000, but the Resettlement Administra-

[4] Tugwell, "Meaning of the Greenbelt Towns," p. 42; Mayer, "Greenbelt Towns: What and Why," p. 59; Will W. Alexander, "Housing Activities of the Resettlement Administration," *Housing Officials' Yearbook, 1937* (Chicago, 1937), p. 20; Memorandum initialed by Franklin D. Roosevelt, n.d., R.G. 96, National Archives.

tion received only $31,000,000 for greenbelt cities, necessitating a reduction in plans to five cities. After plans for a proposed greenbelt city near St. Louis were dropped because of disagreement with the St. Louis Plans Commission, the program was reduced to four communities—on the outskirts of Washington, D.C., Cincinnati, Ohio, Milwaukee, Wisconsin, and New York City. Before construction began, the last was blocked by a court injunction.[5]

After the selection of four urban areas as suitable for greenbelt cities, the actual suburban sites were selected on the basis of a careful study of population trends, topography, land prices, and availability to employment. On this basis the sites were selected for the future Greenbelt at Berwyn, Maryland, about seven miles from Washington, for Greenhills, a site about five miles north of Cincinnati, and for Greendale, a valley three miles southwest of Milwaukee. The ill-fated Greenbrook was to have been near Bound Brook, New Jersey, in the New York metropolitan area. Meanwhile a staff of town planners, architects, and engineering designers had been assembled. Land was quickly optioned at the selected sites and, even as plans were hurriedly made ready, the Construction Division moved into the forests north of Washington and began work on Greenbelt in October, 1935, less than a month after the approval of the greenbelt program by President Roosevelt. "A new chapter in American town planning and community architecture" was under way.[6]

The Suburban Resettlement Division was completely responsible for the planning of the greenbelt cities. Under its head, John S. Lansill, were four relatively autonomous planning teams, one for each city. Since the greenbelt cities were experimental and demonstrational, the vertical form of organization, which, except for a few over-all policies, permitted complete freedom to each team of planners, was adopted in order to allow the maximum possibility for new ideas and new approaches. Each greenbelt city became a distinct experiment in itself. Each planning team was headed by a group of planning principals, each of equal rank. These included one or more town planners, one or more engineers, one or more architects, and a regional co-ordinator,

[5] "Greenbelt Towns," *Architectural Record*, LXXX (1936), 216; Rexford G. Tugwell to Harry Hopkins, July 18, 1935, R.G. 96, National Archives.

[6] "Greenbelt Towns," *Architectural Record*, LXXX, 215–217; Resettlement Administration, *Interim Report*, p. 17.

who maintained liaison with local agencies in the project area and between the planners and Lansill. On a large tract of land, which would permit unified ownership, the planners and architects were directed to create a community for low-income families, designed to encourage the kind of family and community life not previously enjoyed by these families. They were not to plan for a coercive, theoretical, or untested type of discipline. They were to plan for corporate ownership, for perpetual leasing, and for a municipal government suited to the local area. They were to develop a land-use plan for the whole tract, were to devise a system of rural economy co-ordinated with the land-use plan for the rural belt, and were to integrate the plans of the rural and urban areas. Beyond this they were on their own.[7]

The Suburban Resettlement Division was finally lodged in the extravagant old Walsh mansion which had formerly belonged to a multimillionaire, the late Senator Edward B. McLean. The drafting rooms, in which the homes of the poor were to be designed, surrounded a monumental marble staircase said to simulate the rococo central hall of the Atlantic liner on which the Senator had made his first trip abroad. Halfway up the stairs the planners collided with a "monstrous sculptural group of naked figures, so bulky and heavy that the government could not afford to resettle it." Here the young architects and planners at first produced designs that seemed destined for Westchester villas, but, ultimately, created "a great and unified beauty out of essential requirements and simple designs."[8] Critics pointed to the early confusion in the Walsh mansion, the constant shifting of furniture, the scarcity of drawing paper, the expensive equipment, and the lack of clear plans and of co-ordination between planning teams.[9]

Although construction began on the greenbelt cities in October, 1935, it was not until the spring of 1936 that extensive progress was made. The early construction, especially at Greenbelt, was delayed because of a lack of co-ordination between the planning staff and the construction crews. As the first work began at Greenbelt, the Construction Division did not know exactly what type of project was planned. Final plans were also delayed by the failure of the concrete-slab construction attempted at Hightstown and originally considered for Green-

[7] Stein, *Toward New Towns*, pp. 102–103.   [8] *Ibid.*, p. 102.
[9] New York *Sun*, July 11, 1936.

belt. But in 1936 and 1937 the progress was rapid, with an average monthly employment of over 7,000 on the three projects. At Greenbelt the construction program absorbed all the unemployed relief labor in Washington and in the adjacent Maryland counties. The first units were occupied at Greenbelt in September, 1937, at Greenhills in May, 1938, and at Greendale in June, 1938. When completed the three projects contained 2,267 family units and complete community facilities, all costing over $36,000,000.[10]

One project, Greenbrook, never proceeded beyond the planning and land-option stage because of the successful opposition of local citizens, which culminated in the court injunction that was sustained by the District of Columbia Court of Appeals in May, 1936. Greenbrook had been planned by Henry Wright, coplanner of Radburn, and was the only one of the four greenbelt cities that would probably have had local industries, making it a complete garden city such as Letchworth rather than an economically dependent satellite. The Greenbrook decision practically assured that the greenbelt program would not be expanded beyond the three cities already under construction and, at the same time, placed each of them in danger of similar local injunctions.

Greenbelt, Maryland, was the first of the greenbelt cities to be completed, was slightly the largest of the cities, and, perhaps because of its proximity to Washington, received much the larger share of publicity. For $1,124,480 the Resettlement Administration purchased 12,259 acres of submarginal land located next to the Department of Agriculture's National Research Center near College Park, Maryland. Of this large acreage, 8,659 acres were placed under the jurisdiction of the Research Center, which formed part of the greenbelt, and 3,600 acres were retained for Greenbelt proper. Of this, 217 acres were used for the town, 500 acres were reserved for future expansion, 250 acres were used for parks, 107 acres were reserved for allotment gardens, 20 acres were used for a county high school, and the rest remained in waste and woodland, both available for recreation. Greenbelt was planned as a dormitory town for Washington, which was

[10] Department of Agriculture, Resettlement Administration, *Report of the Administrator of the Resettlement Administration, 1937* (The second annual report of the Resettlement Administration; Washington, 1937), p. 17. Joseph L. Dailey to John Sansill, Oct. 19, 1935, R.G. 96, National Archives; Farm Security Administration, Report on the Greenbelt Cities, n.d., *ibid.*

Greenbelt Towns

experiencing a rapid growth and a severe housing shortage. Unlike the English garden cities, Greenbelt was not planned for any industry of its own, although it was hoped that several employees of the Research Center could live at Greenbelt. Finally, unlike the other greenbelt cities and again contrary to garden city principles, Greenbelt did not contain any farms in its greenbelt, primarily because the land was not suitable for farming. However, the Research Center was a contiguous farming area.[11]

The physical design of Greenbelt became famous. The completed plan envisioned a future expansion to approximately 3,000 family units, although the Resettlement Administration planned to construct only 1,000 units. The design combined the ideas of the garden city exponents with the Radburn plan. As a garden city it was to be limited in size by the greenbelt, and was to be under public ownership. As its older sister, Radburn, it was to have extra-large blocks, internal parks, the rigid separation of pedestrians and automobiles, and pedestrian underpasses. The town of Greenbelt was constructed on a crescent-shaped plateau which formed a half-moon around the central community shopping center and recreational area. The dwelling units were largely located in five superblocks of from fifteen to twenty acres each. As at Radburn the houses or apartments faced two ways, toward a central park and pedestrian walkways on one side and toward the service entrances or cul-de-sacs on the other. Skirting the large blocks were the streets, which, because of the design, amounted to only six miles. The parks in the center of each block were connected to each other by pedestrian underpasses costing about $5,000 each. An underpass also connected the housing areas with the community center. A man-made lake of twenty-five acres near the community center enhanced the beauty of the site.[12] (See Figure 2.)

Because of limited funds, the Resettlement Administration completed only 885 dwelling units at Greenbelt. Of these, only five were detached, single-family homes, whereas 574 were in multiple-dwelling

---

[11] Cedric Larson, "Greenbelt, Maryland: A Federally Planned Community," reprinted from the *National Municipal Review*, XXVII (1938), by the Farm Security Administration, pp. 2–3.

[12] Stein, *Toward New Towns*, p. 113; Larson, "Greenbelt, Maryland," p. 4; "Greenbelt Towns," *Architectural Record*, LXXX, 220–221; M. E. Gilford, "Introducing: 'Greenbelt, Maryland,'" *Christian Science Monitor Magazine*, Aug. 11, 1937, p. 5.

row houses and 306 in larger apartment buildings. Despite the multiple dwellings the housing density was only seven families per acre. The dwellings were partly of brick veneer with pitched roofs and partly of cinder blocks with flat roofs. The city contained its own sewage system and disposal plant, a water storage tank and mains, and a central electrical distribution system. Water and electricity were purchased in bulk from Washington and a private company, respectively. The housing units varied in size from tiny one-bedroom apartments to seven-room dwellings. They were unfurnished, except for the range and refrigerator, but, as in each of the three cities, the Resettlement Administration had given simplified furniture designs to private manufacturers and would, if the tenant desired, furnish his unit at a very low price. The units were heated by centrally located hot-water furnaces. All utilities were planned for a city of 3,000 families.[13]

The community center was planned as the heart of Greenbelt. It contained the community building, which was leased during the day to the county for an elementary school, the fire engine, the gas station, an inn and restaurant, the movie theater, and a mercantile center, which included a food and general merchandise store, a drugstore, a barbershop, a beauty shop, and a dry-cleaning and valet shop. The community center also had a playground, an outdoor swimming pool, and an athletic field. Other playgrounds, play boxes, and open areas were interspersed throughout the town, and the lake and greenbelt formed perfect natural playgrounds. The shopping center followed Ebenezer Howard's idea of a restricted market. Only one shop was allowed for each business or service, and all were under community control. A consolidated county high school was constructed by Prince George County near the town and on the very edge of the greenbelt. The University of Maryland was only four miles from the community.[14]

In September, 1935, the Resettlement Administration optioned 5,930 acres of farm land about eleven miles north of downtown Cincinnati.

[13] Larson, "Greenbelt, Maryland," pp. 4–5; "Greenbelt Towns," *Architectural Record*, LXXX, 220–222; "Farm Security Administration Housing Projects," *Architectural Forum*, LXVIII (1938), 416–417.

[14] Stein, *Toward New Towns*, pp. 132, 137; "Greenbelt Towns," *Architectural Record*, LXXX, 220–222; "Greenbelt Takes Over: Consumers Now Own Co-op Stores Launched with Filene Money," *Business Week*, Feb. 3, 1940, p. 35.

Figure 2. Greenbelt, Maryland. 1, water tower; 2, disposal plant and incinerator; 3, picnic center and lake; 4, community center; 5, retail stores; 6, areas planned for rural homesteads; 7, areas reserved for allotment gardens. From *Architectural Record*, LXXX (Sept., 1936), 219.

Greenbelt Towns 313

This was the site for Greenhills, which was, according to original plans, to be as large as Greenbelt. The Cincinnati area was picked for a greenbelt city because of the density of industry, the proportionately large number of people engaged in industry, and the local housing shortage. The particular site was selected because it was only thirty minutes from 53,800 jobs and because of its beauty, its distance from existing subdivisions, its transportation facilities, and its excellent farm land. Only about 1,300 acres of the roughest terrain were utilized in the central town, leaving over 4,000 acres in farm or woodland. Unlike Greenbelt, the site for Greenhills contained about thirty large farms and an equal number of subsistence farms. These farms already had homes and outbuildings and were only repaired by the Resettlement Administration. The farms were leased to tenants under five-year leases, with the rent determined by production. Some eroded areas were reforested. Soil analyses were made by the Ohio State University, and the Resettlement Administration helped the farmers work out crop plans. It was hoped that the farms could supply Greenhills with farm products, which were to be marketed through a farmers' market in the town. In actuality the farmers sold most of their products in Cincinnati.[15]

The plot design at Greenhills varied considerably from that at Greenbelt, although many of the Radburn features remained. Greenhills was scenically placed in a wild area sharply cut by ravines. Unlike Greenbelt, the site was crossed by a main highway. The roads and topography led to several narrow curving building areas separated from each other by the ravines or the roads. Thus, although there were several superblocks with cul-de-sacs and central park areas, much of the town consisted of single, fingerlike cul-de-sacs or small circular drives, both surrounded by the natural scenery. The community center, roughly in the center of the town and on the main highway, was not as easily accessible by foot to all the homes as was the one at Greenbelt, but, unlike that at Greenbelt, was designed for automobile travel. Thus, Greenhills, adapted to different terrain, was not planned with all the unique pedestrian facilities of Greenbelt, such as a complete underpass system. On the other hand, Greenhills was situated in a much more beautiful natural setting, with the homes always fronting

[15] Cincinnati *Enquirer*, Oct. 13, 1936; Washington *Star*, Nov. 20, 1938; "Greenbelt Towns," *Architectural Record*, LXXX, 224–226.

both on streets and on central parks or on a back-yard wilderness.[16] (See Figure 3.)

As completed, the town of Greenhills contained only 676 of a contemplated 1,000 family units. These were divided into 24 detached, three- or four-bedroom, single-family dwellings, 152 one- and two-bedroom apartments, and 500 two-, three-, or four-bedroom units in row or group houses. The housing units were of stucco over terra-cotta blocks, with slate roofs and insulation. They were heated by hot-water radiators connected with boiler-type oil furnaces. Many of the homes had attics, basements, and attached garages. Water was secured from Cincinnati, and sewage was disposed of in a regional trunk line. The Greenhills community center included the administration building, the combined community center, high school, and elementary school building, a restricted retail center as at Greenbelt, an arcade planned as a farmers' market, and a swimming pool. Connected with it was a park and, at a short distance, athletic fields. An area near the town was reserved for allotment gardens, and the wooded banks of a creek which bisected the town provided a perfect area for hiking.[17]

The third greenbelt city, which contained 3,510 acres just to the west of Milwaukee, was radically different in design from the other two greenbelt towns. It was placed near Milwaukee because of the housing shortage and the large percentage of people employed in industry. Planned for only 750 family units, Greendale was less like Radburn than its two sisters. Alone among the three cities, it had a small, ten-acre area reserved for light industry, although none was established by the Resettlement Administration. Approximately 1,830 acres were in farm land, with 13 full-time dairy farms of from 75 to 240 acres and 53 small farms or subsistence units. A farm adviser was provided by the Farm Security Administration, which remodeled or repaired many of the farm buildings.[18]

Greendale was planned as a conventional country village, with a

[16] "Site Plans of 'Greenbelt' Towns," *American City*, LI (Aug., 1936), 58–59; "Greenbelt Towns," *Architectural Record*, LXXX, 224–226.

[17] "Farm Security Administration Housing Projects," *Architectural Forum*, LXVIII, 418–419, 424; "Greenbelt Towns," *Architectural Record*, LXXX, 224–226.

[18] Farm Security Administration, "Greendale: Final Report of Project Costs to June 30, 1938," in R.G. 96, National Archives; Sherwood L. Reeder, "A Report on the First Two Years of the Greendale Community," A Project Report of the Bureau of Agricultural Economics, April 30, 1940, R.G. 83, National Archives.

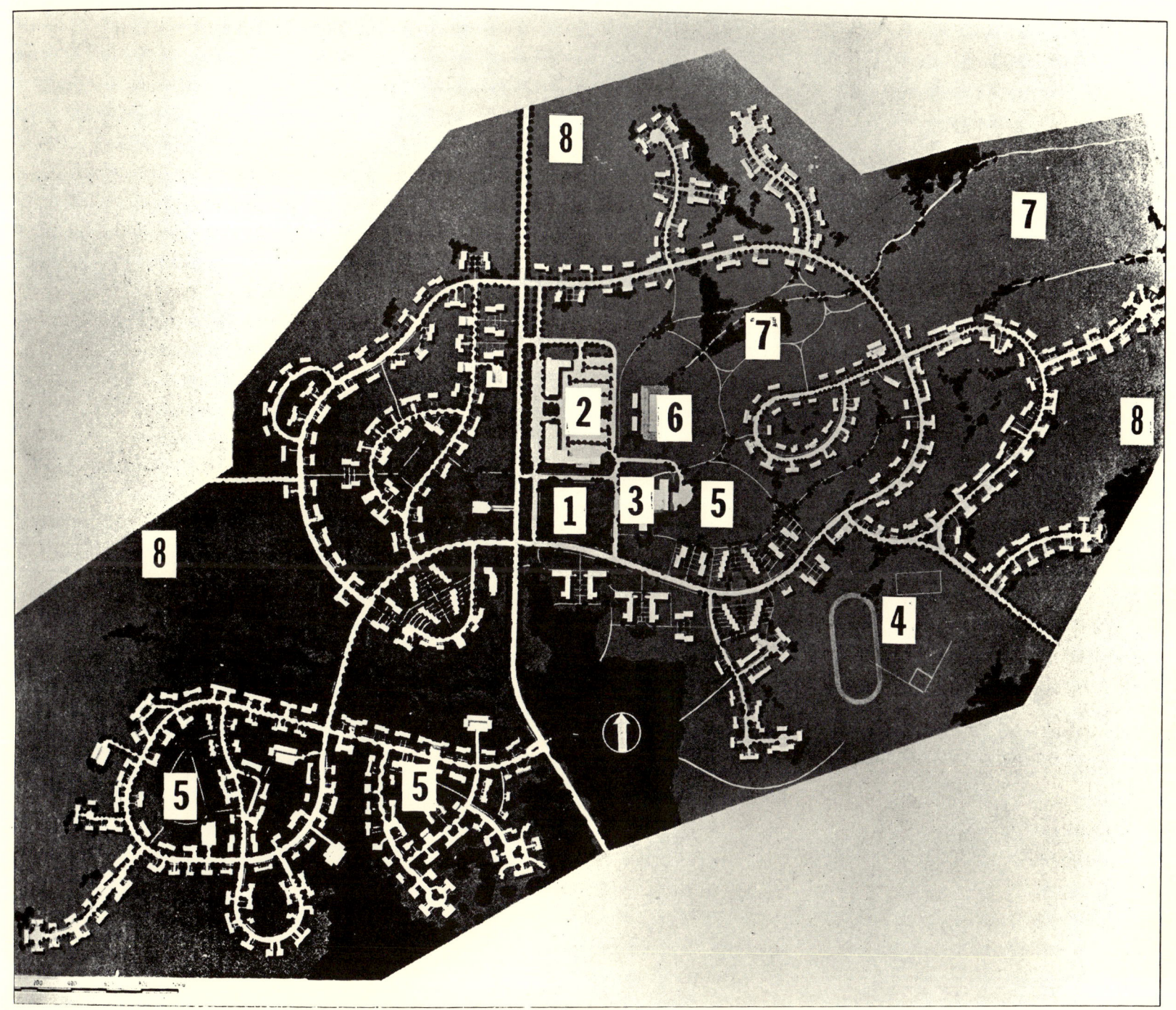

Figure 3. Greenhills, Ohio. 1, town common; 2, commercial center; 3, community building; 4, athletic field; 5, interior park; 6, swimming pool; 7, sites for future residential development; 8, rural greenbelt. From *Architectural Record*, LXXX (Sept., 1936), 223.

few cul-de-sacs and several normal city blocks. It contained only individual or small-group housing, being the largest housing project of this nature in the northern United States. The community and business section resembled the business area of an average village. Each home faced either a main street or a service entrance; each contained a back yard and a garden area. The large village park was separated from the homes, and the nearby farms contributed to the rural atmosphere. Although in every way more conventional than its sister cities, Greendale was usually adjudged more desirable by most tenants because of the predominance of individual houses. Located in a green valley, protected from winter storms by wooded hillsides, and close to the Milwaukee park system, Greendale was also a very pretty town.[19] (See Figure 4.)

Greendale, when completed, contained only 572 dwelling units in the city proper. Of these, 274 were two- and three-bedroom, detached, family dwellings, 90 were one-, two, and four-bedroom duplexes, whereas only 208 were in multiple-family units. All houses were of cinder blocks, with clay tile roofs, insulation, maple floors, and individual hot-air furnaces. Unlike those in the other two cities, the tenants at Greendale were individually responsible for their utilities. Most of the homes had garages and screened porches. The electric and telephone wires were underground, with enough utilities laid for 5,000 people. Each family that desired more garden space than was provided in the back yards could have an extra allotment near the village.[20]

Greendale's community center included an administration building, a combination community and elementary school building, a fire and police station, a store, a movie theater, a tavern, a post office, and a service station. Its streets were bordered by sidewalks, again in the conventional manner, and the community area was fully landscaped. Alone among greenbelt cities, Greendale's community center was constructed by contract rather than by relief labor.[21]

---

[19] Clarence S. Stein, "Greendale and the Future," *American City*, LXIII (June, 1948), 106–107; "Site Plans," *American City*, LI, 56; "Greenbelt Towns," *Architectural Record*, LXXX, 227–230.

[20] Milwaukee *Journal*, Sept. 17, 1936; "Farm Security Administration Housing," *Architectural Forum*, LXVIII, 420–421; "Greendale: Final Report of Project Costs," R.G. 96, National Archives.

[21] "Greendale, Final Report of Project Costs," R.G. 96, National Archives.

The first tenant moved into Greenbelt on September 30, 1937. By December, 1938, approximately 2,000 of the more than 2,200 units in all three cities were occupied. By the time of the first occupancy, the Resettlement Administration had been besieged with over 12,000 applications for Greenbelt alone, necessitating a careful process of selection. The express purpose of the greenbelt towns, to serve low-income workers, led to a wage ceiling of $2,200 for each family, and the rent scales necessitated a minimum income of about $1,200. Preference was given to young married families with children, who were living in poor housing but who could, nevertheless, afford the rent to be charged at the greenbelt cities. The rent scale at Greenbelt and Greenhills, where utilities were included, ranged from about $18.00 to $42.00, depending on the size of the unit. At Greendale, where the individual was responsible for utilities, the rent varied from $19.00 to $32.50. The first 885 families at Greenbelt were composed primarily of wage earners and government workers. Most had high school educations; the religious composition followed the national average. At Milwaukee and Cincinnati the tenants were usually industrial workers. In all cases they were predominantly young people, with the adults at Greenbelt averaging only thirty-one years of age. In order to maintain high standards, the Resettlement Administration enforced strict rules in the greenbelt cities. At Greenbelt no dogs were permitted, and no clothes were allowed to remain on the lines after four in the afternoon. Contrary to many of the rural communities, a strict rent discipline was maintained, with payments due in advance and eviction an ever-present reality. For the first four years the amount of accumulated delinquency totaled only 0.3 per cent.[22]

The original occupants at the three greenbelt cities were an enthusiastic group, with the highest of morale. This fact was reflected in the amazing number of community activities. One visitor to Greenbelt concluded that the citizens were "overstimulated" socially. There were so many activities, so many things planned, that the citizens' association provided for a "stay-at-home week" for the last week of the year.

[22] Will W. Alexander, "A Review of the Farm Security Administration's Housing Activities," *Housing Yearbook, 1939* (Chicago: National Association of Housing Officials, 1939), p. 139; Larson, "Greenbelt, Maryland," p. 6; Stein, *Toward New Towns*, p. 110; Philip S. Brown, "What Has Happened at Greenbelt?" *New Republic*, CV (1941), 184; a report on the greenbelt communities, n.d., R.G. 96, National Archives.

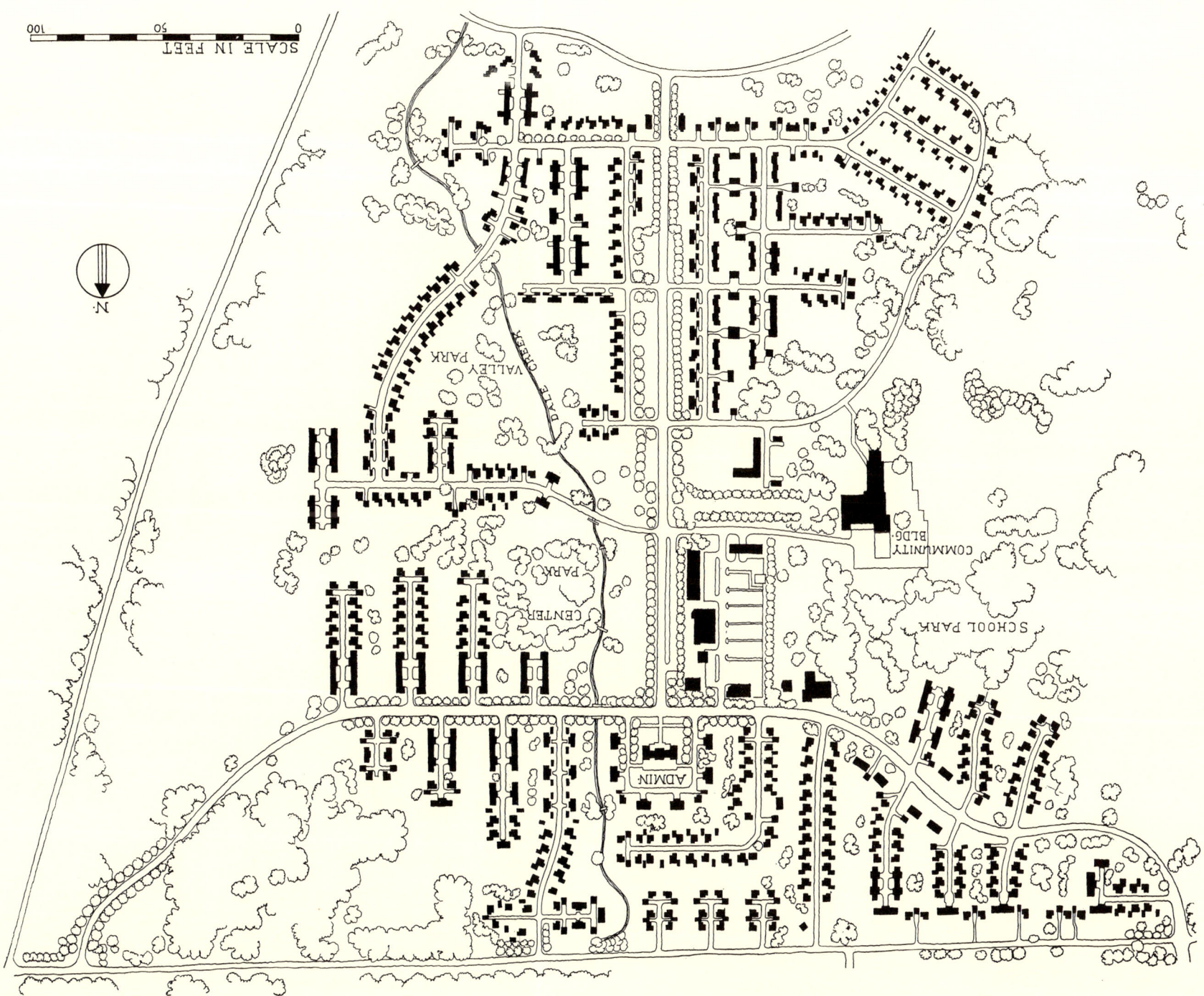

Figure 4. Greendale, Wisconsin. From *Architectural Forum*, LXVIII (May, 1938), 420.

During this week there was to be a moratorium on all club and civic activities. At Greenbelt there was the Greenbelt Citizens' Association (the most important civic organization), a Junior Citizens' Association, a hobby club, boy scouts, girl scouts, cub scouts, a garden club, a bridge club, an American Legion chapter, a dance band, an athletic organization, a preschool mothers' club, a school-age mothers' club, a radio club, a glider club, a widows' club, a swimming club, a camera club, a better buyer's club, the Greenbelt Players, a choral group, and a journalistic club.[23] Greendale had its citizens' group, a marionette class, a drama club, a tap-dancing class, an organized sports league, scout activities, and a newspaper. Perhaps fortunately for the overworked citizens, this social activity soon lessened, and the greenbelt cities settled down to a very normal small-town existence, with much apathy, many cliques, and a continually large turnover in tenants.[24]

Although the greenbelt cities were satellites, economically dependent upon their parent cities, they did contain their own retail shopping centers. These permitted the usual stress upon co-operation. Edward Filene, a merchant of Boston, gave $1,000,000 to further the co-operative movement as the greenbelt cities were being constructed. The Consumer Distribution Corporation, founded with this Filene grant, leased the commercial centers in the three greenbelt cities and had the stores ready for operation when the residents arrived. The externally financed co-operative service was to operate the stores only until the citizens could establish their own consumers' co-operative. Co-operation became a rage at Greenbelt, with the children operating a co-operative commissary in the school. But not until 1940 was a local co-operative organized and ready to take over the retail services, which were returning a regular profit. The consumers' co-operative, as organized, included 456 of the 885 families. At Greenhills and Greendale similar consumer groups took over the retail stores at an even earlier date. The co-operatives paid limited dividends to each stockholder, with one share of stock costing $10.00 at Greenhills and $15.00 at Greendale. Other savings, if any, were passed on to the consumers. Also organized co-operatively were the credit unions and the

[23] Hugh A. Bone, "Greenbelt Faces 1939," *American City*, LIV (Feb., 1939), 59–61; Larson, "Greenbelt, Maryland," p. 7; O. Kline Fulmer, *Greenbelt* (Washington: American Council on Public Affairs, n.d.), pp. 26–36; George A. Warner, *Greenbelt: The Cooperative Community* (New York, 1954), pp. 84–85.

[24] Brown, "What Has Happened at Greenbelt?" p. 184.

group medical services. A typical medical plan, the one at Greendale, cost one dollar a month per person, or three dollars for a family.[25]

The educational program in the greenbelt cities was for adults as well as for children. The early enthusiasm resulted in a flurry of adult classes. Under the direction of an educational committee of the Greenbelt Citizens' Association, adults took courses in art, home economics, political science, and accounting, many under instructors from the nearby University of Maryland. In all three cities the elementary schools were held in the community buildings. At Greenbelt the school was used as an experiment in progressive education, with the unit plan being used. This did not receive support from all the parents, since some of them desired a more traditional system for their children. For many years the religious services were also held in the community buildings.[26]

According to the earliest plans, the greenbelt cities were to be complete, incorporated towns with their own municipal governments. In April, 1937, months before completion, Greenbelt received a charter from the Maryland legislature, which officially established it as the first Maryland town with a city-manager type of government. Greenhills and Greendale were similarly incorporated in 1938, each with the city-manager system. In each town the city manager was appointed by a democratically elected city council. Since the Farm Security Administration had its own community manager in each town, the town councils, for many years, also appointed him town manager. The existence of three or four governmental units (state, county, city, and federal) inevitably led to problems. The Farm Security Administration made payments in lieu of taxes not only to the county and state, but also to the city government for specific services. Since the city government could not tax the landowner—the federal government—most of the money for public utilities, street repairs, maintenance, and police and fire protection had to be provided by the

---

[25] Warner, *Greenbelt: The Cooperative Community*, pp. 72–74, 133–141; Ralph Adams Cram, "What Is a Free Man?" *Catholic Rural Life Objectives*, III (1937), 38; Memorandum for Mordecai Ezekiel, Sept. 9, 1937, R.G. 16, National Archives; "Greenbelt Goes Completely Cooperative," *Reader's Digest*, XXX (Oct., 1938), 36; "Greenbelt Takes Over," p. 35; Fulmer, *Greenbelt*, pp. 27–31; Washington *Star*, Nov. 20, 1938; Reeder, "A Report on . . . Greendale," R.G. 83, National Archives.

[26] Bone, "Greenbelt Faces 1939," pp. 60–61; Stein, *Toward New Towns*, p. 135.

federal government. Thus the city council and town manager could only make suggestions as to needed expenditures, receiving the needed funds at the discretion of the Farm Security Administration. This led to some indications of irresponsibility on the part of the local governments.[27] Fortunately, many of the problems in local administration and government had been anticipated by John O. Walker, long-time mayor of Radburn, who had been brought to the Management Division of the Resettlement Administration on the suggestion of M. L. Wilson, and by Clarence Stein, who made a study of anticipated operation and maintenance costs in the three greenbelt cities.

The greenbelt communities were constantly in the public eye from the beginning of construction until long after full occupancy. Since they were close to large urban areas, over 1,200,000 people visited them between July 1, 1936, and June 30, 1937. Every innovation, every petty detail was scrutinized. One critic stated that, whether or not a person felt the government had any business building greenbelt cities, "you can't help admit they're interesting."[28] But, interesting or no, local opinion prevented Greenbrook's completion, and a suit against Greendale was attempted unsuccessfully by the Milwaukee building and loan associations. In Cincinnati the Real Estate Board, the building and loan associations, and the Chamber of Commerce all opposed Greenhills. Real estate owners often feared lowered land values, and local governments, such as Bound Brook, New Jersey, feared a loss in tax revenue. The greenbelt cities—like all of Tugwell's ventures—were treated unfairly in a majority of newspapers, with the New York *American* describing Greendale as "the first Communist town in America."[29]

As in many of the subsistence homesteads, much of the greenbelt criticism was directed at minor details. Many of the new concepts in planning, partly because of their newness, were unappreciated or disliked. The row houses and flat roofs at Greenbelt were described as ugly. The community ownership was described as either socialism or communism. Tenants often disliked the stiff discipline and desired to

[27] Stein, *Toward New Towns*, pp. 148, 155.
[28] Resettlement Administration, *Report of the Administrator of the Resettlement Administration, 1937*, p. 17; New Brunswick *Daily Home News*, May 11, 1936.
[29] New York *American*, Oct. 29, 1936; Warren Bishop, "A Yardstick for Housing," *Nation's Business*, XXIV (April, 1936), 69; Milwaukee *Journal*, Sept. 17, 1936.

own their own homes as soon as possible. Many viewed the rigid ceiling on income as an attempt to stifle initiative by rewarding poverty. The relative isolation of Greenbelt led to constant transportation difficulties. For one year the Farm Security Administration subsidized the Washington city transportation system in order to have regular buses. After this was declared illegal by the Attorney General, the people at Greenbelt had to form car pools or make several bus changes. Some citizens disliked the monopoly over consumer outlets enjoyed by the local co-operatives. Yet most inhabitants were proud of their homes and would suggest no basic changes. As for the children, they were in a heaven as compared with most low-cost city housing areas.

The most valid criticism of the greenbelt cities was directed at their costs. Tugwell, when first beginning the greenbelt towns, had thoroughly condemned private enterprise for not entering the field of low-cost, prefabricated housing. Yet the average unit cost at Greenbelt was $15,395, at Greenhills $16,093, and at Greendale $16,623. This was not low-cost housing. At the price rented it was highly subsidized housing. The net income from rent at Greenbelt in 1941 was only $30,744; this meant that, not regarding interest, it would take over 300 years for Greenbelt to pay for itself. In defense of the high costs the Farm Security Administration had some very logical arguments. The use of unskilled relief labor, it was argued, added over a third of the cost. Beyond this, the unused greenbelt could not be charged to the homes, since it had certainly retained its original value. Moreover, the public and community facilities, usually furnished by local governments, had been added to the costs. Finally, the greenbelt cities had been constructed to care for over three times the original population, meaning that any future expansion would cost only a fraction as much per unit, an argument proved at Greenbelt by the addition of wartime housing. But, on the other hand, the greenbelt towns indicated that no private corporation could build complete towns, with all their facilities and an expensive greenbelt, and then be able to rent them to low-income families.[30]

Nevertheless, the greenbelt cities had many enthusiastic admirers. When visiting Greenbelt in December, 1936, President Roosevelt pro-

---

[30] George Morris, "$16,000 Home for $2,000 Incomes: Typical Government Experiments Is Greenbelt," *Nation's Business*, XXVI (Jan., 1938), 21–22; Tugwell, "Meaning of the Greenbelt Towns," p. 42.

claimed: "This is a real achievement and I wish everyone in the country could see it."[31] In England, Sir Raymond Unwin, the coplanner of Letchworth, enthusiastically lectured on the greenbelt cities to those familiar with garden cities. The greenbelt towns influenced housing and town planning around the world, being second only to the Tennessee Valley Authority in interest to foreign guests. The Department of State received requests for information on the towns from several foreign governments.[32] To town planners the towns had their greatest significance. Said Henry Churchill, one of the architects at Greenbelt, of the three towns: "The prevailing philosophy of self-liquidation, of constipated conservatism, must not be allowed to interfere with what is, by any philosophy, next to the T.V.A., the most significant of the New Deal's attempt to be a New Deal."[33] Another housing and planning expert, Walter H. Blucher, though critical of some aspects of greenbelt planning, conceded: "Greenbelt, Greenhills, and Greendale provide the first American demonstration of how adequate communities can be built."[34] A colleague, Tracy B. Augur, believed that the greenbelt cities marked "the birth of an urban nation," with a new dependency on community and group action. He concluded:

They mark the beginning of a new urban era in the United States, an era in which the emphasis will no longer be on more and bigger cities, but on better ones. They mark the beginning of an era in which the establishment and expansion of cities will become recognized as the people's business, to insure, through the process of democratic government, an urban environment worthy of the American ideal of life.[35]

Greenbelt was the only one of the three towns to be enlarged while under government ownership, though they all had facilities for at least doubling their population. Even as the Resettlement Administra-

[31] Mount Rainier, Maryland, *Prince Georgian*, Dec. 25, 1936.

[32] Henry Wallace to Sir Raymond Unwin, May 28, 1937, R.G. 16, National Archives; a series of letters from the Secretary of State to the Secretary of Agriculture, 1938, R.G. 96, National Archives.

[33] Henry Churchill, "America's Town Planning Begins," *New Republic*, LXXXVII (1936), 97.

[34] Tracy B. Augur and Walter H. Blucher, "The Significance of the Greenbelt Towns," *Housing Yearbook, 1938* (Chicago: National Association of Housing Officials, 1938), p. 224.

[35] *Ibid.*, pp. 218, 221.

tion and the Farm Security Administration completed the construction of Greenbelt, they leased some acreage to a private corporation which completed ten inexpensive prefabricated houses under a limited-dividend arrangement. These houses shared the community facilities and utilities. In July, 1940, the Farm Security Administration announced that private housing could be erected at the greenbelt sites by any company that would complete as many as 200 homes, that would accept a ninety-nine-year lease on the land, and that would permit the Farm Security Administration to pass upon house plans. No company accepted these terms, although a co-operative group was interested at Greenbelt. Just before the entrance of the United States into World War II, the Federal Works Agency, under the supervision of the Farm Security Administration, added 1,000 defense units at Greenbelt under the provisions of the Lanham Housing Act. These homes were constructed on 217 acres of reserve land, utilized existing community facilities, and were in harmony with, even if somewhat inferior to, the older units. In proof of the contention that all later additions would profit from the original expenditures for community facilities, these homes cost less than $3,950 each.[36] This defense housing brought in a new type of tenant, for the defense workers could not be carefully selected, were older on the average, and had more children. Older residents at Greenbelt, perhaps naturally, believed that the defense housing ruined their city. Both the defense needs and the wartime inflation made meaningless the original income limitations on Greenbelt residents.

With the virtual completion of the greenbelt cities in June, 1938, the Suburban Resettlement Division was abolished in the Farm Security Administration. In 1942 the three greenbelt cities were transferred to the Federal Public Housing Authority, since they were strictly nonagricultural housing developments. Until 1947 they were retained by the Federal Public Housing Authority without any attempts at liquidation, since they represented renting property and, with some exceptions, could not be sold separately to individuals. In 1947 Congress

[36] Will W. Alexander, "Housing Activities of the Farm Security Administration," *Housing Yearbook, 1938*, p. 38; U.S. Department of Labor, Bureau of Labor Statistics, "Private Housing in Greenbelt Towns," *Monthly Labor Review*, LI (1940), 643; C. Benham Baldwin, "Farm Security Administration's Sixth Year in Rural Housing," *Housing Yearbook, 1941* (Chicago, National Association of Housing Officials, 1941), p. 251.

Greenbelt Towns

authorized the Public Housing Administration, which had replaced the Federal Public Housing Authority, to spend $39,500 for land surveys and other steps looking toward the sale of the greenbelt cities. Another $40,000 was authorized in 1948. These grants were accompanied by an authorization for the Public Housing Administration to insure mortgages on the projects, with a maximum interest of 4 per cent and a maturity date of not over twenty-five years. With the completion of the appraisals, fourteen acres at Greenbelt were sold to five churches in 1948. The Public Housing Administration found that there were "numerous unusual problems" involved in disposing of whole cities, particularly since they had authority only for selling to the highest bidder. In addition, the tenants believed that they should have a special opportunity collectively to purchase their homes. Beyond this there was the desire among garden city advocates to retain community ownership of the town and the encircling greenbelt in order to preserve the planning objectives of the Resettlement Administration.[37]

In 1949 Representative Mike Monroney of Oklahoma introduced into the House of Representatives a bill which was intended to permit the Public Housing Administration to sell the greenbelt cities by negotiated sale, at an appraised value, to nonprofit co-operatives, corporations, or other organizations, including veterans' groups. In the House this bill, which was described as a "fine way for the Government to get out of the real-estate business," was amended to give first choice only to organized veterans' groups, provided the present tenants were accepted on the same terms as the veterans. The conditions in the bill required a down payment of 10 per cent and the rest at 4 per cent interest over twenty-five years. The bill passed the House by voice vote. In the Senate, Senator Paul Douglas of Illinois, who wished to preserve the publicly owned greenbelt areas around the three cities, added an amendment to the House bill which permitted the Public Housing Administration to transfer public facilities to appropriate nonfederal governmental agencies. It passed the Senate as amended and became Public Law 65.[38]

[37] Warren Farmer to M. Kinzer, June 16, 1938, R.G. 96, National Archives; U.S. Housing and Home Finance Agency, *Second Annual Report for Calendar Year 1948* (Washington, 1949), pt. IV, p. 321, and *Third Annual Report for Calendar Year 1949* (Washington, 1950), pt. IV, pp. 346–347.

[38] *C.R.*, 81st Cong., 1st Sess., 1949, pp. 932, 4011, 4471, 4493, 5291, 5833–5834.

With these new instructions from Congress, the urban section of Greenhills was sold on December 6, 1949, to a Greenhills Home Owners Corporation, a nonprofit co-operative group composed of veterans and tenants. The sale price was $3,511,300, including not only the 680 dwellings but also 600 acres of vacant land. Earlier the electric system had been sold for $98,055, and 1,125 acres of land had been sold to the Department of the Army for $213,665. In 1950 all sales negotiations were halted because of the Korean War. When negotiations resumed in 1952 at Greenhills, 457 acres were sold to the Cincinnati Park Service for $71,150, and the rest of the greenbelt, 3,378 acres, was sold to the Cincinnati Development Corporation for $1,200,000. The total sale price for Greenhills was $5,094,170; it cost $11,860,628.[39]

No organized veterans' group qualified for the purchase of Greendale, so it was subdivided (more easily done because of the large number of individual houses) and offered for sale to the tenants in 1951, with offers being received on 97 per cent of the homes. The village was sold to the tenants for $4,666,825, and the greenbelt was purchased by the Milwaukee Community Development Corporation for $825,000, or a total price of $5,491,825. Greendale cost $10,638,465.[40]

Negotiations for the sale of Greenbelt to a veterans' group began in 1950. On December 30, 1952, this group purchased 1,580 dwellings (including the defense housing) for $6,285,450 and 708 acres suitable for residences for $670,219. The remaining 307 units (the apartment buildings) were sold by competitive bids in 1953 for $914,342 to six different purchasers. In addition to these major sales, the fourteen acres for churches sold for $14,800, the electric system for $67,600, and 1,362 acres of the greenbelt was transferred to the Department of the Interior without reimbursement. Three parcels of land totaling 818 acres were sold for $576,912, and, in 1954, the shopping center was sold for $444,444 in competitive bidding.[41] Greenbelt thus sold for

---

[39] Letter to author from Casey Ireland, Special Assistant to the Commissioner, Public Housing Administration, Nov. 28, 1956; U.S. Housing and Home Finance Agency, *Third Annual Report for Calendar Year 1949*, pt. IV, pp. 346–347, and *Sixth Annual Report for Calendar Year 1952* (Washington, 1953), pt. IV, pp. 430–431.

[40] Letter to author from Casey Ireland, Nov. 28, 1956.

[41] *Ibid.;* U.S. Housing and Home Finance Agency, *Seventh Annual Report for Calendar Year 1953* (Washington, 1954), pt. IV, pp. 399–400.

$8,973,767. All the greenbelt cities liquidated at $19,559,762, which, not even counting the cost of the defense housing at Greenbelt, was only approximately 53 per cent of the total cost of $36,200,910.

With the final liquidation of the greenbelt cities in 1954, the direct role of the federal government in community building was ended. Yet the communities still survived, for, in a larger sense, the government had only set in motion a self-perpetuating process. The community building would continue far into an unpredictable future, for the government merely withdrew its paternal direction from its very youthful offspring, leaving each fledgling community to grow toward adulthood without external supervision. Very appropriate are the words of Vachel Lindsay in his "The Building of Our City":

> Record it for the grandson of your son—
> A city is not builded in a day:
> Our little town cannot complete her soul
> Till countless generations pass away.

In Retrospect

THE many attempted reforms of the New Deal period were not all part of one consistent program. The term "New Deal," like the label "Progressive Era," defies analysis in terms of one, dominant philosophy. In both periods there were many reformers and many reform programs, many philosophers and many diverse philosophies of reform. No one doctrinaire, thoroughgoing pattern for reform has ever been implemented in the United States, a country which never has had a strong socialist-labor, or any other one-class, party. Yet the term "New Deal" is not meaningless. It symbolizes the most overwhelming sentiment for reform (or for a new deal) in American history. The three years of depression from 1930 to 1933 did more to arouse a widespread demand for effective reform than the many years of less intense distress and of public education that preceded the Progressive Movement. But the depression, although leading to a demand for action and creating an atmosphere favorable to even drastic reforms, did not in itself reveal any one, widely accepted pattern for this reform.

Limited by certain assumptions and attitudes—and surprisingly traditional and conservative ones they were—Franklin D. Roosevelt still was open minded and impressible almost to a fault. By 1932 he would lend a sympathetic ear to almost any well-sounding program for relief, recovery, or reform. As a result, Washington, in 1933, became a haven for literally thousands of zealous men with

In Retrospect

widely varied ideas for saving America, for conserving the best of the past, for creating a new America, for thwarting radicalism, and for implementing radicalism. Sooner or later many long-overdue and much-advocated reforms were achieved, such as more favorable legislation for labor, a social security program, and more controls over banking and investment. Roosevelt was not immune to experimenting with appealing, all too simple panaceas, such as government-induced inflation through currency manipulation, and was not too dogmatic to be converted to a "sound money" policy. Closely related to the tremendous relief program were the many public works programs and new ventures into such fields as public housing. Action, on many different fronts, was certainly the keynote of the New Deal.

Compared to many other New Deal experiments, the community program was relatively small in terms of final accomplishments. This fact should not obscure the early enthusiasm, from Roosevelt on down the line, that greeted the early community program. The back-to-the-land movement, which eventuated in the first subsistence homesteads legislation, was a very romantic and appealing panacea in 1933. Its appeal, basically conservative or even reactionary, won the support of numerous congressmen who were opposed to many of the other New Deal experiments. The community idea itself, whether connected with subsistence homesteads or resettlement, was flexible enough to appeal, and appeal strongly, to people with very diverse political creeds, from the most reactionary to the most radical, from Ralph Borsodi to Rexford G. Tugwell. In the abstract, most people favored planned communities or towns, decentralization of industry, subsistence gardens, handicrafts, and even co-operation. The community program was not to flounder and die because of any deep-seated repudiation of the community idea, which still has both its romantic and rational appeal to most Americans. The program succumbed because of the controversial ideas of some of its directors, the unforseen practical difficulties encountered in implementing the community idea, the many problems that inevitably resulted from the unco-ordinated and hasty accretion of activity on the part of a rather inflexible federal government, an organized opposition to the New Deal itself, and a declining sentiment for reform after 1936.

With the enactment of the subsistence homesteads legislation, the community idea had to be implemented in accordance with the philosophy of one or only a few policy makers. Many diverse philosophies can contribute to the legislative enactment of an abstract idea; many diverse or even contradictory philosophies cannot be reflected at the same time in the concrete implementation of an idea, at least not without complete confusion and near inaction. In a larger sense this was a dilemma faced not only by the community program but by many other agencies and by the New Deal as a whole. The New Deal had an overwhelming mandate for action, a mandate coming from all classes and all interests. But action leads to concrete programs, and in the presence of conflicting interest groups and varying political philosophies, no major, significant program can long win overwhelming support. The early honeymoon period of the New Deal was doomed to a quick end in spite of the severity of the economic depression. Back at the level of the community program, any policies set up in the Division of Subsistence Homesteads were sure to displease some of the sponsors of the legislation. The source of this opposition was to be determined by the controlling ideas of the men who directed the community-building agencies. The severity of the opposition was to be determined by the degree that these directors expressed the most popular views of the American people.

The most critical decision affecting the New Deal communities was Roosevelt's choice of Tugwell to head the newly created Resettlement Administration in 1935. The communities then became only one element in an ambitious program to reshape the face of rural and suburban America. They also were soon to share the notoriety of the controversial Tugwell. As a director of the community program, Tugwell's collectivist ideas did not express the majority sentiment in the United States, particularly since that majority sentiment was slowly shifting toward the right. To say that Tugwell was unpopular is not to pronounce judgment. More than almost any other person in the New Deal, Tugwell advocated a logical, consistent, and thoroughgoing program of reform that touched on every aspect of the economy. As few other men, he saw through the superficial gloss of the many panaceas of the New Deal period. He lacked neither personal magnetism nor an incisively logical, and not always academic, appeal to American liberals. His famed political ineptitude, if such existed, often indicated only tenacious honesty and high personal integrity. As a director of a practical program he did compromise, and he was

In Retrospect

a better, more conservative administrator than his opponents would ever concede. Tugwell soon realized that all his sweeping reforms could not be achieved during the New Deal, but fatalistically, pessimistically, Tugwell had to act his part anyway, striving for the unachievable. And his ideas of a collective society, to be achieved slowly and not without hard work and costly sacrifices, were far too radical for most Americans. He and his successors, who shared his philosophical orientation, set the community program on a pathway that could lead only to disaster. At a time when public opinion was becoming more conservative, the community program was becoming more daringly experimental, and departing farther from traditional institutions, than ever before.

The community idea, so appealing in the abstract, was much more difficult to achieve in actuality than almost anyone believed possible in 1933. The raw material for the completed communities was both physical and human, and the latter proved very unpredictable and sometimes intractable. All too often the settlers were not anxious to participate in experimental reforms leading to a new America which they could not understand or appreciate. They simply wanted economic security. Despite some few precedents, the community planners of the New Deal were largely exploring new territory. The first communities were frankly experimental. The planners soon faced hundreds of unexpected problems. The methods for detailed social planning were unknown or else not available in a free society. In most cases the more extensive the reforms attempted within a community, the more often that community was a failure. The time and expense required in developing successful communities proved to be much above earlier expectations. In a period when quick results were demanded, the community idea soon appeared to be very impractical.

By Roosevelt's second term, an anti-New Deal coalition had solidified in Congress. Conservative Democrats joined with Republicans to police relief expenditures and to oppose any new, large-scale reforms. By 1938 the New Deal was completed. Roosevelt himself was becoming preoccupied with foreign developments and, seeking wide support, was accepting more conservative advisers. During World War II conservative forces dominated Congress, whittling away at such vulnerable New Deal programs as the Farm Security Administration. Just when the conservative opposition solidified in 1937 and 1938, the New Deal communities were at a critical period of development. Most were yet uncompleted or had just been completed. The difficult task of community management was just under way. The actual construction cost of individual communities was just being appraised by critical congressmen. The most radical experiments in co-operative farming and in long-term leases were introduced either in 1937 or even later. For the conservative opponents of the New Deal, the unsuccessful communities offered perfect ammunition. They were to be exploited for propaganda purposes until after the congressional investigation of the Farm Security Administration in 1943. If Tugwell had launched his Resettlement Administration program in 1933, and could have completed it by 1936, he probably would have achieved many of his goals without serious congressional opposition. This was not possible after 1936 in a period when the whole New Deal was more and more on the defensive.

The tremendous, frenzied governmental activity of the early New Deal can be understood only in relation to the depression. The depression resulted in both fear and anger among large groups of people. For a brief time the old individualistic, capitalistic society was widely condemned. The caution, complacency, and natural conservation of most Americans were shattered, and millions looked to the federal government for a new, more secure society. But this early movement for reform rapidly lost momentum, although it never disappeared completely. Whether because of returning prosperity or because of a regained sense of security, there was not nearly so much enthusiasm for a new society in 1937 as there had been in 1933. By the time of the Farm Security Administration investigation in 1943, any challenge to the old society was branded as treason, or at least heresy. The renewed popularity of the older, more established institutions doomed the experiments being carried on within many of the New Deal communities. Many changes had been wrought by the New Deal, and many were to remain. But the day for launching extensive new reforms was in the past. The New Deal produced no more Tennessee Valley Authorities, despite Roosevelt's wishes. Congress had decided that there should be no more new communities and no expansion of the ones already developed. Furthermore, the existing communities were to be forced back into the traditional patterns of complete individual ownership, private enterprise, and local control. This all happened after 1943.

Despite the fact that the New Deal communities were repudiated as part of government policy and that government controls over the communities were removed before most of the social experiments had been completed, the program resulted in approximately 100 completed communities and housing for approximately 10,000 families, about one-half of which were rural. The construction and management of the communities provided direct or indirect employment for countless thousands of workers. For each dollar expended, the communities represented more tangible, enduring achievements than most other relief expenditures.

In retrospect, the program appears to have been most valuable in revealing the problems of detailed social planning and of effecting a rapid transition from an individualistic to a more collectivised society. For the historian, the community program was most valuable in providing new insight about American reform efforts and in revealing or suggesting the many ideas, ideals, and values that were competing for acceptance, or were seemingly at stake, in the New Deal period. From a more tangible viewpoint, the green belt cities have been widely influential in the city planning movement, and the excellent physical designs and the present-day prosperity of most of the New Deal communities seem to have redeemed some of the early mistakes. It is unfortunate that the long political controversy that swirled around the Resettlement Administration and the Farm Security Administration has completely colored the memory of the New Deal communities, obscuring most of their virtues and magnifying all their shortcomings.

Appendix: Complete List of New Deal Communities [1]

Table 1. Communities planned and initiated by the Division of Subsistence Homesteads

Name	Location	Type	Units	Total cost	Unit cost
Arthurdale	Reedsville, W. Va.	Stranded community	165	$2,744,724.09	$16,635
Cumberland Homesteads	Crossville, Tenn.	Stranded community	262	3,267,345.10	12,471
Tygart Valley Homesteads	Elkins, W. Va.	Stranded community	195	2,080,213.99	10,668
Westmoreland Homesteads	Greensburg, Penn.	Stranded community	255	2,516,469.81	9,869
Jersey Homesteads	Hightstown, N.J.	Co-operative industrial	206	3,402,382.27	16,516
Penderlea Homesteads	Pender County, N. Car.	Farm community	195	2,277,685.60	11,680

[1] Most of the statistics in this Appendix were compiled from U.S. House of Representatives, Select Committee of the Committee on Agriculture, *Hearings on the Farm Security Administration*, 78th Cong, 1st Sess., 1943–1944, pp. 1118–1127.

Table 1. By the Division of Subsistence Homesteads (cont.)

Name	Location	Type	Units	Total cost	Unit cost
Piedmont Homesteads	Jasper County, Ga.	Farm community	50	649,650.88	12,993
Richton Homesteads	Richton, Miss.	Farm community	26	216,468.82	8,626
Shenandoah Homesteads	Five counties in Virginia	Resettlement communities (seven)	160	1,060,125.49	6,626
Cahaba (Trussville Homesteads)	Near Birmingham, Ala.	Industrial (small garden city)	287	2,760,610.47	9,619
Austin Homesteads	Austin, Minn.	Industrial	44	213,227.87	4,846
Bankhead Farms	Jasper, Ala.	Industrial	100	1,046,420.80	10,464
Beauxart Gardens	Beaumont, Tex.	Industrial	50	143,027.62	2,861
Dalworthington Gardens	Arlington, Tex.	Industrial	79	325,712.35	4,123
Dayton Homesteads	Dayton, Ohio.	Industrial	35	50,000.00 (loan)	—
Decatur Homesteads	Decatur, Ind.	Industrial	48	157,279.94	3,277
Duluth Homesteads	Duluth, Minn.	Industrial	84	983,984.30	11,714
El Monte Homesteads	El Monte, Calif.	Industrial	100	292,476.81	2,925
Granger Homesteads	Granger, Iowa	Industrial	50	216,189.87	4,324
Greenwood Homesteads	Near Birmingham, Ala.	Industrial	83	827,835.27	9,974
Hattiesburg Homesteads	Hattiesburg, Miss.	Industrial	24	75,648.78	3,152
Houston Gardens	Houston, Tex.	Industrial	100	283,568.10	2,836
Lake County Homesteads	Chicago, Ill.	Industrial	53	554,745.53	10,469
Longview Homesteads	Longview, Wash.	Industrial	60	194,097.52	3,235
Magnolia Homesteads	Meridian, Miss.	Industrial	25	73,556.46	2,942
McComb Homesteads	McComb, Miss.	Industrial	20	91,452.52	4,573
Mount Olive Homesteads	Near Birmingham, Ala.	Industrial	75	618,162.84	8,242
Palmerdale Homesteads	Near Birmingham, Ala.	Industrial	102	938,865.08	9,205

Table 1. By the Division of Subsistence Homesteads (cont.)

Name	Location	Type	Units	Total cost	Unit cost
Phoenix Homesteads	Phoenix, Ariz.	Industrial	25	104,859.28	4,194
San Fernando Homesteads	Reseda, Calif.	Industrial	40	102,065.23	2,552
Three Rivers Gardens	Three Rivers, Tex.	Industrial	50	162,943.43	3,259
Tupelo Homesteads	Tupelo, Miss.	Industrial	35	139,247.12	3,978
Wichita Gardens	Wichita Falls, Tex.	Industrial	62	187,527.85	3,025
Aberdeen Gardens	Newport News, Va.	Garden city for Negroes	159	1,353,896.29	8,515
Totals for all 34 subsistence homesteads communities			3,304	$30,112,467.38	$9,114

Table 2. Communities planned or initiated by the Federal Emergency Relief Administration

Name	Location	Type	Units	Total cost	Unit cost
Dyess Colony	Mississippi County, Ark.	Farm community	275 *	$2,306,250.00 †	$8,386
Cherry Lake Farms	Near Madison, Fla.	Farm and rural industrial	132 *	1,913,811.00 †	14,499
Pine Mountain Valley	Harris County, Ga.	Farm and rural industrial	205 *	2,207,572.00 †	10,769
Burlington Project	Burlington, N. Dak.	Stranded community	35	213,172.15	6,091
Red House	Red House, W. Va.	Stranded community	150	1,506,397.82	10,043
Albert Lea Homesteads	Albert Lea, Minn.	Industrial	14	38,160.68	2,726
Arizona Part-Time Farms	Phoenix, Ariz.	Industrial	91	564,013.05	6,198
Fairbury Farmsteads	Jefferson County, Neb.	Farm village	11	67,895.87	6,172
Fall City Farmsteads	Richardson County, Neb.	Farm village	10	102,755.42	10,276
Grand Island Farmsteads	Hall County, Neb.	Farm village	10	68,126.52	6,813

* As of 1943, after many consolidations.
† The original investment of the FERA. This does not include later expenditures.

Table 2. By the Federal Emergency Relief Administration (*cont.*)

Name	Location	Type	Units	Total cost	Unit cost
Kearney Homesteads	Buffalo County, Neb.	Farm village	10	98,238.96	9,824
Loup City Farmsteads	Sherman County, Neb.	Farm village	11	101,281.82	9,207
Scottsbluff Farmsteads	Scotts Bluff County, Neb.	Farm village	23	231,520.02	10,276
Sioux Falls Farms	Minnehaha County, S. Dak.	Farm village	14	218,660.71	15,619
South Sioux City Farmsteads	Dakota County, Neb.	Farm village	22	115,395.98	5,245
Two Rivers Farmsteads	Douglas and Saunders counties, Neb.	Farm village	40	547,746.49	13,694
Woodlake Community	Wood County, Tex.	Farm village	101	648,255.81	6,418
Ashwood Plantation	Lee County, S. Car.	Farm community	161	1,874,268.56	11,641
Bosque Farms	Valencia County, N. Mex.	Farm community	42	677,725.45	16,136
Chicot Farms	Chicot and Drew counties, Ark.	Farm community	85	578,338.60	6,804
Irwinville	Irwin County, Ga.	Farm community	105	899,815.34	8,571
Roanoke Farms	Halifax County, N. Car.	Farm community	294	2,191,568.39	7,454
Ropesville Farms	Hockley County, Tex.	Farm community	76	667,489.03	8,783
Scuppernong Farms	Tyrrell and Washington counties, N. Car.	Farm community	127	779,327.49	6,136
Skyline Farms	Jackson County, Ala.	Farm community	181	1,230,333.06	6,797
St. Francis River Farms	Poinsett County, Ark.	Farm community	86	546,767.43	6,358
Wichita Valley Farms	Wichita County, Tex.	Farm community	91	931,086.53	10,243
Wolf Creek	Grady County, Ga.	Farm community	24	233,351.21	9,723
Totals for all 28 Federal Emergency Relief Administration communities			2,426	$21,559,325.39	$ 8,887

Table 3. Communities initiated by the Resettlement Administration

Name	Location	Type	Units	Total cost	Unit cost
Greenbelt	Berwyn, Md. (near Washington D.C.)	Garden city	890	$13,701,817.17	$15,395
Greendale	Milwaukee, Wis.	Garden city	640	10,638,465.62	16,623
Greenhills	Cincinnati, Ohio	Garden city	737	11,860,627.53	16,093
Ironwood Homesteads	Ironwood, Mich.	Small garden city	132	1,373,138.48	10,403
Drummond Project	Bayfield County, Wis.	Forest homesteads	32	246,376.88	7,699
Sublimity Farms	Laurel County, Ky.	Forest homesteads	66	419,824.85	6,361
Casa Grande Valley Farms	Pinal County, Ariz.	Co-operative farm	60	817,548.17	11,959
Lake Dick	Jefferson and Arkansas counties, Ark.	Co-operative farm	97	663,850.81	6,844
Terrebonne	Terrebonne Parish, La.	Co-operative plantation	73	514,504.21	7,048
Biscoe Farms	Prairie County, Ark.	Farm community	77	373,224.39	4,847
Christian-Trigg Farms	Christian County, Ky.	Farm community	106	971,424.99	9,164
Clover Bend Farms	Lawrence County, Ark.	Farm community	91	483,534.82	5,314
Desha Farms	Desha and Drew counties, Ark.	Farm community	88	511,872.94	5,817
Escambia Farms	Okaloosa County, Fla.	Farm community	81	585,818.99	7,232
Flint River Farms	Macon County, Ga.	Farm community	146	727,611.42	4,984
Gee's Bend Farms	Wilcox County, Ala.	Farm community	100	418,505.30	4,185
Hinds Farms	Hinds County, Miss.	Farm community	81	294,484.96	3,636
Kinsey Flats	Custer County, Mont.	Farm community	80	874,741.08	10,934
La Forge Farms	New Madrid County, Mo.	Farm community	101	769,534.69	7,619
Lakeview Farms	Lee and Phillips counties, Ark.	Farm community	141	899,652.21	6,381
Lonoke Farms	Lonoke County, Ark.	Farm community	57	254,484.84	4,465

Table 3. By the Resettlement Administration (cont.)

Name	Location	Type	Units	Total cost	Unit cost
Lucedale Farms	George and Greene counties, Miss.	Farm community	93	449,945.75	4,838
McLennan Farms	McLennan County, Tex.	Farm community	20	244,050.17	12,203
Mileston Farms	Holmes County, Miss.	Farm community	110	744,721.40	6,770
Mounds Farms	Madison and East Carroll parishes, La.	Farm community	149	803,616.30	5,393
Orangeburg Farms	Orangeburg and Calhoun Counties, S. Car.	Farm community	80	535,518.55	6,694
Osage Farms	Pettis County, Mo.	Farm community	86	976,055.87	11,349
Pembroke Farms	Robeson County, N. Car.	Farm community	75	613,267.98	8,177
Plum Bayou	Jefferson County, Ark.	Farm community	200	1,634,921.84	8,175
Prairie Farms	Macon County, Ala.	Farm community	34	201,683.79	5,932
Sabine Farms	Harrison County, Tex.	Farm community	80	436,674.00	5,458
Saginaw Valley Farms	Saginaw County, Mich.	Farm community	33	365,958.14	11,090
Sam Houston Farms	Harris County, Tex.	Farm community	86	607,777.78	7,067
Tiverton Farms	Sumter County, S. Car.	Farm community	29	117,987.93	4,069
Townes Farms	Crittenden County, Ark.	Farm community	37	163,733.93	4,425
Transylvania Farms	East Carroll Parish, La.	Farm community	163	847,640.34	5,200
Trumann Farms	Poinsett County, Ark.	Farm community	57	278,937.13	4,894
Totals for all 37 Resettlement Administration communities			5,208	$56,423,535.25	$10,834
Grand totals for all 99 communities			10,938	$108,095,328.02	$ 9,691

Bibliographical Note

THE National Archives are the one indispensable source of information about the New Deal communities. Here are records of high-level policy decisions and of the most minute details concerning local projects. Record Group 96, Records of the Farmers' Home Administration, contains literally hundreds of cubic feet of official records on the Division of Subsistence Homesteads, the Federal Emergency Relief Administration, the Resettlement Administration, and the Farm Security Administration. No adequate history of the communities could be written without these all-important records. Since the Resettlement Administration (soon to become the Farm Security Administration) was absorbed by the Department of Agriculture in 1937 and since Rexford G. Tugwell was Assistant Secretary of Agriculture, Record Group 16, Records of the Office of the Secretary of Agriculture, contains much valuable correspondence relating to the community program. Record Group 48, Records of the Office of the Secretary of the Interior, contains a few cubic feet of very valuable records on the early subsistence homesteads program. A few scattered records of the Federal Emergency Relief Administration communities are contained in Record Group 69, Records of the Work Projects Administration and Its Predecessors; and Record Group 83, Records of the Bureau of Agricultural Economics, contains the records of several valuable studies conducted on various aspects of the community program.

Second in importance only to the National Archives are the many public documents, reports, and bulletins relating either directly or indirectly to the New Deal communities or to their background. Since the fate of the communities was ultimately in the hands of Congress, the *Congressional Record* provides a running account of the developing congressional displeasure

Bibliographical Note 339

with the communities. Even more valuable are the many congressional committee hearings, reports, and documents, beginning with those relating to soldier settlement and reclamation (House and Senate Committees on Irrigation and Reclamation, Labor, Public Lands, and Agriculture) and culminating with the annual hearings and reports of the House and Senate Agricultural Subcommittees of the Committees on Appropriations from 1936 through 1949. Two congressional documents deserve special mention. The first is the result of the monumental investigation of the Farm Security Administration in 1943–1944: Select Committee of the House Committee on Agriculture, *Hearings on the Farm Security Administration,* 78th Cong., 1st Sess., 1943–1944. These hearings provide a controversial but most valuable source of information on the financial records of the individual communities. The second document is Senate Document no. 213, *Resettlement Administration Program,* 74th Cong., 2d Sess., 1936, which represents a statistical analysis of the resettlement program as compiled for Congress by the Resettlement Administration. A glorified, dressed-up view of the communities is contained in the many reports, bulletins, and circulars issued by the Division of Subsistence Homesteads, the Resettlement Administration, and the Farm Security Administration from 1934 through 1943. The final disposition of the communities is recorded in the annual reports of the United States National Housing Agency (1945–1947) and its successor, the United States Housing and Home Finance Agency (1947–1953).

The New Deal communities were both centers of controversy and objects of curiosity from their very beginning. Almost the same thing can be said of the back-to-the-land movement, the garden city crusade, and Elwood Mead's work in rural resettlement. In each of these cases there was a wealth of contemporary publicity in magazines and newspapers. A list of such articles would probably fill a book. Over 200 are cited in the footnotes of this study; many more were consulted. The articles varied in size and in merit. Some were pure propaganda, and only a few were balanced. One news release by the Resettlement Administration might result in twenty different articles, all recounting the same basic information with varying interpretations. In retrospect, it is surprising that so many words were written and so little revealed. The popular articles tended to concentrate almost entirely on the curious and the ridiculous, on the errors, or on human interest. The following four bibliographies provide a nearly complete list of articles related to the early community program and its background: Louise O. Bercaw and Annie M. Hannay, *Bibliography on Land Utilization, 1918–1936* (United States Department of Agriculture, Miscellaneous Publication no. 284; Washington, 1938); Louise O. Bercaw, Annie M. Hannay, and Esther M. Colvin, *Bibliography on Land Settlement, with Particular Reference to Small Holdings and Subsistence Homesteads* (United States Department of Agriculture, Miscellaneous Publication no. 172; Washington, 1934); Helen E. Heunefrund, *Part-Time Farming in the United States* (United States Department of Agriculture, Bureau of Agricultural Economics, Agricultural Economics Bibliography no. 77; Washington, 1939); Katherine McNamara, *Bibliography of Planning, 1928–35* (Cambridge, Mass., 1936).

There are no published studies of the whole New Deal community program. The most valuable book to appear so far was the result of a sociological research project on the part of the Bureau of Agricultural Economics and was published as: Russell Lord and Paul H. Johnstone, eds., *A Place on Earth: A Critical Appraisal of Subsistence Homesteads* (Washington, 1942). It includes an introductory background by the editors and field reports on several individual subsistence homesteads communities. Another valuable study was limited to five communities, Paul W. Wager, *One Foot on the Soil: A Study of Subsistence Homesteads in Alabama* (University of Alabama, 1945). An intimate view of the early years at Greenbelt is contained in George A. Warner, *Greenbelt: The Cooperative Community* (New York, 1954). One other major work was completed very early and also was limited in scope, Raymond P. Duggan, *A Federal Resettlement Project—Granger Homesteads* (School of Social Work, Monograph no. 1, Catholic University of America; Washington, 1937).

The community program generally has not received detailed attention in the growing number of works related to the New Deal. A significant exception is Arthur M. Schlesinger, Jr., *The Age of Roosevelt*, vol. II: *The Coming of the New Deal* (Boston, 1958), which includes a detailed account of the work of the Resettlement Administration. Russell Lord, in *The Wallaces of Iowa* (Boston, 1947), provides biographical information on Rexford G. Tugwell and Milburn L. Wilson and shows the relationship of the community program to the over-all agricultural program. Unfortunately some of the minor factual details in this well-written but rambling study are inaccurate. The struggle over the Farm Security Administration in World War II is recounted by Grant McConnell in *The Decline of Agrarian Democracy* (Berkeley, 1953). The intellectual background of the New Deal is interpreted by Arthur M. Schlesinger, Jr., in *The Age of Roosevelt*, vol. I: *The Crisis of the Old Order, 1919–1933*, (Boston, 1956). Alfred W. Griswold, in his *Farming and Democracy* (New Haven, 1952), traces the life history of the agrarian myth that was upheld by the back-to-the-landers. Rexford G. Tugwell, in a series of articles and in his *The Democratic Roosevelt* (Garden City, N.Y., 1957), has proved that an economist can write interesting history. His insights into the Roosevelt personality and into the development of the New Deal program are among the best that have yet appeared.

Index

Aberdeen Gardens, 113, 162, 167, 173, 201-202, 217, 334
Ackerman, Frederick L., 69-70
Adams, Henry C., 74
Adams, Thomas, 64, 68, 70, 280
Agar, Herbert, 27
Agger, Eugene E., 155, 247
Agrarianism, 11-12, 24-27, 44-45, 51-52, 96-97, 257, 294-295
Agricultural Adjustment Administration, 80, 94, 96, 134, 143, 152, 154, 174
Agricultural price supports, 78
Agricultural supervision, *189-191*, 286-287, 291
Agriculture, Department of, 7, 55, 57, 75, 79, 84, 94, 122, 134, 142, 152, 155, 160, 171, 181-184, 194, 281, 310
Agro-industrial communities, 260
Albert Lea Homesteads (Minn.), 334
Alexander, Will W., 154, 172, 181, 223, 295
Alliance, N.J., 257
Amana, Iowa, 13, 210
American Country Life Association, 74
American Economic Association, 74
American Farm Bureau, 100, 123, 222-225
American Farm Economic Association, 74

American Federation of Labor, 101, 170, 225
American Friends Service Committee, 35-36, 98, 114, 193-194, 197, 238, 244-245, 248
American Liberty League, 250-251
American Medical Association, 198-199
Arizona Part-Time Farms, 334
Arthur, Richard M., 238
Arthurdale (W. Va.), *237-255*, 108, 114-116, 118, 122, 124-125, 136, 142, 159, 164-165, 173, 177, 191, 194, 197, 204, 207-208, 216-217, 233, 259, 273, 277, 296, 332
Arts and crafts, *195-196*, 35, 45, 108, 159, 191, 193-194, 267, 302
Ashwood Plantation (S. Car.), 335
Augur, Tracy B., 321
Austin Homesteads (Minn.), 112, 162, 193, 217, 333
Australia, 43-46

Back-to-the-land movement, *28-35*, 12-24, 87, 93, 256-257, 259-260, 262, 294, 296, 327
Bailey, Josiah W., 117
Baker, Jacob, 203
Baker, Oliver E., 74
Baldwin, Calvin B., 154, 224, 226, 228-229, 295

341

Bankhead, John H., 56, 87-88, 100, 111, 180, 183
Bankhead, William B., 56, 87, 175, 183
Bankhead Farms (Ala.), 111, 162, 207, 217, 333
Bankhead-Jones Farm Tenant Act, 183-184, 220-221, 223-225, 227
Banks, Nathaniel P., 14
Barbour, W. Warren, 178, 274
Baruch, Bernard, 245-246, 254
Beauxart Gardens (Tex.), 111, 162, 215, 333
Bellamy, Edward, 61
Belloc, Hilaire, 25
Belmont, August, 66
Berle, Adolf A., Jr., 181
Bing, Alexander, 69-70
Biro-Bidjan, Russia, 261
Biscoe Farms (Ark.), 336
Black, John D., 32, 74, 78-80, 82, 87, 100
Black, Loring M., Jr., 33
Bland, Schuyler O., 201
Bliss, William D. P., 66
Blitzer, Max, 262-265
Blucher, Walter H., 321
Borsodi, Ralph, 26-27, 97, 99, 107-108, 123, 201, 203, 294, 327
Bosque Farms (N. Mex.), 334
Brand, Charles J., 75
Brown, Benjamin, 261-269, 273-274
Brownlow, Louis, 100
Brunner, Felix, 175-178
Buckingham, James Silk, 61
Bureau of Agricultural Economics, 75, 78, 80, 98, 154-155, 157, 185
Bureau of Biological Survey, 134
Burlington Project (N. Dak.), 334
Burnham, Daniel, 61
Butler, Benjamin F., 15-16
Byrd, Harry F., 163-164, 177, 224, 275

Cadbury, George, 61
Cahaba (Ala.), 111, 162, 167, 202, 217, 233, 333
California Commission on Colonization and Rural Credits, 46
California Land Settlement Board, 47, 49

Carden, Philip V., 100
Carver, Thomas Nixon, 20
Casa Grande Farms (Ariz.), 169, 210-211, 277, 336
Castle Hayne (N. Car.), 279
Catholic rural movement, 14-15, 25; see also National Catholic Rural Life Conference
Chapman, Oscar L., 94, 143
Chase, Roy P., 223
Chase, Stuart, 69
Cherry Lake Farms (Fla.), *140*, 137, 192, 334
Chicot Farms (Ark.), 335
Christian-Trigg Farms (Ky.), 336
Churchill, Henry, 321
City planning: in Colonial America, 60; in the 19th century, 61; by Ebenezer Howard, 62-66; and the Garden City Association of America, 66; in spacious American cities, 67; and zoning, 67; in World War I housing, 68; growth in the twenties, 68; and the New York Regional Plan, 68-69; by the Regional Planning Association, 69; in the greenbelt towns, 304-315, 321, 330-331
Civil Works Administration, 80, 98, 133, 244-245
Civilian Conservation Corps, 196
Clapp, Elsie, 246-248
Clark, John Bates, 74
Clover Bend Farms (Ark.), 336
Collective farms, 169-170, 182, 210-211, 220-222, 224-229
Collectivism, 3-4, 150, 160, 210-211, 222, 225, 329-333
Committee for Soil Surveys, 114
Committee on the Bases of a Sound Land Policy, 79
Commons, John R., 74, 77, 94
Commonwealth Club of California, 46
Communitarian colonies, 13
Community idea, 102, 127, 305, 327-329
Community management, 125, 156, 181, 185, 189-190, 203-204, 212-213, 287-292
Congress of Industrial Organizations, 225, 229

Index

Conservation movement, 41
Consular Service, 157
Consumer Distribution Corporation, 317
Cook, Nancy, 242-243, 249
Cooley, Harold D., 224-228
Coolidge, Calvin, 56, 68, 78
Cooper, Thomas, 94
Co-operation, *202-211*, 45, 50-52, 102-103, 128, 153, 158-159, 162-165, 168-170, 183, 189, 192-193, 197-198, 215, 221, 238, 248, 251-253, 259, 261-262, 266-267, 270-271, 273, 276-277, 287-290, 300-304, 317, 327, 330
Co-operative farm colonies, 169-170, 182, 210-211, 220-222, 224-229
Council of Social Agencies, Morgantown, W. Va., 238-239
Country Life Commission, 74
Cox, Edward E., 223
Crosser, Robert, 49-50
Cumberland Homesteads (Tenn.), 108, 115, 164-165, 207-208, 213, 217, 332

Dailey, Joseph L., 155
Dalworthington Gardens (Tex.), 111, 162, 215, 333
Davis, Chester C., 76
Dayton Homesteads (Ohio), 107-108, 114, 121, 123, 294, 333
Debt adjustment, 153
Decatur Homesteads (Ind.), 113, 115, 162, 173, 216, 333
Delano, Frederic A., 65, 68, 71, 79
Delhi, Calif., 47-48
Delta Co-operative Farm (Miss.), 210-211
Desha Farms (Ark.), 336
Dewey, John, 4, 191, 247
Dirksen, Everett M., 230
Distributists, 24-27, 294-296
Division of Land Economics, Department of Agriculture, 75
Division of Self-Help Co-operation, 203
Domestic Allotment Plan, 78-79, 81-82, 84
Dornbush, Adrian J., 195-196
Douglas, Paul, 323
Drummond Project (Wis.), 336
Dubinsky, David, 263-265

Duffy, F. Ryan, 199
Duluth Homesteads (Wis.), 112, 162, 217, 333
Durham, Calif., 47-48
Dyess Colony (Ark.), *137-138*, 140, 197, 233, 334

Eddy, Sherwood, 210
Educational programs, *192, 246-248*, 128, 142, 205, 286-287, 302
Einstein, Albert, 262-263
El Monte Homesteads (Calif.), 111-112, 162, 216, 296, 333
Ely, Richard T., 73-77, 79-80, 84
Emergency Committee for Food Production, 223
Emergency Fleet Corporation, 67, 118
Emergency Relief Act of 1935, 142, 174
Escambia Farms (Fla.), 336
Ezekiel, Mordecai, 75

Fairbury Farmsteads (Neb.), 334
Fairway Farms experiment, 76-77
Fall City Farmsteads (Neb.), 334
Farm City Corporation of America, 280
Farm Credit Administration, 134, 228, 261
Farm Security Administration, *220-230*, 7, 137-138, 140, 146, 154, 160, 168, 171-172, 182, 185, 189-190, 197-199, 202, 204, 207-214, 217-219, 231-232, 253, 255, 269, 272, 275-276, 287-294, 301-302, 314, 318, 329-331
Farm tenancy, 77, 180, 182-184, 221
Farm Tenancy, Presidential Committee on, 180, 182-185, 227
Farmers' Home Administration, 230, 293
Farmers' Home Corporation, 184-185, 227, 230
Federal Arts Project, 196
Federal Emergency Relief Administration, *131-145*, 7, 80, 154-155, 157, 161, 169-170, 197, 201, 203, 218
Federal Farm Board, 78-79
Federal Land Bank, 114, 141, 297
Federal Public Housing Authority, 7, 218, 227-228, 231-232, 255, 273, 276, 303, 322-323

Federal Subsistence Homesteads Corporation, 106, 119, 123-124, 281
Federal Surplus Relief Corporation, 134
Federal Theatre and Music Division, 196
Federal Works Agency, 322
Filene, Edward, 317
Flanders, Ralph E., 100-101
Flannigan, John W., Jr., 226
Flint River Farms (Ga.), 336
Ford, Henry, 23-24, 27, 29
Foreman, Clark, 101
Forest Service, 110
Foster, Philip W., 280
Fourier, Charles, 13
Fritts, Frank, 281
Fulmer, Hampton P., 129

Galpin, Charles J., 74
Garden City Association (England), 63-64
Garden City Association of America, 65-66
Garden city planning, *61-75*, 154, 159-160, 280, 305-311
Gee's Bend Community (Ala.), 188, 230, 336
General Accounting Office, 118
George, Henry, 61, 126
Geraldson, Gerald, 158
Goldstein, Philip, 273, 276
Gorman, John J., 302
Gould, Elgin R. L., 66
Grand Island Farmsteads (Neb.), 334
Granger Homesteads (Iowa), *294-304*, 113, 162, 217, 333
Gray, Lewis C., 74-75, 80, 154
Greeley, Horace, 14
Green, Robert A., 33
Green, William, 101, 170
Greenbelt, Md., *310-312*, 166, 176, 196, 308-309, 313-325, 336
Greenbelt towns, *305-325*, 60, 69, 71, 156, 160-161, 166-167, 173-174, 188, 217-218, 221-233, 331
Greenbrook, N.J., *173-175*, 178-179, 275, 308, 310, 319
Greendale, Wis., *314-315*, 166, 308, 310, 316-321, 324, 336

Greenhills, Ohio, *312-314*, 166, 308, 310, 317-321, 324, 336
Greenwood Homesteads (Ala.), 111, 162, 217, 333
Grimes, Bushrod, 239

Hacker, Louis M., 124
Hall, Bolton, 18
Hancock, Frank, 229
Handicraft program, *193-194*, 35, 45, 108, 159, 191, 302, 327
Harding, Warren G., 20, 54, 75, 78
Harriman, Henry I., 82, 93, 100
Harris, Hayden B., 100
Hattiesburg Homesteads (Miss.), 111, 162, 216-217, 231, 333
Hayden, Eustace, 77
Hebrew Emigrant Aid Society, 257
Heilprin, Michael, 257
Hendrickson, Roy, 98-99
Hibbard, Benjamin H., 74
Hightstown, N.J., *see* Jersey Homesteads
Hildebrandt, Fred H., 179
Hillman, Sidney, 229
Hinds Farms (Miss.), 336
Hirsch, Baron Maurice de, 258-259
Hofflin, Elizabeth, 195
Home supervision, 189-190, 285-286, 291
Homestead associations, *215-218*, 162-163, 209, 231, 254, 276, 302-303
Hoover, Herbert, 35, 67, 78-79
Hopkins, Harry, 133, 137, 142-143, 161
Hormel, George A., 112
Housing and Home Finance Agency, 232
Housing experiments, 170-172, 241-242, 248, 265
Houston Gardens (Tex.), 111, 115, 162, 173, 215, 333
Howard, Ebenezer, *61-65*, 68, 71, 159, 305, 312
Howe, Frederic, 52, 157
Howe, Louis M., 105, 122, 237, 240-243, 246, 250
Hyde, Arthur M., 32, 79

Ickes, Harold L., 80, 93-94, 97, 100, 106, 115-116, 119-122, 124-126, 142-143, 239-243, 245, 282

Index 345

Ickes, Mrs. Harold L., 245
Indians, 200-201
Individualism, 1-2, 6, 160, 225, 295-296, 330
Industrial decentralization, 23-24, 62, 80, 82, 84, 99, 105, 136, 159, 168, 240, 251, 256, 259, 295, 327
Industrial-type subsistence homesteads, 110-113, 128, 131, 162-163, 184, 216, 277, 296
Institute of Land and Public Utility Economics, 75-76
Interior, Department of the, 49-52, 55, 57, 80, 98, 200, 324
International Federation for Town and Country Planning and Garden Cities, 64-65, 68, 281
International Ladies' Garment Workers' Union, 263
Iowa State College, 297-299, 301
Ireland, John, 14-15
Ironwood Homesteads (Mich.), 167, 217, 336
Irwinville (Ga.), 335

Jacobstein, Meyer, 101
James, Edmund J., 74
Jefferson, Thomas, 12, 40, 60, 295
Jeffersonianism, 1-6, 12, 25-27, 295
Jersey Homesteads (N.J.), 256-276, 109, 121, 145, 162, 171, 173, 178, 210, 217, 233, 277, 296, 309, 332
Jewish Agricultural Society, 257, 259-261
Jewish colonization, 256-262, 109
Jewish Colonization Society, 258
Johnson, Alvin, 124
Johnson, Hiram W., 46
Johnson, Hugh, 6, 78
Jones, Marvin, 183
Julian, William A., 100

Kearney Homesteads (Neb.), 335
Kelley, Fred J., 247
Kinsey Flats (Mont.), 336
Kohn, Robert D., 69, 93

Labor, Department of, 49-50
La Cognina, Henry, 195
La Follette, Mary, 195-196

La Follette, Robert, 179, 195
La Forge Farms (Mo.), 336
LaGuardia, Fiorello H., 33
Lake County Homesteads (Ill.), 112, 162, 173, 217, 333
Lake Dick (Ark.), 169, 210-211, 277, 336
Lakeview Farms (Ark.), 336
Land-leasing associations, 220-221, 225
Land Policy Section, Agricultural Adjustment Administration, 134, 143-144, 154
Land-purchasing associations, 220-221, 225
Land retirement, 78-83, 133-134, 142, 153, 182
Land settlement: in Colonial America, 40, 60; in the 19th century, 40-41; on reclamation projects, 42, 54-55; in Australia, 43; as conceived by Elwood Mead, 44-45; in the California colonies, 46-48; as advocated by the Department of Labor, 49; and soldier settlement proposals, 50-54; and Southern reclamation colonies, 56; in the Lake States, 75; and Fairway Farms, 76-77; as a problem for farm economists, 78; and New Deal studies, 79-80, 158
Land tenure, 45-49, 77-78, 126-128, 158-160, 168-170, 182, 215-216, 218, 222, 225-228, 279, 286, 289-290, 302, 330
Land-use planning, 77-83, 86, 99, 133-134, 143, 153, 155-156, 161, 182-184, 306
Land Utilization Conference of 1931, 79-80
Lane, Franklin K., 20, 50, 51-53
Lansill, John S., 155, 308
Laura Spelman Rockefeller Foundation, 76
Letchworth, England, 63-65, 310, 321
Lever, William H., 61
Lewis, John L., 170
Liberalism, 1-3
Ligutti, Luigi, 25, 113, 294, 296-303
Little Landers, 19-20
Longview Homesteads (Wash.), 112, 115, 162-163, 216, 296, 333

Lonoke Farms (Ark.), 336
Loup City Farmsteads (Neb.), 335
Ludlow, Louis, 116-117, 201
Lumsden, Edith R., 32, 87
Lund, Mr. and Mrs. Haviland H., 20-21, 32

McCarl, John R., 119-120, 128-129, 173
McComb Homesteads (Miss.), 111, 162, 217, 333
Macfadden, Bernarr, 31-32, 34, 87, 94, 99, 114
Mackaye, Benton, 69
McKellar, Kenneth D., 117, 224
McLean, Edward B., 309
McLennan Farms (Tex.), 337
McNary, Charles L., 31
McNary-Haugen bills, 78
MacRae, Hugh, 277-284, 32, 94, 99, 109, 123, 289, 294
MacRae colonies, 277-280
Magnolia Homesteads (Miss.), 111, 162, 216-217, 231, 333
Marland, Ernest W., 118
Marshall, Alfred, 61
Matanuska, Alaska, 137, 177
Maverick, Maury, 179
Mead, Elwood, 42-58, 80-81, 87, 94, 279-280
Medicine and health services, 196-199, 128, 205, 248, 266, 318
Melvin, Bruce, 94, 98, 129, 200
Migratory workers, 140, 153, 222, 224
Mileston Farms (Miss.), 337
Mitchell, George S., 229
Mitchell, Morris R., 192
Mondell, Frank W., 53
Monroney, Mike, 323
Morgan, Arthur E., 93
Morgenthau, Henry, Jr., 82, 261
Morgenthau, Mrs. Henry, Jr., 249
Mormon villages, 13-14, 81, 100
Moser, Guy L., 223
Mounds Farms (La.), 337
Mount Olive Homesteads (Ala.), 111, 162, 171, 217, 333
Mountaineer Craftsmen's Co-operative Association, 193-194, 244, 251, 253
Mumford, Lewis, 68-69

National Advisory and Legislative Committee on Land Use, 80
National Advisory Committee on Subsistence Homesteads, 100-101, 123
National Catholic Rural Life Conference, 25, 294-296, 302
National Catholic Welfare Council, 225
National Council of Churches, 225
National Farmers' Union, 222, 225
National Forward to the Land League, 20-21
National Grange, 53, 100
National Housing Agency, 218
National Industrial Recovery Act, 88, 93, 129
National Land Use Planning Committee, 80
National Park Service, 134, 217
National Planning Board, 80
National Recovery Administration, 83, 174, 263
National Resources Board, 142
National Resources Committee, 66, 72, 80
Negroes, 199-202, 101, 104, 113, 141, 154, 167, 270
Nolen, John, 61, 67, 94, 114, 280-281, 285
Norris, Tenn., 113
Norton, Charles D., 71

Office of Indian Affairs, 134
Olmsted, Frederick Law, 60-61
O'Neal, Edward A., 100, 123, 224
Orangeburg Farms (S. Car.), 337
Osage Farms (Mo.), 337
Owen, Robert, 13-14, 61

Palmerdale Homesteads (Ala.), 111, 162, 217, 333
Parker, Barry, 64
Part-time farming, 80-82, 98, 105, 159, 256, 260, 296
Patten, Simon, 73-74, 84-85, 148
Peek, George N., 78
Pembroke Farms (N. Car.), 337
Penderlea Homesteads (N. Car.), 277-293, 109, 114, 121, 123, 192, 199, 207-208, 213, 230, 296, 332

Index

Phoenix Homesteads (Ariz.), 111, 115, 162, 216, 334
Pickett, Clarence E., 35-36, 98, 105, 108, 114, 193, 238-239, 248-249
Piedmont Homesteads (Ga.), 109, 123, 332
Pinchot, Gifford, 280
Pine Mountain Valley (Ga.), *138-140,* 137, 192
Planning, as a concept, *37-39,* 59-60, 96, 121, 153
Plum Bayou (Ark.), 337
Political Action Committee of the CIO, 229
Post Office Department, 116
Pragmatism, 4
Prairie Farms (Ala.), 337
Pressman, Lee, 155
Progressive Movement, 326
Provisional Commission for Jewish Farm Settlements in the United States, 262
Public housing, 67, 105, 115, 170-172, 303, 306, 311
Public Housing Administration, 7, 232-233, 276, 323
Public land policies, 40-42
Public Works Administration, 80, 93, 116, 119-120, 175, 307
Purdom, Charles B., 69
Pynchon, Charles E., 124-125, 282

Radburn, N.J., 70, 76, 175, 242, 280, 305, 310-311, 313-314, 319
Randolph, Jennings, 118, 245
Reclamation, 41-43, 54-57
Red House (W. Va.), 136-137, 141, 166, 204, 207, 334
Reed, Daniel, 117
Regional Plan of New York City, 68
Regional Planning Association, 68-69, 72, 93
Religion, 199
Relocation corporations, 221
Resettlement Administration, *152-185,* 7, 80, 109-113, 125, 127-128, 130, 134, 136, 140-146, 187-192, 194, 196-209, 214-215, 218-221, 224, 229, 245, 248, 251-252, 256, 259-260, 263-275, 284-289, 305, 307, 310-314, 316, 321, 323, 328, 330-331
Retirement homesteads, 141
Rich, Robert F., 182
Richardson, Charles L., 30
Richton Homesteads (Miss.), 110, 333
Roanoke Farms (N. Car.), 141, 201, 335
Robinson, Charles M., 61
Roosevelt, Franklin D.: and Jeffersonian ideas, 5; on agrarianism, 34, 83, 260; and Rexford G. Tugwell, 35, 148, 161, 180-181, 215, 328; on planning, 37, 70-71, 83; on public land policy, 41; on industrial decentralization, 82-84; and advocacy of rural-industrial towns, 83; and support of land-use planning, 83, 133; and New Deal agricultural planning, 83-84; and the Division of Subsistence Homesteads, 99, 103, 115, 119; and the Resettlement Administration, 129, 142-144; and Pine Mountain Valley, 138-139; and the Farm Security Administration, 225-226; and Arthurdale, 237, 240, 243, 255; and Penderlea Homesteads, 282; and the greenbelt towns, 307-308, 320-321; and experimentation, 327, 330
Roosevelt, Mrs. Franklin D., 36, 99, 103-105, 108, 114-115, 122, 193, 200, 237-249, 251, 253, 255
Roosevelt, N.J., 276
Ropesville Farms (Tex.), 335
Rosenwald Foundation, 198
Roseworth Colony, 22
Rural colonies: and socialist inspiration, 13; and religious inspiration, 13-14; at Greeley, Colo., 14; and the Catholic Church, 14-15; as proposed by congressmen, 15-16; as initiated by the Salvation Army, 17-18; and the Little Landers Movement, 19-20; as proposed by the National Forward to the Land League, 20-21; at Roseworth, 22; at Sunrise, Mich., 30; at Durham and Delhi, Calif., 46-47; established by the Division of Subsistence Homesteads, 109-110; estab-

Rural colonies (*cont.*)
lished by the Federal Emergency Relief Administration, 136-141; established by the Resettlement Administration, 167-170; established by Jewish immigrants, 256-260; established by Hugh MacRae in North Carolina, 277-280
Rural-industrial communities, 132, 135-137
Rural rehabilitation, 133, 135, 143, 153, 155, 157, 159-160, 168, 178-179, 182-184, 197-198, 220-221, 225, 227, 256, 260
Rural Rehabilitation, Division of, 133-136, 142, 144
Rural rehabilitation corporations, 134-135, 141, 144, 154, 161, 264, 270
Rural resettlement, 141, 153, 155-156, 159, 161, 167-170, 182, 218
Ruskin, John, 61
Russell, George (or A. E.), 81
Russell, William, 247
Ryan, John A., 101

Sabine Farms (Tex.), 337
Saginaw Valley Farms (Mich.), 337
St. Francis River Farms (Ark.), 335
St. Helena, N. Car., 278
Sale of communities, *214-220*, 162-163, 220, 223, 228-233, 255, 275-276, 292-293, 303, 322-325
Salt, Titus, 61
Salvation Army, 17-18, 30
Salvation Army colonies, 17-18
Sam Houston Farms (Tex.), 337
San Fernando Homesteads (Calif.), 111, 162, 216, 334
Schafer, John C., 34
Schall, Thomas D., 118
Schmiedeler, Edgar, 32
Schnurr, Mae A., 32
School garden movement, 17
Schurz, Carl, 41
Scott, William D., 22
Scottsbluff Farmsteads (Neb.), 335
Scrugham, James G., 87-88
Scuppernong Farms (N. Car.), 210, 335

Settler selection, *186-188*, 45-46, 55, 115, 126, 141, 215, 244, 279, 285-286, 297, 299, 316
Shenandoah Homesteads (Va.), 113, 163-164, 333
Sheppard, Morris, 67
Sioux Falls Farmsteads (S. Dak.), 335
Skyline Farms (Ala.), 207-208, 335
Smith, Alfred E., 69
Smith, Joseph, 14
Smith, Russell, 223
Smythe, William E., 19-20, 22
Social planning, 186, 193, 211, 256, 272-273, 300, 317, 329-330
Soil Conservation Service, 152
Soldier settlement, 21, 50-54
Soule, George, 101
South Sioux City Farmsteads (Neb.), 335
Southard, Keith, 159
Southern agrarians, 25-26
Southern reclamation movement, 56
Spillman, William J., 75, 78-79
Stafford, William H., 33
Stein, Clarence S., 69-70, 305, 306, 319
Stranded communities, 108-109, 131, 136, 164-166, 188, 203, 205, 239, 251
Sublimity Farms (Ky.), 336
Subsistence homesteads, *86-130*, 11, 18, 26, 32-34, 45, 80, 82, 131, 140, 142, 144, 156, 159, 161-162, 164, 167, 186, 203, 214-218, 231-232, 238-239, 246, 250, 256, 260, 262, 272, 280-282, 294, 296, 300, 319, 327
Subsistence Homesteads, Division of, *98-130*, 7, 13, 26, 80, 135-136, 141-145, 154, 156-157, 161, 163-164, 167, 169, 172-173, 187, 191, 194, 197, 200-203, 216-217, 237, 239-240, 243, 244-246, 248-251, 256, 262-264, 277, 280-284, 289, 296, 297-299, 328
Suburban resettlement, 155-157, 167, 218, 305-309, 322
Sunrise Co-operative Community, 30, 261
Swope, Gerard, 251

Taber, Louis J., 100
Tarver, Malcolm C., 224

Index

Taussig, Charles A., 181
Taylor, Carl C., 98, 122, 155, 281, 297
Taylor, Henry C., 74-76
Taylor, John, 12
Tenant-purchase programs, 77, 180, 183-184, 225, 227
Tennessee Valley Authority, 93, 113, 167, 179, 305, 321, 330
Terrebonne Plantation (La.), 169-170, 210, 336
Three Rivers Gardens (Tex.), 111, 162, 215, 231, 334
Tiverton Farms (S. Car.), 337
Tolley, Howard, 75
Torrance, Jared S., 66
Townes Farms (Ark.), 337
Transylvania Farms (La.), 337
Trumann Farms (Ark.), 337
Tufts, James H., 77
Tugwell, Rexford G.: and collectivism, 6, 202; and Franklin D. Roosevelt, 34-35, 143-144; on agricultural planning, 73-74, 84-86; on national economic planning, 86; and the subsistence homesteads communities, 94, 100, 163-166, 295; and the origins of the Resettlement Administration, 142-144; character and economic theory, 146-152, 164-165, 295, 328-329; and the policies of the Resettlement Administration, 153-160, 194, 215, 229, 330; and other New Deal agencies, 160-161; and resettlement communities, 166-171, 174-176; on housing methods, 170-171; and resignation from the Resettlement Administration, 171, 180-181; and unpopularity, 175-176, 180; and congressional friends, 179; and farm tenancy, 180, 182; on co-operation, 202, 204, 300-301; and class feelings, 221; and the Farm Security Administration, 225, 228, 230; and Jersey Homesteads, 263, 265, 268; and the greenbelt towns, 305-307, 319-320
Tupelo Homesteads (Miss.), 111, 162, 216-217, 334
Twentieth Century Fund, 198
Two Rivers Farmsteads (Neb.), 335

Tygart Valley Homesteads (W. Va.), 108, 114-115, 136, 164-165, 206-208, 212, 231, 332

United Mine Workers, 170
United States Employment Service, 170
United States Extension Service, 105, 134, 160, 228, 259
United States Housing Corporation, 67
United States Public Health Service, 197
Unwin, Raymond, 64, 68, 70, 280, 321

Vacant-lot gardens, 17, 29
Valiant, Margaret, 196
Vandenberg, Arthur, 117
Veblen, Thorstein, 74, 148

Wadsworth, James W., 53
Wakefield, Edward G., 61
Walker, John O., 319
Wallace, Henry A., 76, 82, 84, 94, 142, 152, 180, 182, 185, 196
Wallace, Henry C., 57-58, 75, 78, 82
Waring, Bernard G., 101
Warren, George F., 77, 83
Weltner, Philip, 101
Welwyn, England, 64-66
West Virginia University, 238-239, 242, 244, 247
Westbrook, Lawrence, 132-133, 135-137, 142
Wester, Otto, 195
Westmoreland Homesteads (Pa.), 108, 145, 164-165, 205-208, 213, 232, 332
Whitaker, Charles H., 69
Wichita Gardens (Tex.), 111, 162, 215, 334
Wichita Valley Farms (Tex.), 335
Williams, David, 132-133, 135-136, 138
Williams, Ralph C., 198-199
Wilson, Milburn L.: and the Mormon colonies, 13; on agricultural planning, 73, 121; biographical data, 76-77; and Fairway Farms, 76-77; on the domestic allotment system, 79, 81, 82; on land utilization, 80-81, 83; on agrarianism, 81, 295; and ideas on subsistence homesteads, 81-82; and New Deal agricultural policy, 82-84,

Wilson, Milburn L. (*cont.*)
86; philosophical outlook, 94-97; and policies of the Division of Subsistence Homesteads, 97-105, 109, 112, 114, 127-128, 135, 193; and end of work in the Division of Subsistence Homesteads, 110, 115, 120, 122, 124-125; and ideas on decentralized administration, 119-121; on co-operation, 202-203; as Undersecretary of Agriculture, 207; and Arthurdale, 245; and trip to Russia, 261; and Jersey Homesteads, 262-263, 267; and greenbelt towns, 319

Wilson, William B., 49

Wilson, Woodrow, 50-51
Wise, Stephen S., 262, 274
Wolf Creek (Ga.), 335
Woodbine, N.J., 258-259
Woodlake (Tex.), 132, 135, 141, 166, 218, 335
Woodruff, Roy O., 177
Work, Hubert, 55
Workers' Aim Association, 265, 268
Works Progress Administration, 7, 137-139, 144, 160-161, 170, 173, 196, 265
Wright, Hendrick B., 15
Wright, Henry, 69-71, 175, 305, 310

Zeuch, William E., 197, 203

Recent books published for the American Historical Association from the income of the Albert J. Beveridge Memorial Fund

THE AGRICULTURAL HISTORY OF THE GENESEE VALLEY. By Neil A. McNall.

STEAM POWER ON THE AMERICAN FARM. By Reynold M. Wik.

HORACE GREELEY: NINETEENTH-CENTURY CRUSADER. By Glyndon G. Van Deusen.

ERA OF THE OATH: NORTHERN LOYALTY TESTS DURING THE CIVIL WAR AND RECONSTRUCTION. By Harold M. Hyman.

HISTORY OF MARSHALL FIELD & CO. By Robert W. Twyman.

ROBERT MORRIS: REVOLUTIONARY FINANCIER. By Clarence L. Ver Steeg.

A HISTORY OF THE FREEDMEN'S BUREAU. By George R. Bentley.

THE FIRST RAPPROCHEMENT: ENGLAND AND THE UNITED STATES, 1795–1805. By Bradford Perkins.

MIDDLE-CLASS DEMOCRACY AND THE REVOLUTION IN MASSACHUSETTS, 1691–1780. By Robert E. Brown.

THE DEVELOPMENT OF AMERICAN PETROLEUM PIPELINES: A STUDY IN PRIVATE ENTERPRISE AND PUBLIC POLICY, 1862–1906. By Arthur Menzies Johnson.

COLONISTS FROM SCOTLAND: EMIGRATION TO NORTH AMERICA, 1707–1783. By Ian Charles Cargill Graham.

PROFESSORS AND PUBLIC ETHICS: STUDIES OF NORTHERN MORAL PHILOSOPHERS BEFORE THE CIVIL WAR. By Wilson Smith.

THE AXIS ALLIANCE AND JAPANESE-AMERICAN RELATIONS, 1941. By Paul W. Schroeder.

A FRONTIER STATE AT WAR: KANSAS, 1861–1865. By Albert Castel.

BRITISH INVESTMENTS AND THE AMERICAN MINING FRONTIER, 1860–1901. By Clark C. Spence.

RAILS, MINES, AND PROGRESS: SEVEN AMERICAN PROMOTERS IN MEXICO, 1867–1911. By David M. Pletcher.

LAGUARDIA IN CONGRESS. By Howard Zinn.

TOMORROW A NEW WORLD: THE NEW DEAL COMMUNITY PROGRAM. By Paul K. Conkin.

MAR 0 8 1993